On revolutions and progress in
economic knowledge

By the same author

On revolutions and progress in economic knowledge

T. W. HUTCHISON

MITSUI PROFESSOR OF ECONOMICS
UNIVERSITY OF BIRMINGHAM

CAMBRIDGE UNIVERSITY PRESS

CAMBRIDGE

LONDON · NEW YORK · MELBOURNE

Published by the Syndics of the Cambridge University Press
The Pitt Building, Trumpington Street, Cambridge CB2 1RP
Bentley House, 200 Euston Road, London NW1 2DB
32 East 57th Street, New York, NY 10022, USA
296 Beaconsfield Parade, Middle Park, Melbourne 3206, Australia

First published 1978

Printed in Great Britain at the
University Press, Cambridge

Library of Congress Cataloguing in Publication Data

Hutchison, Terence Wilmot.
On revolutions and progress in economic
knowledge.

Bibliography: p.
Includes indexes.
1. Economics – History. 2. Economics –
Methodology. I. Title.
HB75.H79   330'.09   77-82498
ISBN 0 521 21805 5

Contents

For L.

Foreword

I

Most of the component parts of this volume started as separate papers written at various times and in various contexts. What these papers had in common was that they were all concerned with one or other of the three (or perhaps four) major turning-points in the history of economic thought, associated with the names of Smith, Jevons, and Keynes (and, in a rather different way, with that of Ricardo). As I reconsidered and revised these essays, I became more and more interested in the nature and variety of the changes and processes of which these major turning-points, 'shifts in research programmes', or 'revolutions', consisted, and in how far, and in precisely what sense, they can be said to have represented 'progress' in the subject. Therefore, in the course of being revised, rearranged, and rewritten, in most cases quite comprehensively, these papers have developed interconnections and inter-relations in respect of their common concern with these turning-points, or processes of major change, or 'revolutions'. Comparisons and contrasts have suggested themselves between the different cases. So on one level the chapters in this volume may be read – by those less interested in their methodological aspects – simply for such contributions as they may make to the study of particular episodes, and of particular economists and their works. But they may also be regarded as attempted contributions to the study of the three or four major changes, turning-points or transformations in the history of political economy and economics, and of the processes by, and senses in which, 'progress' might be held to have come about.

II

Finding a suitable title has presented considerable difficulties because the subject-matter, or processes, with which this book is centrally concerned, are so complex and imprecise, blending general qualities with particular historical characteristics. The first question to be answered was: what word, or brief caption, sums up best the profound and variegated changes in economic theorising and political economy which were summed up in, or followed from, the works of Adam Smith and Keynes? And are there any other cases which are near enough to being parallels as to justify the same description? We do not wish to get involved in purely, or mainly, verbal issues. We have mentioned such terms as 'major changes', 'turning-points' and 'transformations', which are descriptive terms not actually at all widely used by historians of economics. Much the most widely, and recently increasingly used term is 'revolutions', for which we have eventually settled. Certainly there have been disparities and disagreements about its use, and also some exaggerations, but many of those who have recently been employing it have done so in a sense reasonably close to that in which it is used in this book, which does not need, at any rate initially, to be very precise.

However, some writers have denied the existence of 'revolutions' in the history of economic thought, or have allowed hardly more than a single valid case.[1] They have asserted a kind of 'inevitability of gradualness' and continuity, or rather the historical actuality of gradualness and continuity, as regards the change and development of the subject. But though, of course, change has always been more or less continuous, it has not by any means been absolutely uniform, at all times and places, in pace, or in profundity, or comprehensiveness. (This may be regarded as a, or the, basic *aperçu* of T. S. Kuhn's work on 'scientific revolutions'.) There have been periods mainly consisting of relatively minor controversies and amendments, and other phases dominated largely by much more fundamental confrontations and reconstructions. In fact there seems to be much support for the idea that the historical record in political economy and economics, in the last two hundred years, does show some three (or perhaps four) relatively fundamental turning-points. Some writers seem to envisage several more cases of smaller-scale turning-points, or 'revolutions', especially during the last four or five decades, applying the term to various sub-divisions or sectors of the subject (for example, imperfect competition, 'welfare' analysis, etc.). But we propose to take a middle course between this wider and less discriminating use of the term, and the denial that *any* – or more than one – 'revolution' has taken place in the entire history of political economy and economics. For the beginnings of some measure of agreement seem to have been emerging regarding these three or four cases in the subject as a whole. In fact, these three or four major turning-points, or transformations, have long provided the main divisions and framework for many or most histories of economic thought.[2]

[1] See M. Blaug, 1973, pp. 13–14; A. W. Coats, 1969, D. F. Gordon, 1965, and G. Routh, 1975, p. 27.

[2] On revolutions in the history of political economy and economics, see the earlier discussions by D. F. Gordon and A. W. Coats mentioned in the preceding footnote.

The increasing interest in, or recognition of these processes of major change or revolution in the subject seems to have come about in three main phases. It probably originated mainly with the Keynesian phenomenon – which is still considered by some to be the only valid case of a 'revolution'. Further interest was then sharply stimulated in the 1960s by T. S. Kuhn's challenging book, already mentioned, *The Structure of Scientific Revolutions*. (This work was, however, primarily concerned with the natural sciences, and has not always been very carefully or accurately interpreted. Furthermore its conclusions were later considerably modified by the author himself.) Then, thirdly, in the early 1970s, interest in the concept of a revolution in economics was further reinforced by the actual emergence in those years of what was widely referred to, or claimed to be, some kind of fundamental 'crisis', or 'revolutionary situation', in the subject.[3] Hence understanding the present state and prospects of the subject involved understanding the nature of 'revolutions'.

Anyhow, the term 'revolution' had come into frequent use – and/or misuse – by economists long before T. S. Kuhn's very stimulating, and briefly very fashionable, work first appeared in 1962. Soon after 1936 'The Keynesian Revolution' began to become a familiar concept (and, in fact, in 1947 the phrase, of course, became the title of Professor L. R. Klein's well-known book). This term 'revolution', therefore, can be, and has been, widely applied to the history of political economy and economics without any implications or commitments whatsoever regarding Kuhnian ideas as to the philosophy of science and the nature of scientific progress. This is the kind of fairly loose, and even simple-minded, sense in which the term is initially introduced here. But at a later stage after having studied our three or four main cases from various angles – (and for several hundred pages) – we seek to suggest briefly some very tentative general conclusions about revolutions and progress in the history of economic thought, and to compare and contrast our conclusions with the Kuhnian ideas based on, or derived from, the leading natural sciences.[4] The construction and method of this book may therefore be said to be, to some extent, inductive.

See also, more recently: C. D. W. Goodwin's tabular analysis in 1973, p. 303; M. Bronfenbrenner, 1971; L. Kunin and F. S. Weaver, 1971; H. G. Johnson, 1975; Sir John Hicks, 1975 and 1976; A. Leijonhufvud, 1976. See also, for what he calls the 'Jevonian' and 'Sraffa' revolutions, M. H. Dobb, 1973, Chapters 7–9.

[3] See Hutchison, 1977, Chapter 4.

[4] See Chapter 11: On revolutions and progress in economic knowledge: definitions and conclusions.

III

So far, the discussion of major changes, or revolutions, in the history of economic thought has mostly been in terms of the kind of sweeping generalisations inevitable when some two hundred years of intellectual history are surveyed in the space of a single essay of ten or twenty pages. It is an aim of this book to assemble more of the relevant materials about the more important cases and elements, from which answers can be built up regarding the nature of the main changes or turning-points, or 'major shifts in research programmes' – or 'revolutions' – in the subject, and also regarding the 'progress' (such as it may have been) that comes about, or is claimed. We are certainly not attempting to put forward anything like complete, precise, or cut-and-dried answers.

Anyhow, questions regarding the kind of progress which takes place in economics, and regarding the nature of the major changes in the development of the subject, are not only of some importance to students of the history and philosophy of science (and economics). They may be, and perhaps should be, of importance to economists. In his paper on '"Revolutions" in economics', Sir John Hicks has stated:

> The history of science is a fascinating subject; it is important (as has been shown) for the philosophy of science; but it is not important to the working scientist in the way that the history of economics is important to the working economist. When the natural scientist has come to the frontier of knowledge, and is ready for new exploration, he is unlikely to have much to gain from a contemplation of the path by which his predecessors have come to the place where he now stands. Old ideas are worked out; old controversies are dead and buried...
>
> Our position in economics is different; we cannot escape in the same way from our own past. We may pretend to escape; but the past crowds in on us all the same. To 'neoclassical' succeeds 'neomercantilist'; Keynes and his contemporaries echo Ricardo and Malthus; Marx and Marshall are still alive. Some of us are inclined to be ashamed of this traditionalism, but when it is properly understood it is no cause for embarrassment [1976, p. 207].

Many, perhaps most, economists would probably reject Sir John's 'traditionalism'. Certainly there have been plenty of economists – beginning with J. B. Say[5] – who would emphatically deny, or confidently dismiss, this historical dimension in economics, which significantly differentiates it, and its methodology, from the natural sciences. This readiness to disregard the history of economics is partly based on the confidently held assumption that, as is assumed for the natural sciences, their history has, since their origins, been one of

[5] See the opening quotation of Chapter 8: Economists and the history of economics: revolutionary and traditional versions.

smooth, more-or-less unbroken progress, recognisable as such by the professionally qualified, or by those with sufficient knowledge to form a judgment. As we shall see (in Chapter 8, Section III) economists, especially the more influential, have long been liable to break out in extremely confident assertions regarding the progress represented by some recent revolutionary development in the subject, which had rendered past theorising completely obsolete, and which, it could be assumed, like advances in the natural sciences, would retain its practical validity and relevance, without danger of any obsolescence.

Recently certain doubts have grown up, and, indeed, certain patches of sackcloth and ashes have even become, briefly, quite fashionable garb (discardable, of course, at the outbreak of the next 'revolution'). Anyhow, it may be timely to examine briefly the question as to how far, and in what sense, 'progress' can, or cannot, be said to have come about in political economy and economics. Again, it is not claimed that any cut-and-dried answers are supplied here; only that materials are assembled and arranged out of which answers may eventually be put together.

Moreover, the interest and importance of the study of 'progress' – if any – in economic knowledge, how this comes about, and what part 'revolutions', or major transformations, or turning-points, may have in bringing it about, extend well beyond the boundaries of economics. T. S. Kuhn, at one point, draws a comparison of 'an esoteric, isolated and largely self-contained discipline, with one that still aims to com-municate with and persuade an audience larger than their own profession' (1970, p. 254).

Although some of the current work of economists may sometimes seem to belong to 'an esoteric, isolated and largely self-contained discipline', the traditional aims and claims of the subject (still largely upheld and by no means explicitly renounced) require that its prac-titioners 'still aim to communicate with and persuade an audience larger than their own profession'. Among the vitally important mes-sages that must be communicated to the larger audience of politicians and public are not only those regarding particular policies for solving, or mitigating – rather than exacerbating – the pressing problems of the day – of inflation, unemployment, poverty etc. Perhaps just as, or even more, important a message at this particular time to get across to this larger audience, than any conclusions regarding some particular current problem, is the general clarification as to what can, and what cannot, reasonably be expected in the way of more enlightened, or less unsuccessful, economic policy-making. For misleading and over-optimistic expectations about what the economic policies of govern-ments can deliver might seriously undermine the political framework of a free society. In turn, clearer and more accurate understanding and expectations as to what economic policy-making can and cannot reasonably be expected to achieve must depend on clearer and more accurate understanding and expectations as to the limits and extent of economic knowledge, and as to what kind of 'progress' therein has taken place and can reasonably be expected. Certainly a very rapidly reached and complete consensus regarding such problems is most unlikely. But it is naive and philistine to suppose that trying to promote such clarification may not prove at least as fruitful, in terms of less unsuccessful policy-making, as more 'normal' or 'mainstream' work on the 'real' problems of the subject.

It would certainly seem that in recent years, politicians, the public, and indeed some economists, have not always been sufficiently cautious, realistic and clear regarding what the economic policies of governments may reasonably be expected to achieve, and, therefore, regarding the limits, extent, and possible progress of economic knowledge. A fuller and clearer understanding of the past record over the last 200 years, in the first instance more widely disseminated among economists, might, or could, have a useful part to play in promoting a clearer grasp of the possibilities of economic knowledge. It is presumably one of the tasks of historians of economic thought to attempt to promote this kind of understanding. Studying the major changes, turning-points, or revolutions in economic knowledge may help to clarify the kind of progress in such knowledge which it is reasonable to expect in the future, and what it is reasonable, and unreasonable, to expect economics as a subject to deliver.

Acknowledgements

I am grateful to a number of editors and publishers under whose auspices earlier and/or partial versions of chapters in this volume have appeared. Details are as follows:

A shorter, modified version of *Chapter 1* (on *The Wealth of Nations*) was delivered in March 1976 as part of a Bicentennial lecture series at the University of Chicago and appeared in a special issue of the *Journal of Law and Economics* (vol. XIX (3), October 1976) edited by Professor Ronald Coase, to whom I am very much indebted.

Of *Chapter 2*, one section (IV), plus one or two other paragraphs, appeared in *The Cambridge Journal* published by Bowes and Bowes, November 1953, in an article entitled 'James Mill and the Political Education of Ricardo'.

Chapter 3 is based on an article contributed to *The Marginal Revolution in Economics*, 1973, edited by R. D. C. Black, A. W. Coats, and C. D. W. Goodwin (copyright 1972 by Duke University Press). This article has been very much rearranged, revised and supplemented.

Chapter 4 is a considerably revised version of an article which appeared in *History of Political Economy*, Fall 1969 (copyright 1969 (1972) by Duke University Press).

Origins of *Chapter 5* are to be found in my articles: 'Berkeley's *Querist* and the Economic Thought of the Eighteenth Century' (*British Journal for the Philosophy of Science*, vol. IV, No. 13, 1953); and 'Keynes und die Geschichte der Klassischen Nationalökonomie' (*Zeitschrift für Nationalökonomie*, Band XVIII, Heft 4, 1958). This chapter is three or four times longer than those earlier essays. Some parts of it were delivered as lectures at Keio University in 1973 and have been published in Japanese translation by Professor Tamotsu Matsuura and Professor Hayasaka, to whom I am deeply grateful for their work as translators and also for their generous hospitality in October 1973.

Chapter 6 is based on the Appendix to *Economists and Economic Policy in Britain 1946–1966* (G. Allen and Unwin, 1968). Considerable alterations, additions and subtractions have been made.

Chapter 7 starts from some quotations from an article entitled 'Expectation and Rational Conduct', which appeared in the *Zeitschrift für Nationalökonomie,* 1937, Band VIII, Heft 5.

An earlier version of Section II of *Chapter 8* has appeared in the Report of the International Congress of Economic History and History of Economic Theory held at the Piraeus in 1975. I should like to express my thanks to Professor L. Houmanidis the editor and organiser of the conference.

An earlier draft of *Chapter 9* appeared as a Discussion Paper in January 1974 under the title of 'The Cambridge Version of the History of Economics'. The text has been much revised and extended.

An earlier version of *Chapter 10* was delivered at the Conference of the International Economic History Association at Leningrad in August 1970.

I would add my thanks to Diana Sheedy for her devoted work on the typescript.

I

The Wealth of Nations and the Smithian revolution

I

The centenary in 1876 of the publication of *The Wealth of Nations* was celebrated in London by a 'grand dinner and special discussion' held by the Political Economy Club, with Mr Gladstone presiding. As a London daily newspaper stated at the time, the centenary celebration of 1876 did not, in Britain, 'coincide with an auspicious moment in the history of the science which Adam Smith founded'.[1] In fact, the first centenary took place at a time in Britain especially – not so much elsewhere – of fundamental challenge and uncertainty. Rather suddenly, in the late 1860s, the doctrines of classical political economy, in respect of theories, policies, and methods, which had achieved in Britain such an extraordinary dominance over the subject, and which had enjoyed such confidence and prestige among the articulate public and political élite, were shaken by fundamental criticisms and seemed to lose rapidly and heavily in credibility. By 1876 little firm consensus had emerged regarding the nature and methods of the subject. The centenary celebration in London consisted, therefore, to a considerable extent, of conflicting claims and opposing interpretations regarding the methods and significance of *The Wealth of Nations*. Representatives of a somewhat desiccated orthodoxy – such as Robert Lowe – were claiming Adam Smith as the founder of 'a deductive and demonstrative science of human actions and conduct'. On the other hand, for some years, historical rebels and critics, like Cliffe Leslie, had been directing fundamental attacks on the abstract and deductive methods of orthodoxy, while calling for a return to the methods of *The Wealth of Nations*.[2] Briefly, on a much smaller scale, something resembling the great Austro-German *Methodenstreit* was played out in Britain (with something of a reversal of roles regarding the 'orthodoxy' of the deductive and historical methods respectively).

Fifty years later, in 1926, at the sesqui-centennial celebration in Chicago, in spite of institutionalist criticisms in the United States, there

---

[1] See Political Economy Club, 1876; also T. W. Hutchison, 1953a, pp. 1–6.
[2] See, for example, Leslie's essay of 1870 'The Political Economy of Adam Smith' (in n.d., pp. 21ff).

was not so much fundamental uncertainty and challenge, but indeed something like comparative 'normalcy', or a lull before the storm. On the occasion, on the other hand, of the bicentenary, though the scale and many other aspects, were, of course, very different, one could discern certain broad, if distant, parallels with the state of the subject in Britain a hundred years previously. It could perhaps, therefore, again have become relevant to start by focussing on rather fundamental questions of the scope and method of *The Wealth of Nations*. Such questions often are, and certainly are in Smith's work, significantly related to the treatment of policy-issues, and they have not received as much attention as other less significant aspects of Smith's work, or as much as their unusual, and in some ways unique, features deserve.

II

Sometimes, with very great men who have some outstanding deed, or epoch-making achievement, to their name, it is possible to look at their previous life simply or mainly as a preparation, brief or lengthy, leading up to the fulfilment of their supreme task or historic role. In the second half of the eighteenth century there was, as Smith himself was definitively to demonstrate, a great historic work to be written on Political Economy, which would pull together and systematise the subject, lay down new or reformed principles of perennial significance, or, at any rate, valid for decades to come, and at the same time instigate a long revolution in economic policy just at the juncture when England was about to enter upon one of the most crucial phases in her, or any other country's economic history. What better intellectual grounding, for the person destined to produce this supreme work, could then have been found, anywhere in the world, than in Francis Hutcheson's Moral Philosophy class (reading Grotius at 15) in Glasgow from 1737 to 1740? (Scott, 1938, p. 6). As Smith claimed decades later, though surely he would have maintained that it held also in his student days:

> In the present state of the Scotch universities, I do most sincerely look upon them as, in spite of all their faults, without exception the best seminaries of learning that are to be found anywhere in Europe. They are, perhaps, upon the whole, as unexceptionable as any public institutions of that kind, which all contain in their very nature the seeds and causes of negligence and corruption, have ever been, or are ever likely to be.[3]

The next stage for our historic author-to-be was Oxford – a sharp contrast with Glasgow in educational terms – where, as *The Wealth of Nations* of course tells us: 'The greater part of the public professors

[3] See the letter to William Cullen of 20 September 1774, reproduced in full in J. Thomson, 1859, vol. I, p. 473.

have, for these many years, given up altogether even the pretence of teaching' (1937, p. 718).

We have strangely little knowledge of how Smith spent these six years in Oxford – except that he evidently was not, *formally*, taught much. W. R. Scott maintained that 'the Oxford of his time gave little if any help towards what was to be his life-work' (1937, p. 40).[4]

On the other hand, even if Oxford was not exactly ideal for this purpose, it was surely invaluable for Smith to obtain some direct, first-hand acquaintance with the social, political and economic institutions of England (to which, indeed, significant tributes are paid in *The Wealth of Nations*). For though, in mid-century, philosophically somewhat in the shade compared with Scotland and France, England was, as we just noted, at that time approaching a supremely important passage in her and the world's economic development. *The Wealth of Nations* may well have been vitally enriched by its observant author's first-hand experience of English life and society.

Then, coming home to Scotland again, to emerge remarkably rapidly as a successful young lecturer rewarded with a major chair at 28, what could have been more valuable for our future master, than *first*, the closest friendship with (as Adam Smith himself called David Hume) 'by far the most illustrious philosopher and historian of the present age' (1937, p. 742) who, in his *Political Discourses* of 1752, was about to contribute significantly to emerging revolutionary ideas on political economy? And *secondly* what could have been more stimulating and fruitful than the contacts with the merchants of Glasgow – doubly important for a scholarly philosopher in imbuing his work with a vitally realistic, practical, concrete power? For as John Rae tells us: 'It was amid the thickening problems of the rising trade of the Clyde, and the daily discussions they occasioned among the enterprising and intelligent merchants of the town, that he grew into a great economist' (1895, p. 87).[5]

[4] On the other hand, Sir George Clark has maintained: 'Adam Smith is still by common consent the greatest of economic historians, as he is the greatest of economists, and we shall not do well if we tamely acquiesce in the belief that the six years which he spent without interruption in Oxford contributed little to the formation of his mind. It is to be hoped that one of the present fellows of Balliol will publish what he knows about the remarkable coincidence between the books referred to in the footnotes to *The Wealth of Nations* and the books which are known to have been in the college library when its future author was in residence' (see G. N. Clark, 1932, p. 73). This suggestion does not so far seem to have been followed up.

[5] In a letter of Sir T. Munro to Kirkman Finlay (15 August 1825) he wrote: 'I remember about the time of the appearance of *The Wealth of Nations*, that the Glasgow merchants were as proud of the work as if they had written it themselves: and some of them said it was no wonder that Adam Smith had written such a book, as he had the advantage of their society, in which the same doctrines were circulated with the punch every day' (James Finlay and Co., 1951). Doubtless the influence of the Glasgow merchants on Smith was not *all* in one direction or only of the kind they claimed. They

Meanwhile there followed a longish period of teaching and lecturing, in part on political economy, to foster a solid mastery of the subject. For, as *The Wealth of Nations* explains:

> To impose on any man the necessity of teaching, year after year, any particular branch of science, seems, in reality, to be the most effectual method of rendering him completely master of it himself. On being obliged to go every year over the same ground, if he is good for anything, he necessarily becomes, in a few years, well acquainted with every part of it. If upon any particular point he should form too hasty an opinion one year, when he comes in the course of his lectures to reconsider the same subject the year thereafter, he is very likely to correct it [1937, p. 764].

Very likely: and up to a point...But these learning-by-teaching processes seem sometimes to be liable eventually to a kind of diminishing returns, or exhaustion of investment opportunity. So, after a dozen years, as Lord Keynes appreciated: 'At the age of 41 (just at the right moment neither too soon nor too late)' Smith 'launched himself on the great world' (1938, p. 33)[6] notably making contact in the *salons* of Paris with the leading 'economists' of France, where, at the same time, he had an instructive view of the French economic policies of the day, which then rendered France, according to Walter Bagehot, 'on all economic matters...a sort of museum stocked with the most important errors' (1881, p. 264).

Finally our future author returns home once more, endowed with the financial resources enabling him to concentrate for most of a decade on the composition of his masterpiece published in 1776.

In spite of some teleological overemphasis, there is clearly, from the point of view of a modern economist, much that is valid in the foregoing account. It sets out the main intellectual sources, experiences, and ingredients, which went into the making of *The Wealth of Nations*. But one thing about it is entirely out of focus: Smith himself would never, for one moment, have entertained or accepted – even in his later years, after 1776, when *The Wealth of Nations* was bringing him such resounding and rewarding success – an interpretation of his intellectual career as having been centred round, or dominated by, political economy – even in the broadest possible sense of the term.

For Adam Smith was, in fact, and undoubtedly always considered himself to be, a philosopher, in a highly comprehensive sense, not as interested in epistemology as Locke, Berkeley and Hume, but pene-

---

may also have provided him with material for his attacks on 'mercantile' practices and ideas. But a powerful realistic influence they almost certainly had, in one direction or another.

6 Regarding coincidences between Smith and Keynes, it is incorrect that they were both certainly born on 5 June. What we know is that Smith was *baptised* on that day. But they did publish their major works at almost exactly the same age: Smith at a few days *over*, and Keynes at a week or two *under*, 52 years and 9 months.

trating much more deeply into social and legal philosophy and the psychology of ethics. Smith remained a philosopher from the beginning to the end of his life. He would never have regarded his work as a whole as primarily economic. He thought of economics, or political economy, as only one chapter, and not the most important chapter, in a broad study of society and human progress, which involved psychology and ethics (in social and individual terms), law, politics, and the development of the arts and sciences.[7] Smith did not merely start life with a youthful enthusiasm for philosophy, and then eventually narrow down his interests in his maturity to become an economist. Fortunately for our subject, as it turned out, he did devote a decade or so of his prime years to political economy (using up, perhaps, quite a lot more scarce time than he had originally intended in completing his work in that particular section of his vast field). But having finished *The Wealth of Nations* Smith moved on, or back, to the history and philosophy of law and of the progress of the arts and sciences. When he lamented in his last days that 'he had done so little', Smith did not, of course, mean that he had planned, but failed to complete, further volumes on political economy (as Alfred Marshall originally planned a multi-volume *Principles of Economics*, which very unfortunately for the subject in the twentieth century was never completed in the form originally intended). What Smith, with excessive modesty, was lamenting was that he had not completed more than a small part (which fortunately included the politico-economic part) of his original vast philosophical–historical plan.[8] Therefore, that *The Wealth of Nations* played such an important role in establishing political economy as an

[7] A number of earlier and more recent writers have recognised this point. For example James Bonar: 'Adam Smith undoubtedly started with the purposes of giving to the world a complete social philosophy' (1922, p. 149). A. L. Macfie wrote: 'He himself would not have regarded his work as primarily economic. For him it was broadly social, fitting into that title the political as well as the psychological and ethical aspects of individuals living in societies... They in the eighteenth century thought of economics only as one chapter (not the most important) in a general theory of society involving psychology and ethics, social and individual, law, politics, and social philosophy as well' (1967, pp. 13–16). Again, Glen Morrow, in his Chicago lecture of 1926, maintained of *The Wealth of Nations*: 'This an economic work? It is far more than that; it is a history and criticism of all European civilisation...a philosophical work' (1928, p. 157). More recently Professor J. R. Lindgren has very strongly insisted that 'all who are familiar with Smith's life and writings recognize that he was a philosopher by profession and that all his writings were conceived and executed as works of philosophy' (1973, p. ix). Moreover the sociologists have staked a claim to Smith's work: 'The apostolic succession in social philosophy from Adam Smith is through the sociologists rather than the economists. The sociologists have kept alive the vital spark of Smith's moral philosophy', A. Small, 1907, p. 4, quoted by D. A. Reisman, 1976.
[8] See Smith's letter of 1 November 1785, to the Duc de la Rochefoucauld, reproduced in the *Economic Journal*, 1895, p. 165; also Dugald Stewart's account, 'prefixed' to Smith's *Essays on Philosophical Subjects*, 1795, p. cxlv; and both the preliminary 'Advertisement' and the closing paragraph of the 1790 edition of *The Theory of Moral Sentiments*.

independent subject is one of those felicitous, unintended and quite unplanned outcomes to which Smith himself assigned such an important, and often beneficent, role in human affairs. In his own celebrated words Smith himself was 'led by an invisible hand to promote an end which was no part of his intention' (1937, p. 423) – the end, that is, of establishing political economy as a separate autonomous discipline.

Moreover, it is not simply that Smith held that an *Inquiry*, and the conclusions thereof, into the wealth of nations, or the progress of opulence, must be regarded as a subordinate part of a far more comprehensive whole. There is also, in fact, at every important point within his 'Inquiry' a constant *interdependence and interpenetration* between questions and factors of economics and political economy and those of law, morals, psychology and politics.

One of the most important themes of Smith's vast, uncompleted life-work, seems to have been centred around the idea of human progress, or the progress of society.[9] In fact, as Walter Bagehot, in his essay of 1876, illuminatingly observed regarding *The Wealth of Nations*:

> It was not the exclusive product of a lifelong study...It was in the mind of its author only one of many books, or rather a single part of a great book, which he intended to write...He spent his life accordingly, in studying the origin and progress of the sciences, the laws, the politics, and all the other aids and forces which have raised man from the savage to the civilised state...
>
> He investigated the progress of opulence as part of the growth and progress of all things...
>
> The last way in which he regarded Political Economy was as a separate and confined speciality; he came upon it as an inseparable part of the development of all things, and it was in that vast connection that he habitually considered it [1881, pp. 248–50; and 1895, p. 129].

But what interest, it may well be asked, for economists today, have Smith's apparently vast intellectual ambitions regarding the intended scope of his life-work, and the somewhat limited and subordinate place of *The Wealth of Nations* in that intended work? Are Smith's comprehensive intellectual ambitions and concepts more than a rather magnificent, 'period', museum specimen of eighteenth-century intellectual design, which, in any case, Smith himself came nowhere near to completing, and which have become quite obsolete and irrelevant in scale for the tasks of today?

Of course it can be validly claimed that for nearly two centuries the concentration and specialisation carried through by successive gener-

---

[9] See Duncan Forbes, 1954, pp. 643–70. As Mr T. D. Campbell points out, the theme of progress is not so prominent in *The Theory of Moral Sentiments*. But we would suggest that there too it is significantly present. See 1971, p. 8on.

ations, beginning with Ricardo and Senior, has largely paid off, in spite of objections advanced from time to time by Historical, Comteist, Marxist and Institutionalist critics. But this specialisation and concentration in political economy and economics has depended, to a large extent, on the assumption of a fairly stable social and political environment which would not too seriously or irregularly interfere with economic processes, which processes, therefore, could be studied more or less in isolation. This assumption of a stable social framework – or what Pigou (1929, p. 21), before the world depression, was describing as a 'stable general culture' – permitted the development of classical, neoclassical and Keynesian economics in Britain. Indeed, there may always be plenty of more narrowly and specifically economic questions which will not require the kind of comprehensive social and historical setting envisaged by Adam Smith. But to the extent that the assumption of a more or less stable social framework, and the kind of specialisation in economics which it permits, *may be* becoming significantly less valid than it used to be, there may well be reasons for regarding Smith's conceptions of the scope of the subject, and its close inter-relationships and interpenetration with other fields, especially that of law, not simply as an obsolete, impracticable, intellectually unfeasible irrelevance, of no more than period interest for economists today. What, at least, might be concluded is that Adam Smith would not have neglected, or underestimated, the legal, social and social–psychological factors in our contemporary economic problems (for example, the problem of inflation) just because such factors may be outside what have more recently come to be regarded as accepted 'professional' or departmental frontiers.

III

Conceptions of the scope of the subject are naturally related to conceptions regarding methods, and in turn are related to the kind of conclusions regarding policy which are considered intellectually feasible or justified. The combination and balance of methods employed in *The Wealth of Nations* have been as rarely followed by subsequent economists as have Smith's comprehensive conceptions of the scope, and of the wide-ranging interdependencies of social and economic enquiry. There was surely some justification for the claim of the historical economist Thorold Rogers, at the centenary celebrations in 1876, that there was 'nothing more significant than the differences of the process by which Adam Smith collected his inferences, and that by which his followers or commentators have arrived at theirs'.[10]

[10] Political Economy Club, 1876, p. 32. Thorold Rogers' successors as economic historians have also laid claim, methodologically, to *The Wealth of Nations*. George Unwin (1908)

In fact, following what may be described as the James Mill–Ricardo methodological revolution, the comprehensiveness and balance of methods deployed in *The Wealth of Nations* has hardly ever been regained in a general work on the subject of major stature. It is a tribute to the remarkable balance which Smith achieved that he has been both acclaimed and criticised from both or all sides in subsequent methodological debates. But there is certainly a most striking contrast with the Ricardian methods which later obtained such prestige.[11] For the bulk of the text of *The Wealth of Nations* consists of descriptive and historical material. As one of Smith's recent successors at Glasgow has noted:

> He was rather a rich inductive thinker than a rigidly logical system-builder...though he was both. He had the modesty and wisdom always to give true weight to the facts...[He had a] genius for choosing and using factual data. He was at home in facts. He enjoyed ferreting them out, and giving them their proper weights [Macfie, 1967, pp. 13 and 139].

Sixty years after the appearance of *The Wealth of Nations*, Nassau Senior, in formulating the viewpoint established by the Ricardian methodological revolution, was to complain of 'the undue importance which many economists have ascribed to the collection of facts' (1836, p. 6).

According to Senior, the Science of Political Economy, apart from its multifarious applications, was not, '*avide de faits*'. *Adam Smith emphatically was 'avide de faits'*, and overwhelmingly demonstrated his avidity, and the conception of the subject which this avidity implied, in *The Wealth of Nations*.

In his *Lectures on Rhetoric and Belles Lettres*, Smith is reported as referring to 'abstract and speculative reasonings, which perhaps tend very little to the bettering of our practice' (1963, p. 37).

maintained: 'Adam Smith was the first great economic historian, and I do not scruple to add that he is still the greatest. There is scarcely a page of *The Wealth of Nations* where history and theory are sundered from each other.' According to R. H. Tawney (1932): 'It is a truism that the central theme of *The Wealth of Nations* is historical.' (See N. B. Harte (ed.) 1971, pp. 39 and 91.) In his outstanding bicentennial tribute, Professor H. M. Robertson suggests that 'the reader himself has to be something of an economic historian fully to appreciate *The Wealth of Nations*, whilst other economists, who are without a true historical bent, somehow truncate it in their own minds' (1976, p. 383).

[11] See H. J. Bitterman, 1940, p. 504: 'Smith's work is not deductive in the sense that the term could be applied to, say, the major works of Ricardo and Senior. The bulk of Smith's text consists of descriptive, historical, and statistical data, with a few inferences from "conjectural history". There are some deductions from definition and arguments supported only by common knowledge or casual observation, which give parts of the work an abstract tone. But Smith had argued that valid generalizations could be reached only by induction from observation, and he tried to apply this technique.' However, the views of one distinguished dissenter should be recorded: 'Smith's frame of mind was on the whole essentially unhistorical...historical narration and inductive reasoning were with him subordinate to a deductive movement of thought' (W. J. Ashley, 1900, p. 310).

In fact, in *The Wealth of Nations* 'abstract reasonings' are kept on a very tight rein. Smith is certainly not one for taking off into the Ricardian stratosphere of 'strong cases' or extreme, arbitrary abstractions. Of course Smith employed a 'system', as he called it, by which he meant an abstract, deductive model. But he sharply denounced 'the man of system' who indulges in, what Viner called, 'over-attachment or an exaggeration of the applicability to concrete issues without qualification of abstract and therefore at its best partial and incomprehensive theorizing...

He [Smith] very much doubted that abstraction could provide either understanding of the real world or, by itself, safe guidance for the legislator or statesman.'[12]

When Smith wanted to use a simple case for its illustrative value he seldom invented an abstraction. He sought to go back in history and find a factual illustration in a simpler kind of economy, such as the hand-to-mouth hunting and fishing economy which is so frequently referred to from the first page onwards in *The Wealth of Nations*. How far Smith's history, or sometimes what has been called his 'conjectural history', or conjectural anthropology, was always accurate, is beside the point methodologically. Smith did not consider that students of society, or of the wealth of nations, could, or should seek to compensate very far for their inability to experiment by setting up abstract models.

Smith was methodologically comprehensive. Though sharing much of the intellectual confidence of his age, he realised that significant or useful social and philosophical truth, including economic truth, was always a *very* scarce commodity, and especially so in relation to the extravagant needs for it implicitly postulated by, though often not explicitly understood to be an essential prerequisite for, the plans and projects of reformers and revolutionaries. So the student of society, or of the economy, cannot afford to overlook *any* method by which some grain or crumb of truth, however insubstantial and fragmentary, may be picked up. As John Neville Keynes said of Smith: 'He rejected no method of enquiry that could in any way assist him in investigating the phenomena of wealth' (1917, p. 10).[13]

---

[12] See 1797, vol. II, p. 110; J. Viner, 1965, p. 32; and 1968, p. 327.

[13] Smith's readiness to use different methods was not of course accompanied by any fervent professional over-confidence regarding actual results. On the subject of quantitative methods, Schumpeter (1954) castigated Smith for remarking that he placed 'no great faith in political arithmetic' or in the 'exactness' of its 'computations': 'It was the inspiring message, the suggestive programme which wilted in the wooden hands of the Scottish professor...A. Smith took the safe side'. After the pretentious over-confidence regarding 'the quantitative revolution', which has taken place since Schumpeter was writing – with its marvellous results for economic policies – it may be possible today to discern more intellectual merit in the sobering attitude of someone who was ready to 'take the safe side' (see 1954, p. 212; and A. Smith, 1937, p. 501).

In fact, Smith employed methods which recently have been power-fully denounced by some philosophers and economists. For Smith was a historical economist not only in the sense that he was empirical, but in that the theme of *progress through natural stages of development* runs all through his *Inquiry into the Nature and Cause of the Wealth of Nations*. Smith was in fact, with Adam Ferguson and Smith's pupil John Millar, a leader of the Scottish historical school,[14] and they might well be described as proto-historicists. Smith did not claim to have discovered 'laws' of economic development, or indeed, *any* economic laws, and so might not be describable as a 'historicist' in the fullest sense. But, especially in the often rather neglected Book III of *The Wealth of Nations*, 'Of the Natural Progress of Opulence', Smith seeks to lay down 'the natural course of things' or an 'order of things which necessity imposes in general', though he allowed that this natural course or order could be 'inverted' by misconceived government policies.

Of course, as with most methods (including, for example, quanti-tative methods) 'historicist' procedures, as Sir Karl Popper has demon-strated, have been grossly misused, and wildly exaggerated claims have been made on their behalf. But if one is interested in different kinds of economy, existing at different times and places, and their different actual and potential levels of development, then one cannot afford fastidiously to dismiss 'historicist' concepts, questions, and methods, however uncertain and unreliable. Though the economist should test and scrutinise results or predictions with the utmost feasible strictness, he cannot dismiss in advance *any* method which may yield some fragment of insight – and certainly not just because such a method is not employed in what are called the most 'mature' natural sciences such as physics.

Therefore, even more definitely than with regard to the scope of the subject, there may seem in 1976 to be important lessons to be found in the methodological comprehensiveness and balance of Smith's *Inquiry*, which has, in this respect, virtually never been emulated in a book of general principles of major importance. Though Marshall discerned and wrestled with the problem of meshing history and analysis in an exposition of general principles, following the metho-dological revolution of James Mill and Ricardo,[15] no one has really been able to put it all together again with the balance and compre-hensiveness achieved in *The Wealth of Nations*.

[14] See Roy Pascal, 1938, pp. 167ff; and R. L. Meek, 1971, pp. 9ff.
[15] See the next chapter: James Mill and Ricardian economics: a methodological revolution?

IV

Adam Smith's *Inquiry*, with its abundantly marshalled empirical and institutional data, evidence, and illustrations, with its sometimes extensive historical digressions (for example, on silver, or on the corn trade, or on the Bank of Amsterdam), and with its exhaustive surveys of institutions (for example, educational institutions), is all eventually held together, securely but flexibly, by the thread provided by a single *type* of model or 'system': what Smith called 'the simple system of natural liberty', or what we might call the freely competitive, self-adjusting, market model. The conditions for 'natural' values and prices, wages, profits and rents, having been analysed the model is applied generally – but not dogmatically, universally, or exclusively – both to domestic and foreign trade as well as to the allocation of particular resources and to their accumulation and employment in the aggregate. Moreover, Smith uses his simple system of natural liberty as a historically 'dynamic' model, in that it is concerned not only with a static criterion, or ideal condition, but with the *progress* of the economy – an essential part of Smith's central theme. What Smith's *Inquiry* is primarily about is how 'the simple system', starting from individual initiative, allocates, accumulates, and reallocates resources *via* free markets so as to release and stimulate, more effectively than any other 'system', the economic forces which make for progress. The essential unique contribution of 'the simple system' is this vital and attractive complementarity between individual freedom and the economic progress of society.

This assertion of the simple 'system', or the free-market model, in such broad, general terms (but not universally or exclusively) provides one of the main grounds for maintaining that Smith's *Inquiry* marks an epoch in the history of economic thought, or even a revolution in the subject. For it was Adam Smith who really generalised the theory of market self-adjustment as operating effectively, by and large – though with several and, in some cases, important exceptions – throughout the economic cosmos, domestically and internationally, micro-economically and macro-economically. Of course, others before Smith had discerned self-adjusting forces at work in particular sectors, and had also sometimes urged that in some areas these forces should be allowed to work themselves out free of government intervention: for example, Gervaise and Hume for international trade, North, Mandeville, and Josiah Tucker for domestic markets, and with regard to labour or capital markets. But it was Smith who asserted the 'system', or model in general terms, as a general answer regarding most economic processes of a 'natural' or normal kind. It must also be emphasised that for Smith self-adjustment was not assumed as a hypothetical abstraction, but was asserted as an imprecise and qualified empirical theory, open, in principle, to refutation, regarding how particular market processes actually and usually worked out. Smith discerned and asserted that market processes worked out in general, given some reasonably simply specifiable, and practically feasible, conditions, in a very different way from that which had mostly been stated or implied in previous economic writings.

In *The Wealth of Nations* there are two great economic forces or processes making for economic progress, which depend, in their turn, on the psychological factor of the individual's striving to better his condition, and on a favourable legal framework (especially regarding property and land tenure). The first of these two great economic forces is the division of labour. It has been justifiably asserted that the initial and basic proposition of Smith's *Inquiry*, that the division of labour depends on the extent of the market, 'is one of the most illuminating generalisations which can be found anywhere in the whole literature of economics' (A. Young, 1928, p. 529).

What might be called Smith's micro-economics and international economics are concerned with how free competitive markets allow the division of labour to contribute with its full power to economic progress. The second great force, or process, making for economic progress is individual frugality or parsimony; and Smith's 'macro-economics' shows how, under his simple system of natural liberty, individual frugality, or parsimony can be fully implemented in the progress of the economy.

Of course, as we have already emphasised, Smith does not assert the empirical validity of the 'simple system', or model, in dogmatic, unqualified, or universal terms. In the mass of historical evidence and illustration, which it is an essential part of Smith's method to bring to bear, and to assign its due weight, a variety of qualifications and exceptions are to be found, certainly in micro-economic and inter-national applications of 'the simple system' or model.

In the first place Smith emphasises the basic preconditions to be satisfied, such as a favourable legal and property framework. It was laws and customs relating to land tenure which 'have perhaps con-tributed more to the present grandeur of England, than all their boasted regulations of commerce taken together' (1937, p. 369).

Smith is, of course, also constantly emphasising (and denouncing) the striving after monopoly and the persistence of monopolies and restrictive practices, 'which may endure for many centuries,' or 'for ages together,' and which are based sometimes on 'particular accidents' and sometimes on 'natural causes', as well as government legislation (1937, pp. 60–1).

The important qualifications and exceptions, which Smith cites, to the beneficent working of his simple system are well known.[16] They include, notably, defence and shipping, justice, public works (a potentially capacious category), and building methods and standards. Smith is even prepared to allow the government to fix or limit the rate of interest (for which he was logically rebuked by Jeremy Bentham). As regards foreign trade, he was ready to support an export duty on wool and moderate import duties for the purposes of revenue and retaliation or bargaining.

V

There is one feature of Smith's 'micro-economics' which had important consequences in the subsequent history of economic thought and about which some disagreements have appeared in recent years: this is his labour and cost-of-production analysis of value. It has been authoritatively maintained (and we would agree) that Smith's treatment of value (1) marked a significant shift of emphasis as compared with his predecessors; and (2) involved a serious *under*emphasis, or confusion, regarding the role of utility and demand. Recently these views have been challenged.[17]

As regards the historical question, it seems doubtful whether the generalisation can be sustained (against the writings of de Roover) that the Scholastics generally placed greater emphasis upon costs than upon demand and utility. But it is not necessary, at this point, to go back to the Scholastics and argue over such a massive generalisation. It is simply relevant to point up the contrast with *Francis Hutcheson*, with regard to the definition of utility or 'use'. For Hutcheson employs a comprehensive concept of use, or utility which includes that of giving 'any satisfaction, by prevailing custom or fancy, as a method of ornament or distinction...for this will cause a demand as well as natural use' (1755, vol. II, pp. 53–4). Smith, on the other hand, in *The Wealth of Nations* maintains that 'utility', which 'may be called "value in use"', is *not necessary at all* for 'the greatest value in exchange'. Smith is thus amputating the utility concept, in a manner rejected by most economists before and since.

In any case, it hardly seems deniable that this initial assertion by Smith, in a crucial passage, that goods which may even possess the greatest value in exchange may have *no* 'value in use', or 'utility', was highly confusing. This proposition of Smith has been defended by maintaining that he must have meant by 'value in use' and 'utility', not what has been meant by economists before and after Smith, that is 'desiredness' – or satisfying a want of whatever kind – but that he

---

[16] See J. Viner's essay 'Adam Smith and Laissez Faire,' 1928, pp. 116ff.
[17] See S. Hollander, 1973, pp. 133ff; and M. Bowley, 1973, pp. 110ff.

must rather have meant a kind of objective, biological, or 'moralistic' usefulness – as P. H. Douglas called it. But this attempt at an explanation seems unsatisfactory because (1) Smith is changing the meaning of the term 'use' (or 'utility') compared with his predecessors (e.g. Francis Hutcheson); and (2) because in any case Smith's usage is economically irrelevant and need not have been adopted simply to make the point which he may have wished to make, that is, the familiar point that economic values are not 'objective', moralistic, or biological values.[18]

Seen in proportion and perspective, in the whole vast setting and sweep of *The Wealth of Nations*, this seems a rather petty analytical point, or 'a little local difficulty', regarding the dissection of which Smith himself might have felt some impatience. But historically his treatment of value, and the new shift of emphasis which he introduced in that consequential paragraph at the end of Chapter IV of Book I, along with his unusual definition of utility and value-in-use, had a significant influence on orthodox theorising in Britain for much of the next century until Jevons, and it provided a cue for the revival by Marx of the ideology of labour value, originally propounded by Locke as a defence of private property. Of course, for ideological or persuasive purposes the labour-value pseudo-theory has much to be said for it. But it is largely useless in terms of allocation formulae or for predicting economic behaviour in a non-primitive economy.

In fact, Smith's treatment of value, and his objective concept of utility, was certainly not helpful to his own major purpose, that of establishing the case for economic freedom, which requires, or is much assisted by, a value analysis which gives a full role to subjective utility and individual choice and demand. Smith's objective biological or 'moralistic' concept of utility contains possible implications from which Smith himself would have recoiled in horror: that is, that there are objective biological or moral questions, or 'utilities' which experts, of one sort or another, may be qualified to instruct us about. Moreover, the 'objective' labour and cost analysis of value can lead, and has led, in the totally opposite direction to that of Smith's supreme message regarding economic freedom. In fact it is not too much to maintain that a subjective concept of utility is essential, and fundamental for a pluralist and free economy, and therefore for a pluralist and free society. (That is, of course, precisely why Marxists are so keen to get rid of such a concept.) We must, therefore, agree strongly with Professor P. H. Douglas's conclusion, in his Chicago lecture of 1926, that historically it turned out to be highly unfortunate that Smith

[18] As Marshall observed, in his treatment of utility and values, Adam Smith 'makes himself the judge of what is useful to other people and introduces unnecessary confusion' (1975, p. 125).

shifted the emphasis, along with a crucial definition, in the analysis of value, from the scarcity approach developed by his predecessors, Pufendorf, Carmichael, and Hutcheson, along the road which led to Ricardo, Marx and their successors.[19]

VI

The second of the two major economic factors, by or through which progress is promoted, is that of saving, investment and accumulation. Smith's stress on the role of capital accumulation in promoting economic progress has even been described as the greatest innovation in *The Wealth of Nations*, and there are clearly some grounds for such a claim. But Smith's point is not simply the importance of accumulation: *but how – within the simple system of natural liberty – individual frugality and initiative in free markets will be fully and smoothly implemented and converted into capital accumulation, and the economic progress of society, without any intervention of government*. It is the 'simple system' which enables the frugal or parsimonious man, concerned simply to 'better his own condition', to be a public benefactor. Throughout his macro-economics, in both his analysis of saving and investment and his treatment of money, Smith holds to the logic of his 'simple system' and its implications for government policy, in a highly, though not absolutely, consistent manner (apart from his incongruous approval of a maximum rate of interest).[20]

[19] See Douglas, 1928, pp. 77ff. I would agree with the recent summary of Professor Denis O'Brien: 'Adam Smith laid the foundations for classical value theory. What he did, and the way he did it, were to prove extremely important because he seems deliberately and consciously to have rejected the value theory which he inherited. He inherited a subjective value theory: and instead of developing this he largely substituted for it a cost of production theory...The dismissal of utility as a determinant of value is justified by reference to the "diamonds and water" paradox although, as we have seen, Smith solved this in his *Lectures*. It is interesting to see that Smith so far purges his analysis of the subjective elements as to redefine utility. As understood by Hutcheson and Smith's predecessors, utility was subjective; and this was also the view adopted by the other Classical economists from Ricardo onwards. But for Smith "having utility" meant not being productive of subjective satisfaction but having objective usefulness' (1975, pp. 78–80). On the other hand, I cannot quite follow Professor O'Brien's explanation of Smith's having 'to rework his value theory', in this way between the *Lectures* and *The Wealth of Nations*, because in the latter book he had a distribution theory and in the former he did not. Smith *could* have followed the line taken soon after by J. B. Say in terms of 'relative productive contribution'.

It seems, however, to go too far to assert as does Professor R. L. Meek, that: 'It cannot be too strongly emphasised that any approach to the problem of the determination of value from the side of utility and demand (as opposed to that of cost and supply) would have been regarded by him [Smith] as quite alien to the general outlook of *The Wealth of Nations*. Smith makes it perfectly clear that in his opinion demand has nothing directly to do with the determination of exchange value ' (1973, p. 73).

[20] On Smith as the major founder of what Keynes was to call 'classical economics', see below: The Keynesian revolution and the history of economic thought, Chapter 5, Section VI.

Smith's macro-economics, that is, both what Schumpeter called the Turgot–Smith saving-and-investment theory, as well as his treatment of money and the money supply, represent a sufficiently sharp novelty and contrast, as compared with what had gone before, such as also fully to deserve the description 'revolutionary'. There had been only a few intimations previously of the new, unconditionally pro-saving model in the writings of one or two of Smith's predecessors (as, for example, in Francis Hutcheson's notable denunciation of Mandeville's eulogy of luxury spending, as well as, of course, in Turgot's *Réflexions*).[21]

We noted the flexibility and qualifications with which Smith applies his 'simple system' in the fields of micro-economics and international trade. But his macro-economics, on the other hand, is the one major area where he applies this 'system' without sufficient regard to qualifications and exceptions, or to the necessary conditions, *which very much need specifying*, with regard to the monetary and banking framework.[22]

First, there is Smith's bald, unqualified assertion about saving and investing that: 'what is annually saved is as regularly consumed as what is annually spent, and nearly in the same time too'.

Consequently: 'Every prodigal appears to be a public enemy, and every frugal man a public benefactor' (1937, pp. 321–4).

Secondly, there is Smith's treatment of the money supply. He seems at times to suggest that it is simply a crude fallacy of 'the mercantile system' to be concerned about the money supply any more than, say, the wine supply:

> We trust with perfect security that the freedom of trade, without any attention of government, will always supply us with the wine which we have occasion for: and we may trust with equal security that it will always supply us with all the gold and silver which we can afford to purchase or to employ, either in circulating our commodities, or in other uses...Upon every account, therefore, the attention of the government, never was so un-necessarily employed as when directed to watch over the preservation or increase of the quantity of money in any country [1937, pp. 404–5].

At some points it seems that Smith is implying that his 'simple system' of competitive freedom can and will always be so flexible as to adjust satisfactorily to any variations in the money supply. Elsewhere Smith seems to recognise that a growing economy needs a growing money supply, while pointing out, in the Digression on Silver, that the world supply of precious metals, or international liquidity, may be extremely uncertain and unreliable. However, Smith seems also to assume that, internally, if the quantity of gold and silver is not main-

---

[21] See T. W. Hutchison, 1953b, pp. 52ff; 1958, p. 393.
[22] One such qualification or exception mentioned by Smith might be his 'vent for surplus' idea about export trade. But this seems a rather doubtful and not very large breach. See S. Hollander, 1973, pp. 268–76.

tained in a country, then paper money will automatically be created to the appropriate amount, without giving rise, apparently, to any serious problems of central regulation (1937, pp. 181, 188, 207, 281, and 304).

Of course, the monetary and banking conditions, or framework, required for the reasonably smooth working of Smith's 'simple system' can be worked out. But Smith did not get very far towards doing this. His rather cavalier treatment generated a long-persistent over-optimism, first regarding the intellectual and practical difficulties of devising and implementing, *through governments*, a satisfactory framework of monetary and banking rules and institutions, and secondly, regarding the seriousness of defects in these rules, or in their implementation, for economic stability. With regard to money and macro-economics, Smith did not adequately develop the conditions and qualifications for his simple system which had been suggested by the less 'revolutionary' but more perceptive insights on these subjects of his greatest friend, David Hume, or of his eclipsed rival Sir James Steuart – sometimes referred to as 'the last of the mercantilists'.[23]

VII

Smith's intellectual horizons in *The Wealth of Nations* ranged with tremendous spaciousness, in time and place, and with regard to levels of development, over every variety of society, economy, and human specimen, from the primitive savage to the eighteenth-century Scotsman. Geographically, there is hardly any major area of the world, except Australasia, nor any significant period of history, which Smith does not call upon, at some point, for evidence and illustration. Peoples and countries, literally from China to Peru, not omitting the Tartars and the Hottentots, and including, of course, frequently and at length, the ancient Greeks and Romans, all have their contribution to make to the empirical or historical comprehensiveness of *The Wealth of Nations*. When Smith declares what 'are the two greatest and most important events recorded in the history of mankind' (1937, p. 590), he does not include a fundamental invention, a decisive battle, a great political declaration or religious revelation: the two greatest and most

[23] In his illuminating article 'Adam Smith and the Bankers', Professor S. G. Checkland concludes: 'The banking expression of Smith's system of natural liberty was a set of institutions composed of many enterprises, none capable of monopolistic power or even leadership, each guided by prudential rules, and all trading within an environment of law provided by the state. Acting in aggregate they would, Smith implied, provide an optimal money supply or an effective approximation to it. But in the light of Banking conditions in the Scotland of Adam Smith's time, not to speak of the years to follow when matters approximated even less to his assumption, his view of banking omitted important aspects of reality which, if properly attended to, might have damaged his view of economic processes' (1976, p. 523).

important events in the history of mankind are, for Smith, 'the discovery of America and that of a passage to the East Indies by the Cape of Good Hope'; that is, two vast potential extensions of the market (and the second of Smith's greatest historic events is not even an extension in area, but an improvement of the means of communication).

These vast extensions of the world market had, in Smith's day, given rise to the most important process or problem in international or world-wide politico-economic relations of the period, that of colonisation. Colonisation, as Smith saw it, was essentially the expression in the international arena, of the constant mercantile striving after monopoly. If, according to Clausewitz, war was the continuation of foreign policy by other means, then, according to Smith, colonisation was the continuation of monopolisation by other means. Nothing is more passionately and constantly condemned, throughout *The Wealth of Nations*, than this monopolistic drive, both generally, and in its particular manifestation in colonial policies: 'To prohibit a great people...from making all that they can of every part of their own produce, or from employing their stock and industry in the way that they judge most advantageous to themselves, *is a manifest violation of the most sacred rights of mankind*' (1937, p. 576).

The colonial policies of Britain were, according to Smith, 'less illiberal and oppressive' than those of other countries. At home, also, the bad effects of monopoly had been countered especially by 'that equal and impartial administration of justice which renders the rights of the meanest British subject respectable to the greatest, and which, by securing to every man the fruits of his own industry, gives the greatest and most effectual encouragement to every sort of industry' (1937, p. 576).

But her colonial policies were, nevertheless, in Smith's estimation, causing Britain herself very serious harm: 'The whole system of her industry and commerce has thereby been rendered less secure; the whole state of her body politic less healthful, than it otherwise would have been...Under the present system of management, therefore, Great Britain derives nothing but loss from the dominion which she assumes over her colonies' (1937, pp. 571 and 581).

If his cherished plan of a federal union, or commonwealth, of the colonies and mother country was unattainable, then (though it was vain, Smith believed, to hope that this would be conceded) it would be preferable for Britain to abandon gradually but completely the restrictions on colonial trade, and to give up altogether all authority over her colonies – and, in the first place over those in North America:

> By thus parting good friends, the natural affection of the colonies to the mother country, which perhaps, our late dissensions have well nigh

extinguished, would quickly revive. It might dispose them not only to respect, for whole centuries together, that treaty of commerce which they had concluded with us at parting, but to favour us in war as well as in trade, and, instead of turbulent and factious subjects, to become our most faithful, affectionate, and generous allies [1937, p. 582].[24]

In the very last paragraph of *The Wealth of Nations* Smith repeats the demand that 'if any of the provinces of the British empire cannot be made to contribute towards the support of the whole empire' then, it was surely time for Great Britain to give up her 'project of an empire'. In that case, in the very last sentence and last words of the book Smith instructs his country 'to accommodate her future views and designs to the real mediocrity of her circumstances' (1937, p. 900).

Commenting in *1876*, Walter Bagehot found this 'a strange passage considering all that has happened since, and all the provinces we have since taken' (1881, p. 275).

In *1976*, on the other hand, perhaps these famous last words did not seem so 'strange'.

VIII

Smith once described his treatment of economic policy in *The Wealth of Nations* as a 'very violent attack upon the whole commercial system of Great Britain' (Scott, 1937, p. 283).

Moreover, when he delivered that attack it was from what was still a heretical or minority point of view. As Walter Bagehot said, a hundred years ago, 'It is difficult for a modern Englishman, to whom "Free Trade" is an accepted maxim of tedious orthodoxy, to remember sufficiently that a hundred years ago it was a heresy and a paradox. The whole commercial legislation of the world was formed on the doctrines of Protection' (1895, p. 128).

But if Smith could be 'violent' in denunciation, and revolutionary in policies and objectives, he tended to be moderate and gradualist regarding timing and methods. As an empirical and historical economist, and as something of a historical relativist, Smith does not resort to abstract, absolute optima and maxima in his criticisms and appraisals of economic institutions and policies – which highly abstract criteria can be and often are used by economists in such misleading and question-begging ways. In *The Theory of Moral Sentiments* Smith's approach to policy-making even bears a somewhat conservative cast, in that he urges 'the man whose public spirit is prompted altogether

---

[24] Of course Smith's first preference in colonial policy was for a union or commonwealth involving both representation for, *and taxation of*, the colonists. In fact C. R. Fay seems to have gone so far as to place an immense responsibility on Smith for having pressed on Townshend in 1766 the case for American taxation: 'In the last analysis it was professorial advice which lost us the first empire' (1956, p. 116).

by humanity and benevolence' to be prepared to bear with the faults and injustices of the existing order of society:

> He will content himself with moderating, what he often cannot annihilate without violence. When he cannot conquer the rooted prejudices of the people by reason and persuasion, he will not attempt to subdue them by force...he will accommodate, as well as he can, his public arrangements to the confirmed habits and prejudices of the people; and will remedy, as well as he can, the inconveniences which may flow from the want of those regulations which the people are averse to submit to. When he cannot establish the right, he will not disdain to ameliorate the wrong; but like Solon, when he cannot establish the best system of laws, he will endeavour to establish the best that the people can bear [1797, vol. II, p. 109].[25]

It is here that Smith's methodological approach implies an attitude to policy differing very significantly from the narrowly abstract, *a priori*, deductive, 'rigorous' *laissez-faire* of Quesnay – and Ricardo.[26] For Smith accuses Quesnay of irrelevantly and misleadingly applying the criteria of absolute or perfect optimality, in imagining that an economy and polity 'would thrive and prosper only under a certain precise regimen, the exact regimen of *perfect* liberty and *perfect* justice...If a nation could not prosper without the enjoyment of *perfect* liberty and *perfect* justice there is not in the world a nation which could ever have prospered' (1937, p. 638).

In his theory and advocacy of free markets Smith did not concern himself with the Utopian abstractions of perfect maxima and optima.[27] After the Ricardian methodological 'revolution' such concepts became, and have remained, the focus for a great deal of vacuous,

[25] Smith returned to the comparison with the laws of Solon in *The Wealth of Nations* (p. 510) on the subject of the prohibition of wheat exports: 'This law...though not the best in itself, it is *the best which the interest, prejudices and temper of the times would admit of*' (italics added).

[26] As Professor J. M. Buchanan has observed: 'Smith did not, however, seek to accomplish his didactic purpose by elaborating his theoretical model. Instead he applied the analysis variously, sometimes repetitively, but always with great skill, to the actual economy in which he lived. The starting-point remained always the institutions that he observed, the effects of which were to be explained, along with the effects that might be forthcoming under alternative arrangements. Modern economic theorists proceed quite differently. They analyse abstract and formal models which may bear little or no relationship to the institutions that may exist. (Indeed it is this disparity between the conceptual models and reality that often makes the attempted derivation and testing of empirically refutable hypotheses seem bizarre.)' ('Public Goods and Natural Liberty', in *The Market and the State*, eds. T. Wilson and A. Skinner, 1976, p. 271.)

[27] Nor did Smith employ the concept of '*perfect*' competition. See on this subject the essay by Mr G. B. Richardson, 'Adam Smith on Competition and Increasing Returns' (1976, pp. 350–60). It is surely quite mistaken for Mr M. H. Dobb, in the same volume (p. 335), to describe Smith as '*par excellence* a theorist of perfect competition'. Smith explicitly took into account the pervasiveness of ignorance, for example with regard to the prime motivator: 'Profit is so very fluctuating, that the person who carries on a particular trade cannot always tell you what is the average of his annual profit' (1937, p. 79).

irrelevant, or misleading 'rigour'. Adam Smith's conclusions regarding policies were empirically based on historical and psychological
judgments.

IX

It was noted earlier how Smith was able, plausibly and validly, to
make the complementarity of freedom and economic growth, or
progress, a central theme of *The Wealth of Nations*, and also how
attractive a message is which proclaims that more of each of two great
highly-valued *desiderata* are obtainable, so that it is unnecessary to
sacrifice one of them to obtain more of the other. But there can be
no doubt as to which of this happily complementary pair Smith would
have chosen if he had felt forced to do so.[28] Smith was, at least,
ambiguous about the value or significance of an increase in wealth as
a value or objective.[29] While greater wealth for a society had a part
in rendering it more civilised, and more free, or was an indicator of
social progress, regarding individuals, at any rate: 'In ease of body
and peace of mind, all the different ranks of life are nearly upon a
level, and the beggar, who suns himself by the side of the highway,
possesses that security which kings are fighting for' (1797, vol. 1, p.
467).[30]

[28] 'Smith may be understood as a writer who advocated capitalism for the sake of
freedom, civil and ecclesiastical' (J. Cropsey, 1957, p. 95).
[29] As Mr D. A. Reisman puts it: 'On the one hand, he *appears* to have been a commodity-
utilitarian concerned with free trade, economic growth, the ending of restrictive
practices and other ways of providing "a plentiful revenue or subsistence for the
people"; while on the other hand, he seems to have been determined to prove that
higher material standards of living do not, except for the poor, represent a significant
change in human happiness.' As Mr Reisman shows, there is no contradiction here.
See Reisman, 1976, p. 102.
[30] Just before this quotation comes the marvellous passage on the rat race and 'gracious
living' (cited by Professor George Stigler, 1950, p. 3): 'The poor man's son, whom
heaven in its anger has visited with ambition, when he begins to look around him,
admires the condition of the rich. He finds the cottage of his father too small for
his accommodation, and fancies he should be lodged more at his ease in a palace.
He is displeased with being obliged to walk a-foot, or to endure the fatigue of riding
on horseback... To obtain the conveniences which these afford, he submits in the first
year, nay in the first month of his application, to more fatigue of body and more
uneasiness of mind than he could have suffered through the whole of his life from
the want of them. He studies to distinguish himself in some laborious profession. With
the most unrelenting industry, he labours night and day to acquire talents superior
to all his competitors. He endeavours next to bring those talents into public view... For
this purpose he makes his court to all mankind; he serves those whom he hates, and
is obsequious to those whom he despises. Through the whole of his life he pursues
the idea of a certain artificial and elegant repose which he may never arrive at, for
which he sacrifices a real tranquillity that is at all times in his power, and which if
in the extremity of old age he should at last attain to it, he will find to be in no respect
preferable to that humble security and contentment which he had abandoned for it.
It is then, in the last days of his life, his body wasted with toil and diseases, his mind

This belief, perhaps, explains why Smith does not seem to show much interest in policies concerned with the distribution of wealth or income. Anyhow, Smith would always have put freedom first and would surely have done so more than ever two hundred years later when he would so often have found himself faced with the paradox that tremendous technical progress, and in some respects higher material living standards, seem to be accompanied rather by more insidious threats to freedom than a greater abundance of it. Smith valued economic freedoms not mainly or simply because he believed that they promoted a more rapid growth of GNP per head, but *for their own sake*, because they were a kind of freedom which ordinary people value highly and an essential component of civil freedom. The paradox has recently been pointed out of how today – in some countries at any rate – we have the most strident demands and assertions regarding many new kinds of cultural and social 'liberation', combined with a disdain, or even a concentrated hostility towards economic freedoms.[31] For Smith's great enemy, monopoly, is more than ever on the march, in ever more powerful forms. The monopolisers, of one type or another, seem often to be aided both by the trend of technology, which gives new opportunities, or pretexts, for their encroachments, as well as by the upsurge of centralised government expenditure by democratic governments, which Smith himself referred to as 'the thoughtless extravagance that democracies are apt to fall into' (1937, p. 770).

In some countries at any rate, Smith's description of monopolists seems truer than ever today:

> Like an overgrown standing army, they have become formidable to the government, and upon many occasions intimidate the legislature. The member of parliament who supports every proposal for strengthening this monopoly is sure to acquire not only the reputation of understanding trade, but great popularity and influence... If he opposes them, on the contrary, and still more if he has authority enough to be able to thwart them, neither the most acknowledged probity, nor the highest rank, nor the greatest public services, can protect him from the most infamous abuse and detraction, from personal insults, nor sometimes from real danger, arising from the insolent outrage of furious and disappointed monopolists [1937, p. 438].

Today, indeed, the monopolists and monopolisers, in some cases of types and forms almost unknown to Smith, are certainly as insolent, outrageous, and furious as ever, but unfortunately they do not seem

galled and ruffled by the memory of a thousand injuries and disappointments which he imagines he has met with from the injustice of his enemies, or from the perfidy and ingratitude of his friends, that he begins at last to find that wealth and greatness are mere trinkets of frivolous utility, no more adopted for procuring ease of body or tranquillity than the tweezer-cases of the lover of toys...'

[31] See Samuel Brittan, 1973.

so often to be disappointed.[32] It is just this dangerously adverse trend, discernible here and there, which makes all the more precious today the message of *The Wealth of Nations*, and which makes the cause of the economic freedom for which it stands all the more vital. But this cause was not fought for by Adam Smith, and cannot with full effect be fought for today, from the narrow base of modern economics. *The Wealth of Nations* was not founded on abstractions, nor on the particular abstraction of economic actions and processes from their historical interdependence and interpenetration with social, legal and political actions and processes.

X

Was there, or can one validly or appropriately write – as we have – of a Smithian 'revolution'? If a comparison is drawn between *The Wealth of Nations* and the *Principles of Political Economy*, which Sir James Steuart – 'the last of the mercantilists' as he has been described – published just nine years earlier, surely the transformation in terms of theories and policy-conclusions can be regarded as so rapid, extensive, and profound, as to deserve the adjective 'revolutionary'. But this could be regarded as a misleading contrast. For many decades before the publication of Smith's (or Steuart's) great work, the central ideas, which were to be so powerfully expounded in *The Wealth of Nations*, had been gaining ground in one form and direction or another. Especially in the early 1750s there had been a remarkable cluster of significant writings and new ideas, with Galiani's *Della Moneta* (1751), Hume's *Essays* (1752), the early works of Josiah Tucker (1751–2), Cantillon's *Essai* (1755), followed by Quesnay's works in the later 1750s. But the fact that, as in the case of most important 'revolutions', a long preparatory or premonitory build-up can be traced, decades before the 'revolutionary' event (in this case the publication of *The Wealth of Nations* in 1776) does not seem necessarily to render invalid or inappropriate the term 'revolution'.

Let us briefly categorise the main contributions of *The Wealth of Nations* so as to fix more precisely where, if anywhere, its revolutionary significance may lie.

First, the immense importance and indeed near-uniqueness, of the

---

[32] Op. cit., p. 438. With regard to professional–academic monopolies, the remarkable letter (already quoted) to William Cullen (1774) should be remembered: 'Had the Universities of Oxford and Cambridge been able to maintain themselves in the exclusive privilege of moderating all the doctors who could practice in England the price of feeling a pulse might by this time have risen from two or three guineas, the price which it has now happily arrived, to double or treble that sum, and English physicians might have and probably would have been the most ignorant and quackish in the world' (see John Rae, 1895, pp. 273–80, and J. Thomson, 1859, vol. I, p. 473).

scope and method of *The Wealth of Nations* must surely be emphasised. At the same time, however, the methodological significance of *The Wealth of Nations* would not seem to justify any 'revolutionary' claims. Certainly Smith's marvellous use of history was largely unprecedented, as regards political economy, in 1776 (though not entirely so since Sir James Steuart's *Principles* are admirably enriched by a great deal of comparative economic and institutional history). But presumably a contribution, however important and outstanding, which does not successfully influence and dominate, or set a pattern for, much or any subsequent work, can hardly be said to have brought about a 'revolution'.

The justification for the concept of a Smithian 'revolution' must be based on the generalisation in *The Wealth of Nations* (though not in universal or dogmatic terms) of the notion of a 'natural', effective self-adjusting mechanism as being usually at work throughout competitive economies or markets. As we have noted, the idea that the economy, or rather, to start with, particular sectors, such as the labour market, or foreign trade, should be regarded as more or less effectively self-equilibrating had been gaining ground. The development can be traced at least from the closing decade or two of the previous century, though the self-adjusting mechanism was not always regarded as operating sufficiently rapidly or smoothly as to justify, in terms of policies, an exclusive reliance on market processes, or the denial of any role to government, in the sector or field concerned – as in Cantillon's treatment of international trade.

In more or less positive terms, *The Wealth of Nations* was a main force in establishing an archetypal model for economic analysis, that of a competitive market, or economy, the insights from the analysis of which are still relatively fruitful after two hundred years – though returns in operational significance to the more and more 'rigorous' refinements and elaborations of the model have for some time been sharply decreasing.

In terms of policies, *The Wealth of Nations*, which in its own day constituted a strong attack, from a minority position, against established ideas on economic policy, remained a main intellectual force behind the long transformation (or revolution) in English economic policy over, roughly, the next seventy years (not to mention the book's influence in other countries).

More specifically, the most definitely and sharply 'revolutionary' contribution of *The Wealth of Nations* was surely that relating to economic growth and the theory of employment, interest and money, with its extreme emphasis on the beneficence of individual saving and on the smoothness with which this was implemented in capital accumulation. This left little or no macroeconomic role for governments, apart from an extremely simple one with regard to the money and banking framework. Again, it is regarding the theory of employment and money that the contrast is greatest and most clear-cut between *The Wealth of Nations* and Sir James Steuart's *Principles*. Nor had David Hume in his essays made the full revolutionary transition brought about in *The Wealth of Nations*. Both in terms of the break with what had gone before, and its dominance of what came after, Smith's macro-economics has the strongest claims on the adjective 'revolutionary'.

Regarding 'micro-economics', or, more particularly, the development of the theory of value and price, Smith's treatment of utility, and his emphasis on the idea of labour-value, though not perhaps, by themselves deserving the adjective 'revolutionary', nevertheless can be regarded as introducing a distinctive and extremely consequential feature of the new 'classical' regime, which Smith did so much to establish, and which was to dominate, in England, for the next hundred years. As regards this contribution, different economists would assign very different weights on the favourable or unfavourable side of the balance. This would also be the case with what has been called 'the dark side' of *The Wealth of Nations*, that is, the intimations of monopsony in labour markets, the falling rate of profit and the sombre possibilities of the stationary state, and the cultural stultification brought about by the intensification of the division of labour.

Finally, we should not conclude without emphasising that as a result of the Smithian revolution, as with most or all intellectual revolutions, there were significant losses of one kind or another. A 'revolution' in political economy or economics usually or inevitably involves, or consists of, some drastically new selection and simplification, *either* with regard to the questions given priority, *or* possibly, with regard to important elements in the answers – or both.[33] In the case of the Smithian revolution, questions and theories, to which economists before and since Smith have attached great importance, were submerged by its triumph, mainly questions and theories regarding employment, interest and money, but possibly also regarding utility and value. Any intellectual cost–benefit analysis will, of course, inevitably involve subjective valuations. However, in the case of the Smithian 'revolution', although Keynesians – and those dubious regarding the validity for theory and policy of self-adjusting models – would stress the losses, there would appear to have been an overwhelming consensus, supported by almost all schools of economists, as to the epoch-making intellectual gains represented by *The Wealth of Nations*.

[33] See below the concluding essay: On revolutions and progress in economic knowledge (Chapter 11).

2

James Mill and Ricardian economics: a methodological revolution?

I

It hardly seems useful to start by discussing whether there was or was not – or whether one can properly write of – 'a Ricardian revolution'. Sir John Hicks and Professor H. G. Johnson have expressed themselves in favour of this concept which at least seems *prima facie* to be well worthy of serious consideration.[1] But in any case, if the changes brought about by Ricardo's work, and the influence which it exercised, may validly be regarded as 'revolutionary', this must surely be primarily, or largely, because of the novelty, and subsequent importance for the subject, of its *methodological* contribution. Certainly Ricardo's pronouncement that 'the principal problem in Political Economy' was 'to determine the laws which regulate this distribution' – that is, distribution between aggregate rent, profits and wages – signified a certain shift in interests or priorities, although this problem had already been broached in *The Wealth of Nations*. But it can be argued that of *much* more fundamental and lasting significance than the shift of interest or priorities regarding the subject of distribution, was the *methodological* claim that problems in political economy are problems of '*determining laws*'. Moreover, of equally fundamental and lasting significance was the *method* of extreme abstraction (or 'strong cases') by which, in his *Principles* Ricardo sought to 'determine' the 'laws' of political economy, which he claimed his new Science was establishing. The transformation in method and epistemology as between *The Wealth of Nations* and Ricardo's *Principles* is profoundly significant because it altered the mood in which the 'problems' of political economy were treated and in which 'theories', and policy-recommendations were put forward. In fact, Walter Bagehot opened his essay on Ricardo by stressing his most important contribution: 'The true founder of abstract Political Economy is David Ricardo' (1895, p. 197).

It has long been known that James Mill played a considerable part in the intellectual development and political career of Ricardo. But the full extent of Mill's influence, and just how vital and substantial

[1] See Sir John Hicks, 1975, p. 322, and 1976, pp. 207ff; and H. G. Johnson, 1975, pp. 23ff.

it was for Ricardian political economy, in a crucial, perhaps 'revolutionary' phase of the subject, and for the subsequent development
and methodology of political economy and economics, does not
seem to have been fully recognised.

II

The nature of the relationship between James Mill and Ricardo was
first clearly revealed, at least with regard to an important phase after
1815, in Mr Sraffa's edition of Ricardo's Correspondence (1951). We
can follow there in detail the story – the rough outline of which had
long been known – of the triumphantly successful twofold plan which
James Mill brought off for and through Ricardo: of how he got the
modest, unlettered paterfamilias and wealthy retired-stockbroker-
turned-country-gentleman, first to publish to the world a treatise on
the *Principles of Political Economy and Taxation*, and then, following up
the written with the spoken message, how Mill pushed the still reluctant
Ricardo into Parliament to proclaim the new politico-economic doctrines from the stage of the House of Commons. For the first part of
the project Mill acts as an impatient professorial supervisor, admon-
ishing, encouraging, cajoling, and bullying his gifted but inarticulate
pupil through the labours of large-scale literary composition. Then,
as a preparation for his parliamentary career, Mill puts Ricardo
through a rapid and wonderfully confident correspondence course in
what he describes as 'the science of legislation' – an *exact* science as Mill
presents it.

Whatever may be thought of the directions in which Mill influenced
Ricardo and his career, and of the political and philosophical principles
which he sought so vigorously to instil in his much less sophisticated
friend, it is impossible not to respect the warmth and affection they
had for one another. Ricardo drew out the least forbidding side of
Mill, and they seem to have been much closer to one another personally
as well as intellectually than were Ricardo and Malthus. Partly it was
a case of the attraction of opposites. As a writer Ricardo always felt
himself something of an amateur, at any rate outside the narrower
field of monetary and banking problems, and he admired the strenuous professional intellectual, or 'hackneyed stager' as Mill called
himself, who wielded such a fluent and incisive pen on any subject from
India to Education.[2] Mill, on the other hand, respected the practical,
successful, financial acumen and expertise of Ricardo. But it was not

[2] As late as 18 September 1820 Ricardo writes to Mill: 'It is impossible that I should
be offended by any offer of a fee which Mr. Napier might make me – nor does my
pride stand in the way of my accepting it, if it is usual for persons who are amateurs,
and not worthy to be called authors, to be paid for their articles.'

contrasts, but close intellectual affinities, which made possible their partnership, and which made Ricardo such a 'natural' for Mill's great project or promotion. (See E. Halévy, 1928, p. 266.)

According to Mr Sraffa, Mill and Ricardo first met 'as a result of the publication of Mill's early pamphlet *Commerce Defended* in 1808'. Bain states that Mill's acquaintance with Ricardo began in 1811.[3] In any case, the earliest extant letters show that they were on terms of close, man-to-man friendship by December or January of 1810–11. Down to the middle of 1814, while both were constantly in London, apparently they walked and talked together almost daily, and there are very few letters. In view of the later commanding role which we can now see Mill exercising in his letters of 1815–18, the question obviously arises as to the part which Mill had earlier played in Ricardo's intellectual development down to 1815, in particular in the decisive broadening out of Ricardo's economic theorising from the narrower monetary problems of his early pamphlets, a field in which he had great first-hand knowledge and expertise, and in which he made significant use of statistics, to his far more general and overwhelmingly deductive analysis of 'the laws of distribution', as presented in his *Essay on Profits* (1815), the embryo of his *Principles*. Halévy has said that when they were in London together (1811–14), 'Mill during the long walks which he loved to take with Ricardo, was chiefly concerned to give him lessons in method.'[4]

However, further significant, if indirect, evidence regarding this remarkable relationship between Mill and Ricardo, perhaps very crucial in the history of political economy, appeared with Professor Winch's valuable edition of *James Mill's Selected Economic Writings* (1966). In particular, this volume made easily available the previously not unknown, but relatively disregarded and inaccessible, early essay of Mill, *An Essay of the Impolicy of a Bounty on the Exportation of Grain* (1804),[5] as well as a similarly little known, and remarkably significant, later article on methodology entitled 'Whether Political Economy is Useful' (1836). It appears that one of these works was the first, and the other the last, of all Mill's publications.

---

[3] See D. Ricardo, 1952, vol. VI, p. xv, and A. Bain, 1882, p. 74.

[4] E. Halévy, 1928, p. 272. As Walter Bagehot emphasised regarding 'the doctrines of James Mill': 'If Ricardo had never seen James Mill he would probably have written many special pamphlets of great value on passing economic problems, but he would probably not have written *On the Principles of Political Economy and Taxation*, and thus founded an abstract Science' (1895, p. 204).

[5] Professor George Stigler refers to this Essay of 1804 as 'a first, very poor pamphlet on foreign trade' (1965, p. 306). We are not concerned here with the quality of the pamphlet but with its influence on Ricardo.

III

In considering the possible intellectual influence of Mill on Ricardo in the seven years or so before the opening of the correspondence of 1815 and after, it seems especially worth emphasising that although, *in 1815*, Mill is proclaiming himself as having been out of touch 'for a good many years' with the subject of political economy, *when he and Ricardo first met*, some time after 1808, it was Mill who was the senior economist, or contributor to political economy, with two trenchant publications to his name and a number of reviews, while Ricardo may not yet have published a line. Doubtless Ricardo had a first-hand knowledge and expertise in finance and banking, but Mill had expounded and developed the central, general theories of economics, which had the most decisive policy significance regarding population and natural wages, and aggregate demand and supply.

So in the early years of the Mill–Ricardo friendship, before Ricardo broadened his interests in, and grasp of, political economy, Mill may not only have been Ricardo's educator in philosophy, method, literary composition, and political presentation, but may also, in his masterful way, have decisively shaped the substance of Ricardo's general economic assumptions and theorising, in accordance with Mill's own already well-articulated doctrines regarding the central theories of political economy. Anyhow, two of the main Ricardian doctrines of political economy, and the two with the most immediate and weighty implications for policy, had been developed by Mill in his works of 1804 and 1808, though the extent of Ricardo's debts to, or indoctrination by, Mill, is impossible to estimate precisely.

In these two works, *The Impolicy of a Bounty on the Exportation of Grain* (1804), and *Commerce Defended* (1808), Mill closely follows Adam Smith, at times almost reproducing Smith's arguments word for word. But, as he does so, Mill drastically and decisively sharpens and hardens Smith's theories, putting them in a much starker and more unqualified form, imbuing them with his own particular confident dogmatism, and giving them a much more definite cutting-edge in terms of policy applications, to the extent of making them new and different doctrines. This is more especially the case with regard to his earlier work on the grain bounty than it is in *Commerce Defended*, where Smith's original doctrine, including the policy applications, was already pretty clear-cut and unqualified.

This essay on the grain bounty has not attracted much attention, but it is closely relevant to what became Ricardo's central question, or 'model', of macro-distribution and 'progress'. Following very closely Smith's treatment of grain bounties, Mill opens his essay with the idea of the uniqueness of 'corn',[6] which is 'the only necessary article' and 'a peculiar commodity':

> the very elements of society are interwoven with the laws which regulate the production of this primary article. . .
> If it be said that wool is the material of one of our most important manufactures; corn is the most important material of all our manufactures. If it be of importance that the raw material of any of our manufactures should be got cheap, surely it is of importance that what is the great material of them all should be got cheap [1966, pp. 55 and 67].

Mill proceeds to elaborate on the crucial significance of this 'basic' commodity:

> *No proposition is established more thoroughly to the conviction of those who have studied the scientific principles of political economy than this; that the money price of corn, regulates the money price of everything else.* The wages of the common labourer may in general be reckoned his maintenance. He must earn a sufficient quantity of corn to feed himself, otherwise he cannot exist. If he is paid in money, the sum of money he daily receives must always be equivalent to the quantity of corn he must use. If the price of corn is high he must receive the greater sum of money, as his day's wages, to buy with. *This is so obviously necessary, that we need spend no more time in proving it. The money price of labour therefore is entirely regulated by the money price of corn* [1966, p. 63, italics added].

The idea of the uniqueness of 'corn' is then combined by Mill with an extremely hard-line version of the natural wage doctrine and with the 'great law of society' regarding the relation between wage rates and population changes – a far more drastic, unqualified, and immediate version of the doctrine than that in *The Wealth of Nations*, or, at many points, in the writings of Malthus himself. In fact Mill's natural-wage doctrine amounts to a very different proposition from that of Smith, with far more definite and immediate policy implications:

> The multiplication of the human species is *always* in proportion to the means of subsistence. *No proposition too is more incontrovertible than this*, that the tendency of the human species to multiply is much greater than the rapidity with which it seems possible to increase the produce of the earth for their maintenance.
> . . . *No one however will hesitate to allow all that is necessary for our argument*, that the tendency of the species to multiply is *much* greater than the rapidity with which there is *any* chance that the fruits of the earth will be multiplied in Britain, or any other country in Europe. What is the consequence of *this great law of society*, but that the production of corn creates the market for corn? Raise corn as fast as you please, mouths are producing still faster to eat it. Population is *invariably* pressing close upon the heels of subsistence; and *in whatever quantity* food be produced, a demand will always be produced greater than the supply.

<hr />

[6] See A. Smith, 1937, p. 482.

Mill then draws the conclusion that, except in quite extraordinary circumstances, the voluntary export of corn will never take place except possibly in the very short-run or after a bumper harvest: 'The nature of *this elementary principle of society*, of which we never ought to lose sight, is such that *a sufficient market is always provided at home, for all the corn which the land, with the utmost exertions of the farmer, can ever be made to produce.*'[7]

Having dealt with the proposal for a bounty on export, Mill goes on to advocate the free importation of corn arguing that 'at *all* times when the trade in corn is free, the interests of the traders in corn, and those of the people at large, are *exactly* the same'.

It is clear that several of the key concepts, assumptions, and building blocks of the Ricardian models and 'theories' are presented, trimmed, polished and ready for use, in this essay of 1804 by James Mill: notably (1) the simplified concept of 'corn' as a short-hand for workers' subsistence, a unique commodity in that it is a raw material for all production; (2) an extremely drastic, hard-line version of the Malthusian proposition regarding the relations between population changes and wages; and (3) the idea that adjustments take place so rapidly and completely that lags, or 'disequilibria', can be left out of the argument. Therefore, it seems that Mr Sraffa's statement regarding the influence of Mill on Ricardo's *Principles* may be highly questionable that: 'On the theory there is little doubt that his influence was negligible' (1951, p. xxi).[8]

We do not propose to discuss at length the second, and much better-known, of Mill's early works, which, also, he had produced before his meeting with Ricardo, that is, *Commerce Defended*. Here the 'classical' doctrine of the impossibility of general over-production is elaborated – as Mill acknowledges – from Smith's seminal and epoch-making analysis of saving and investing. Mill simply adds a mixture of dogmatism and ambiguity:

> No proposition however in political economy seems to be more certain than this which I am going to announce, however paradoxical soever it may at first sight appear; and if it be true, *none undoubtedly can be deemed of more importance.*

[7] Op. cit., p. 56 (italics added). Over half a century later J. S. Mill was still upholding the same argument just when the importation of grain into this country, exported from America and other overseas countries, was expanding massively. See J. S. Mill, 1909, I.XIII.3, and IV.IV.7.

[8] On the other hand, Professor Ingrid Rima has convincingly argued that the Ricardian problem of distributive shares comes from Mill's essay of 1804 and that 'analytically speaking, the behaviour of the distributive shares was Mill's chief concern' in this essay. Professor Rima goes on to emphasise how Mill's work 'paved the way *attitudinally* for the Ricardian model', and 'contributed to the development of the conceptual framework within which Ricardo's positive economics took shape' (1975, pp. 115 and 118. I am grateful to Professor W. Thweatt of Vanderbilt University for this reference).

The production of commodities creates, and is the one and universal cause which creates a market for the commodities produced...
The demand of a nation is always equal to the produce of a nation...
...*Every individual in the nation uniformly makes purchases, or does what is equivalent to making purchases, with every farthing's worth which accrues to him*[9]

These doctrines, and the policy implications that followed, already had behind them the considerable prestige and authority of Smith. But they were by no means, in 1808, as dominant as they were later, thanks to Mill and Ricardo, to become. They were fundamentally challenged, not only by Spence, Mill's immediate opponent in *Commerce Defended*, but by Lauderdale and Bentham – and of course, later, in a rather confused way by Malthus. Lauderdale's arguments are equated by Mill with those of Spence, who is told that his questioning of Smith's analysis is 'pretty much as if a follower of the Ptolemaic astronomy should accuse the reasonings of Sir Isaac Newton of vagueness and confusion'.[10]

It may be said that the Smith–Mill–Say doctrine of saving, investment, and the impossibility of general over-production is not closely related to the main Ricardian problem of macro-distribution. But it was pretty completely, consistently, and unswervingly accepted and upheld by Ricardo. Moreover Ricardo expounded the massive, *laissez-faire* policy implications of the doctrine in Parliament, in opposing public works in the depressed year of 1819. What subsequently came to be called 'The Treasury View' is really '*The Ricardo View*'.

Between the publication of *Commerce Defended* and the crucial correspondence which began in 1815 two episodes in the Mill–Ricardo relationship may be briefly mentioned.

The *first* episode, as recorded in the earliest Mill–Ricardo letters extant (1811), relates to Bentham's essay on inflation, *The True Alarm*, which rejected the Turgot–Smith saving-is-investing doctrine, and its consequences, which had been so stoutly maintained in *Commerce Defended*. In correspondence of 1811 Mill and Ricardo agreed to advise Dumont, who had sent them Bentham's manuscript, that no attempt was worth making to prepare it for publication. Against Bentham's argument Ricardo maintained: 'The increase of money in my opinion can have no other effect than raising the prices of commodities.'[11]

The *second* episode, or example, where traces of Mill's influence may perhaps be discerned, relates to the most celebrated of Ricardo's early monetary writings, his *Reply to Bosanquet*, also of 1811. Here Ricardo

[9] 1966, pp. 135–6 (italics added). Mill's strong anti-landlord opinions are expressed in this essay of 1808: 'The fact is that land in this country bears infinitely less than its due proportion of taxes, while commerce is loaded with them' (p. 96).
[10] Op. cit., pp. 133n and 144. See below: The Keynesian revolution and the history of economic thought (Chapter 5, Section VII).
[11] See Ricardo, vol. VI, 1952, p. 16. See also my article: 'Bentham as an Economist', 1956.

deploys a kind of trenchant, even aggressive, methodological criticism which is most emphatically on Millian lines. A favourite section of Mill's Commonplace Book was devoted to 'Theory or Speculation versus Practice', in which he brings a mass of authorities to check the over-weening presumption of the practical man.[12] This is precisely Ricardo's line in his *Reply to Bosanquet*. Ricardo's denunciations of the man 'who is all for fact and nothing for theory', as having 'no standard of reference', and as providing a 'melancholy proof of the power of prejudice over very enlightened minds', might, as regards substance and language, have been penned by the master himself.[13] In fact it would not be at all surprising if Mill had some direct responsibility for these controversial gambits, which can hardly be paralleled else-where in Ricardo's writings.

It is difficult to suppress the conjecture that those Millian 'lessons in method', mentioned by Halévy, may already have been influencing his pupil as early as 1810. Exactly how far Ricardo, from the earliest stages of his career as a political economist, was fashioned by Mill as the intellectual partner, or instrument, for Mill's projects, is bound to remain doubtful. But there does seem to be considerable evidence for such conclusions of Halévy as that Mill exercised 'a profound influence on Ricardo's intellectual destiny'; and that he 'intended to make of Ricardo the Quesnay of nineteenth-century England'.

Halévy maintains that Mill did not so much give Ricardo a doctrine, 'as develop in him the doctrinal leaning and make him a doctrinaire'.

We may agree on the latter point, but would observe that in his two early economic writings Mill may in fact have 'given' Ricardo two or three of his *central economic theories or doctrines*, or essential components of them.[14] We may suggest also that what Halévy writes of the relation

[12] See A. Bain, 1882, p. 465, Professor R. S. Sayers has pointed out that the sweeping triumph of Ricardo in this controversy was by no means an unqualified gain for nineteenth-century monetary theory, as the sound points in Bosanquet's argument tended to be overlooked. Professor Sayers maintains that many of Ricardo's monetary doctrines were permeated and vitiated by the assumption 'of instantaneous adjust-ment to a long-run equilibrium' and concludes that Ricardo's influence 'was a major disaster'. (See 1971, p. 37 et *passim*.)

[13] It is typical that Ricardo starts by castigating Bosanquet for 'availing himself of the vulgar charge, which has lately been so often countenanced, and in places too high, against theorists. He cautions the public against listening to their speculations before they have submitted them to the test of fact' (see Ricardo, 1951, vol. III, pp. 160 and 181). Mill and Ricardo obviously resisted and rejected suggestions of empirical testing – like many of their 'model'-building successors.

[14] Professor W. O. Thweatt has concluded that we owe the early development of the doctrine of comparative advantage to James Mill rather than to Ricardo or Torrens. Regarding Mill's influence on Ricardo, Professor Thweatt emphasises the use of 'Mill's words' by Ricardo in his *Economical and Secure Currency* and endorses Patten's view, approvingly cited by Sraffa, that 'Mill wrote or at least inspired the first three paragraphs of the Preface' to the *Principles*. He holds that Mill's hand may also be noted in the translations from J. B. Say and in the – according to Sraffa – 'unmistakeably characteristic' phrases in the conclusion on the poor laws of the chapter 'On Wages'. (See 1976, pp. 222 and 232.)

between Mill and Bentham may be applied also to that between Mill and Ricardo: 'In Bentham [sc. Ricardo] he had found a great man, *his* great man, and he set it before himself to give Bentham [sc. Ricardo] an influence in his own time and in his own country' (1928, pp. 282 and 307).

But from 1815 onwards there is no need to rely so much on conjecture or speculation. We can follow out precisely Mill's influence and methods of persuasion in his letters.

IV

The opening letter of Mill's campaign, and the first between him and Ricardo for nearly a year, was that written on 23 August 1815.[15] Before that there had been only a few miscellaneous exchanges in 1810–11, and four letters, all from Mill, in 1814. There is no suggestion that Mill is taking up a subject they had previously discussed together face to face. Mill expresses the hope that now Ricardo has 'made quite as much money for all your family, as will be conducive to their happiness', he will have leisure for 'other pursuits' and first of all for the science of political economy. For Mill explains that he is satisfied

> that you can improve so important a science far more than any other man who is devoting his attention to it, or likely to do so for Lord knows how many years.
> ...I have other projects upon you, however, besides. You now can have no excuse for not going into Parliament, and doing what you can to improve the most imperfect instrument of government.

Ricardo will find the problems of politics extremely simple, once he turns his mind to them: 'There is not more difficulty in finding out the principles on which alone good government *must of necessity depend*; and when all this is as clearly in that head of yours, as that head knows how to put it, the utility in Parliament, of even you, in spite of all your modesty, would be very great' (italics added).

However, for the time being, Mill drops the subject of Parliament; for his first main task is to urge Ricardo on with his treatise on the science of political economy. In his next letter (9 November 1815) Mill writes:

> As I am accustomed to wield the authority of a school master, I therefore, in the genuine exercise of this honourable capacity, lay upon you my commands to begin to the first of the three heads of your proposed work, rent, profit, wages – viz. rent, without an hour's delay. If you entrust the inspection of it to me, depend upon it I shall compel you to make it all right before you have done with it.

[15] References to letters to and from Ricardo are given by the dates by which they are ordered in *The Works*, ed. P. Sraffa, vols. VI–IX inclusive, 1952.

Soon Mill is explaining to Ricardo how a treatise on the principles of political economy should be set out, that is, like a text book of geometry, an analogy which Mill had suggested in previous writings:

> Never set down any material proposition without its immediate proof, or a reference to the very page where the proof is given...On this subject (improvements in cultivation), I ordain you to perform an exercise...My meaning is that you should successively answer the question, what comes first? First of all is the improvement. What comes next? Ans. The increase of produce. What comes next? Ans. A fall in the price of corn. What comes next? – and so on [22 December 1815].

Mill breaks off at the difficult point of the analysis, but his suggestions are methodologically typical, and Ricardian economic 'theorising' (or analysis) is in the main conceived after this pattern and based on a highly simplistic and mechanical conception of economic behaviour and processes which are to be accounted for in terms of 'proofs'.

At length, after some further robust encouragement from Mill, Ricardo sends him the draft of a large part of the *Principles* (October 1816). Mill's impression of the work is absolutely clear-cut: 'I think you have made out all your points. There is not a single proposition the proof of which I think is not irresistible' (18 November 1816). A month later, having examined some further chapters by Ricardo, Mill writes: 'Your doctrines are original and profound. I have no hesitation whatsoever in saying that they are fully and completely made out. I embrace every one of them; and am ready to defend them against all the world' (16 December 1816). Mill hardly raises one single point of doubt or difficulty.

It might indeed be said that whatever else can be claimed for Ricardo's *Principles*, certainly they possess 'originality and profundity' (though there is nothing *necessarily* virtuous in either of these qualities). But Ricardo's *Principles* certainly represented a big new departure from previous conceptions of the scope and method of Political Economy, as represented in the writings of British economists. But only a year before, Mill had confessed that 'not withstanding my passion for the science of Political Economy, it has so happened that for a good many years I have not been able to think of it [except through Ricardo's writings or conversation]'. Of course, Mill wanted to encourage the diffident Ricardo. But his immediate and complete adoption of Ricardo's new doctrines, in the exposition of which subsequent economists, even the most enthusiastic, have found serious difficulties, was almost certainly perfectly sincere. It can only be explained by the fact that Mill saw Ricardo to be applying *not only exactly the same method but also the same important assumptions* on which Mill himself had based his conclusions 7–10 years previously, and this guaranteed the soundness, and fully justified (for Mill) his unquestioning acceptance of Ricardo's new doctrines.

Soon, however, Mill is looking forward to further advancing Ricardo's political education by means of his forthcoming book, *The History of British India*:

> The subject afforded an opportunity of *laying open the principles and laws of the social order in almost all its more remarkable states, from the most rude to the most perfect with which we are yet acquainted*; and if I have been capable of explaining them, will be of some help to you, in exploring what I wish to see you thoroughly acquainted with, the course which human affairs, upon the great scale, have hitherto taken, the causes of their taking these different courses, the degree in which these courses have severally departed from the best course, and by what means they can best be made to approximate to that course. That is the field of application; and none of the pretexts you set up will avail you. *There is nothing in this knowledge mysterious, or hard – there is nothing but what anybody, who has common application, a common share of judgement, and is free from prejudice, and sinister interest, may arrive at* [19 October 1817, italics added].

In fact, in Mill's eyes, Ricardo at this point seems to begin to bear some significant resemblance to Martin Luther: 'All great changes in society, are easily effected when the time is come. Was it not an individual, without fortune, without name, and in fact without talents, who produced the Reformation? Before I have done with you you will reason less timidly on this subject because you will know more certainly'.[16]

Ricardo in reply (9 November 1817) expresses an eager interest at the prospect of Mill's great work on the laws and progress of society: 'I am eager for information on the causes which are constantly obstructing man in the rational pursuit of his own happiness. Legislation would be comparatively an easy science if it were not so much influenced by the characters and dispositions of the people for whom it is to be undertaken.'

Perhaps we can detect in this wistful remark Ricardo's hankering after a simplified political 'model', or one of those 'strong cases', by means of which he could deal with the political world and enunciate impressively sweeping pronouncements 'in the nature of mathematical truths', by the method he had applied in political economy.

Mill, however (3 December 1817), is perfectly confident of his ability to deal with Ricardo's doubts and difficulties:

---

[16] Mill had made a considerable study of Luther when he translated and edited with copious notes, *An Essay on the Spirit and Influence of the Reformation of Luther*, by C. Villers, 1805. Among Mill's 'copious notes' is one lending the most enthusiastic support to the doctrine of Perfectibility: 'That impulse which every individual experiences to better his condition, and which is the inexhaustible source of improvement in the individual, is an equally necessary and inexhaustible source of improvement to the species' (p. 25).

I have no doubt about removing all your difficulties; and showing you that instead of being a science, the practical results of which must always be uncertain, rendering it always prudent to try to remain in the state we are in, rather than venture the unknown effects of a change, *legislation is essentially a science the effects of which may be computed with an extraordinary degree of certainty*; and the friends of human nature cannot proceed with too much energy in beating down every obstacle which opposes the progress of human welfare [italics added].

At last, Ricardo gets his copy of the *History* (18 December 1817): 'The long-desired book has at length arrived.' For Ricardo, it comes as a revelation:

> If I before had had doubts of what legislation might do, to improve society, I should have none after reading what I have read of your book. . .My plea for caution and timidity was ignorance. . . Legislation may not be as difficult as I imagine – I wish it may not be, for I am anxiously disposed to understand it. One of the great difficulties of the science appears to me to be that. . .of the government and laws of one state of society being often very ill adapted for another state of society [italics added].

We must linger for a moment over Mill's *History of India* if only to deplore the very small attention paid to this remarkable work in studies of philosophic radicalism and of the politics of classical political economy.[17] Leslie Stephen gives us no idea of it, while Halévy's hints, though penetrating and important, are all too brief. But John Stuart Mill described his father's great work as:

> one of the most instructive histories ever written, and one of the books from which most benefit may be derived by a mind in the course of making up its opinions. The Preface, among the most characteristic of my father's writings, as well as the richest in materials of thought, gives a picture which may be entirely depended on, of the sentiments and expectations with which he wrote the History [1924, p. 21].

The vast labours of research devoted by Mill to the historical narrative, which makes up a large part of the *History*, made it for many decades an indispensable authority.[18] But Book II of the work is

---

[17] See the valuable article by Duncan Forbes (1951): 'James Mill and India'. Mr Forbes described Mill's *History* as 'a good and perennially useful example of the influence on the minds of administrators and politicians of half-baked "philosophical" history'. Mr Forbes further points out that 'it is clear that Mill's method in the *History of India* was really deductive, as in the *Essay on Government in which the "experience test" is purposely rejected, as also in the abstract political economy of Ricardo*' (italics added).

[18] Mill's *History* was edited and continued by H. H. Wilson, FRS, Professor of Sanskrit at Oxford (and it is his edition, published in 1858, a year after the Mutiny, that we have used). Wilson worked on Mill's *History* because he regarded it as 'the most valuable work upon the subject which has yet been published', but he nevertheless considered it necessary to criticise Mill's judgments on Hindu civilisation in extraordinarily severe terms: 'He has elaborated a portrait of the Hindus which has no resemblance to the original and which almost outrages humanity. . . *The History of British India* is open to censure for its obvious unfairness and injustice; but in the effects which it is likely to exercise upon the connection between the people of England and the people of India, it is chargeable with more than literary demerit:

concerned, as Mill had informed Ricardo, with determining 'laws of society', 'laws of human nature', 'stages of social progress', 'steps' in 'the progress of civilization', and in particular with the place of the Hindus in the 'scale of civilization', that is, with an appallingly hubristic, imperialist historicism. Mill had, of course, never been further East than, let us say, perhaps Southend, and hardly knew a word of any Oriental language. However, as he explains in his Preface, such merely empirical equipment may well be highly misleading for the historian, and is of far less importance than a grasp of 'the laws of society' and what Mill calls 'a masterly use of evidence'. Anyhow, Mill has no hesitation in pronouncing the most severe, definite, and detailed condemnation of every aspect of Hindu civilisation (except perhaps cloth-making) including manners, mathematics, sculpture, laws, painting, science, architecture and religion, and he concludes that the Hindus are at almost the lowest possible level in 'the scale of civilization'.

Ricardo is especially pleased with Mill's treatment of Hindu civilisation. He writes off to Say (18 December 1817), and to Trower (26 January 1818):

> His views on the subjects of Government, Law, Religon, Manners are profound; and his application of these views to the actual, and past state of Hindustan...cannot, I think, be refuted...*He endeavours to refute the prevailing opinion that the Hindus are now, or ever have been, a highly civilized people...I am exceedingly pleased with the work* [italics added].

Meanwhile, Mill is reassuring Ricardo as to his difficulties about the fitting of legislation to the particular state of society, or position on 'the scale of civilization', to which it is to apply (27 December 1817):

> On the subject of legislation I have no doubt that we shall now understand one another. Doubtless, the laws which are adapted to an improved state of society, would not be adapted to a state of society much behind. But *it will not be difficult when we have a standard of excellence, to determine what is to be done, in all cases. The ends are there, in the first place, known – they are clear and definite.* What you have after that to determine is the choice of the means, and under glorious helps for directing the judgement [italics added].

its tendency is evil; it is calculated to destroy all sympathy between the rulers and the ruled; to preoccupy the minds of those who issue annually from Great Britain, to monopolise the posts of honour and power in Hindustan, with an unfounded aversion towards those over whom they exercise that power, and from whom they enforce that honour; and to substitute for those generous and benevolent feelings, which the situation of the younger servants of the Company in India naturally suggests, sentiments of disdain, suspicion, and dislike, uncongenial to their age and character, and wholly incompatible with the full and faithful discharge of their obligations to Government and to the people. There is reason to fear that these consequences are not imaginary, and that a harsh and illiberal spirit has of late years prevailed in the conduct and councils of the rising service in India, which owes its origin to impressions imbibed in early life from the *History* of Mr. Mill' (p. xiii).

However, Ricardo's healthy doubts are not completely flattened by Mill's steamroller, and with much native insight he cautiously directs attention to a fundamental difficulty in Mill's 'science of legislation' as applied to the government of India. May not the great criterion of utility, or the greatest happiness of the greatest number, be used to justify or even demand, the wholesale imperialistic conquest of the sub-Continent? (except in so far as the House of Commons at home might find the operation rather expensive):

> Are we to fix our eyes steadily on the end, the happiness of the governed, and pursue it at the expense of those principles which all men are agreed in calling virtuous? If so, might not Lord Wellesley, or any other ruler, disregard all the engagements of his predecessors, and by force of arms compel the submission of all the native powers of India if he could show that there was a great probability of adding to the happiness of the people by the introduction of better instruments of government. If he accomplished this end at the expense of much treasure to England, I do not think the plea would be admitted by a British House of Commons, however freely chosen. The difficulty of the doctrine of expediency or utility is to know how to balance one object of utility against another – there being no standard in nature, it must vary with the tastes, the passions and the habits of mankind. This is one of the subjects on which I require to be enlightened [6 January 1818].

Unfortunately, there is no record in these letters showing that the enlightenment which Ricardo requested from Mill was forthcoming.[19] However, Mill continued to reassure his pupil as to 'the plain rule of utility, which will always guide you right, and in which there is no mystery' (23 September 1818). We would, however, point out that on another problem of internal policy Mill had previously suggested to Ricardo that though the principle of utility was consistent with obligations between individuals being held sacred, where *states* were concerned it was justifiable to overturn contractual obligations which clashed with the one great over-riding principle: 'There is utility in making bargains between individuals strict, unless where fraud appears to have intervened. There would be utility in holding all

---

[19] It should be noticed that Mill does give a partial answer to Ricardo's question, further on in the *History* (vol. VI, p. 286): 'Even where the disparity of civilization and knowledge were very great; and where it was beyond dispute that a civilized country was about to bestow upon a barbarous one the greatest of all possible benefits, a good and beneficent government; even here, it would require the strongest circumstances to justify the employment of violence or force.' But what are 'the *strongest circumstances*', and who is the judge of them? Obviously Mill does not clear up the question of principle as to the implications of the magic formula of utility 'which will always guide you right, and in which there is no mystery'. The formula becomes no plainer when it appears as the criterion of civilisation as well as of all action: 'Exactly in proportion as *Utility* is the object of every pursuit may we regard a nation as civilized. Exactly in proportion as its ingenuity is wasted on contemptible and mischievous objects, though it may be, in itself, an ingenuity of no ordinary kind, the nation may safely be denounced as barbarous' (vol. II, p. 105).

bargains between the public and individuals null, in which the interests of the public are sacrificed' (22 December 1815).[20]

V

Before we leave this remarkable correspondence there is one further exchange between Mill and Ricardo from the year 1821 which raises the question of class antagonism, and clashes of interest. Mill remarks (23 August 1821): 'It is very curious that almost every body you meet with – whig and tory – agree in declaring their opinion of one thing – that a great struggle, between the two orders, the rich and poor, is in this country commenced.'

Ricardo replies (28 August 1821) with a less pessimistic view and expresses confidence in the political wisdom of the English governing class:

> The only prospect we have of putting aside the struggle which they say has commenced between the rich and the other classes, is for the rich to yield what is justly due to the other classes, but this is the last measure which they are willing to have recourse to. I cannot help flattering myself that justice will prevail at last, without a recurrence to actual violence.

We may note, first, that this discernment of class antagonisms by Mill and Ricardo dates from 1821 when, according to Marx, 'the class struggle was still undeveloped', that is, before his cut-off date of 1830, at a period which 'was notable in England for scientific activity in the domain of political economy',[21] most notably by Ricardo. But, in fact, James Mill denounced in the most ferocious terms those who advocated the pursuit of class conflict, while Ricardo expounded doctrines of the harmony of class interests, between labourers and capitalists, in more extreme terms than any subsequent, important bourgeois 'apologist'. Ricardo argued not merely that this harmony of class interests was a fact, but that it was so 'self-evident' a conclusion of the science of political economy (as expounded by him) that 'even the lowest' would accept the point. Even Bastiat hardly went as far as this.

Regarding Mill, it must be emphasised that he was a middle-class radical, not a champion of the working class. Professor Donald Winch has very clearly pointed out how sternly Mill denounced the advocacy of labour's right to the whole product (including, for example, 'the mad nonsense of our friend Hodgskin', later so highly esteemed by Marx and Marxists and sometimes grossly misdescribed as a 'Ricardian Socialist'). According to Mill:

[20] James Mill and his pupil Ricardo may be seen as propagators of that 'false individualism' which leads towards absolute state power. See F. A. Hayek on 'Individualism: True and False' (1949, pp. 1–32).

[21] See the 'Nachwort' to the second edition (1873) of *Das Kapital*, and Chapter 8, section III below.

These opinions, if they were to spread, would be the subversion of civilised society; worse than the overwhelming deluge of Huns and Tartars. This makes me astonished at the madness of people of another description who recommend the invasion of one species of property, so thoroughly knavish, and unprincipled, that it can never be executed without extinguishing respect for the rights of property in the whole body of the nation, and can never be spoken of with approbation, without encouraging the propagation of those other doctrines which directly strike at the root of all property.[22]

Mill continues:

I should have little fear of the propagation of any doctrines hostile to property, because I have seldom met with a labouring man (and I have tried the experiment upon many of them) whom I could not make see that *the existence of property was not only good for the labouring man but of infinitely more importance to the labourers as a class, than to any other*.[23]

Ricardo certainly agreed with Mill's 'middle-class' view that respect for property is good for 'the workers' too. He said so himself.

In Marxist versions of the history of political economy a very important role is attributed to Ricardo as a propagator of 'the antagonism of class interests'. It is, therefore, necessary to emphasise that Ricardo believed preponderantly in the over-riding harmony of class interests much more than in the kind of antagonism which Marx and Marxists ('vulgar' or otherwise) have subsequently ascribed to him, and which is a prime article of their own faith. It might be suggested that Ricardo emphasised the clash of interests between landlords and the rest of the community. But Ricardo himself *indignantly rejected*, as the most serious misrepresentation, the suggestion that he was lending any countenance to ideas of class antagonism:

Perhaps in no part of his book has Mr. Malthus so much mistaken me as on this subject – he represents me as supporting the doctrine that the interests of landlords are constantly opposed to those of every other class of the community, and one would suppose from his language that I consider them as enemies of the state.

Mr. Malthus is not justified by anything I have said in pointing me out as the enemy of landlords, or as holding any less favourable opinion of them, than of any class of the community.[24]

[22] Letter to Brougham, 3 September 1832, quoted in A. Bain, 1882, p. 364, and by D. Winch, 1966, p. 202. Professor Winch emphasises that 'Mill wished to substitute middle-class rule for aristocratic domination. He was quite unable to understand the nature of the working-class movement.' Positively, Mill held quite a different view of the class struggle from that of Marx.

[23] See A. Bain, 1882, p. 365 (italics added).

[24] *Works*, 1951, vol. II, pp. 117–19 (italics added). Again, in a letter to Trower (21 July 1820), Ricardo insists: 'I do not consider landlords as enemies to the public good.' Here is a contemporary, Marxistically-inclined interpretation (unsupported by any actual quotations or texts) which Ricardo himself would have repudiated with the same indignation as he did Malthus's misinterpretation: 'His account of the landowner's interests, and his assertion of the need to import cheap food to England, amounted to a declaration of war on the established authorities, and pointed to a serious class

Otherwise Ricardo hardly went further than, first, a qualified suggestion that technical progress *might* (not necessarily would) damage the
interests of labourers; and, secondly, the logically impeccable proposition that if something is divided into three relative or percentage
shares, and the first of these is held constant, then an increase in the
second relative or percentage share must mean a decrease in the third.
Whatever partial clashes Ricardo envisaged, he regarded as decisively
over-ridden by the broad, fundamental harmony of interests which he
held to inhere in the competitive market economy, based essentially
on full private property rights. Ricardo's glowing ideas about the
economic harmonies are expounded as regards both the international
economy, and internally, as follows:

> Under a system of perfectly free commerce, each country naturally devotes
> its capital and labour to such employments as are most beneficial to each.
> This pursuit of individual advantage is admirably connected with the uni-
> versal good of the whole. By stimulating industry, by rewarding ingenuity,
> and by using most efficaciously the peculiar powers bestowed by nature, it
> distributes labour most effectively and most economically; while, by increas-
> ing the general mass of productions, it diffuses general benefit, and binds
> together by one common tie of interest and intercourse, the universal
> society of nations throughout the civilized world [vol. I, 1951, p. 134].

What Ricardo thought about the harmony of class interests is also
indicated in the following passage about the franchise, *in which not only
are the interests of 'the poor labourer' and 'the rich capitalist' held to be in
harmony, but it is claimed that this harmony has been so conclusively
demonstrated and understood (presumably thanks to the new Science of Political
Economy, as embodied in Ricardo's own teachings) that the franchise can
suitably be conferred even on 'the very lowest'*:

> So essential does it appear to me, to the cause of good government, that
> the rights of property should be held sacred, that I would agree to deprive
> those of the elective franchise against whom it could justly be alleged that
> they considered it their interest to invade them. But in fact it can be only
> amongst the most needy in the community that such an opinion can be
> entertained. *The man of a small income must be aware how little his share would
> be if all the large fortunes in the kingdom were equally divided among the people.
> He must know that the little he would obtain by such a division could be no adequate
> compensation for the over-turning of a principle which renders the produce of his
> industry secure.* Whatever might be his gains after such a principle had been
> admitted would be held by a very insecure tenure, and the chance of his
> making any future gains would be greatly diminished; for the quantity of
> employment in the country must depend, not only on the quantity of
> capital, but upon its advantageous distribution, and, above all, on the

conflict at the heart of the new system. In addition, Ricardo's theory implied that
capitalism was subject to a process of internal degeneration' (G. Duncan, 1973, p. 51).
Professor Duncan also writes (p. 114) of how Marx 'approved of Ricardo's clear-eyed
cynicism'. It surely involves a total misreading of Ricardo's character and writings
to discover in them the slightest drop of cynicism.

conviction of each capitalist that he will be allowed to enjoy unmolested the fruits of his capital, his skill, and his enterprise. *To take from him this conviction is at once to annihilate half the productive industry of the country, and would be more fatal to the poor labourer than to the rich capitalist himself. This is so self-evident that men very little advanced beyond the very lowest stations in the country cannot be ignorant of it,* and it may be doubted whether any large number even of the lowest would, if they could, promote a division of property [1952, vol. v, p. 501, italics added].[25]

One can certainly agree with Marx regarding a certain 'naïveté' in Ricardo and also, possibly, regarding 'the scientific impartiality and love of truth characteristic of him' with which Ricardo is writing here. But though a passage similar to the above, regarding the harmony of interests between 'the poor labourer' and 'the rich capitalist', might possibly be found in the writings of Mrs Marcet – which Ricardo so warmly recommended for his daughter[26] – it seems improbable that any other major British economist in the nineteenth century would ever have penned such an extremely optimistic statement regarding politico-economic harmonies.

A certain economic pessimism is sometimes ascribed to Ricardo in respect of his forebodings about diminishing returns and the falling rate of profit. But, it seems very doubtful whether, in his view of the politico-economic prospects for the then existing system, Ricardo was basically pessimistic.[27] Certainly *politically*, Ricardo expressed a

[25] B. Inglis (1972, p. 205) points out how the premise was constantly appearing in Ricardo's writings: 'that the legislature must not be allowed to infringe the rights of property'. Dr Gunnar Myrdal has explained Ricardo's 'labour' theory of value in terms of Locke's doctrines regarding property. He asks: 'Is there any other way of accounting for Ricardo's labour theory of value? *It is no more than an unsupported hypothesis which leads to insuperable difficulties without being of any analytical use*' (1953, p. 73, italics added). Of course the labour theory is of great *ideological* use in extruding notions of subjective utility and hence of individual choice, and so justifying authoritarian, or even Stalinist, regimes.

[26] Ricardo believed enthusiastically in the popularisation of political economy. He writes to Mill (6 January 1818): 'You are correct in an opinion I have heard you give that the most intricate parts of Political Economy might be made familiar to the people's understanding...and a subject which appears at first view so difficult is within the grasp of a moderate share of talents'. On Mrs Marcet, see his letter to Mill of 10 December 1821, in which, regarding Mill's own elementary textbook, Ricardo regrets 'that you had used the word "procreation" so often in a book you call a school book'. Presumably Ricardo, no more than Malthus, would have discussed publicly the subject, or methods, of birth control.

[27] See Professor Samuel Hollander (1974), who produces a great deal of evidence for attributing to Ricardo a high degree of economic *optimism* regarding the British economy of his day, suggesting a quite Malthus-like ambiguity, on Ricardo's part, regarding the 'tendencies' set out in his 'model'. This model certainly lends itself, perhaps very misleadingly, to highly pessimistic interpretations – which have, of course, been seized upon and magnified for the purposes of political propaganda. Professor Hollander emphasises (p. 45) 'Ricardo's confidence in future prospects', and quotes Professor G. S. L. Tucker's 'careful' observation: 'Ricardo's principal conclusion, immanent throughout his work, was that profits and the rate of new capital accumulation were lower in Britain than they must otherwise have been under

buoyant, even naive, optimism. But, in any case, economic pessimism cannot be equated with a belief in class-antagonism. Moreover, the very moderate extent to which Ricardo recognised certain clashes of class-interest did not move him one inch from upholding a strict regard for the *laissez-faire* principle in distribution. If the existence of 'conflicts' implied that there must be losers – whether these losers were labourers or landlords – *nothing must be done by government, according to Ricardo, to compensate the losers, or intervene in the free market processes which caused their losses.* In 1819 Ricardo was reported as proclaiming in Parliament:

> It could not be denied, on the whole view of the subject, that machinery did not lessen the demand for labour...It might also be misapplied by occasioning the production of too much cotton, or too much cloth, *but the moment those articles ceased in consequence to pay the manufacturer, he would devote his time and capital to some other purpose* [16 December 1819] [1952, vol. v, p. 30, italics added].

However, four years later 'the Oracle' was instructing honourable members on quite opposite lines: 'It was evident, that the extensive use of machinery, by throwing a large portion of labour into the market, while, on the other hand, there might not be a corresponding increase of demand for it, would, in some degree operate prejudicially to the working classes' (op. cit., p. 305). But however fascinating may be the analytical subtleties behind Ricardo's well-known change of view about machinery, his steadfast policy-conclusion remains as an essential implication of his philosophy of political economy. In spite of the possible damage to the working classes:

> He would not tolerate any law to prevent the use of machinery. The question was, – if they gave up a system which enabled them to undersell in the foreign market, would other nations refrain from pursuing it? Certainly not. They were therefore bound, for their own interest, to continue it. Gentlemen ought, however, to inculcate this truth on the minds of the working classes – that *the value of labour, like the value of other things, depended on the relative proportion of supply and demand. If the supply of labour were greater than could be employed, then the people must be miserable.* But the people had the remedy in their own hands. A little forethought, a little prudence... [op. cit., p. 303, italics added].

Professor George Stigler has remarked that 'Ricardo is as much to be censured for his preoccupation with maximum output as certain modern economists for their preoccupation with equality' (1950, p. 10).

Perhaps this excessive preoccupation is illustrated by Ricardo's attitude to policies aimed at relieving the distress of hand-loom cotton weavers in 1820. It had been proposed that power looms should be

a more enlightened economic policy...But even if the Corn Laws were not repealed, *Englishmen could still look forward to a long period of economic progress*' (1960, p. 162, italics added).

taxed and public money applied to provide lands for those who could find no employment at their hand-looms. Ricardo's opposition to such proposals was indignant and total: 'If government interfered, they would do mischief and no good. They had already interfered, and done mischief by the poor laws. The principles of the hon. mover *would likewise violate the sacredness of property, which constituted the great security of society*' (1952, vol. v, p. 68, italics added).

VI

Perhaps to a greater extent even than with most economic theorising the, or a, main meaning and intention of the Millian–Ricardian theories and methods can be found in the nature of the policy conclusions derived from them. Ricardo's policy conclusions, which he went into Parliament to proclaim with all the authority of the new science behind him, followed from, and depended on, with great exactness and rigidity, his 'strongly' simplified assumptions or theories. The Millian–Ricardian abstract, deductive method started from starkly unqualified assumptions (or 'strong cases') based on no systematic observation of the behaviour and knowledge of buyers and sellers, savers and spenders, parents and wage-earners. They led immediately and inevitably to sharply *laissez-faire* policy doctrines. There was little or no room for judgments of probabilities or qualifications, or for weighing up, or striking a balance between, contrasting tendencies, or for broadly political considerations, all of which belong essentially among the problems of responsible, real-world policy-making. Moreover, *Ricardo was overwhelmingly interested in policy conclusions. Abolishing the Poor Laws, cutting down the Corn Laws, stopping Public Works to relieve unemployment during depressions: this is what Ricardo was centrally concerned with, however extreme the abstractions he indulged in and however remote from the real world his models may seem to us (but not to him) to have been.* Ricardo did not buy a seat in Parliament simply to expound blackboard exercises or to read out articles for *Econometrica*. As Cannan, in terms of Ricardo's intentions, quite rightly insisted: 'Among all the delusions which prevail as to the history of English political economy there is none greater than the belief that the economics of the Ricardian school and period were of an almost wholly abstract and unpractical character' (1917, p. 302).

It may be quite legitimate, if the logical or mathematical niceties of extremely abstract 'models' are what one is primarily interested in, to concentrate one's account of Ricardo's work simply on this aspect of it. But it involves a complete misinterpretation of Ricardo's own interests and purposes to appraise his works and his purposes simply in terms of highly abstract 'model'-building for its own sake.

In fact, Ricardo's economics were of the most dangerous type: on the one hand extremely abstract, based on highly restrictive assumptions used largely for deductive facility, but also, on the other hand, intended to supply, *and regarded as supplying*, direct and trenchant implications, of immediate policy relevance, for the real world. *Laissez-faire* followed immediately and directly with inescapable logic: (1) in aggregate, macroeconomic management and policy; (2) in a very stark form with regard to distribution, the labour market and the relief of poverty; and (3) with regard to the operation of markets generally, in view of their assumed, extremely rapidly self-equilibrating properties.

Taking (1) Ricardo's views on macroeconomic management and policy: *Laissez-faire* conclusions, against government action, followed logically from his (and Smith's) model. Professor Hollander has pointed out with what inexorable logic Ricardo followed out the implications of his assumptions: 'Even in the depth of economic depression Ricardo consistently insisted on the impossibility of a general deficiency of aggregate demand. The fact of unused capacity did not in any way shake his conviction that an increase in aggregate demand could not expand output' (1974, p. 23).

It must certainly be acknowledged, however, that Ricardo went much further than Adam Smith with regard to specifying a monetary framework for *laissez-faire*, which he did in his *Proposals for an Economical and Secure Currency* (1816) and his *Plan for the Establishment of a National Bank* (1824). This was a major contribution *in an area where he could claim real experience and expertise*, but a subject quite separate from his main general-theoretical interests in 'the laws of Political Economy'. Moreover, his proposals regarding the monetary framework can hardly be said to represent major qualifications or diminutions of *laissez-faire* (unless this doctrine is interpreted as equivalent to anarchism) but rather amount to proposals for the rules within which *laissez-faire* can effectively operate. The same can also be said, though considerably more questionably, regarding Ricardo's proposals for a capital levy, to reduce or remove the national debt incurred under war conditions in order to establish a peace-time normality in public finance.

(2) But it is with regard to distribution, wages, and the relief of poverty, that Ricardo emerges as a much more drastic and thoroughgoing champion of *laissez-faire* than any other leading English economist. Again, his policy conclusions followed inexorably from his very clear-cut postulates, which in turn followed those of James Mill regarding the relationship between wages, subsistence, and population. The Mill–Ricardo postulates, or 'model', were so much more sharply and more rigidly applied than in the corresponding much

looser Smithian doctrine of the natural wage, that they should be considered as amounting to a different proposition or theory. In the *Principles* Ricardo lays it down: 'Like all other contracts, wages should be left to the fair and free competition of the market, and should never be controlled by the interference of the legislature' (1951, vol. i, p. 105).

But it was to Poor Law policy that Ricardo applied the full logic of his natural wage theory. In his maiden speech in Parliament he argued: 'If parents felt assured that an asylum would be provided for their children, in which they would be treated with humanity and tenderness, then there would be no check to that increase of population which was so apt to take place among the labouring classes' (1952, vol. v, p. 1).

To his friend, the magistrate Trower, Ricardo urged: 'The population can only be repressed by diminishing the encouragement to its *excessive* increase – by leaving contracts between the poor and their employers perfectly free.'

Otherwise the prospect seemed to Ricardo to be alarming: 'The population and the rates would go on increasing in a regular progression till the rich were reduced to poverty, and till there would no longer be any distinction of ranks.'

As Ricardo put it, the aim must be to cut poor relief to the limit: 'Is not this to be done by refusing all relief in the first instance to any but those whose necessities absolutely require it – to administer it to them in the most sparing manner and lastly *to abolish the poor laws altogether*?' (1952, vol. vii, p. 125, italics added).

Again Ricardo insisted: 'Great evils...result from the idea which the Poor Laws inculcate that the poor have a *right* to relief' (op. cit., p. 248).

It is almost totally irrelevant to protest that Ricardo, as a generous, warm-hearted man, would, of course, have rejoiced to see a rise in the living-standards of the labouring class, or that he believed that such a rise might *possibly*, or eventually, come about. A rather vague, humane hope cannot be said to become an objective of economic policy unless some means are specified for approaching the objective. A belief in, or the promotion of, the progress of the British economy did not, of itself, imply the lifting of 'the great Malthusian difficulty' (as Cairnes was to call it half a century later); nor would simply the removal of what Ricardo regarded as the abuses of the Poor Laws. If the account is correct that J. S. Mill was detained at a police station for distributing pamphlets about contraception, at least he can be said to have envisaged and propagated *some kind* of means *via* which the natural wage might eventually and permanently be raised. But as an admirably respectable family man of his time such a topic was publicly unmentionable for Ricardo.

Anyhow, he certainly went considerably further with regard to the natural wage than simply making the 'assumption for certain theoretical purposes of wages at subsistence level due to pressure of population'; or merely engaging in 'grown-up talk about the implications of certain assumptions' (Robbins, 1952, pp. 84 and 215).

(3) Ricardo's 'model' of self-adjusting markets moving smoothly and rapidly to a beneficent equilibrium, depended crucially on his assumption of perfect (or adequate) knowledge. He employed this absolutely vital basic postulate more drastically and consequentially than any economist before him. As with other methods and models, James Mill and Ricardo rigorously pressed this postulate to extremes, or to the 'strong case'. In fact, to Ricardo must be ascribed the responsibility for placing the perfect knowledge postulate firmly in position at the foundations of equilibrium economics, with uncertainty – or most of the problems of the real world – 'rigorously' excluded. For example, in his *Principles* Ricardo assumes: 'Whilst every man is free to employ his capital where he pleases, he will naturally seek for it that employment which is most advantageous; he will naturally be dissatisfied with a profit of 10 per cent, if by removing his capital he can obtain a profit of 15 per cent.'

In a letter to Malthus (1811) on international payments Ricardo acknowledged the perfect knowledge postulate *as basic to his method*:

> The first point to be considered is, what is the interest of countries in the case supposed? the second what is their practice? Now it is obvious that I need not be greatly solicitous about this latter point; it can clearly demonstrate that the interest of the public is as I have stated it. It would be no answer to me to say that men were ignorant of the best and cheapest mode of conducting their business and paying their debts, because that is a question of fact and not of science, and might be urged against almost every proposition in Political Economy.[28]

Keynes wrote: 'I accuse the classical economic theory of being itself one of those pretty polite techniques which tries to deal with the

---

[28] See 1951, vol. I, p. 88 and 1952, vol. VI, p. 64. The following earlier (1937) comments of mine on these two passages seem reasonable. 'With Ricardo there is no uncertainty as to the relative advantages of different lines of investment. The assumption is tacitly made that it is perfectly foreseen that one will yield 10% and the other 15% and people "naturally" select 15%.' And regarding the second passage: 'The only possible interpretation of this passage...seems to be that economists are not to concern themselves with what actually happens in the economic world, as this is a question of fact and not of science. The *scientist* assumes that people are fully equipped with certain knowledge.' (See Chapter 7 below.)

Ricardo, at one point, remarks that 'Adam Smith has justly observed, that it is extremely difficult to determine the rate of profits of stock'. But he takes this simply as a historical difficulty regarding past periods and concludes: 'Undoubtedly if the market rate of interest could be accurately known for any considerable period, we should have a tolerably correct criterion, by which to estimate the progress of profits' (1951, vol. I, p. 296).

present by abstracting from the fact that we know very little about the future' (1937, p. 186).

It is Ricardo and Ricardian economics against whom this accusation should pre-eminently be directed.[29]

Ricardo's assumptions regarding the rapidity and smoothness with which markets moved to a beneficent equilibrium emerged logically from this basic postulate of perfect knowledge. His treatment of agricultural protection illustrates his conceptions as to the smoothness and rapidity of economic adjustments, as well as his occasional doubts. It is true that in his pamphlet *On Protection to Agriculture* (1822) Ricardo conceded that such protection should be withdrawn gradually, 'with as little delay as possible, consistently with a due regard to temporary interests' (1952, vol. VI, p. 266).

But in Parliament he had expressed extraordinary optimism about the speed of the adjustment process so far as labour was concerned. With regard to allowing free imports of corn: 'He would endeavour to show what would be the real effect. The prices of corn would be reduced immediately, and agriculture might be distressed more than at present. *But the labour of this country would be immediately applied to the production of other and more profitable commodities, which might be exchanged for cheap foreign corn*' (1952, vol. V, p. 82, italics added).

The idea that masses of agricultural workers and farmers, with their traditional way of life – even if they had the resources to do so – *know whither* to move off '*immediately*' to the 'production of other and more profitable commodities', seems to suggest a failure to distinguish between a hyper-abstract model and the real world, which points to something having gone seriously astray with regard to the vitally important and delicate relationship between analysis and policy.[30]

---

[29] Ricardo apparently regarded as quite valid the assumption that 'the wants of society were well known'. For he used this proposition in criticising the treatment by Malthus of demand in relation to value. Naturally this Ricardian assumption appeals to neo-Ricardian advocates of centralised planning, who are eager to assume that 'the wants of society' are as well known to them (or even better known) than they are to consumers themselves. Ricardo wrote: 'When the wants of society are well known, when there are hundreds of competitors who are willing to satisfy those wants, on the condition only that they shall have the known and usual profits, there can be no such rule for regulating the value of commodities' (i.e. any dependence on 'the wants of mankind'). See 1951, vol. II, p. 24. This passage was pointed out to me by Mr M. Harvey-Phillips.

[30] See T. W. Hutchison, 1953, pp. 269–71. Certainly Ricardo at times entertained doubts. There is a very interesting letter written during the depressed year 1819 in which he writes: 'We all have to lament the present distressed situation of the labouring classes in this country, but the remedy is not very apparent to me. The correcting of our errors in legislation with regard to trade would ultimately be of considerable service to all classes of the community, but it would afford no immediate relief: on the contrary I should expect that it would plunge us into additional difficulties. If all the prohibitions were removed from the importation of corn and many other articles, which could not fail to follow, would ruin most of the farmers, and many

Like some economists subsequently, Ricardo promised tremendous, Utopian gains, if only just one or two of his favourite measures were adopted, thus bringing the British economy up to the full individualist, market ideal:

This would be the happiest country in the world, *and its progress in prosperity would be beyond the power of imagination to conceive, if we got rid of two great evils* – the national debt and the corn laws... If this evil were removed, *the course of trade and the prices of articles would become natural and right*; and if corn were exported or imported, as in other countries, without restraint, this country, possessing the greatest skill, the greatest industry, the best machinery, and every other advantage in the highest degree, *its prosperity and happiness would be incomparably, and almost inconceivably great* [1952, vol. v, p. 55, italics added].[31]

Certainly political preconceptions played some part in reinforcing Ricardian policy conclusions. As Professor Fetter has observed:

Ricardo's belief that self-interest was the well-spring of economic development also went beyond Smith in Ricardo's almost pathological feeling that the government did everything badly. *The difference between Smith and Ricardo on the role of government was a subtle but nevertheless important one, and one that I believe most economists have neglected or underplayed. The Wealth of Nations* has far more examples than the *Principles of Political Economy* of appropriate fields for government action. But this was not the whole difference...Ricardo gives the impression of the universal ineptness of government [1969, p. 73, italics added].

Of course governments seem especially inept insofar as one is tacitly assuming that individuals are omniscient. This political preconception against government activity had also been expressed by James Mill who maintained, regarding government generally that: 'Every farthing which is spent upon it, beyond the expense necessary for maintaining law and order, is so much dead loss to the nation, contributes so far to keep down the annual produce, and to diminish the happiness of the people' (1966, p. 157).

of the manufacturers; and although others would be benefited the derangement which such measures would occasion in the actual employments of capital, and the changes which become necessary, would rather aggravate than relieve the distress under which we are now labouring' (13 October 1819). Certainly there is great wisdom here in the realisation of ignorance and the scepticism regarding conclusions deduced from long-run, rapidly self-equilibrating modes. It amounts to an extreme contrast with the more typical kinds of Millian–Ricardian policy analysis.

[31] Brougham commented, not unfairly, on this speech as follows: 'His hon. friend, the member for Portarlington, had argued as if he had dropped from another planet; as if this were a land of the most perfect liberty of trade – as if there were no taxes – no drawback – no bounties – no searchers – on any other branch of trade but agriculture; as if, in this Utopian world, of his hon. friend's creation, the first measure of restriction ever thought on was that on the importation of corn; as if all classes of the community were alike – as if all trades were on an equal footing; and that, in this new state, we were called upon to decide the abstract question, whether or not there should be a protecting price for corn? But we were not in this condition

These sturdy sentiments were echoed by his pupil: 'The country had a right to insist, and I hope will insist, on the most rigid economy in every branch of the public expenditure' (Ricardo, 1952, vol. VII, p. 90).

Moreover: 'We very soon arrive at the knowledge that agriculture, commerce, and manufactures flourish best when left without interferences' (1952, vol. VIII, p. 133).

Millian–Ricardian political economy was much more incisively *laissez-faire* in its policy implications than *The Wealth of Nations* partly because of political preconceptions, but partly, or mainly, *because Ricardo had so sharpened and hardened the assumptions and hypotheses of The Wealth of Nations, especially in relation, (1) to natural wages and the vast policy implications which this assumption contained; and (2) with regard to the perfect knowledge postulate with its implication of smooth and immediate equilibration.*

In his eloquent defence of the classical economists against the charge of advocating any crude or harsh *laissez-faire* doctrines, Lord Robbins can be considered well-justified with regard to Adam Smith, Malthus, Senior, J. S. Mill and others: *but not with regard to Ricardo*, who is not merely the *only*, but outstandingly the *most*, thoroughgoing advocate of *laissez-faire* among the major British economists. Of course political preconceptions do, as they must, play some part in such an attitude, but such preconceptions were powerfully aided and abetted by the Millian–Ricardian abstract method and the particular positive economic assumptions which Ricardo took over from Mill.

VII

Shortly before his own death, and thirteen years after Ricardo's, James Mill made a further remarkable contribution to Millian–Ricardian political economy in his essay 'Whether Political Economy is Useful' (1836). This is another work, previously rather inaccessible and little known, which has been made conveniently available by Professor Winch's edition (1966). It is reasonable to assume that this work presents a view of economic knowledge which Mill had long held and which he had pressed upon his pupil Ricardo. The argument is developed by means of a dialogue between A and B, B being Mill himself and A a pupil (perhaps originally Ricardo). Mill brings out very clearly the extent and nature of the authority, and 'the extraordinary degree of certainty', as Mill put it, which was claimed by him, and also more widely and generally, for political economy. This had been indicated by Mill's references to Newton, and Ricardo's to Euclid, and

– we were in a state of society in which we had manufactures of almost every description, protected in every way' (op. cit., p. 56). Brougham might well have added perfect knowledge to the Utopian assumptions of Ricardo.

by means of their comparisons with mathematics.[32] The significance
of this final essay by Mill justifies lengthy quotation. Mill is concerned
to establish and explain the basis for the scientific authority of political
economy:

> *J.M.:* Political Economy, therefore, possesses one of the qualities which you
> represented as essential to a science, that it should explain the whole of
> the subject to which it relates.
> *Pupil:* It is so.
> *J.M.:* The next of your essentials was, that the doctrines should be true.
> What, then is the test to which we shall apply the doctrines of political
> economy, in order to know whether they are true?
> *Pupil:* The disagreement about them, of political economists themselves, is
> a sufficient proof of the uncertainty, at least, of all their conclusions.
> . . . . . .
> *J.M.:* Is it, then, your opinion, that truth is never disputed; never after it
> is proved? You would, in that case, reduce the number of established truths
> to a short catalogue. It is even denied that the establishment of property
> is useful, or the institution of government.
> *Pupil:* I do not consider it a presumption against an opinion, that it is
> disputed by a few wrong-headed people. . . The opinion of people who are
> capable of understanding the subject, and who have used the due means
> of understanding it, are the only people whose opinions afford a presump-
> tion either for or against any proposition or propositions regarding it.
> . . . . . .
> *J.M.:* Now all political economists, in whatever else they disagree, are all
> united in this opinion, that the science is one of great importance. There
> is, therefore, according to you, the strongest presumption of its importance.
> *Pupil:* I do not dispute the importance it might be of, were a set of
> propositions embracing the whole subject actually established. But I am
> justified in holding it of no importance, so long as nothing important is
> established.
> . . . . . .
> *J.M.:* But what proof have you that the generality of those who study and
> know political economy, are not agreed about its doctrines?
> *Pupil:* See what contradiction there is, on almost all the leading points,
> among the writers on the subject.
> *J.M.:* I believe you are here led into an error, by a superficial appearance
> . . . *You take the proportion of the writers who oppose the standard doctrines, for
> the proportion of the well-instructed people who oppose them; but the fact is very
> different. The writers are some half-dozen individuals, or less. And who are the people
> who write in such a case? Why, any creature who takes it into his head that he sees
> something in a subject which nobody else has seen.* On the other hand, they who,
> after studying the subject, see the truth of the doctrines generally taught,
> acquiesce in them, hold to them, act upon them, and do not write. Every
> creature who objects, writes: those who believe, do not write [1966, pp.
> 378ff, italics added].

The Pupil's last words are simply: 'I cannot but agree with you.'
James Mill presents here the standard self-sealing mechanism:

---

[32] See 1951, vol. v, p. 38, and vol. viii, p. 331. See also Section ii below of *Economists
and the history of economics: revolutionary and traditional versions* (Chapter 8).

anyone who seriously criticises 'the standard doctrines' automatically disqualifies himself. Thus the authority of the new science of political economy, and its great 'laws of society', is based on the authority of 'the well-instructed people' who include a number of recognised writers together with an allegedly dominant silent majority, who do not write but 'believe' in the 'standard doctrines' – such as that, for example: 'Every individual in the nation uniformly makes purchases, or does what is equivalent to making purchases, with every farthing's worth which accrues to him' (1966, p. 136).

Or, as announced by Ricardo to the House of Commons in a time of serious unemployment: 'When he heard honourable members talk of employing capital in the formation of roads and canals, they appeared to overlook the fact that the capital thus employed must be withdrawn from some other quarter' (1952, vol. v, p. 32).

On basic principles Ricardo had claimed epistemological parity with Newton's achievements in physics for his extremely abstract proposition about economic progress, the rise in rents and fall in profits: 'It appears to me that the progress of wealth, whilst it encourages accumulation, has a natural tendency to produce this effect and *is as certain as the principle of gravitation*' (1952, vol. vi, p. 204, italics added).

Meanwhile, as we have seen, according to his mentor James Mill: 'No proposition is better established than this, that the multiplication of the human species is always in proportion to the means of subsistence' (1966, p. 157).

Indeed such 'standard doctrines' as these, faithfully 'believed' by an alleged silent majority, are always of the kind, in the Mill–Ricardo language, of which 'none but the prejudiced are ignorant'.

Or they are: 'a truth which admits not a doubt'.

Or such that 'no proposition is more incontrovertible', or 'seems to be more certain'.[33]

It has been held that Ricardo's great contribution, over-riding that of any particular one of the various propositions and theories which are associated with his name, was that of method, or 'the technique of analysis': 'The classical economists, and *Ricardo in particular,*

---

[33] A contemporary observer, J. L. Mallet, noted this contrast in Ricardo: 'It is impossible to be in company with Ricardo and not to admire his placid temper, the candour of his disposition, his patience and attention, and the clearness of his mind; but he is as the French would express it 'herissé de principes', he meets you upon every subject that he has studied with a mind made up, and opinions in the nature of mathematical truths...His entire disregard of experience and practice...makes me doubtful of his opinions on political economy' (quoted by P. Sraffa, 1952, vol. viii, p. 152). Could this contrast be one between Ricardo's own innate nature and the results of Mill's influence? Alfred Marshall's religious or racial explanation does not seem very convincing: 'The faults and virtues of Ricardo's mind are traceable to his Semitic origin; no English economist had a mind similar to his' (Pigou, 1925, p. 153).

discovered something more important than any single generalisation; they discovered *the technique of economic analysis itself.*'[34]

Of course it is possible to take a different view of the method developed by Ricardo – as Schumpeter, in fact, did:

> The comprehensive vision of the universal inter-dependence of all elements in the economic system that haunted Thünen probably never cost Ricardo as much as an hour's sleep. His interest was in the clear-cut results of direct, practical significance. In order to get this he cut that general system to pieces, bundled up as large parts of it as possible in cold storage – so that as many things as possible should be frozen and 'given'. He then piled one simplifying assumption upon another until, having really settled everything by these assumptions, he was left with only a few aggregative variables between which, given these assumptions, he set up simple one-way relations so that, in the end, the desired results emerged almost as tautologies. For example, a famous Ricardian theory is that profits 'depend upon' the price of wheat. And upon his implicit assumptions and in the particular sense in which terms of the proposition are to be understood, that is not only true, but undeniably, in fact trivially, so. Profits could not possibly depend upon anything else, since everything else is 'given', that is, frozen. It is an excellent theory that can never be refuted and lacks nothing save sense. The habit of applying results of this character to the solution of practical problems we shall call the Ricardian Vice [1954, p. 472].

The Millian–Ricardian contribution to method, of which Mill's share was certainly a very large one, has had, and still has, a vast influence on the subject a century and a half later, and has persisted longer and more consequentially even than the role or influence of most of Ricardo's particular propositions or theories. Far from being confined to recent 'neo-Ricardian' fashions, the Mill–Ricardo method can be seen at work in neoclassical and in some branches of 'Keynesian' theorising and in the treatment of the principles of economic policy (1954, p. 472).[35]

The contrast in method with *The Wealth of Nations* seems sufficiently profound, extreme and consequential, as to justify the adjective 're-volutionary'. The integration of history with analysis and theory so superbly, and uniquely, achieved in Adam Smith's work was shattered, hardly ever after to be fully recovered in a major treatise (except, perhaps, in its own historicist way, in Karl Marx's *Capital*). Economic

---

[34] *The Economist*, 1 September 1951, p. 502, italics added, quoted in T. W. Hutchison, 1952, p. 427.

[35] Professor Thomas Sowell has explained the significance of the Millian–Ricardian methodological 'revolution' as follows (1974, p. 113): 'With Ricardo economics took a major step toward abstract models, rigid and *artificial* definitions, syllogistic reasoning – and the direct application of the results to policy. The historical, the institutional, and the *empirical* faded into the background, and *explicit* social philosophy shrank to a few passing remarks. Comparative statics became the dominant – though usually implicit – approach: Ricardo declared: "I put those immediate and temporary effects quite aside, and fixed my whole attention on the permanent state of things which will result from them"' (italics added).

history was left largely to rebels and outsiders. As an economic historian has described the consequences of the methodological revolution of Ricardo (and James Mill):

> The historical aspects of the subject during a period of enormous structural change in the economy were left, by and large, to a handful of non-academic Victorian worthies. Why was the genesis of economic history so long delayed in a country and in a period which presents so much of crucial importance to the economic historian today? The simple answer is that economics as understood by the classical economists *of the nineteenth century* was an a-historical subject, not to say an anti-historical one, while history was not conceived as being concerned with things economic. The method adopted by what became known as 'the dismal science' was that of logic and deduction from abstract principles rather than that of empirical investigation and historical inquiry. The ample historical digressions employed by Smith in *The Wealth of Nations* (1776) conspicuously did not relieve the pages of David Ricardo's *Principles of Political Economy* (1817), and it was the approach laid down by Ricardo which dominated classical political economy in England. John Stuart Mill's *Principles of Political Economy* (1848), though concerned to some extent with what he called 'applications' as well as with the 'principles' themselves, followed Ricardo in treating economics in a basically non-historical manner. Economic thought in England in the generations dominated by Ricardo, Mill and the Benthamite distaste for the study of the past is to be contrasted with the line of development taking place at the same time in Germany. While Mill's system of economic principles became entrenched in English thought, the approach to economics in Germany was radically altered during the 1840s and after by the so-called 'historical school' of economists [Harte, 1971, p. xiii].[36]

In the second edition of his *Essay on Population* (1803) and again in the Introduction to his *Principles of Political Economy* (1820), Malthus did *something* to uphold the empirical–historical method of Adam Smith. But the methodological protests of Malthus, like his fundamental theoretical protests regarding effective demand, had little effect compared with the orthodoxies so triumphantly established by Ricardo and the Mills (in spite of the various criticisms and alternatives which emerged for a time in the 1830s and 1840s).

Malthus implicitly contrasted his own views on method with those of Mill and Ricardo when he wrote: 'The science of political economy bears a nearer resemblance to the science of morals and politics than to that of mathematics.'

A similar reference was implied when Malthus was denouncing the avoidance of empirical testing and oversimplified monocausal 'models' and theories: 'These writers...do not sufficiently try their theories by a reference to that enlarged and comprehensive experience...In political economy the desire to simplify has occasioned an

---

[36] Mr Harte's conclusions are rather unfair regarding J. S. Mill in about the last five years of his life, when, under the influence of Cliffe Leslie and the Irish Land problem, he was moving towards a historical and inductive approach. See G. Koot, 1975, pp. 320–2.

unwillingness to acknowledge the operation of more causes than one' (1836, pp. 4–5).[37]

Referring simply to their doctrines on 'macro-economics', Keynes, rather controversially, exclaimed: 'If only Malthus, instead of Ricardo, had been the parent stem from which nineteenth-century economics proceeded, what a much wiser and richer place the world would be to-day' (1933, p. 144).

Whether or not one is prepared to conclude, on the basis of Keynes's speculative historical hypothesis, that the world would have been a much *richer* place had Malthus's views had more influence, it may well be reasonable to claim that the world would have been a *wiser* place, if Malthus's later modest caution regarding the dangers of abstraction, and the limits of economic knowledge, had prevailed over the excessive pretensions and overconfidence of the Millian–Ricardian philosophy and method of political economy.

The Millian–Ricardian philosophy, or methodology, was supported by a newly elaborated version of the history of the subject in the construction of which J. R. McCulloch and J. S. Mill – as well as James Mill – played notable parts. According to this version, political economy was relatively a very new subject, born in 1776 with *The Wealth of Nations*; but it was one which had made triumphantly rapid progress in the next half or three quarters of a century. Scientific laws of production, distribution, exchange and consumption, had been discovered, regarding the 'certainty' of which there was as much perfect and valid concurrence, *among those entitled to hold an opinion*, as existed in the science of physics, for example. In fact, regarding some vital, central theories, the subject had reached perfection with nothing for future generations to clear up.[38]

The tendency to generalise about the English 'classical' economists has fostered the erasing of vital distinctions, notably, for example, of this important methodological contrast between *The Wealth of Nations* and Ricardo's *Principles*. The fruitful combination of history and empirically significant theory in *The Wealth of Nations* was broken. History was largely extruded from the orthodox conception of the subject for decades to come. The legacy of the Mill–Ricardo methodological revolution was one of insufficiently controlled abstraction and over-simplification on the one hand, and of over-confident pretensions on the other hand. Traces of this legacy were still discernible

---

[37] As Ricardo complained to Mill in a letter of 1 January 1821 regarding the errors of Malthus: 'Another of his great mistakes is, I think, this; Political Economy, he says, is not a strict science like mathematics.' Malthus had, of course, matured, methodologically, as contrasted with the dogmatic, *a priori* deductivism of his first *Essay*, which was on somewhat Millian–Ricardian lines.

[38] See below the essay on Economists and the history of economics: revolutionary and traditional versions (Chapter 8).

in economics a century and a half after Ricardo's death. In other words, in respect of the Ricardian methodological revolution there were very serious intellectual losses. Again, the consensus or majority view, as in the case of the Smithian revolution, would be that the gains far outweighed the losses (if these were admitted as significant). For Ricardo is the intellectual hero both of Marxists ('vulgar' and other-wise) and of the more dogmatic, non-Smithian kind of classical liberal. Especially, he is the patron saint of the devotees of – an often misleading and largely irrelevant – 'rigour', and of those who like to assume an air of intense intellectual strenuousness and 'profundity'. To mention fundamental doubts regarding his contribution will seem to be bad form, or even unprofessional. Nevertheless, though we were happy to subscribe to the consensus view regarding the Smithian revolution, we are *not* regarding the methodological transformation brought about by James Mill and Ricardo. In fact, we would conclude, as Walter Bagehot concluded:

> It must be remembered that Ricardo...had no large notion of what science was...To the end of his days, indeed, he never comprehended what he was doing. He dealt with abstractions without knowing that they were such; he thoroughly believed that he was dealing with real things. He thought that he was considering actual human nature in its actual circumstances, when he was really considering a fictitious nature in fictitious circumstances. And James Mill, his instructor on general subjects, had on this point as little true knowledge as he had himself. James Mill, above all men, believed that you could work out the concrete world of human polity and wealth from a few first truths [1895, p. 205].

Bagehot then goes on to maintain that the kind of abstractions worked out by Mill and Ricardo might constitute useful 'preliminary work', before the real-world problems, or 'life and practice', were reached. But neither Bagehot, nor subsequent economists recognised the extent to which the Ricardian abstractions, and the descendants thereof, depended on the perfect knowledge postulate, nor the magnitude of the simplification, or over-simplification, which this postulate represents.

3

The decline and fall of English classical political economy and the Jevonian revolution

I

The chapter in the history of the subject entitled 'English Classical Political Economy' has probably been more thoroughly and extensively expounded, sometimes critically, but recently more often highly eulogistically, than any other section in the history of economic thought. Perhaps latterly, for English economists, it has had a certain wistful, nostalgic charm to hark back to a period when The Science of Political Economy enjoyed such power and prestige, at the same time as the English economy itself was held in awe as 'the workshop of the world'. How fascinating it is today to contemplate Nassau Senior, soon after the Great Exhibition of 1851, pointing to the flourishing prosperity and leadership of the English economy and proclaiming triumphantly to an admiring Frenchman: 'It is a triumph of theory. We are governed by philosophers and political economists.'[1] Anyhow, it is certain that the particular, peculiar English classical doctrines or 'theories' had an influence, dominance and authority, *in their home country*, in a vital and triumphant period of its economic history, hardly equalled by any other economic ideas before or since. But just how and why this almost uniquely influential and dominant body of economic theory came to lose its hold and credibility has been comparatively very little examined or discussed in serious terms. In fact, in the space of a few years in the late 1860s and early 1870s the classical structure of 'theory' underwent a remarkably sudden and rapid collapse of credibility and confidence, considering how long and authoritative had been its dominance in Britain. In view of the rapidity and central importance of this change in ideas, what took place, *in Britain*, might not unreasonably be said to have had something 'revolutionary' about it, though mainly in a destructive, negative sense.[2] For there was much less agreement between the rebels, who were attacking from very different directions, regarding what should

[1] 1878, vol. I, p. 169, quoted by A. Gerschenkron, May 1969, p. 6.
[2] Many indications that a general breakdown in confidence had taken place, both among economists and the wider interested public, in the previously prevailing orthodoxies, can be cited from economic writings in the early and middle 1870s. For a number of these see T. W. Hutchison, 1953, p. 6. There were, for example, the well-known

replace the orthodox theories, than that these theories should be rejected. For nearly two decades there was in Britain a somewhat confused interregnum. But in a negative sense the term 'revolution' may be justifiable, even though some aspects or components of the orthodox system survived the attacks, some never were attacked, and some sort of pious counter-revolutionary restoration, or retention of some of the 'classical' terminology and concepts, was subsequently attempted by Marshall.

The collapse in confidence seems to have been common to, and more or less simultaneous among, both the handful of competent contributors to economic theorising and the wider 'educated class' of the general reviews. The upheaval which began in the late 1860s, and the 'watershed' of the 1870s, were, of course, concerned with policy and method as well as theory. Clearly, after the extension of the franchise in 1867 fundamental new departures in policy would probably have had to be considered sooner or later. (See Hutchison, 1966.) Regarding method, the historical and Comteist attacks, though in due course largely repulsed, contributed to the uncertainty and loss of confidence. As regards the central theoretical structure some of the main pillars seemed to have lost the ability – insofar as they ever may have had it – to bear the weight of generalisation which they had previously been assumed to be capable of sustaining.

The main outlines of what happened to political economy in England at this time were quite clearly, and apparently quite accurately, described by Henry Sidgwick at the beginning of his *Principles* (1883). He wrote as someone reasonably detached, nicely combining a certain perspective with some first-hand acquaintance, while the scrupulous quality, balance, and fairness of his judgment hardly ought to need emphasis. Sidgwick's opening words described the transformation in England:[3] 'Some twenty years ago (c. 1863), both the Theory of

words of Walter Bagehot, writing, in the middle 1870s, of political economy: 'It lies rather dead in the public mind. Not only does it not excite the same interest as formerly but there is not exactly the same confidence in it' (1895, p. 3). In 1876 Jevons found that 'respect for the names of Ricardo and Mill seems no longer to preserve unanimity...We find the state of the science to be almost chaotic' (1905, pp. 190–1). In 1877 Sir Francis Galton was leading an attempt to exclude political economy from the British Association for the Advancement of Science (1877, p. 468). Regarding attitudes to policy there is the evidence of Lord Milner about the Oxford of 1872–6, years 'marked by a very striking change in the social and political philosophy of the place, a change which has subsequently reproduced itself on the larger stage of the world. When I went up, the *laissez faire* theory still held the field. All the recognised authorities were "orthodox" economists of the old school. But within ten years the few men who still held the old doctrines in their extreme rigidity had come to be regarded as curiosities' (Introduction to A. Toynbee, 1908, p. xxv).

[3] Sidgwick supports his account with a quotation from the *Edinburgh Review* (vol. 114) 'which seems to me to represent accurately the view of the subject which was current about the time (1861) that it was written'. The quotation epitomises what W. J. Ashley referred to as 'the confident dogmatism of the last generation of the period which

Political Economy in its main outlines, and the most important practical applications of it, were considered as finally settled by the great majority of educated persons in England' (1883, p. 1).

He goes on to maintain that 'comparatively little notice was taken' of the attacks of the middle 1860s, such as Frederic Harrison's Comteist diatribes, the criticisms of MacLeod, and Longe's refutation of the wages-fund theory (1866), and then concludes: 'In 1871, however, these halcyon days of Political Economy had passed away. Their termination was of course not abrupt; but so far as any date can be fixed for it, I should place it at the appearance of Mill's notice of Mr. Thornton's book *On Labour* in the *Fortnightly Review* of March, 1869.'

So, classical orthodoxy was already crumbling when, as Sidgwick puts it, 'a second shock was given in 1871 by the publication of Professor Jevons' *Theory of Political Economy.*'

Sidgwick attributed the supreme authority of and confidence in the orthodox theories in the 1850s and early 1860s to two causes: (1) the prosperity that had (in due course) followed on the abolition of the Corn Laws, and (2) the impressive mastery of J. S. Mill's lucid and authoritative exposition of the principles of the subject.

As regards the first 'cause', *there was certainly little in the way of major policy challenge in the 1850s* – unlike the earlier decades of the century. The framework of the free-market, free-trade economy had been established in the 1830s and 1840s. This seemed to have been followed in the 1850s and early 1860s by a convincing measure of fairly widespread prosperity, and so the conclusion seemed plausible – at any rate, for the wider public – that the major policy problems of political economy had been solved, if not for all time, at any rate, for the foreseeable future.[4] Moreover, the theories of the subject, having borne fruit in such successful policies, might thereby be

extended from the publication of John Stuart Mill's treatise to the sounding of the first note of revolt in Cliffe Leslie's Essays' (1893, p. 3). According to the *Edinburgh Review* (1861): 'That some departments of human conduct are capable of being classified with sufficient exactness to supply the materials of a true science is conclusively proved by the existence of Political Economy...The conclusions of those who understand the science are accepted and acted on with a degree of confidence which is felt in regard to no other speculations that deal with human affairs. *Political Economists can appeal to the only test which really measures the truth of a science – success – with as much confidence as astronomers.*'

[4] This kind of presumption may be behind the view, several times expressed in the 1870s that in political economy 'the great work has been done', as Robert Lowe said (1876); or as Cairnes had put it (1870): 'It is not denied that the science had done some good, only it is thought that its task is pretty well fulfilled' (1873, p. 240). Professor Checkland writes of the 'apparent exhaustion of application'. He cites Jowett's belief that, 'with the exception of the field of distribution, Political Economy, like Benthamism, has done its work', and Gladstone's view that 'the application of economics to public policy was almost complete' (1951, pp. 417–18).

considered to have received a convincing kind of general corroboration.[5]

Secondly, with regard to the dominance of J. S. Mill and his *Principles*, it is not always realised how near he was literally to monopolising the British market in economic ideas at this time. When one looks at the vital dates of the leading or near-leading economists in England in the nineteenth century one finds a comparatively large and distinguished cohort born about fifteen years before Mill (including McCulloch, Torrens, and Senior) who were naturally beginning to fade away by the middle 1850s. There were, however, *very* few born during about the next quarter century, that is, within about a dozen years either side of Mill.[6]

[5] For Anglo-centric chauvinism, it would be difficult to beat the opening sentences of Cairnes's essay 'Political Economy and *Laissez faire*' (1870): 'Great Britain, if not the birthplace of Political Economy, has at least been its early home, as well as the scene of the most signal triumphs of its manhood. *Every great step in the progress of economic science (I do not think an important exception can be named) has been won by English thinkers*; and while we have led the van in economic speculation, we have also been the first to apply with boldness our theories to practice. Our foreign trade, our colonial policy, our poor-laws, our fiscal system, each has in turn been reconstructed from the foundation upwards under the inspiration of economic ideas; and the population and the commerce of the country, responding to the impulse given by the new principles operating through these changes, have within a century multiplied themselves manifold. This London, in the midst of which we find ourselves, what is it but a mighty monument of economic achievement? – the greatest practical illustration which the world has seen of the potent influence of those principles which it is the business of the political economist to expound?' (italics added). Cairnes goes on to estimate the total number of students of the subject in 1870 in London at 'very much short of a hundred individuals'. By 1970 this number had been multiplied perhaps a hundred times over, or more. But whether this 'mighty monument' was a correspondingly greater 'practical illustration' of 'the potent influence' of economic principles, seems open to doubt. (See 1873, p. 232.)

[6] In his fascinating pioneer paper 'Statistical Studies in the History of Economic Thought' (1965, pp. 31ff), Professor Stigler lists 56 'Important English Economists' born between 1712 and 1861 (that is at an average rate of nearly 4 per decade). So one is dealing with pretty small numbers in attempting to distinguish changes and transitions in economics, and even more so in contributions to economic theory or analysis (for the Stigler list includes a fair proportion of historical and statistical economists). Obviously, also, there are some rather marginal inclusions and omissions which might be suggested, but we shall follow strictly the Stigler list.
  This shows a remarkable fluctuation in the birth-rates relevant to the period with which we are concerned:
  (1A) The 11-year period 1787–97 (inclusive) is extremely prolific, with 13 births, against what would be an 'average' of about 4. (These are Hodgskin, Whately, McCulloch, Senior, Torrens, Jones, Bailey, Joplin, Lloyd, Wakefield, Scrope, Porter, and Babbage – almost a quarter of the entire list).
  (2A) Then for 22 years (1798–1819 inclusive) there is a 'great depression', with only 3 births altogether – compared with an 'average' of about 9 (Longfield, J. S. Mill, and W. T. Thornton).
  (3A) From 1820 the birth-rate recovers again, with 7 (including Cairnes, Bagehot and Leslie) in the 1820s, and 4 more, all highly distinguished, in the 1830s (Giffen, F. Jenkin, Jevons, and Sidgwick). Many of the leading neoclassicals follow in the 1840s, notably Marshall (1842).
  As might be expected, corresponding with this cycle of boom, slump, and

In the middle and late 1860s, however, a new cohort of writers, all under forty in 1865, born about 20 years or more *after* Mill, were beginning to assert themselves. The most important members of this new and varied cohort were Cliffe Leslie, Fleeming Jenkin, Bagehot, and Jevons, who all rejected the central Ricardo–Mill theories of value and distribution. Of those who had a significant theoretical contribution to make, only J. E. Cairnes,[7] born slightly earlier, was left on the other side, and his attempts at defending the Ricardo–Mill orthodoxy could be said only to have weakened its position, either by the extent of the concessions he made (on the wages-fund doctrine and by the 'non-competing groups' analysis) or by the extremity of his hard-line Malthusian gloom.[8] It was the emergence of this new

recovery in the birth-rate, there is a subsequent cycle in the output of important works. Professor Stigler also gives a column stating the year of his economist's major publication in economics, or the mean year of his range of publications. The cyclical fluctuation here corresponds fairly closely with that of birth-rates, after intervals of between 41–7 years:
(1B)   The 15-year boom period, 1830–44, yielded 14 major works.
(2B)   A long 21-year slump, 1845–65, yielded only 3.
(3B)   The 5-year recovery, 1866–70, yielded 5.

Period A	*Births*	*Period B* (A+41/47 years)	*Major works*
I 1787–97 (Boom 11 yrs)	13	1830–44 (15 years)	14
II 1798–1819 (Slump, 22 yrs)	3	1845–65 (21 years)	3
III 1820–29 (Recovery, 10 yrs)	7	1856–70 (5 years)	5

Thus, in, say, 1852, there were only 3 'important' English economists between the ages of 32 and 55 – the other 2 being Longfield and W. T. Thornton. Longfield had long previously completed his main contributions, while Thornton was, much later, to have his crucial date with Mill in 1869. These quantitative observations from Professor Stigler's table, are not put forward in order to *explain* Mill's extreme pre-eminence, but in order to underline the literal fact of it. An explanation of the great mid Victorian depression in political economy in Britain would have to allow for many different kinds of factors, including individual or personal 'accidents'. The more general hypothesis for which I would seek to marshal evidence would be in terms of the absence of major policy challenge. This is how Walter Bagehot explained the boom in the subject of c. 1815–45: 'For the thirty years succeeding the peace of 1815 England was always uncomfortable. Trade was bad, employment scarce... While the economic condition of countries is bad, men care for Political Economy, which may tell us how it is to be improved; when that condition is improved, Political Economy ceases to have the same popular interest' (1895, p. 202).

   The mid Victorian 'depression' was, of course, a depression in numbers, not in prestige and influence, which was in important respects at a peak in this country. It may be noted that the slump in the birth-rate of 'important' *English* economists (1798–1818) coincided with a peak in France and Germany with regard to the great pioneers of marginal analysis such as Cournot (1801), Dupuit (1804), Gossen (1810), as well as A. Walras (1801). Karl Marx, of course, dated from 1818.
[7]   Henry Fawcett might be added to Cairnes as a surviving defender of English 'classical' orthodoxy; but Stigler finds him 'an easy exclusion' from his list of 'important' English economists and we accept this judgment.
[8]   See F. W. Taussig, 1896, pp. 263–5, for Cairnes's retreat on the wages-fund doctrine.

cohort of economists, with important critical or constructive contributions to make to economic theorising, who all rejected the central theories of value and wages of 'the Ricardo–Mill Economics', which makes a comparatively brief span of years in the late 1860s and early 1870s so important a turning point in the history of economic theory in England.[9] But what is especially intriguing is that Mill himself in these years, his own last years, seems to have come to share the disillusion and impatience with prevailing doctrines, or some of them, which had owed so much to his own prestige and earlier support. Mill has been accused, for example, of having unnecessarily sold the pass by his excessive concessions to critics of the wages-fund doctrine. But this was not simply an isolated lapse on a particular point. In a letter to Thornton of 1867 Mill was expressing warm support for

> the emancipation of political economy – its liberation from the kind of doctrines of the old school (now taken up by well-to-do people) which treat what they call economical laws, demand and supply for instance, as if they were laws of inanimate matter, not amenable to the will of the human beings from whose feelings, interests, and principles of action they proceed. This is one of the queer mental confusions which will be wondered at by and by [1972, vol. XVI, p. 1320].

Just what were these doctrines from which 'emancipation' and 'liberation' were so desirable? And *exactly who were the members and founders of this 'old school'* who were responsible for their formulation and influence? Could they *possibly* have included James Mill and Ricardo, with their comparisons with Newton and Euclid?

Then again, in 1870, there is some remarkable support by Mill for the radical attacks of Cliffe Leslie, the most fundamental historical and methodological critic of classical doctrines at this time. (For Leslie was not a theoretical, 'neoclassical' critic.) Discussing Leslie on the Land Question, Mill denounced what he called

> this routine school of political economists who have mostly had things their own way; the more easily, as they comprise in their ranks some men of more than ordinary talents and acquirements, but who share the common infirmity of liking to get their thinking done once for all, and be saved all further trouble except that of referring to a formula [1967, vol. V, p. 671].[10]

---

9   Dr Pedro Schwartz writes aptly of 'a long Indian Summer, which, because of Mill's exceptional authority lasted until about 1870, almost totally paralysing the development of economic science in Great Britain' (1972, p. 17).

10 On Leslie see the valuable article by G. M. Koot (1975). As Dr Koot observes regarding Mill's concessions to the critics, or his 'half-way house', they 'tended to deepen rather than alleviate the crisis of English political economy during the 1870s' (op. cit., p. 322). It would certainly seem that one of 'the routine school' of economists was Robert Lowe whom Mill answered in Parliament on the subject of Ireland declaring that 'no one is at all capable of determining what is the right political economy for any country until he knows its circumstances'. (See Koot, op. cit., p. 321, and *Hansard's Parliamentary Debates*, 3rd series 190, 12 March 1868, 1489–1526.) Mill put forward a forthright historico-relativism against the rigid, Ricardian, deductive absolutism of

Again, Mill does not identify his target. But these aspersions certainly possess a certain piquancy coming, as they do, from one who twenty-two years previously had proclaimed that 'happily there is nothing in the laws of value which remains for the present or any future writer to clear up'. These 'routine' economists, according to Mill, 'believe themselves to be provided with a set of catch-words, which they mistake for principles – free-trade, freedom of contract, competition, demand and supply, the wages fund, individual interest, desire of wealth, etc. – which supersede analysis and are applicable to every variety of case without the trouble of thought' (1967, vol. v, p. 67).

But who exactly these 'routine' economists were, about whom Mill was so concerned in 1870, is left unclear. Mill describes Leslie – an even more radical rebel than Jevons – as 'one of the best living writers on applied political economy', and he goes on to quote approvingly Leslie's own denunciations of orthodoxy:

A school of economists of no small pretensions, strongly represented in Parliament, supposes itself to be furnished with a complete apparatus of formulas, within which all economic knowledge is comprised – which clearly and satisfactorily expounds all the phenomena of wealth, *and renders all further investigation of the causes and effects of the existing economy of society needless, and even mischievous, as tending to introduce doubt and heresy into a scientific world of certainty and truth,* and discontent and disturbance into a social world of order and prosperity [Leslie, 1870, p. 89, italics added].

It is a pity that Mill did not identify who these economists were, and, in particular, *just what the relation was, in 1870, between their writings and his own 'Principles'*, which for the preceding twenty-two years had been so overwhelmingly and almost exclusively the dominant influence and authority on the subject. Anyhow it seems that the time must indeed have been ripe for a Reformation when the Pope himself was to be found supporting and encouraging the most radical Protestant critics.[11]

Lowe. According to Lowe: 'As regards the laws of political economy, I believe they are the same on both sides of the Channel.' According to Mill: 'My Rt.Hon. Friend thinks that what is good political economy for England must be good for Ireland – or perhaps for the savages of the backwoods of America...I do not know in political economy...a single practical rule that must be applicable to all cases.' This confrontation in Parliament, and Mill's abrupt challenge to Lowe on the political economy of Irish policy, must have been a significant factor in the loss of public credibility which the subject underwent in the late 1860s. Certainly Mill gives some earlier suggestions of his thorough-going relativism – for example in a review of Harriet Martineau (1834) and in the well-known distinction regarding the laws of distribution (see vol. iv, 1967, p. 225, and *Principles*, ii.i.i). But this relativism does not otherwise figure at all strongly or prominently elsewhere in the *Principles* or in his essay on Definition and Method.
[11] Mill's *Principles* and its great authority undoubtedly played a major role in upholding the influence and implications of the three main pillars of classical political economy. Professor T. Sowell sees Mill as 'turning the clock back': 'John Stuart Mill was as

II

The note of challenge and revolt against the central theories of the dominant orthodoxy, described by Jevons as 'the Ricardo–Mill Economics,' is prominently featured throughout his *Theory*, and at once emphasised on the first pages of his original preface (1931, p. 11).[12]

It must be emphasised, next, that, as we have noted, Jevons's call to revolt was not an isolated, individual challenge against the prevailing theories, although it was the first of Jevons's public writings in which he proclaimed this kind of protest. (His paper of '62 had simply stated 'a Theory of Economy' without any criticism of, or challenge to, other theories.) Jevons, in fact, in 1871 was giving a weighty and spirited shove to a bandwagon of revolt which had begun to roll two or three years previously. In 1862 his paper had made no impact, but by 1870 he saw that the time was now ripe for a fundamental questioning of the prevailing orthodoxies. For in the late 1860s a series of attacks had begun on the central body of orthodox theory, notably on the wages-fund theory and more broadly on the method and policy conclusions of the dominant English school of thought.

We would like to emphasise that, in his *Theory*, Jevons attacks the central pillars of the Ricardo–Mill theory of *distribution*, as well as the theory of value; and that, in any case, *because of the logical and conceptual links between the two the attack on the one implied an attack on the other*. In the preface to the first edition of his *Theory* Jevons at once joins the assault on the wages-fund doctrine (already launched in the later 1860s by Longe, Thornton, Leslie, and, incidentally, Karl Marx).[13] In the

steadfast in his defence of the third pillar of classical orthodoxy – the Malthusian population theory – as he was in defending Say's law or the cost of production theory of value...Probably only a man with Mill's massive reputation for an open and forward-looking mind could have so successfully turned the clock back on fundamental developments in economics' (1972, pp. 160–4). It was in his policy ideas, or 'political economy', as Dr Pedro Schwartz calls it, that Mill was trying to break away from the doctrines of his 'classical' predecessors.

12 Jevons 'insists' on taking 'a view, however, which when properly followed out, will overthrow many of the principal doctrines of the Ricardo–Mill Economics'. Finding an apposite description for the enemy to be 'overthrown' ('The Mercantile System', 'Ricardo–Mill Economics', 'Classical Theory') is an essential element in a successful attempt at 'revolution', probably more important than simply a positive statement of some fundamentally new idea. Jevons's 1862 paper had, of course, contained no attack on dominant theories and was disregarded. Similarly what made Keynes's *General Theory* 'revolutionary' was not so much new developments in his ideas since the *Treatise* of six years previously, *but the identification of 'Classical' theory as a formidable, ubiquitous enemy to be overthrown.*

13 The young Marshall, though he had not yet published anything, might well be included in the new cohort of critics of the Ricardo–Mill distribution 'theories'. It is significant that (as pointed out by Sir John Hicks) his early papers (1867–70) reveal that it was from J. S. Mill's teachings on *distribution* that Marshall most fundamentally dissented. For Marshall, Mill's recantation on the wages-fund doctrine 'did not go

second edition he goes on to demand that we 'cast ourselves free from the Wage-Fund Theory, the Cost of Production doctrine of Value, the Natural Rate of Wages, and other misleading or false Ricardian doctrines' (1931, p. vi and p. xiv).

It is often insisted that in contrast with their close unification in fully developed marginal analysis, in the 'English' or 'classical' system the theories of value and distribution were 'separate' or not analytically connected. Certainly they were not unified in the same close-knit way. But the Ricardian labour-cost theory of value, with the theory of natural wages, and, in a looser sense, the wages-fund theory, were closely linked by common assumptions or simplifications. If (possibly partly because of changing economic conditions, or 'environmental' factors) these simplifications came to seem less plausible or justifiable, then *both* the Ricardo–Mill theory of value and that of wages or distribution, were being rejected as general explanations of the workings of actual goods and labour markets, as these had in fact become.

Jevons clearly perceived this interdependence in his call to revolt against the prevailing orthodoxy. Moreover, although he did not elaborate the marginal productivity analysis, he strongly asserted its basic principle in insisting that the distribution to factors must be explained by their contribution to production, an idea suppressed in the 'classical' or, at any rate, the Ricardo–Mill theories. Jevons expressed the idea in the 'Concluding Remarks' in the first edition of the *Theory*, and, as recognised by Walras, with great force at the end of the Preface to the second edition. He also sees that although this productivity type of explanation, or 'the true theory of wages', is: 'not new as regards the French school, it is new, or at any rate renewed, as regards our English Schools of Economics' (1931, pp. 269–70 and xiv).[14] The wages-fund and natural wage theories both failed to link wages with productivity; a link which would, in turn, have pointed towards a greater emphasis on final, consumer demand. The common assumption in both the labour-cost theory of value, the natural wage theory, and, also, to a lesser extent, in the wages-fund

far enough'. Moreover, following Thünen, Marshall first developed a marginal productivity doctrine, years before turning to utility and value. (See Hicks, 1976, pp. 367–9.)

For Cliffe Leslie on the wages-fund doctrine see his *Essays*, n.d., p. 43 (in his review of Cairnes's '*Leading Principles*'). For Fleeming Jenkin's rejection of 'this fallacy', see his essay of 1870 on 'The Laws of Supply and Demand', in 1931, p. 94.

[14] As Professor R. D. C. Black points out, it seems to involve some misconception of Jevons's thought to look for a unified approach to the analysis of distribution in his chapters in the *Theory* on 'Rent, Labour, and Capital', in which there is undoubtedly 'a certain asymmetry of treatment'. It is unjustifiable to conclude from this asymmetry that Jevons did not clearly discern the marginal productivity principle though he did not work it out. There are clear suggestions of the outline of a general marginal productivity approach both in the later chapters of the *Theory* and in the Introduction to the second edition (as Walras maintained). (See R. D. C. Black, 1970, pp. 17–19.)

theory, was that it was empirically justifiable to assume that 'labour' could be treated as broadly and generally homogeneous, *or* that different types or qualities were reducible to a common homogeneous 'labour' by some stable scale. This was the necessary basis both for a labour-cost theory being justifiable, and for a theory of a general 'natural wage', or even a significant general average wage, being a reasonably adequate approximation. This simplification is assumed by Mill at the outset of his chapter, 'Of Wages' (II. XI. I.) where he begins by claiming that it is 'convenient' to 'proceed in the first instance as if there was no other kind of labour than common unskilled labour of the average degree of hardness and disagreeableness' (1909, p. 343).

In one of his crucial passages Ricardo (opening Section II of the first chapter of his *Principles*) had written:

> In speaking, however, of labour, as being the foundation of all value, and the relative quantity of labour as almost exclusively determining the relative value of commodities, I must not be supposed to be inattentive to the different qualities of labour, and the difficulty of comparing an hour's or day's labour, in one employment, with the same duration of labour in another. The estimation in which different qualities of labour are held, comes soon to be adjusted in the market with sufficient precision for all practical purposes, and depends much on the comparative skill of the labourer, and intensity of the labour performed. *The scale, when once formed, is liable to little variation.* If a day's labour of a working jeweller be more valuable than a day's labour of a common labourer, it has long ago been adjusted, and placed in its proper position in the scale of value [1951, vol. I, p. 20, italics added].[15]

This is what Jevons emphatically rejected in the much-quoted concluding paragraph of his chapter on the 'Theory of Exchange':

> But it is easy to go too far in considering labour as the regulator of value; it is equally to be remembered that labour is itself of unequal value. Ricardo by a violent assumption, founded his theory of value on quantities of labour considered as one uniform thing. He was aware that labour differs infinitely in quality and efficiency, so that each kind is consequently paid at a higher or lower rate of wages. He regarded these difficulties as disturbing circumstances which would have to be allowed for; but his theory rests on the assumed equality of labour. This theory rests on a wholly different ground. I hold labour to be *essentially variable, so that its value must be determined by the value of the produce, not the value of the produce by that of the labour* [1931, pp. 165–6, original italics].

[15] See also Mill's *Principles*, Book III, Chapter IV, and J. E. Cairnes, 1874, pp. 87–8. As Professor G. J. Stigler expounds Ricardo: 'the wages of labor are also diverse, varying with skill, cost of education, and the like. Yet the occupational wage structure is very stable, so we may treat a skilled laborer as (say) three unskilled laborers if the former's wage is three times that of unskilled labor. Thus the expenditure on wages may be taken as proportional to the number of "equivalent unskilled" laborers. (Ricardo should also have specified that the occupational structure of laborers is stable.)' (1965, p. 188; see also p. 330.)

Jevons was not alone at this time in attacking this central simplification of the Ricardo–Mill value and distribution theory. Walter Bagehot in his chapter on 'Cost of Production' quotes *exactly* the passage cited above from Ricardo and goes on to emphasise why this simplification had become less plausible in the fifty years since Ricardo wrote:

> And fifty years ago, when manufactures grew but slowly, and when the arts were comparatively stationary, this mode of speaking may not have been wholly incorrect – at any rate was not perfectly false. But nowadays the different skill used in different employments varies incessantly; it tends to increase with every improvement in quality; it tends to diminish with every improvement in machinery. Even between the same employment at different times it is difficult to compare it, and between two different employments it is impossible to compare it [1895, p. 262].

Actually J. S. Mill, apparently without fully realising the implications, and J. E. Cairnes more explicitly, had introduced a fatal qualification to the Ricardian simplification regarding the homogeneity of labour in their concept of 'non-competing groups'. Indeed Cairnes conceded that in 'no inconsiderable proportion of all the exchanges which take place within such a country as this', value cannot be explained by cost of production, and that the demand side, in the form of the principle of reciprocal demand, has to be invoked (as in J. S. Mill's theory of international values):

> Therefore, the action of cost of production in regulating value is by no means as extensively prevalent, even within the limits of the same country, as the current theory would lead us to suppose. The same commodity follows the law of cost of production in some exchanges and does not follow it in others; nor is it true that the value of any commodity conforms to the principle of cost in all exchanges [1874, p. 80].[16]

[16] In this part of my argument I am much indebted to the paper by K. J. Arrow and D. A. Starrett, 'Cost- and Demand-Theoretical Approaches to the Theory of Price Determination', read to the Symposium at the University of Vienna, June 1971, celebrating the centenary of Carl Menger's '*Grundsätze*'. Arrow and Starrett write: 'Apart from the problem of capital, the classical structure gradually faced new challenges, partly due to more detailed study of the real world, partly due to changes in that world. By the middle of the nineteenth century, the course of real wages was certainly inconsistent with any subsistence theory. The value placed by the market on labor could not be explained by its cost of production; the most natural alternative was to explain wages by the productivity of labor, an explanation only useful if labor was intrinsically scarce. In short, labor had to be treated like land. Also, the only explanation of relative wages in a classical model was Smith's doctrine of equalizing differences, due to unpleasantness, riskiness, and the like. Individuals were supposed to have equal abilities but were not indifferent among alternative jobs. But this is already a multi-factor model; not only raw labor but also willingness to do unpleasant work or to engage in risk-bearing are scarce primary factors. Further, the most casual observation of the world suggested that equalizing differences were an inadequate explanation of relative wages; it was frequently remarked that the most highly paid positions were the most, not the least preferred. When Cairnes started talking about "non-competing groups", the classical model was completely vitiated. The multiplicity of primary factors required a new theory. The great founders of the neoclassical

In fact the exceptions to the Ricardo–Mill theory were now becoming more important than the general case and the general explanation. As Jevons subsequently wrote to Foxwell (14 November 1869): 'Cairnes professedly supports the theory [of the wage fund] but his arguments really tend against it in a deadly manner. He cannot stop at any non-competing groups, and his ideas followed out lead to entire rejection of the theory' (1886, p. 408).[17]

III

Let us now look in rather more detail at the collapse of the two main pillars of the Ricardo–Mill distribution theory, (a) the wages-fund doctrine and (b) the natural wage theory. We are concerned to emphasise the common elements as between the inadequacies of these wage theories, and the inadequacy of the Ricardo–Mill value theory.

(a) The extent and suddenness of the collapse of confidence in the prevailing orthodoxies was most prominently exhibited with regard to the wages-fund doctrine in the late 1860s and early 1870s. F. D. Longe's '*Refutation*' in 1866 was slightly too early to make an impact.[18] But Cliffe Leslie and Fleeming Jenkin (both 1868) were followed by W. T. Thornton (1869), who extracted the capitulation from Mill, which Sidgwick saw as the critical episode in the collapse of confidence in 'classical', or 'Ricardo–Mill' political economy. We would emphasise that we are not necessarily insisting that the wages-fund doctrine was totally untenable, or should have been abandoned as completely as it was by Mill and others. It may be that the consensus of the time should be considered wrong in some respects. But there is no question in

school, Carl Menger, W. S. Jevons, and Leon Walras, and their precursors, A. A. Cournot and H. H. Gossen, understood the glaring omission of demand from the classical model. They took as an expository point of departure a model which was the polar opposite of the classical, the model of pure exchange.' Arrow and Starrett conclude that *what 'led to the downfall of the classical theory' was 'the failure to explain either absolute or relative wages'*. We would add that this failure came to a head in the late 1860s and early 1870s. (See Arrow and Starrett, in J. R. Hicks and W. Weber, eds., 1973.)

[17] See also S. G. Checkland, 1951, p. 164. As Professor K. J. Arrow has put it: 'The classical theory could solve neither the logical problem of explaining relative wages of heterogeneous types of labour nor the empirical problem of accounting for wages that were rising steadily above the subsistence level' (1968, p. 377). Professor George Stigler has concluded regarding the Ricardian theory of value and distribution: 'One could criticise Ricardo's theory on many grounds. The population was not at a subsistence level, the occupational structure of the labor force and the relative wage structure were not stable, improvements in agricultural technology were neither negligible nor sporadic, technological progress in non-agricultural industries could offset diminishing returns in agriculture etc.' (1965, p. 191)

[18] Pride of place in the 'neoclassical' revolt against the wages-fund doctrine should perhaps be given to Karl Marx. An attack on this Ricardian doctrine opens *Value, Price and Profit* (1865), an address directed specially at trade unionists. See also K. Marx, 1961, Chapter XXII, Section 5, on 'The So-called Wages Fund'.

which direction the consensus then pointed, and it was a consensus led by some of the ablest economists of that or any other date.[19] Interest shifted towards *relative* wages, quite justifiably, and whatever significance the wages-fund doctrine had regarding *aggregate* wages was lost sight of. In the 1870s, as Schumpeter puts it 'killing the wages fund became a favourite sport' (1954, p. 671). We have seen Jevons continuing the attack along with his general challenge to the Ricardo–Mill value theory and the natural wage theory. Cairnes (1874) seemed to regard himself as attempting a defence, but in doing so emptied the doctrine of almost all its earlier content and got listed by Jevons along with those who had abandoned it (1931, p. xliv). Reviewing Cairnes's '*Leading Principles*', Cliffe Leslie emphasised the interdependence between the Ricardo–Mill theories of wages and of value:

> The doctrine of cost of production involves the whole theory of wages and profit, and an immense super-structure which has been built on what Mr. Cairnes would call the orthodox theory, must stand or fall with that theory. The subject may conveniently be approached by an examination of the doctrine of 'the Wages Fund' and an 'average rate of wages', for which Mr. Cairnes contends [Leslie, n.d., p. 43].

Later there was the well-known work of F. A. Walker (1876) and further attacks by such a varied range of economists as Ingram, Toynbee, Rogers, Henry George and Sidgwick. After Cairnes's effort the wages-fund doctrine was maintained only at the level of the successive editions of Fawcett's *Manual*. Certainly there was nothing very elaborate to put in its place, except for what Cannan calls 'the produce-less-deductions' theory of wages, which did, however, point towards marginal productivity analysis (Cannan, 1929, p. 356).

(b) The other part of the Ricardo–Mill distribution theory, and the third of the three basic Ricardo–Mill doctrines from which Jevons demanded that economists 'cast themselves free', was 'the theory of a natural rate of wages, that which is just sufficient to support the labourer'. Jevons added: 'I altogether question the existence of such a rate...I am inclined, therefore, to reject altogether the current doctrines as to the rate of wages' (1931, p. 269).[20]

The theory of the natural rate of wages is a direct implication of the 'hard line' version of the Malthusian population doctrine. It is,

[19] As Marshall put it in 1885: 'Twelve years ago [i.e. in 1873] England possessed perhaps the ablest set of economists that there have ever been at one time' (1925, p. 152). Especially in view of Marshall's considerable regard for the English classicals, this judgment seems significantly to put them in their place *vis-à-vis* their successors.

[20] Jevons continued: 'Even if the theory held true of any one class of labourers separately, there is the additional difficulty that we have to account for the very different rates which prevail in different trades. It is impossible that we should accept for ever Ricardo's sweeping simplification of the subject, that there is a natural ordinary rate of wages for common labour, and that all higher rates are merely exceptional instances, to be explained away on other grounds.'

of course, highly confusing to refer to 'the' Malthusian population doctrine. There was a whole spectrum of Malthusian population doctrines and Malthus himself moved to and fro along this spectrum. At the extreme 'soft' end was a completely empty generalisation, predicting simply that anything might happen – a perfect example of 'a tautology masquerading as a theory' (Blaug, 1962, p. 65). At the 'hard' end – from which the natural wage doctrine derives – there was, perhaps, the most sweeping, weighty, and consequential empirical generalisation ever put forward in the history of economic theory, a proposition which had the most drastic implications for wages, living standards, and economic and social policies, and which, in addition, was an essential component of any appreciable empirical content which classical distribution 'theory' might possess.

The 'hard' and 'soft' Malthusian propositions are utterly different in their meanings and implications and it is thoroughly confusing to try to discuss the extent of support for, or the decline of, 'the' Malthusian doctrine without distinguishing between them.[21] The different propositions were upheld by different people for different, though partly concurrent, periods of time. In between the 'hard' and the 'soft' extremes was a range of propositions of varied and often rather hazy content depending on the precise interpretation of the various particular qualifications introduced by different writers. It is sometimes difficult enough to pin down at all precisely just what any one author understood by his version of the Malthusian doctrine. To generalise about groups of writers, or about general changes in support, is almost impossible in terms of 'the' Malthusian doctrine. (In other words, in the history of economics Lakatosian 'hard cores' are apt to soften into sticky plasticine lumps malleable into any desired shape, or even liable to melt away altogether.)

Ricardo and J. S. Mill took a line well towards the 'hard' end of the spectrum, and *their distribution model only had content to the extent that it could derive this from a 'hard', empirical Malthusian proposition.*[22]

---

[21] Walter Bagehot summed up the crucial and wide difference between the 'hard' and 'soft' Malthusian theories in his dictum: 'In its first form the Essay on Population was conclusive as an argument, only it was based on untrue facts; in its second form it was based on true facts, but it was inconclusive as an argument' (1895, p. 179).

[22] J. A. Schumpeter emphasises the essential role of the 'hard' Malthusian doctrine in the Ricardian model: 'The theory of rent having fulfilled its only purpose, which is to get rid of another variable in our equation, we are left, on the margin of production, with one equation and two variables – still a hopeless business. But, so it occurred to Ricardo, wages are not really a variable either, at least not within that equation. He thought he knew, from external considerations what they will be in the long run: here the old Quesnay theory comes in, reinforced by Malthus' law of population' (1954, p. 569). See also G. J. Stigler's essay 'The Ricardian Theory of Value and Distribution' (1965, pp. 156ff especially pp. 157, 169 and 172). Stigler emphasises that the subsistence level has to have stability if the theory is to have any significance. It could indeed be argued that Mill's treatment of the population doctrine is not as

Although the hard-line doctrine had been rejected by such classical 'soft-liners' as Senior, McCulloch (in his later years), and Torrens – and by many others – *it was still well entrenched in the orthodox theorising of the 1860s in the dominant, authoritative text of J. S. Mill, and in those of his disciples Cairnes and Fawcett.*[23] Jevons, and the others of the new wave of economists of the late 1860s and early 1870s, were not attacking a defunct Aunt Sally. But after their attacks – apart briefly from Cairnes and Fawcett – *no economist of note attempted to resurrect a hard-line Malthusian doctrine, at any rate in Britain.*[24]

consistently 'hard' as Ricardo's. Certainly Mill expresses, here and there, more rather vague hopes about a distant future. But the logic of the Ricardian model, as he restated it, demanded the 'hard' Malthusian doctrine that, as Mill himself put it: 'It is but rarely that improvements in the labouring classes do anything more than give a temporary margin, speedily filled up by an increase of their numbers.' Mill conceded in later editions that 'subsistence and employment in England have never increased more rapidly than in the last forty years' (1862) and that the standard of living of the people was gradually, though slowly, rising in the more advanced countries. But he continued to stress that 'unless...they can be taught to make better use of favourable circumstances, nothing permanent can be done for them' (1909, p. 161). Ashley stressed (1909, p. 984) how 'in the writings of no contemporary economist, in Great Britain or abroad, does the idea that population is constantly tending to press upon the means of subsistence occupy the same conspicuous and primary place as it does with Mill'. More recently Professor S. Hollander has emphasised that 'the significance of the Malthusian population reaction in accounting for Mill's position on key policy issues...*cannot be exaggerated*' (1968, p. 524, italics added). For J. E. Cairnes's hard-line views see 1874, pp. 332–48.

[23] As Professor Mark Blaug puts it: 'In John Stuart Mill's *Principles* (1848) the Malthusian theory of population became, once again, the key to the Ricardian theory of distribution. In his effort to restore Malthus' arguments Mill indeed affected something of a counter-revolution' (1956, p. 48). Blaug ascribes the failure to last of the first comprehensive rejection, in the 1830s, of the 'hard' Malthusian doctrine, to the fact that no one had any other theory of wages to put in its place. It is true that in the 1830s no one *in England* did have any alternative wage theory, though there was Longfield in Dublin and J. B. Say and Hermann on the Continent. But by the 1870s this was not true, even in insular England, when the 'hard' version of the Malthusian doctrine was rejected (for the second time) by almost all the leading economists. On this occasion, though the replacement was not worked out, Jevons pointed quite clearly to the lines on which a new distribution theory could be developed in terms of marginal productivity. There was also by the 1870s a much weightier body of empirical evidence refuting the 'hard-line' doctrine – (weighty enough, though it might be said, the evidence had been forty years before).

[24] There is an important external or 'environmental' reason which could have contributed much to the final elimination of the 'hard' (but not the 'soft') Malthusian doctrine around 1870. This is the first rapid growth at this time of large food imports from outside Europe. For the hard-line doctrine depends not only on the constant pressure of population, but also on the narrow limits for expanding the food supply. Professor W. H. B. Court has written of 'a revolution in the British trade in foodstuffs. This took place with surprising suddenness. In ten years, between 1868 and 1878, the United Kingdom ceased to grow the greater part of the wheat she consumed and began to take from abroad nearly one-half instead of one-seventh of the meat which she needed. This was the beginning of a bulk importation of foodstuffs upon which the national standard of living was to depend in future' (1964, p. 201). Professor R. S. Sayers emphasises the same point: 'When the U.S.A. settled down after its Civil War (1861–5), that country became a major source of cheap wheat for the English market. Total imports into Britain rose from about 1 million tons in the late

'Softer' Malthusian propositions continued to be maintained. Though the extreme form of soft-line Malthusian proposition was without empirical or predictive content, simply amounting to the use of a set of terms and concepts, or a taxonomy of 'checks', there *were* soft (though not so *extremely* soft) Malthusian propositions, which were not entirely empty empirically, and which implied or consisted of rather vague general maxims or warnings to beware of excessively rapid population increases. As well as to some of the Malthusian terminology and concepts, it was allegiance to this kind of tenuous generalisation

fifties to 3 to 4 million tons in the early eighties, and half of this came from the United States. Imports from the United States alone, that is to say, nearly equalled home production' (1967, p. 108).

It was just this development, of which J. S. Mill went on denying the likelihood in successive editions of *The Principles*, even up to when it was beginning to happen. Regarding Australia and the USA, Mill argues: 'Their agriculture has to provide for their own expanding numbers, as well as for those of the importing countries. They must, therefore, from the nature of the case, be rapidly driven if not to less fertile, at least what is equivalent, to remoter and less accessible lands, and to modes of cultivation like those of old countries, less productive in proportion to labour and expense' (I.XIII.3). Again (in IV.IV.7): 'The principal fund at present available for supplying this country with a yearly increasing importation of food is that portion of the annual savings of America which has heretofore been applied to increasing the manufacturing establishments of the United States, and which free trade in corn may possibly divert from that purpose to growing food for our market. This limited source of supply, unless great improvements take place in agriculture, cannot be expected to keep pace with the growing demand of so rapidly increasing a population as that of Great Britain.'

Mill was following here the teachings of his father in his early *Essay of the Impolicy of a Bounty on the Exportation of Grain* (1804), in which – though he admitted that America was then an exception – he maintained: 'In every well governed country, and whose circumstances are not as extraordinary as those of America, there never will be any *voluntary* exportation of corn, unless of the extraordinary produce of a plentiful year; for that people will always be produced to consume at home the *regular* produce, however rapidly it may increase' (James Mill, 1966, p. 57). See above the essay: James Mill and Ricardian economics: a methodological revolution? (Chapter 2).

In his edition of Mill's *Principles* W. J. Ashley, by way of comment on Mill's rather pessimistic predictions, gives an interesting table of the percentages of the population fed from home-grown corn: 1831–5, 96%; 1856–60, 71.9%; 1881–5, 26.4%. It would be strange to assume that economists, from the early 1870s onwards, had no inkling of the great development of overseas food supplies and the consequent falsification of the basic assumptions of the Ricardo–Mill model. In fact, by the middle 1870s, Bagehot was recognising that political economy 'does not teach that of necessity there will be, as time goes on, a greater and greater difficulty in providing for the increase of mankind...That augmentation of difficulty will not arise, first, because some of the inhabitants of old countries can emigrate to new countries, where people may increase as fast as they can; secondly, *because those emigrants produce more than they want in bare subsistence, and can send home a surplus to those who remain behind*; thirdly, because even in the old countries the growing improvement in the arts of production is likely, at least, to counterbalance the inevitable difficulty of a gradual resort to less favoured and fertile soils' (1895, p. 124, italics added). By 1881–2 Toynbee was recognising in his *Lectures* that Malthus could not 'foresee the great importation of food which would take place in later times...Now, we import one half of our food, and pay for it with our manufactures' (1894, p. 112).

that was implied by the lip-service that continued to be paid to 'the Malthusian doctrine'.

For example, when Jevons insisted that he had no doubt of the 'truth and vast importance' of 'the doctrine of population', but dismissed it because 'it forms no part of the direct problem of Economics', it was obviously a soft-line doctrine that he was brushing aside (1931, p. 266).[25] It is easy to do without a doctrine that has nothing to say about wages or anything much else, except that anything may happen. Certainly Jevons was seeking to focus attention on the allocation problem as central to economics and to concentrate on allocation 'given a certain population', as he puts it. But it would have been impossible to exclude from the concerns of economists a *hard*-line Malthusian proposition, with its vast implications for wages, cost-of-production, living standards, and policy possibilities, *unless*, of course, it was regarded as demonstrably falsified and devoid of empirical validity. Jevons was contributing to the final rejection and abandonment by economists in England of hard-line Malthusianism when he demanded that economists 'cast themselves free' from the Ricardo–Mill theory of the natural wage.

Sidgwick and Marshall later kept alive a decidedly 'softish' version of the Malthusian theory, which, though extensively and imprecisely qualified, and difficult to test, was not completely devoid of all predictive content.[26] Somewhat belatedly, indeed, Marshall (1893) recognised that a decisive break with the earlier hard-line doctrine had taken place. He spoke of 'a change...which separates the economics of this generation from the economics of the past'. What Marshall (who was of about the same generation as Jevons) then asserted was separating the economics of the earlier decades of the century from the later decades, was acceptance of the doctrine that: 'If you tax the rich, and give money to the working classes, the result will be that the working classes will increase in number, and the result will be you will have lowered wages in the next generation' (1926, p. 225).[27]

[25] As Fleeming Jenkin wrote (1870) (obviously of the 'soft' version): 'The Malthusian Law, true as it is, gives no help in determining what profit a capitalist will expect, or what comfort a labourer will expect; because, in fact, it gives no help in determining the cost of production either of labour or of anything else.' Jevons could calmly dismiss a doctrine of population which 'gave no help' in determining cost of production, wages, 'or anything else'. But he could not have dismissed from economics any doctrine which *did* give such help (see Jenkin, 1931, p. 98). As with other critics of classical distribution theory at this time, Jenkin was specially interested in the then topical question of the power of trade unions to affect wages. This question had also acquired new and much increased significance as the credibility of the Malthusian natural-wage theory declined.

[26] See Sidgwick, 1883, pp. 147–57; and 1879 (Chapter v) by A. and M. P. Marshall.

[27] Marshall explains the rejection of the older views – valid in their day – by changes in the social environment: 'It seems to me that whenever I read Poor Law literature of today I am taken back to the beginning of the century; everything that is said about

Marshall had tried to play down the change in value theory, and the challenge to orthodoxy, launched by Jevons. At least we would agree that the 'change' regarding the theory of wages (and population) is, in some ways, of wider significance, at any rate in policy terms. But what must be emphasised is that the 'change' in wage theory and the 'change' in value theory, in England, were closely linked, both temporally, and logically or analytically. Temporally, it was the challenge of Jevons on the natural wage theory, developed alongside his final utility theory of value, together with other attacks in the late 1860s and early 1870s by economists of the same new cohort or generation as Jevons, which constituted the decisive rejection – from which it never recovered as it had previously – of the hard-line Malthusian doctrine, till then firmly entrenched in J. S. Mill's *Principles* and supported by Cairnes and Fawcett. Logically and analytically, the same over-simplified concept of 'labour' and 'wages' was involved in *both* the Ricardo–Mill natural wage and population doctrine, *and* in the labour-cost-of-production value theory. To replace this common weak link Jevons called for a much more decisive role for consumer demand and utility in value theory, and for productivity in wage and distribution theory (both of which had always been acknowledged by the leading French and German writers).

The very rapid decline and fall of English classical political economy, as we have noted, from a position of almost unique authority and dominance, has been given comparatively little examination. We have, however, a case almost unparalleled in the history of economic theory, of the comparatively sudden abandonment of a very central theoretical core, which had long and authoritatively prevailed as an established orthodoxy. The over-worked term 'revolution' does not seem far-fetched in describing this process in England in the late 1860s and early 1870s. But if the term 'revolution' is only to be applied where one authoritative regime is replaced more or less *immediately* by another authoritative regime, then we cannot speak of a 'revolution' occurring in England in, or around, 1871 (and certainly, as we shall see, it seems difficult to describe what happened on the Continent as 'revolutionary'). But if the first negative, or destructive, phase, by itself, can be described as 'revolutionary' then it would be difficult to point to a more clear-cut and important example in the history of economic thought.

What Jevons called for, in his *Theory of Political Economy*, was that

economics had the flavour of that old time. Statements which were true then, taking account of the conditions of the working classes and of the state of wealth, are reproduced and made the basis of arguments which seem to me to be not valid now.' Professor Donald Winch has noted also regarding J. S. Mill: 'Mill still felt that the Malthusian problem posed a real threat to hopes of raising the living standards of the majority' (1971, p. 58).

English economists should abandon the peculiar insular eccentricities of their natural wage, labour-cost-of-production, and wages-fund theories, and rejoin the mainstream of Western European thinking. Of course some of the leading ideas of English classical orthodoxy survived into the new period, but only those which it had always shared in common with French and German theorists. For example, the deductive method survived the historical and Comteist attacks, although these attacks had contributed to the uncertainty and upheaval of the 1870s. The assumption of competition as the general, 'normal' case in the main survived. But the new marginal analysis was *much* better equipped to deal with non-competitive markets and its development had been much stimulated by concern with the growing problems of public monopolies. The Turgot–Smith saving and investing analysis and J. B. Say's concepts of aggregate demand and supply survived, but only briefly. The rent analysis can also be said *to some extent* to have survived: but its generalisation in the marginal productivity treatment really involved its wholesale transformation. Marshall, of course, was to carry through something of a restoration of some of the English 'classical' concepts and terms, though this hardly amounted to more than a façade. As Schumpeter says:

> No unbiased reader can fail to perceive...that Marshall's theoretical structure, barring its technical superiority and various developments of detail, is fundamentally the same as that of Jevons, Menger, and especially Walras, but that the rooms in this new house are unnecessarily cluttered up with Ricardian heirlooms, which receive emphasis quite out of proportion to their operational importance [1954, p. 837].

And of course it should be added, that according to Marshall's own record, it was just at the beginning of what we would claim to be the critical 'revolutionary' period – though publication was delayed for nearly a quarter of a century – that, with the aid of Cournot and von Thünen, his 'main position as to the theory of value and distribution was practically completed in the years 1867 to 1870' (1925, p. 416).[28] So Marshall might well be regarded as a member of the new 'cohort' of the late 1860s together with Leslie, Bagehot, and Jevons (as we have suggested above).

It may at least be agreed, however, that the Marshallian regime, in spite of his discovery of, and debts to, Continental writers, for some decades not unsuccessfully revived something of the earlier Anglican insularity, and the orthodox dominance of the single book. For a time, through much of the first quarter of this century, separate 'schools', notably in Cambridge, Vienna, and Lausanne, survived with their particular peculiarities of terminology and assumptions, before in the

---

[28] It now seems that Marshall's claims, later in life, regarding his early writings, were somewhat exaggerated. See J. K. Whitaker's Introduction (1975).

second quarter merging into a general, cosmopolitan North American and Western European melting pot. It was, of course, in Marxist economic theorising that some of the old concepts of English 'classical' orthodoxy continued a form of existence. Certainly, in the economic regimes of Eastern Europe, claiming somewhat questionably to be following out the economic theories of Marx, the neglect of consumer demand, utility, and choice, in the earlier English theories, had a twentieth century practical, political counterpart.

Anyhow, the theoretical changes of what has been called the Jevonian revolution were linked logically, and after a certain time-lag led on, to important policy consequences and changes, which we follow out in the next chapter.

IV

As its title indicates, this chapter is primarily concerned with the theoretical or analytical changes which took place around 1870. But we have already noted, and would briefly emphasise further, that the revolt against the English classical regime, or the Ricardo–Mill orthodoxy in economics, which began in England in the late 1860s included two very different elements. There was first, the theoretical attack on the Ricardo–Mill distribution and value theories, and the policy conclusions derived from them; and secondly there was the much more fundamental historico-methodological attack, which included, but went well beyond, the criticism of particular theories or policies, *and attacked the abstractions of the Ricardo–Mill method.*

In the initial phase of this revolt much the most important and effective methodological critic was Cliffe Leslie, for whom, as we have seen, Mill himself had a very high regard. Leslie followed in the direction of the attacks on Ricardo launched by the isolated historical critic Richard Jones in the 1830s. He derived his historical approach from Sir Henry Maine, the historical critic of natural law ideas, and owed little or nothing to Comteist or German influences, which were at work later on other English methodological opponents of classical political economy. Leslie was among the early critics of the wages-fund doctrine and was moved to attack classical orthodoxy over the question of economic policy towards Ireland. Though critical of what he regarded as the excessive influences of natural law ideas in Smith's work, Leslie called for a return to the historical and inductive method of 'the great Scotsman'. Leslie was, as Dr Koot observes, especially severe on Ricardo: 'Leslie reserved his most bitter condemnation for Ricardo whose deductive method had allowed the formulation of an entire theory of distribution *without any reference to real conditions*' (1975, p. 318, italics added).

Leslie's criticisms of the abstract methods of Ricardian orthodoxy are as penetrating as any ever made and went to the root of the most fundamental and consequential of the Ricardian simplifications, the abstraction from ignorance and uncertainty. In his profound essay 'The Known and the Unknown in the Economic World' (1879) Leslie complained, as Keynes was to do in the preface to *The General Theory*: 'It is a curious characteristic of the deductive political economy that, in spite of its show of logic, its followers have never firmly grasped either their own premises or their conclusions' (Leslie, n.d., p. 227).

Leslie points out that the assumption of a universal desire for wealth, in some form or other, is simply not adequate to yield the conclusions derived from the orthodox theories: 'The orthodox, a priori, or deductive system thus postulates much more than a general desire for wealth. It postulates also...full knowledge' (op. cit., p. 229).

The Ricardian theory, Leslie observed, involves extreme abstraction – or a very 'strong case' – regarding the extent of knowledge. In the real economic world: 'The vastness, complexity, and incessant changes...are absolutely incompatible with the main postulates of the Ricardian theory, that the advantages of all the different occupations are known' (op. cit., p. 231).[29]

With regard to investment decisions Leslie quotes the German historical economist Erwin Nasse: 'All the observations of fixed capital – ships, railways, factories, mines – involve production for the future; but how is the future to be known?' (op. cit., p. 227).

Keynes was to raise exactly these questions about what he called 'classical orthodoxy' in *The General Theory* – though he then proceeded largely to evade them rather than follow Leslie in drawing drastic methodological consequences. For the assumption of perfect or adequate knowledge survived, of course, in the new analysis which was beginning to be constructed. In fact this, or similar over-simplified or arbitrary assumptions, seems almost indispensable for the construction of abstract models of microeconomic behaviour *of any kind of generality*.

Undoubtedly Leslie's powerful and profound attacks had a major part in the decline and fall of the Ricardo–Mill economics. In fact in his comprehensive historical criticism of Ricardian economics, *unlike Jevons*, Leslie included in his target some of the socialistic inferences regarding class-conflict, which had been dubiously extracted from Ricardo's ideas.[30]

---

[29] See below Chapter 7, Section III.

[30] The irony is that the historical critic Cliffe Leslie, while denouncing the abstraction of Ricardo from historical time and processes, and the Ricardian concentration on rapid equilibration, also criticised the intimations regarding the clash of class-interests and of wages and profits. Just the kind of quotation which Marxists would love to be able to pin on Jevons, Marshall, or other neoclassicals, but are unable to find, are

It is notable that the English version of the *Methodenstreit* was initiated by historical critics of the dominant abstract and deductive approach of Ricardian economics. In Austria and Germany, where a much longer and fiercer battle was to begin in the 1880s the opening shot came from a defender of 'theoretical' or deductive methods against the dominant historical approach long strongly entrenched in Germany. The Austro-German *Methodenstreit* was to continue for decades. But in England history and analysis went their separate ways.[31] The 'classical' or Ricardian (not Smithian) method of deduction from abstract models and assumptions (in particular, the perfect knowledge assumption) survived unscathed in the new models: (hence the, to this extent, justifiable descriptive term, 'neoclassical'). Certainly Marshall tried to take seriously the lessons of the *Methodenstreit* in his *Industry and Trade*, but this important aspect of his work was largely neglected and abandoned by his successors. Moreover, Leslie's penetrating criticisms were forgotten, and the fundamental limitations which they indicated for much orthodox theorising and 'model'-building – in spite of the reminders of Knight (1921), Keynes (1936) and others – were largely disregarded until the 1970s.

V

In order to describe, assess, or explain (to the extent that 'explanation' is possible) what happened with regard to economic theory in 1871 and the years either side, it is essential to distinguish between the state of economic theory, or the orthodoxies prevailing in the leading Continental countries in the 1860s and early 1870s, on the one hand, and on the other hand, the peculiar and very different position in Britain, which we have just surveyed. The history of economic thought in the first half, or three quarters, of the nineteenth century was, and still is, often portrayed in very Anglo-centric terms, as though the theories which achieved for so long in Britain such an extraordinary dominance and authority, perhaps almost unique in the history of the subject, enjoyed a similar hold and authority elsewhere in Europe. This was not the case. The contexts and backgrounds from which Jevons's *Theory*, Menger's *Grundsätze*, and Walras's *Elements* emerged differed significantly, at any rate as between the first named and the other two.

supplied by the intellectual radical Cliffe Leslie, who rejected Jevons's neoclassical analysis as fundamentally as he did the 'classical' doctrines of Ricardo. In fact, Leslie (1879) actually drew a parallel between Ricardo and Karl Marx in what must be one of the first references to that name in English by an important figure in the history of economic thought. See below Chapter 9: On recent revolutionary versions of the history of economics, Section III.

[31] T. W. Hutchison, 1953, p. 21. On the *Methodenstreit*, see my essay on Carl Menger's 'Investigations' in J. R. Hicks and W. Weber, eds., 1973, pp. 27–37.

Of course in the broadest and most general terms all three faced the same fundamental questions of the determinants of value, prices, and incomes, and all inherited the same answers which had come down from a common Western tradition extending from Aristotle to Adam Smith. But in the nineteenth century the theories of value and distribution had developed pretty differently in Britain as contrasted with the rest of Western Europe. Moreover, in the middle decades of the nineteenth century, say from the late 1840s to the late 1860s, there was not much in the way of communication regarding economic theory between the economists of Britain and those of the Continent.[32] There

---

[32] See my article, 1955. Neither on the import, nor on the export side were there any very significant movements of ideas, in or out of Britain, regarding economic theory, between the late 1840s and the late 1860s, except perhaps for the influx of Comteist and historical ideas in the late 1860s, which were of methodological rather than theoretical significance. As an example of English insularity, or the barriers against *imports into* England, J. E. Cairnes, as the last of the 'classical' economists provides a relevant example. As Professor S. G. Checkland put it: 'Cairnes had no doubt that political economy was essentially an English business, and that contemporary French and German ideas were scarcely worthy of notice' (1951, p. 149). Also regarding the absence of imports into England, F. W. Taussig wrote: 'The insular condition of social and political speculation in Great Britain in the middle of the century, and the stagnation of economic thought in particular, prevented any breath of influence from reaching English thinkers. The Germans went their way, unnoticed by their English-speaking contemporaries...The French never were much influenced by Ricardo' (1896, p. 266).

British insularity down to the middle 1860s was summed up by Bastable (1894) as follows: 'There is no room for doubt or question. With the exception of Say and Bastiat – who were chiefly valued as popularizers of English opinions – no foreign economist was at all known in England before the last thirty years. The mere suggestion that we had anything to learn from Germany, Holland, or Italy would have appeared ludicrous to Senior or McCulloch, or indeed to the educated public. The true position of the foreigner was that of the humble disciple accepting gladly orthodox English teaching. *This insularity of tone undoubtedly retarded progress in all departments of economics but its evil effect was greatest in preventing any thorough consideration of the social and political groundwork on which all systems of economy rest*, and to which all theories must, if they are to be enduring, pay adequate attention'. (See Bastable's Presidential Address to Section F of the British Association in 1962, p. 128, italics added.) It has been stated by Dr Neil de Marchi (1973, p. 79), that J. S. Mill (and Cairnes), 'were well versed in the writings of the so-called French school'. But easily the most important French writers whose main works were published in the decade before Mill's *Principles*, were Cournot and Dupuit. There seem to be no signs that Mill was 'well versed', or even 'versed' at all in the writings of these great pioneers. No blame, of course, attaches to Mill for not knowing these works. But it seems difficult, and not very complimentary to Mill, to argue that had Mill been 'well versed' in the writings of Cournot and Dupuit his *Principles* would *not* have shown *some* significant effects, for example with regard to the pricing of public utilities. It was surely unfortunate that a work like Mill's *Principles*, which was to have such an extreme and almost exclusive influence and prestige, incorporated nothing from what have come to be regarded as the two outstanding works of the decade before it appeared. Regarding *exports* from England, the great influence of Smith's ideas, especially on policy, belongs to an earlier period than that with which we are concerned. But, as Bagehot observed, 'Political Economy, as it was taught by Ricardo ...has remained insular. I do not mean that it was not often read and understood; of course it was so, though it was often misread and misunderstood. But it never at

was no world market, nor even a Western European Common Market in economic theorising, and the British market was dominated by a monopolistically inclined orthodoxy, indeed, for a time, almost by a single book.

VI

Menger's *Grundsätze* certainly marks an important beginning, but does not mark an end, as does Jevons's *Theory*, which can be said to mark both an end and a beginning. Menger's work marks very definitively the foundation of the Austrian school, and its long and remarkable history. Though the Austrian school is not as homogeneous and monolithic an entity as it is sometimes treated as being, it can be said to possess certain common family features which can mainly be traced to the *Grundsätze*. What made the breakthrough for Menger and his *Grundsätze*, transforming the work from being simply another distinguished but isolated exposition of the marginal utility idea, was the almost immediate adherence of two brilliant and very prolific disciples in Wieser and Böhm-Bawerk, though it was more than a decade before these two were ready to publish their major contributions.

In Menger's *Grundsätze*, the very careful and precise elaboration of the marginal concept (though the term is not used) is the key technical or analytical contribution, being applied from the start both to consumers' goods and services and to producers' goods and services, establishing, at least in outline, much of the complete pattern of marginal, microeconomic analysis. But although he does have a paragraph or two attacking cost-of-production theories in terms similar to Jevons's well-known passage on 'bygones', Menger was certainly not rebelling, as Jevons was in England, against a powerfully entrenched orthodox theory of value and distribution which had given little, and certainly much too little, scope to utility, demand, and consumers' wants. Nor was Menger confronted, regarding the theory of distribution, by the wages-fund and natural wage theories, which were the prevailing orthodoxies for Jevons, and which he attacked alongside

all reigned abroad as it reigns here' (1895, p. 4). Marshall, also, in 1897, wrote of the classical theories being mostly 'bad sailors; if they were met in other lands, they generally had a languishing air as though they had not recovered from sea-sickness' (1925, p. 295). Earlier (1876), Jevons had observed regarding English exports to France: 'Foreign economists, such as de Laveleye, Courcelle-Seneuil, Cournot, Walras and others have taken a course almost entirely independent of the predominant English school' (1905, p. 190). Professor Piero Barucci has noted regarding Italy in the latter part of the nineteenth century: 'Respect for the great tradition of English economists was, almost invariably, perfunctory, and this is why Ricardo was still rarely read and little understood' (1973, p. 248). The one major Continental economist who was significantly influenced by the English classical value and distribution analysis was Karl Marx, who accepted the insular English view that there was no German economic theory worthy of notice in 1873. (See his 'Nachwort' to the 2nd edition of *Das Kapital*, 1873.)

the labour and cost-of-production theory of value. Menger did not even think it necessary to mention the wages-fund theory, which had been severely criticised by Hermann in 1832 and never gained significant support in Germany or Austria.[33] Nor did the Ricardian 'natural wage' doctrine ever gain much adherence.[34] Thus the link between wages, or distribution, and productivity and (ultimately) consumer demand, was not suppressed in Germany, as it had been in the 'English' theory. Therefore Menger's basically unified approach to the valuation of final consumers' goods and of factors of production was not in itself a fundamentally novel or unorthodox departure, but was in harmony with prevailing ideas. What was to some extent novel, and of the greatest technical importance, was simply the introduction, analysis, and application of the marginal concept, though this also *had previously been developed by Menger's great German predecessors*, such as Thünen, Mangoldt, and the long-unknown Gossen.

Certainly Menger was highly critical of the English classicals. He even maintained that the widely diverging views (as revealed in the *Methodenstreit*) regarding the nature and method of economics, were all (or both) reactions to the fundamental errors of the English classicals:

> The conflict of views about the nature of our science, its problems, and its limits...did not originally develop from an interest of economists in epistemological problems. It begins with the recognition, becoming more and more clear, that the theory of economics, as it left the hands of Adam Smith and his followers, lacks any assured basis and that even its most elementary problems have found no solution [1963, p. 27].

In fact, in a tribute to the leader of the German historicals, Wilhelm Roscher, Menger – presumably with Ricardo in mind – wrote approvingly of: 'the historical–empirical reaction against the abstract unempirical schematism ['Schematismus'] of certain followers of Adam Smith as well as against the German representatives of the doctrines of 'Manchester liberalism' ['Manchestertums'] in economic theory and policy' (1935, vol. III, p. 276).

[33] F. W. Taussig, 1896, pp. 266ff, who explains that 'the radical objection' to the wages-fund doctrine given by Hermann and his followers is that: 'Capital, after all, is not the real source from which wages are paid. That real source is the income of those who buy the products made by labourers, or, briefly, the income of consumers.'
  Marshall also noted (perhaps with a touch of chauvinism) that 'the French and German economists, though on the whole they had not done nearly so much good work as the English, have never given any countenance to the doctrine that there is a determinate wages fund' (1961, vol. II, p. 606).
[34] Menger's analysis of the pricing of factors of production, which followed that of German predecessors, notably Hermann, started from the deliberate dismissal as irrelevant of the special characteristics of the different kinds of factors or factor-services as implied in the tripartite classification. He attacks Ricardo's rent analysis and the concept of 'the original powers' of land, as well as any necessary relationship between 'subsistence' and the price obtainable for labour services. (See 1950, pp. 166–8.)

Anyhow, Menger, as he himself originally proclaimed in his preface of 1871, was following out ideas developed most recently by German predecessors. He certainly contributed a fundamental and vital concept which advanced decisively a tradition of value theory which started from utility or human wants and which can be traced back to Aristotle (whom Menger frequently cites as an authority both in the *Grundsätze* and later in the *Untersuchungen*).[35] When, therefore, he felt aggrieved at the very restricted interest for his path-breaking ideas in Germany, this was not because a ruling orthodoxy with regard to value and wage theory was too strongly entrenched, or because it was maintained, in the famous words of John Stuart Mill, that 'happily, there is nothing in the laws of value which remains for the present or any future writer to clear up; the theory of the subject is complete' (1909, p. 436).[36] If Menger's ideas did not at once make much headway, or as much as he had hoped – in spite of his immediately acquiring such brilliant disciples and expositors – it was because there had come to be very little interest, throughout much of Germany, in the advance and refinement of economic 'theory' or abstract analysis (which was the reason for Menger's explosion against the German historical economists in his *Untersuchungen*, twelve years later and for the subsequent *Methodenstreit*).[37]

[35] Menger emphasises in his preface to the *Grundsätze* that 'the reform of the most important principles of our science here attempted is therefore built upon a foundation laid by previous work that was produced almost entirely by the industry of German scholars' (1950, p. 49). The index to the *Grundsätze* contains most of the great names in the European utility tradition from Aristotle onwards, including the major eighteenth-century theorists, Galiani, Condillac, Genovesi, and Beccaria, with J. B. Say and Auguste Walras from nineteenth-century France, and from among Menger's more immediate German forerunners, K. H. Rau, Hermann, and Mangoldt.
  Later Wieser, also, in the preface to *Natural Value* emphasises how much 'Menger is indebted to the German school of political economists... It may be said that, in great part, the German school long ago formulated the conceptions, leaving us only the task of filling them out by adequate observations... The new value theory... is in truth the fulfillment of what German theory had long demanded.' Wieser cites as forerunners of the marginal utility analysis, or of the Austrian or Mengerian version of it, 'all those who have derived value from utility', listing most of those mentioned above from Menger's index and adding the very interesting name of Daniel Bernoulli (1893, pp. xxxii–iv).
[36] It is true that in the Introduction by his son to the posthumous second edition of the *Grundsätze* (1923), there is a quotation (undated) from the notes of Menger *senior* maintaining that he had 'set himself the task of countering the theories of Adam Smith which he saw to be erroneous', and that, as regards himself and Jevons, 'we both stood in strict opposition to Smith's theory' (pp. vii–viii). This is one of those puzzles in Menger's writings – there are a number in the *Untersuchungen* – which are very difficult to interpret owing to the obscurity enveloping Menger's early intellectual development and the main influences acting on him. To counter or come out in opposition to the theories of Adam Smith in Germany and Austria in the 1860s had about as much or as little significance as to counter, or to come out in opposition to, the theories of Keynes in Chicago in the 1960s or 1970s.
[37] See my essay on the *Untersuchungen* in J. R. Hicks and W. Weber (eds.), pp. 15ff. One very discerning contribution on a subject mentioned above in this essay which

VII

The theories of the English school were scarcely more influential in France in the middle of the nineteenth century than they were in Germany and Austria. Léon Walras started from a tradition of French economic theory which emphasised the role of utility and scarcity in the determination of value. This went back to Condillac and, in particular, to J. B. Say (whom Schumpeter describes as Walras's 'true predecessor'). Say not only emphasised the role of utility in value, but based the explanation of the incomes to factors on their productivity. More directly, Walras was indebted to his father and Cournot. As Schumpeter says: 'He paid conventional respect to A. Smith. The rest of the great Englishmen meant little to him' (1954, p. 828).[38]

Walras was indeed something of a rebel and felt himself almost an outcast. But what he was rebelling against were not the orthodox theories of value and distribution, but, first, as a 'socialist', against the particular kind of extreme *laissez-faire* policy dogmas prevailing in France, and, secondly, against the rejection of mathematics by those whom he described as the 'mandarins' of French economic orthodoxy, in whose citadels he had not been able to find employment. Walras certainly did not have to start by contending against an entrenched theoretical orthodoxy on value and distribution, such as was represented in Britain by the wages-fund theory, the labour and cost of production theory of value, and the 'natural wage' theory. Walras rightly describes these theories as those of 'the English school'. They were part neither of the tradition he built upon nor of the orthodoxies with which he contended. But here and there in the *Elements* he turns aside for a page or two in order to criticise them. Indeed he recognises that 'the efforts of the English school to develop a theory of rent, wages and interest were far more sustained and thorough than those of the various French schools', emphasising 'the order and continuity of development and the enduring quality of the English doctrine' (1954, p. 398). Sustained, thorough, and orderly the English doctrines may

Menger makes in the *Untersuchungen*, is the attention which he briefly calls to the vital fundamental assumption of 'Allwissenheit' (which had been stressed four years earlier by Cliffe Leslie). Discussing what he calls 'the dogma of self-interest' Menger emphasises 'a gap in the line of argument', the omission of the factor of '*error*': 'Even if economic humans always and everywhere let themselves be guided exclusively by their self-interest, the strict regularity of economic phenomena would nonetheless have to be considered impossible because of the fact given by experience that in innumerable cases they are in error about their economic interest, or in ignorance of the economic state of affairs. Our historians are too considerate of their scholarly opponents. The presupposition of a strict regularity of economic phenomena, and with this of a theoretical economics in the multiple meaning of the word, is not only the dogma of ever-constant self-interest, but also the dogma of the "infallibility" and "omniscience" of humans in economic affairs' (1963, p. 84).

[38] As Professor G. J. Stigler puts it: 'Say's approach was fundamentally much more modern than that of his English contemporaries' (1965, p. 304).

well have been, but they seemed to Walras to suffer from a certain fundamental error as compared with the traditional French (and German) approach.

On the subject of value Walras writes:

> The science of economics offers three major solutions to the problem of the origin of value. The first, that of Adam Smith, Ricardo and McCulloch, is the English solution, which traces the origin of value to *labour*. This solution is too narrow, because it fails to attribute value to things which, in fact, do have value. The second solution, that of Condillac and J. B. Say, is the French solution, which traces the origin of value to *utility*. This solution is too broad, because it attributes value to things which, in fact, have no value. Finally, the third solution, that of Burlamaqui and my father, A. A. Walras, traces the origin of value to *scarcity* ('rareté'). This is the correct solution [1954, p. 201].[39]

Walras's distinction between his second and third solutions owes much to his eagerness to differentiate his position from that of French orthodoxy, which mainly followed J. B. Say. For both of the French or Continental solutions, though distinguished by Walras, recognise the role of utility and demand, not adequately provided for in the 'English' theory.

On distribution Walras, after expounding the marginal productivity theory, turns aside to demolish the 'English' theories. He recognises, by way of contrast that: 'J. B. Say had a tolerably clear and accurate idea of the combination of the three productive services in the process of production. The terminology he employed was good; we have therefore adopted it ourselves' (op. cit., p. 425). This is almost the highest possible praise from Walras. When he discusses briefly 'the English theory of wages', as enunciated by J. S. Mill, and, in particular, the wages-fund theory, he dismisses, as 'nothing but a long and tedious quibble', one of Mill's essential fundamental propositions to the effect that to purchase produce is not to employ labour. On the other hand Walras later pays tribute to Jevons who:

> wrote ten remarkable pages at the close of the preface in his second edition (pp. xlviii–lvii), in which he clearly stated that the formula of the English school, in any case the school of Ricardo and Mill, must be reversed, for the prices of productive services are determined by the prices of their products and not the other way round [op. cit., p. 45].[40]

[39] The 'scarcity' tradition stems from the same, originally Aristotelian, source as the 'utility' tradition, coming down through the 'natural law' school, and notably through Pufendorf to Carmichael and Hutcheson, as well as *via* Burlamaqui to Walras. Smith, *to some extent*, and Ricardo very markedly, diverged from this tradition. Marshall, however, with his analysis of value in terms of 'both blades of the scissors', could be said to have renewed this line of thought in that the scarcity concept emphasises *both* demand and supply factors.

[40] See also p. 385 where Walras attributes to Jevons 'the germ' of the marginal productivity analysis in Chapters VI and VII of his *Theory*. Walras is only prepared to agree to a very 'soft' version of the Malthusian theory and strongly rejects the 'harder' sorts of policy conclusions derived from it (p. 388).

VIII

To describe the changes of the late 1860s and early 1870s as the Jevonian 'revolution' is, first, to emphasise that it was only in England that any drastically 'revolutionary' processes took place; and secondly to associate these processes with the man who is usually described, on the whole correctly, as having played the most distinguished role both in the attack on the previous classical regime and in laying the foundations of what was to become, eventually, the new system of thought.

1871 has frequently been described as the year of 'the Marginal Revolution'. But the intellectual developments epitomised or foreshadowed in the books of Jevons and Menger in 1871 had, or soon assumed, other features or dimensions besides the introduction of the marginal concept, of which *two* closely associated ideas seem fundamental. Along with the introduction of the marginal concept there was, *secondly*, a gradual turn towards a narrower and more specific focus on 'micro' theorising and analysis which concentrated on individual maximising units exchanging goods and services; and, *thirdly*, there came about a pronounced emphasis – as contrasted with English classical political economy – on utility and demand, and away from cost and labour in the central theories of value and distribution.

Other features could be mentioned regarding the new pattern of economic theorising which was beginning to emerge in addition to these three basic ideas of the marginal concept, the 'micro' focus on the individual unit, and the stress on utility and demand. In putting primary emphasis on these three there is no need to be exclusivist. Sir John Hicks has described *catallactics* – or the analysis of exchange – as the new focus of interest (1975, p. 322). It would be reasonable also to stress *allocation*, or *allocative efficiency*, as the central new concept or question. Indeed, the proposition called by Schumpeter 'Gossen's Second Law', can be seen as the archetype or pattern for much of the analysis that was to emerge: that is, that to secure an efficient allocation, or a maximum of satisfaction from any good that can satisfy different kinds of want (such as money, labour, or factors of production) an individual must so allocate units of it between different uses as to equalise their marginal utilities or returns in all of them. Nor is it necessary to enlarge on the application of mathematical formulation as an important feature of the new pattern that was to emerge. Mathematics was certainly vigorously championed by Jevons, though it was totally rejected by Menger. But the development of mathematical formulation could be held to have been secondary rather than primary in 1871. It was not so much a question for Jevons or Menger in 1871, though it might have been for Cournot in 1838, or for Walras in 1874, of championing mathematical formulation *a priori*, and then developing the marginal concept with its aid. Rather the central significance of the marginal concept and the maximising individual was arrived at *first*, by Jevons at any rate, and mathematical formulation and the calculus were championed secondarily or consequentially, as tools for developing and deploying these concepts. Menger, of course, as well as his leading Austrian followers, maintained a fundamental opposition to mathematics.

As regards, then, our three basic ideas, their development was closely interconnected, indeed, mutually interacting, the sharpening, clarification and application of each of them promoting the sharpening, clarification and application of the other two. But these interconnections were not logically inevitable. In fact, however, each of the three key concepts was fitted together with the other two to give the coherent new pattern which emerged, of the marginal concept as the key tool, and of utility or consumer's demand as the origin, driving-force, or basic 'determinant' in a system of micro-economics built round maximising individual units. But each of the three concepts *could*, logically, have developed in different contexts without the other two.

For example, the marginal concept was sharpened, and found an easy and open, if ultimately not very richly fruitful field of application, in propounding formulae, notably 'Gossen's Second Law', for the individual utility-maximising consumer. But the marginal concept *could*, logically and conceivably, have been developed and defined in 'macro' terms for application in macroeconomic analysis – as it eventually was by Keynes. In fact, in the early inchoate anticipations of the marginal concept, in the classical diminishing returns analysis, there was a certain macro–micro ambiguity.

Again, the marginal and the utility concepts certainly advanced in tandem in the two books of 1871, and to date a 'revolution' from that year would imply that the most important step in the development, or general emergence, of the marginal concept was in its application to utility by Jevons and Menger. Certainly, examination of the utility concept would presumably in due course lead to the diminishing utility generalisation, and from there it is one of those crucial short steps, from the idea of different utilities from each successive individual unit to the marginal utility concept – though, of course, not necessarily to the term. But then the development of the marginal concept *could* have come in respect of costs or physical product, as indeed to some extent it did, without achieving the crucial breakthrough, in the classical diminishing returns analysis and in the productivity analysis of Longfield and von Thünen. Also the *concept* of marginal revenue had been developed by Cournot in his analysis of monopoly, though it was getting on for a century before the *term* actually emerged.

It may be noted that the particular simplified assumptions of the main classical models left little scope for the marginal concept. With competitive markets and constant costs and returns (except in agriculture) these assumptions mostly implied no divergence between average and marginal, and therefore little pressing need for a distinct marginal concept. With utility relegated rather to the sidelines from *The Wealth of Nations* onwards, there was no scope, where the dominance of English classical orthodoxy was maintained, for arriving at the marginal concept in terms of utility *via* the idea of diminishing utility from which it is a short step. Naturally it was in the field of monopoly, and in particular public monopolies or public 'utilities', involved with falling average costs and falling average revenue, that several of the pioneering developments in marginal analysis took place in the works of Cournot and Dupuit, with Dionysius Lardner's *Railway Economy*, as Sir John Hicks pointed out (1934, p. 339) providing a bridge between Cournot and Jevons – though Jevons does not seem actually to have made much use of this bridge. But insofar as the competitive model was the general case both before and after 1871, it was *via* utility, not *via* physical product, cost, or revenue, that the marginal concept can be said to have achieved its main breakthrough.

We have looked at how the marginal and 'micro', and how the marginal and utility, concepts actually, though not inevitably, were fitted and developed together. When we examine the third pairing, that of the utility concept with the microeconomic focus on the maximising individual unit, one perhaps comes nearest to what might be regarded as a logically inevitable connection. Though the marginal concept need not inevitably have developed, and historically was not solely developed, in terms of utility and micro-analysis, it might now seem that the utility concept *must* inevitably be analysed and refined in individual, 'micro' terms. But this would be to avail oneself of hindsight. Here again the utility concept, or at any rate the utilitarian 'happiness' concept, had emerged and been widely deployed in aggregate social terms in the slogan of 'the greatest happiness of the greatest number'. In fact the utility concept was advanced by Bentham as a criterion for legislation and policy, and for that optimistic purpose some aggregate, 'macro' concept of utility was required. The analysis and refinement of the utility concept by Jevons proceeded, and *had* to proceed in 'micro', individual terms. But the fond, if vain, hope persisted, apparently to some extent in Jevons himself, and particularly ardently in Edgeworth's *Mathematical Psychics* (1881), for example, that somehow out of, or on the basis of, the more precise and refined analysis of utility in 'micro', or individual terms, a valid policy concept and policy criterion, in aggregate 'macro' terms, might be constructed. Tentative hopes of this kind seem to have been shared by Walras and Marshall, only eventually and inevitably to fade away in the sterile shadow of the Pareto optimum.

We have been stressing in this section the change of focus, or 'change of attention' (as Sir John Hicks has called it) which took place as the Jevonian 'revolution' developed, a 'change of attention', that is, from 'plutology' – or the production and growth of wealth – to 'catallactics' and allocation (1975, p. 323). (There was no change of attention, *of nearly the same extent*, involved in the discoveries of Menger and Walras.) 'Changes of attention', though perhaps they could conceivably arise for purely 'internal' reasons, are most likely to – and surely have most often – come about for 'external' reasons arising out of the new economic problems, changes in politico-economic institutions, or in the sociology or organisation of the economics 'profession'. So to describe 'revolutions' as simply or mainly 'changes of attention', probably implies an exclusively or mainly 'external' account of the history of economics. We are prepared to go a long way with this view, but certainly not all the way. It seems too restrictive and over-simplified. As regards the Jevonian 'revolution', and other revolutions in economics and political economy, *part* of the explanation must be found in 'internal' reasons arising out of the intellectual inadequacies of the Ricardo–Mill theories of value and distribution.

IX

The Jevonian revolution is in some ways the most disputed or controversial of the revolutions examined in this book. There have been marked differences of view as to whether there really was such a 'revolution', as well as regarding the reasons or motives for it – if there was one – and as to whether the resulting intellectual losses did not far outweigh any gains. Certainly, as its centenary came round, there was recognition from various quarters of its fundamental importance (*including the claim by Mr M. H. Dobb that the Jevonian revolution had a much deeper significance than the Keynesian revolution*) (1973, p. 214).

As regards 'losses' different kinds of 'loss' must be distinguished.[41] But, in any case, there can hardly be said to have been any revolutionary losses resulting from the developments following Menger's *Grundsätze* and Walras' *Elements*. Any losses must have been incurred in respect of the doctrines of 'the Ricardo–Mill economics', following

[41] See below Chapter 11: 'On revolutions and progress in economic knowledge'.

on the Jevonian revolution. Let us consider the most important of these 'lost' doctrines one by one:

(1) First and most important, there was the demise of the hard-line version of the Malthusian population and natural wage doctrine, which had played such a vital role in both Ricardian theory and Ricardian policies. In its hardest form this generalisation possessed a massive empirical content the validity of which, whatever it may have amounted to in Ricardo's own day – and Marshall was prepared to concede some validity for the early decades in the century – had evaporated pretty completely, through historical obsolescence, by the time the last third of the century was opening. But it was history, not any revolution in economic thought, Jevonian or otherwise, which brought out this 'loss'. In fact it could and should be described as a 'gain' for the Jevonian revolution, insofar as this loss of validity was discerned and the due consequences for distribution theory and policy were recognised.

(2) *Secondly,* there was the Ricardian rent analysis. There was hardly any loss here, except regarding the dubious claims for the special or unique characteristics of 'land' and natural resources. In fact, it would be more appropriate to claim an analytical *gain* from the generalis-ation of the Ricardian rent and diminishing returns analysis which was developed in the 1890s.

(3) As regards the wages-fund analysis it must be agreed that there was a certain loss, though hardly in terms of empirical content, in which respect there was little or nothing to lose. But certainly what *might* have been a useful type of macro-distribution *analysis* was 'lost'. It should be emphasised, however, that there was nothing intellectually inevi-table about this kind of loss, since there was nothing logically or empirically incompatible between the new approach to distribution analysis outlined by Jevons, and the wages-fund doctrine when it had been emptied of its dubious empirical content following the with-drawals by Mill and Cairnes. Neither doctrine had much content which could clash, and, anyhow, one was micro-economic and the other macro-economic. Both approaches *could* have been pursued simultaneously without any empirical or logical contradictions arising. The change was largely one of interest, or of the allocation of the scarce time and energy of a very small number of economists.

(4) What many of those who insist on the losses involved in the Jevonian 'revolution' seem to have in mind is the abandonment of class-distribution analysis, and the labour-cost element in value analysis, with the disappearance of the opportunities for ideological exploitation which these had afforded. Of course, such opportunities would have been sternly rejected by Ricardo, but had just been seized upon and massively exploited by Marx in his first volume of *Capital*

published in 1867. However, it seems perfectly clear that the leading protagonists in the Jevonian revolution, and in the contemporary path-breaking work in Vienna and Lausanne at this time, had no knowledge whatsoever of Marx's book and could not have been reacting to it.

In any case, it is and would have been *logically* perfectly possible to propagate the idea of class conflict on the basis of a micro-economic, productivity analysis with the aid of the necessary simplified sociological assumptions contained in, or injected into, the Ricardian analysis. But in terms of political valuations of one kind or another there are not only 'losses' but 'gains' to be listed, as we shall note in a moment.

The general charge is also frequently heard that the Jevonian revolution led to an impoverishing contraction and narrowing of the subject, as represented by the change in title from Political Economy to Economics. We have discussed in the previous section the ways in which the focus on micro-economics developed. But to some extent this concentration on what came to be called 'microeconomic analysis' was unintentional and even illusory and did *not* imply any more limited conception of the subject as a whole. There was nothing in the least narrow about Jevons's conceptions of political economy. *As his writings fully demonstrate, he took macroeconomic problems, or at least some important aspects of them, such as index-numbers and aggregate fluctuations, much more seriously than his classical predecessors and made much more progress with them.* He was also preparing a much more comprehensive treatise on economics than his *Theory of Political Economy* when he died. As regards Menger, Walras, and Marshall, they all planned their *Principles* on a multi-volume scale, which included money and macro-economics, along with the study of government policies with regard to production and the distribution of property (Walras), and such subjects as monopoly and economic progress (Marshall). If Menger, Walras, and Marshall could have carried out their original plans as intended, 'neoclassical economics' would have emerged with a substantially broader framework than it did. Unfortunately all three got diverted from their original patterns; Walras and Marshall by the need to perfect or elaborate the first volumes of their multi-volume *Principles*, which were mainly devoted to competitive price analysis, and Menger by the *Methodenstreit*. Certainly the priority given to 'micro-economics' is significant in itself. But it does not at all imply the very narrow conceptions of the subject as a whole which 'neoclassical economics' has been accused of promoting. Certainly such immediate followers of Menger and Walras as Wieser and Pareto, with their incursions into sociology, were hardly responsible for any narrowing of the subject. In fact, as the neoclassical period advanced, the problem of the business cycle began to receive, from the turn of the century, the attention it deserved, and had failed to receive, from the English classicals.

With regard to the gains from the Jevonian revolution, we would mention briefly, first, the greatly enhanced power which the marginal concepts provided for dealing with public utilities and monopolies. Insofar as economists are able to shed light on the problems of public utilities it is by using the concepts developed and refined by the Jevonian revolution, and by the parallel work of Menger and Walras. The classical theories were useless and impotent in this field. Similarly with regard to the problems of monopoly which were really opened up for analysis by the marginal concepts of the 'neoclassicals'. *Marshall's largest work was about monopoly*; and J. B. Clark, so repeatedly held-up as 'the typical neoclassical', and, allegedly, exclusively concerned with ideal competitive conditions, actually devoted very much attention to problems of monopoly.[42]

Generally, the value or 'gains' from what was the primary (but not the only) 'neoclassical' concern, that of the analysis of allocation, can be held to be relatively significant, whatever background of economic organisation is assumed. If a political or ideological 'loss' is alleged with regard to class antagonism, then on the basis of other valuations a significant 'gain' can be claimed with regard to the emphasis on individual consumer choice. But we shall be discussing more fully in a subsequent chapter various political and ideological implications and interpretations of 'neoclassical' economics.[43] Anyhow, this kind of political explanation has tended to shift to the later developments of neoclassical analysis in the 1890s (or even, in the search for *some* justification, to alleged neo-neoclassical analysis well on in the twentieth century). It has moved away from the decisive initial developments in England in the late 1860s and early 1870s, and the foundation works of Menger and Walras in the early 1870s, with which this chapter has been primarily concerned and which are impossible to represent as reactions to Marx's *Capital*.[44]

Finally it should be emphasised again that the Jevonian revolution was to a vital extent, an abandonment of Ricardian *distribution* analysis, the single massive empirical content of which came from the natural wage proposition. It was this abandonment which opened up the whole

[42] See for example *The Problem of Monopoly*, 1904.
[43] See below the paper: 'On recent revolutionary versions of the history of economics' (Chapter 9).
[44] Another sociological or 'external' explanation, or partial explanation, of the Jevonian 'revolution' is that, in the last third of the nineteenth century, economics became *much* more an academic discipline, and that the cultivation of marginal utility analysis was calculated to cater for an academic taste for precision, mathematical elegance, and for a proto-, or would-be, 'professional' technical display. (See Professor G. J. Stigler, 1973, pp. 310–12, discussed below in Section v of the concluding Chapter 11.)

question of poverty and social reform, just as it was the emphasis on the utility concept and the principle of diminishing utility which fostered ideas about redistribution and progressive taxation in England (if this is to be regarded as a gain for 'neoclassical economics'). Similarly it was through the study of poverty that the idea of relief works emerged, to counter massive cyclical fluctuations in employment, which ideas were to have fundamental consequences for macroeconomics in the twentieth century. Both these ideas were fundamentally opposed to and excluded from Ricardian political economy. We shall examine in the next chapter what use was made of these ideas for economic policy by English 'neoclassical' economists.

4

The Jevonian revolution and economic policy in Britain

I

The turning-point in economic theory in Britain which we have described in the previous chapter as the Jevonian revolution occurred at roughly the same time as a major turning-point in economic policy in Britain. Though either of these turning-points could conceivably have occurred without the other, they are clearly interconnected in that they influenced and interacted on one another as regards the particular forms they took. That they both occurred around 1870 in Britain is surely not entirely coincidental.

The long re- or e-volution in the economic role of government in Great Britain which has continued through succeeding waves, on one sector or another of the front, since the high tide of the 'classical', individualist, competitive market economy began perceptibly to recede, may be dated from somewhere about 1870. This seems, in round figures, to be the most generally suitable starting-date from which this long, vast continuing process may be traced. A few years either side of our round figures we have two significant events in economic ideas and two in politics. As we have already noted, in economic ideas there was (1) in 1869, Mill's retraction regarding the wages fund, which signified a general decline in the credibility of the classical distribution doctrines. This decline had also gradually been coming about regarding the empirically most important element in the classical account of distribution: the hard-line Ricardo–Mill version of the Malthusian population and natural wage doctrine, for which, however, no precise date of any spectacular recantation can be fixed. *Secondly* (2) in 1871 there was Jevons's attack on the Ricardo–Mill value doctrines, and the development of his final utility theory, in his *Theory of Political Economy*, which work also contained – what was much more significant in terms of policy developments – a sweeping attack on the Ricardo–Mill doctrines of wages and distribution.

Either side of these two dates there were two political events with profound consequences for the subsequent development of economic policy: (1) the Second Reform Act of 1867; and (2) in 1871 (and 1875) the Trade Union legislation on which the subsequent rise to power of the unions was founded.

In favour of a later starting point than 1870 for the long policy revolution, it could be argued that it was not until the 1880s that the new trend really becomes unmistakeable, with a marked rise in public expenditure. But, as we shall see, a definite shift in the current of ideas about economic policy is perceptible in the 1870s.

On the other hand, with regard to economic policy-doctrines, one could argue that a considerably earlier date might be taken, which would bring in J. S. Mill and Book v of his *Principles*, since Jevons, Sidgwick, and Marshall on some points hardly go beyond Mill, and on one or two points perhaps not as far, regarding possible developments in economic policy. But it can be countered, first, that though in some respects the post 1870 economists do not immediately go beyond Mill, in more important ways they do; and furthermore, that Mill can be regarded as concerned much more with prophetic hopes than with operational policies. It may be putting it rather strongly to say, as Clapham did, that 'Mill remained to his death in 1873 only the philosopher who raises a standard' (1932, vol. II, p. 391). But two major fundamental conditions put all Mill's discussion of economic policies in a different mood from the proposals which gradually began to gather force after 1870: (1) before 1867 there was no feasible electoral base for the sort of proposals Mill was discussing, especially with regard to redistribution in general and progressive inheritance duties in particular; (2) as Mill himself believed and assumed when writing his *Principles*, 'the great Malthusian difficulty', as Cairnes called it, continued to inhibit proposals aimed at general improvement in the condition of the people.[1]

It is the combination of the new electoral base and the lifting, or what was believed or realised to be the lifting, of 'the great Malthusian difficulty', that made for a new epoch in policy, bit-by-bit transforming prophetic aspirations and speculations into feasible policy proposals.

To assert that around 1870 a turning-point in economic policy occurred is not to deny or overlook the amount of legislation regarding factory conditions, hours of labour, public health and other fields

[1] J. E. Cairnes's essay of 1870 on 'Political Economy and *Laissez-Faire*' was something of a landmark. Cairnes, who is sometimes described as 'the last of the classical economists', maintained that political economy was then 'very generally regarded as a sort of scientific rendering' of the *laissez-faire* maxim, which he asserted 'has no scientific basis whatever'. Cairnes was *primarily* concerned with a methodological point, that is, with claiming a politically neutral, scientific character for the subject. Cairnes certainly stressed 'those violent contrasts of poverty and wealth' in the England of his time, and maintained that 'the rich will be growing richer; and the poor, at least relatively, poorer'. But when considering reforms such as cooperation he objected that 'at bottom *the great Malthusian difficulty* would remain'. (See 1873, pp. 232ff; and 1874, pp. 340 and 348, italics added).

which had been put through in the preceding decades. But this was largely concerned with creating a *framework* for a free-market or *laissez-faire* economy, not so much with intervening in its processes or results. This distinction is not clear-cut, but it helps to account for the nature of the turning-point with which we are here concerned.[2]

A further development, almost simultaneous with these, was the premonitory forebodings – as expressed in Jevons's *Coal Question*, for example – regarding Britain's relative economic position in the world, which was at its peak in the mid 1860s, and which later, towards the end of the century, was to give rise to much debate regarding economic policy, and in particular regarding the principles of commercial policy.

There is one further preliminary regarding the relations between economists' policy proposals and criticisms and the actual historical changes in economic policies. Economists may either provide the basis of positive predictions relevant for new kinds of policies, or they may act persuasively on the public's or the politicians' attitudes and values, or choice of new objectives, or of much higher levels of old objectives. Whichever sort of influence they may have, all one seems able to say is that for better or for worse economists have sometimes kept roughly in step with changes in public or political opinions or aspirations; sometimes they have been a step or two behind; and sometimes they have been a leading force. In the period with which we are here concerned, they seem at least to have been in step, and sometimes a step or two ahead.

All the same, though no simple general thesis about economists will probably stand up for long, in studying their policy proposals it does seem that we are concerned with the proof of the whole intellectual pudding of economics, in that, *according to what might reasonably be regarded as economists' own tenets*, this lies in the improved prescience or heightened success of economic policies which may result from 'what economists do'.

II

Jevons appears as something of a revolutionary, or at any rate as claiming to be a revolutionary, on a central point of theory. On the subject of the role of government he was, if not a 'revolutionary', at least a transitional figure both chronologically and doctrinally. Chronologically he is almost too neatly so. His writing career covered exactly the quarter of a century from 1857 to 1882, pretty precisely bisected by our year 1870. It is not suggested that in or about that year

---

[2] We may cite Professor E. J. Hobsbawm in his *Industry and Empire*, as taking 'around 1860' as 'the peak of British *laissez-faire*', of which '*the foundations...crumbled in the 1860s and 1870s*' (1969, pp. 226 and 237, italics added).

Jevons underwent a sudden Pauline conversion from his earlier adherence to the strictest individualist principles, to his later position, for which he is better known, as, in Clapham's description, 'a cautious empirical innovator' who 'watched with critical impartiality the inroads of the state on individual liberty in the early '80s' (op. cit., pp. 390 and 439). In fact, it can hardly be shown that anything in the way of a change of view by Jevons took place on any important *specific point* of economic policy or the role of government. It is rather that, as the 1870s wore on, more cases occurred to him which seemed to call for governmental action, or at least for detailed empirical examination, and which were no longer to be disposed of by a sweeping application of *laissez-faire* principles.[3]

In his first publication in Australia in 1857, the 22-year-old Jevons had begun by proclaiming comprehensively that 'freedom for *all* commercial transactions is the spirit of improved legislation'.[4] In particular, the earlier Jevons was a strong champion of Malthus and of the more rigorous interpretation of his doctrines in terms of self-help. Jevons considered it worth repeating in 1869 that 'the British Poor Law of 1834 is one of the wisest measures ever concerted by any government' (1883, p. 192). (Twenty-three years later Marshall, though agreeing that the poor law was justifiable in its own day, was to reject the whole basis of that law for *his* day.) Though he supported the Education Act of 1870, Jevons was not only opposed to any extension of state action with regard to health services for the poor but was against private medical charities in that they discouraged self-help.

As regards external commercial policy, for Jevons in 1869 free trade was an unquestioned and almost unquestionable article of faith:

> Freedom of trade may be regarded as a fundamental axiom of political economy; and though even axioms *may* be mistaken, and any different views concerning them must not be *prohibited*, yet we need not be frightened into questioning our own axioms. We may welcome *bona fide* investigation into the state of trade, and the causes of the present depression, but we can no more expect to have our opinions on free trade altered by such an investigation than the Mathematical Society would expect to have the axioms of Euclid disproved during the investigation of a complex problem [op. cit., p. 182].

The earlier and more severely individualistic strain in Jevons comes out especially in his treatment of taxation. He expressed concern in 1870 that 'the working class so long as they make a temperate use of spirituous liquors and tobacco pay a distinctly less proportion of their income to the state, and even intemperance does not make their

---

[3] I would say now that it was a considerable underestimate on my part of the change which took place in Jevons's views on the economic role of government, to have said merely that he 'may have somewhat modified' them (1968, vol. VIII, p. 258).

[4] W. S. Jevons, 1857 (italics added).

contribution proportionally greater than those of more wealthy persons' (1870, p. 34).

In his main work on taxation, his pamphlet *The Match Tax* (1871), Jevons expressed some regret at the repeal of the tax because he wanted to retain taxes on articles of wide popular consumption, rejecting the Malthusian–Ricardian argument about the effects on wages of taxing 'necessaries'. Jevons figured out statistically that the burden of taxation was then very roughly proportional, but that – as he had complained the previous year – half the taxes paid by the poor were from alcohol and tobacco. These were not only avoidable but ought to be avoided. The great exponent of the utility approach to the problems of value and price came down very firmly in favour of proportional taxation on all except paupers:

> The more carefully and maturely I ponder over this question of taxation from various points of view, the more convinced I always return to the principle, that all classes of persons above the rank of actual paupers, should contribute to the state in the proportion of their incomes. I will not say this is a theoretically perfect rule. From feelings of humanity we might desire to graduate the rate of contribution and relieve persons who are comparatively poorer at the expense of those who are comparatively richer. But we must beware of obeying the dictates of ill-considered humanity. If we once professedly enter upon the course of exempting the poor, there will be no stopping [1905, p. 235].[5]

However, already in 1870 Jevons was envisaging massive increases in public expenditure at the local (though not at the national) level. Calling for the reform of local taxation to meet the new needs, Jevons wrote:

> *There is sure to be a continuous increase of local taxation*...All the more immediate needs of society, boards of health, medical officers, public schools, reformatories, free libraries, highway boards, main drainage schemes, water-suppliers, purification of rivers, improved police, better poor law medical science – these, and a score of other costly reforms must be supported mainly out of the local rates [1883, p. 202, italics added].

It is in his Introductory Lecture at University College in 1876 that a shift in Jevons's attitude seems to become prominent. Even here he began by duly noting that 'it is impossible to doubt that the *laissez-faire* principle properly applied is the wholesome and true one.' But the spread of urban industrialism and its all-pervasive 'externalities', or neighbourhood effects led Jevons to predict: 'It seems to me, while population grows more numerous and dense, while industry becomes more complex and interdependent, as we travel faster and make use

---

[5]   In his *Primer of Political Economy*, 1878, Jevons upheld the proportionality principle in the name of equality: 'Equality consists in everybody paying, in one way or another, about an equal percentage of the wages, salary, or other income which he receives.'

of more intense forces, we shall necessarily need more legislative supervision' (op. cit., p. 204). He called for a new empirical branch of economics:

> If such a thing is possible, we need a new branch of political and statistical science which shall carefully investigate the limits to the *laissez-faire* principle, and show where we want greater freedom and where less...I am quite satisfied if we have pointed out the need and the probable rise of one new branch, which is only to be found briefly and imperfectly represented in the works of Mill and other economists [op. cit., pp. 204–6].[6]

Jevons then proceeds to give an example, representing a blend of paternalism and externalities, with regard to slum clearance and public housing:

> I am quite convinced, for instance, that the great mass of the people will not have healthy houses by the ordinary action of self-interest. The only chance of securing good sanitary arrangements is to pull down the houses which are hopelessly bad, as provided by an Act of the present ministry, and *most carefully to superintend under legislative regulations all new houses that are built* [1883, p. 205, italics added].

Jevons went on a year or two later to suggest increased public expenditure over a wide range of elementary paternalist or public goods and services, such as libraries, museums, parks, municipal orchestras, and meteorological services, claiming that these were 'unsanctified by the *laissez-faire* principle'.[7]

More widely, following up his remarks on public housing, Jevons suggested a further move into the field of town and country planning, by laying heavy emphasis on what he called 'the general interests of the public' as against those of private individuals:

> Our idea of happiness in this country at present seems to consist in buying a piece of land if possible, and building a high wall round it. If a man can only secure, for instance, a beautiful view from his own garden and windows, he cares not how many thousands of other persons he cuts off from the daily enjoyment of that view. *The rights of private property and private action are pushed so far that the general interests of the public are made of no account whatever* [1905, p. 206, italics added].

On nationalised or state enterprise Jevons had written as early as 1867 a sentence anticipatory of his later empirical and experimental attitude: 'My own strong opinion is that no abstract principle, and no

---

[6] In *The Theory of Political Economy* Jevons discusses at some length, as 'negative values', the problems of 'the sewage of great towns, the foul or poisoned water from mines, dye-works, etc.', or what would now be regarded as polluting 'externalities'. He supposes: 'Two adjacent landowners, for instance, might reasonably agree that if A allows B to throw the spoil of his mine on A's land, then A shall be allowed to drain his mine into B's mine' (1879, p. 132).

[7] It should be noted, however, that, long before Jevons, Nassau Senior had urged government action with regard to housing and also with regard to public amenities like parks and museums. See his *Lectures 1847–1852* and M. Bowley, *Nassau Senior and Classical Economics*, 1949, pp. 266–72.

absolute rule, can guide us in determining what kinds of industrial enterprise, the State should undertake and what not' (1883, p. 278). After praising the Post Office, he called for the taking over of telegraph services, though when this was done in 1870 he condemned the financial arrangements. Later Jevons advocated a state-run parcel post (1879), but, unlike Walter Bagehot, he was strongly opposed to nationalisation of the railways (1874).[8]

In his final and admirable book, *The State in Relation to Labour*, published in the year of his death, Jevons dealt with consumer protection and government inspection, factory legislation and hours of work, and trade union legislation.

He returned again, long before the days of mass motoring and air travel, to the mounting importance of externalities and neighbourhood effects with the development of urban industrialism and with the threats to freedom deriving from the complex technology of affluence:

> So intricate are the ways, industrial, sanitary, or political, in which one class or section of the people affect other classes or sections, that there is hardly any limit to the interference of the legislator... It is impossible in short that we can have the constant multiplication of institutions and instruments of civilisation which evolution is producing, without a growing complication of relations, and a consequent growth of social regulations [1882, p. 14].

Regarding hours of work, Jevons argued that legislators up till then had 'in fact, always abstained from interfering with the liberty of adult men to work as long or as short a time as they like'. But he went on: 'I see nothing to forbid the state interfering in the matter... neither principle, experience, nor precedent, in other cases of legislation, prevents us from contemplating the idea of State interference in such circumstances' (op. cit., pp. 64–5).

In fact, ten years later (1892) in the House of Commons, championing an eight-hour bill for miners, Joseph Chamberlain, in his radical socialistic, or at any rate, interventionist phase, quoted Jevons in support of his case, though in terms of very general utilitarian principle: 'The State is justified in passing any law, or even in doing any single act, which without ulterior consequences adds to the sum of human happiness.' Chamberlain drew a contrast, as he put it, with 'the strict doctrine of *laissez-faire* which perhaps 20 years ago [i.e., c. 1870] was accepted as preferable'.[9]

---

[8] See his paper 'The Railways and the State' (1874) in *Methods of Social Reform*, 1883.
[9] See J. L. Garvin, 1933, vol. 2, p. 534; J. H. Clapham, vol. 3, 1938, p. 397; and W. S. Jevons, 1882, p. 12. Chamberlain slightly misquotes Jevons. I am indebted to Mr W. H. Richmond of the University of Queensland on this point. *It should be noted that the most thoroughgoing and learned exponent of classical liberal principles today sees these later views of Jevons as a major turning-point:* 'The end of the liberal era of principles might well be dated at the time when, more than eighty years ago, W. S. Jevons

It is for its magnificently eloquent, often-quoted statements of an empirical, experimental anti-*a priori* approach to policy questions that Jevons's *The State in Relation to Labour* is famous. Jevons indeed is a forerunner of Sir Karl Popper both in his conception of scientific method in his *Principles of Science* and consequently also in his advocacy of empirical, piecemeal social experimentation.

Jevons's proposals for increasing governmental action are almost entirely confined to the heading describable as Inadequacies of Individual Choice, with its subheadings (a) paternalism, (b) ignorance, (c) externalities or 'neighbourhood effects', and (d) public goods and services.

Under the heading Monopoly and Restrictive Practices there is only a little in Jevons, including, for example, his treatment already mentioned of nationalisation. But there is also his discussion of trade union monopolies, which he regarded with serious forebodings. He did not, however, propose to undo the favourable legislation of 1871 and 1875, and is curiously optimistic about the future of trade unions. He asks whether 'the lawgiver ought not simply to prohibit societies which tend towards such monopoly'. But he concludes in the negative (1882, p. 101).[10]

Under the other main headings for state intervention there is almost nothing to be found in Jevons. As we have seen, with regard to distribution and redistribution, one of the main fields opened up in the last quarter of the nineteenth century, Jevons seems to have remained strictly, even severely, classical, especially regarding proportionality in taxation.

On the great twentieth-century subject of the Monetary Framework and Macroeconomic Policy, on which before 1900 there were only some anticipatory rumblings, there is hardly an inkling in Jevons, in spite of the fact that he was a pioneer of research into business cycles and price index-numbers. With regard to the then orthodoxy, Professor Fetter has pointed out that 'in his philosophic approach to the limitations of any metallic standard Jevons soared on a high speculative level'. Fetter goes on to quote Jevons: 'But in itself gold-digging has ever seemed to me almost a dead loss of labour as regards the world in general – a wrong against the human race, just such as is that of a government against a people in over-issuing and depreciating its own currency.' Yet Fetter concludes that Jevons, 'either because he was the pure scientist unconcerned with policy-making, or because as a child

pronounced that in economic and social policy, "we can lay down no hard and fast rules, but must treat every case upon its merits"' (F. A. Hayek, 1973, p. 59).
[10] Regarding labour legislation in general Jevons commented: 'The great lesson which we learn, and it is an impressive one, is that legislation with regard to labour has almost always been class-legislation. It is the effort of some dominant body to keep down a lower class, which had begun to show inconvenient aspirations' (op. cit., p. 34).

of an era he was not prepared to fight its myths and its idols, made no public suggestion for a better standard, although he wrote but did not publish a proposal for a tabular standard of value' (1965, p. 248). Also, in spite of his great interest in cyclical fluctuations Jevons held to the Turgot–Smith 'saving-is-investing' doctrine, the basis of 'classical' theory in the Keynesian sense (1878, p. 22).

Finally, under the heading of Commercial Policy, External Economic Relations, or Britain and her Relative Position in the World Economy, Jevons, in his first and brilliant book, *The Coal Question* (1865), had uttered, at the very peak of Britain's relative economic standing in the world, a prescient warning, if rather over-anxious in the shorter term, that our occupation of this supreme position as the workshop of the world might prove highly transient.[11] Before the end of the century the problem of the weakening of Britain's relative economic position was to give rise to much policy debate. But Jevons reasserted in his last work, as Marshall was to do later, his firm adherence to free trade principles.

III

The historical and institutional critics of classical political economy in the 1870s and early 1880s, who come next, were mostly more concerned with theories and methods than with policy. There seems to be little on policy questions in Cliffe Leslie, for example, except with regard to Ireland. But Arnold Toynbee (d. 1883), a figure of some influence in Oxford, 'one of the noblest of the rising generation', as Marshall called him (1925, p. 152), perceived the politico-economic disequilibrium that had come about with the extension of the suffrage: 'Wealth is in the hands of the few rich, the suffrage in the hands of the many poor; in the concentration of wealth and the diffusion of political power lies a great danger of modern society.' Toynbee saw the importance of this politico-economic conjuncture for the problem of distribution, which he affirmed 'is the true problem of political economy at the present time' (1894, pp. 212 and 250).

Toynbee laid down the principles for state action in the following two propositions: '*First*, that where individual rights conflict with the interests of the community, there the State ought to interfere; and *second* that where the people are unable to provide a thing for themselves, and that thing is of *primary social importance*, then again the State should interfere and provide it for them' (1894, p. 216).

[11] See also Jevons's warning of 1869: 'I shudder to think what might be the effect of any serious impediment to our future progress, such as a long-continued war, the competition of other nations, or a comparative failure of our own material resources' (1883, p. 193).

In this connection, almost simultaneously with Jevons, Toynbee raised the question of public housing, or 'the dwellings of the people', a subject

> upon which it is difficult to understand why so little is said...I do not hesitate to say a community must step in and give the necessary aid. These labourers cannot obtain dwellings for themselves; the municipalities, or the State in some form, should have power to buy up land and let it below the market value for the erection of decent dwellings [op. cit., pp. 217–18].

Toynbee was arguing from the point of view of a Tory or even imperialist socialist: 'We demand that the material conditions of those who labour should be bettered, in order that, every source of weakness being removed at home, we, this English nation, may bring to the tasks which God has assigned us, the irresistible strength of a prosperous and united people' (1894, p. 221).

As regards Walter Bagehot there is not much to say here. We have noted his support for railway nationalisation (1865).[12] In his major field of the monetary framework Bagehot seems to have provided or buttressed the orthodoxy of the day which was to survive until 1914 or 1931. Regarding the position of the Bank of England, as Professor Fetter puts it: 'In the eyes of Bagehot banking statesmanship and the profit motive were to be happily married, and his great service to the next half century of central banking was that he convinced his countrymen that this was an honourable union blessed by the laws of free trade' (1965, p. 271).

One year after Jevons's death Sidgwick's *Principles of Political Economy* appeared. These principles run very much on the general lines of Mill, but are more precise and penetrating at some important points. First, Sidgwick brings more precision regarding externalities and public goods: 'There is a large and varied class of cases in which private interest cannot be relied upon as a sufficient stimulus to the performance of the most socially useful services because such services are incapable of being appropriated by those who produce them or who would otherwise be willing to purchase them.'

He then mentions the lighthouse example, as had Mill. Sidgwick goes on to note, however: 'It does not follow, of course, that wherever *laissez-faire* falls short governmental interference is expedient.'

Regarding commercial policy Sidgwick certainly moved away from anything resembling a dogmatic *laissez-faire* position: 'The foundations on which the old short and simple confutations of Protection were once logically erected has been knocked away...The fashion which still lingers of treating the Protectionist as a fool who cannot see – if

---

[12] In *The Economist*, 7 January 1865, under the title 'The Advantages That Would Accrue From an Ownership of the Railways by the State'. See J. H. Clapham, 1932, vol. II, p. 189.

he is not a knave who will not see – what is as plain as a proof of Euclid, is really an illogical survival' (1887, p. 488).

But the new principle of the most fundamental importance introduced by Sidgwick, though he himself did not develop the consequences, was his proclamation of the 'right' distribution of produce as a second main objective of government policy or 'the art of political economy', alongside increased production:

> We may take the subject of Political Economy considered as an Art to include, besides the Theory of provision for governmental expenditure, (1) the Art of making the proportion of produce to population a maximum ...and (2) the Art of rightly Distributing produce among members of the community, whether on any principle of Equity or Justice, or on the economic principle of making the whole produce as useful as possible [1883, p. 403].

However, like, generally, his classical predecessors, Sidgwick takes equality of sacrifice to imply proportionality in taxation and holds this to be 'the obviously equitable principle', going on to oppose progression and the redressing of inequalities of income by taxation:

> Most economists hold that any such communistic tendency should be rightly excluded in the adjustment of taxation; and that whatever Government may legitimately do to remedy the inequalities of distribution resulting from natural liberty should be done otherwise than by unequal imposition of financial burdens. And this is, in the main, the conclusion which I am myself disposed to adopt; but I must interpret or limit it by one important proviso which seems to me necessitated by the acceptance of the principle that the community ought to protect its members from starvation – a degree of communism which, as we have seen, is legally established in England [1883, p. 562].

As regards the monetary framework, Sidgwick, in a chapter entitled 'Cases of Governmental Interference to Promote Production,' raises some fundamental questions regarding what he calls 'currency'. He holds that the state 'ought to guard so far as it can against fluctuations in the value of the medium of exchange. It can only do this, however, to a very limited extent' (op. cit., p. 453). Regarding the position of the Bank of England, Sidgwick questioned the orthodox acceptance of the happy marriage of private profit and social interest advocated by Bagehot:

> When we consider merely from an abstract point of view the proposal to give a particular joint-stock company an exclusive privilege of issuing notes, the value of which will, in the last resort be sustained by the authority of Government, without subjecting its exercise of this privilege to any governmental control whatsoever; it certainly appears a very hazardous measure [1883, p. 462].

Finally, at this point mention should be made of Foxwell's monograph of 1886, *Irregularity of Employment and Fluctuations of Prices.* This was the outstanding anticipation at this time of what was to be the overriding problem and concern – between wars – of much of the first half of the twentieth century. Foxwell starts from the 'conviction, continually increasing in strength, that uncertainty of employment is the root evil of the present industrial system'. He foresaw and emphasised the growing popular concern for 'social security': 'I cannot venture to say what would be the general opinion of the working class upon the point; but my own feeling would be that when a certain necessary limit had been reached, regularity of income was far more important than amount of income' (1886, pp. 7 and 17). Certainly Foxwell's lecture is more notable for its attempt to shatter complacency about a major problem for policy, and to establish the reduction of the irregularity of employment as an objective, than for the particular remedial measures he proposes. But after analysing the effects of changes in the value of money, Foxwell concludes in favour of stability of the price level, or rather a slightly and steadily rising level.

IV

In considering Alfred Marshall's ideas on policy one might, as with Jevons, try to discover and apply some pattern of development, though in Marshall's case the pattern would presumably be the different though very familiar one of a transition from an earlier, youthful, reformist enthusiasm to a much more cautious and sceptical attitude later on. There is quite a lot of evidence for this sort of pattern with regard to Marshall, though there do seem to be one or two important exceptions or irregularities. There are also, in any case, due to his delays of many decades in publishing his ideas, considerable chronological difficulties in trying to trace out at all definitely or precisely *any* simple lines for Marshall's intellectual development.

However, we may suitably start with his early paper of 1873, 'The Future of the Working Classes,' which provides a glowing statement of early aspirations and which begins, incidentally, with an enthusiastic tribute to Mrs Harriet Taylor Mill for her contribution to the chapter of the same title in her second husband's *Principles*.

Marshall warms up in the manner of Marx, by citing contemporary blue books on such mid-Victorian industrial phenomena as 'lads and maidens, not 8 years old, toiling in the brickfields under monstrous loads from 5 o'clock in the morning till 8 o'clock at night'. He goes on:

> Our thoughts from youth upwards are dominated by a Pagan belief...that it is an ordinance of Nature that multitudes of men must toil a weary toil, which may give to others the means of refinement and luxury, but which

can afford to themselves scarce any opportunity of mental growth. May not the world outgrow this belief, as it has outgrown others? It may and it will [1925, pp. 107–9].

It certainly has, nearly a hundred years later, in some very privileged parts of the world; though whether the parallel cultural accompaniments would have met with Marshall's approval seems highly doubtful. Economically, in fact, Marshall was never at all unrealistic or revolutionary. He denounced the socialists 'who attributed to every man an unlimited capacity for those self-forgetting virtues that they found in their own breasts', and whose schemes 'involve a subversion of existing arrangements according to which the work of every man is chosen by himself, and the remuneration he obtains for it is decided by free competition' (op. cit., p. 109).

It was in his social, cultural, and educational hopes that Marshall seems to have been, and for some time to have remained, rather over-optimistic. He saw that education and technological progress could and would raise the earning powers of the masses and reduce hours and physical toil. It was with regard to what would be done with the time and energy left over that Marshall may seem to have been unrealistic. He envisaged a country which

> is to have a fair share of wealth, and not an abnormally large population. Everyone is to have in youth an education which is thorough while it lasts, and which lasts long. No one is to do in the day so much manual work as will leave him little time or little aptitude for intellectual or artistic enjoyment in the evening. Since there will be nothing tending to render the individual coarse and unrefined, there will be nothing tending to render society coarse and unrefined. Exceptional morbid growths must exist in every society; but otherwise every man will be surrounded from birth upwards by almost all the influences which we have seen to be at present characteristic of the occupations of gentlemen; everyone who is not a gentleman will have himself alone to blame for it [op. cit., p. 110].

After this early statement of Marshall's social visions, it seems more convenient to continue by subject headings than entirely chronologically, partly for the reason previously mentioned of Marshall's delays in publication, and also because Marshall, unlike Jevons, contributed at different times proposals regarding most or all of the main sectors of possible governmental action in the economy.

First, let us take the four-part heading, Inadequacies of Individual Choice, under which all or most of Jevons's contributions were made.

On grounds both of paternalism and externalities Marshall strongly advocated, from his paper of 1873 onwards through the decades, increased public spending on education: 'The difference between the value of the labour of the educated man and that of the uneducated is, as a rule, many times greater than the difference between the costs of their education...No individual reaps the full gains derived from educating a child' (op. cit., p. 118). Subsequently Marshall was to emphasise the economic dangers to Britain of lagging behind Germany in technical and scientific education.

As regards housing, though not recommending subsidies in the same way as Jevons or Toynbee, Marshall in 1884 advocates government controls on movement into slum areas: 'To hinder people from going where their presence helps to lower the average standard of human life, is not more contrary to economic principle than the rule that when a steamer is full, admission should be refused to any more even though they themselves are willing to take the risk of being drowned' (op. cit., p. 148). Later (1902), as contrasted with Toynbee and Jevons, Marshall was to proclaim that 'municipal housing seems to me scarcely ever right and generally very wrong. Municipal free baths seem to me nearly always right' (op. cit., p. 445).

In his paper 'Economic Chivalry' (1907) Marshall suggests with regard to town planning:

> The State could so care for the amenities of life outside of the house that fresh air and variety of colour and of scene might await the citizen and his children very soon after they start on a holiday walk. Everyone in health and strength can order his house well; the State alone can bring the beauties of nature and art within the reach of the ordinary citizen [op. cit., p. 345].

In this essay, in which he proclaims 'Let the State be up and doing', Marshall emphasises especially 'the imperative duty to inspect and arbitrate', taking as an illustration 'the careless treatment of milk': 'Let the government arouse itself to do energetically its proper work of educating British farmers up to the Danish standard, if not beyond; and of enforcing sanitary regulations in critical matters such as this' (op. cit., p. 337).

It is under this broad general heading also that we might mention Marshall's abstract criticisms in the *Principles* of the doctrine of maximum satisfaction (Book 5, Chapter 13), where he seems to suggest taxing goods the production of which is subject to diminishing returns and subsidising increasing return industries out of the proceeds. But though Marshall emphasises that his conclusions 'do not by themselves afford a valid ground for government interference', these rather excessively abstract propositions may have produced more confusion than enlightenment.

Our next main heading, Poverty, Distribution, and Redistribution, certainly was of major concern to Marshall. As he told the Royal Commission on the Aged Poor (1893): 'I have devoted myself for the last

25 years to the problem of poverty, and...very little of my work has been devoted to any enquiry which does not bear on that' (1926, p. 205).[13]

Marshall emphasised to the Commission the lifting of 'the great Malthusian difficulty' and the change in the nature of the problem compared with the beginning of the century:

> You can trace the economic dogmas of present Poor Law literature direct from those times; and the doctrines which they laid down I think were fairly true in their time. The doctrine is that if you tax the rich, and give money to the working classes, the result will be that the working classes will increase in number and the result will be you will have lowered wages in the next generation; and the grant will not have improved the position of the working classes on the whole. *As regards this a change has come, which separates the economics of this generation from the economics of the past*; but it seems to me not to have penetrated the Poor Law literature yet; and this is the main thing that I desire to urge. That change insists upon the fact that if the money is so spent as to increase the earning power of the next generation it may not lower wages [1926, p. 225, italics added].

On the question of progressive taxation we have seen that Jevons and Sidgwick were opposed, as was the Irish public finance expert C. F. Bastable. Mr Shehab in his valuable book states that in the 1890s and before, Marshall also 'was preaching against it', though especially later, and as late as 1917, aged seventy-five, he was to come out strongly in favour. But Mr Shehab's evidence for Marshall's earlier opposition to progression is based simply on a footnote in Clapham, which recalls that 'in his lectures in the 1890s Marshall used to tell his pupils that graduated income taxation would weaken the chief pillar of the tax's yield, collection at source'.[14] This does not seem to amount to outright opposition to progression in principle. Admittedly also – though Mr Shehab does not cite this – Marshall himself wrote in 1909 that he had for fifteen years 'somewhat eagerly' opposed death duties, because they checked the growth of capital, but that now he considers them 'a good method of raising a large part of the national revenue'. On the other hand, though admittedly his later statements are much more explicit, Marshall had proclaimed as early as 1889 for example: 'I myself certainly think that the rich ought to be taxed much more heavily than they are, in order to provide for their poorer brethren the material means for a healthy physical and mental development' (1925, p. 229).

Subsequently Marshall was certainly moving more explicitly, though

---

[13] Previously (1884), Marshall had called for a break with the old Poor-Law attitude fostered by Ricardian economics: 'Being without the means of livelihood must be treated not as a crime, but as a cause for uncompromising inspection and inquiry'. (See José Harris, 1972, p. 119.)

[14] F. Shehab, 1953, p. 199; and J. H. Clapham, 1932, p. 40.

still cautiously, towards progression in his Memorandum (1897) to the Royal Commission on Local Taxes. However, for the theoretical case in favour of progressive taxation, such as it was, one would have to go to Edgeworth's paper of the same year (1925, vol. II, pp. 63ff). By 1907 Marshall is praising his contemporaries in that: 'Our age has reversed the old rules that the poor paid a larger percentage of their income in rates and taxes than the well-to-do' (1925, p. 327).

His 1917 paper, one of his last, is much his most forthright statement on progression, expressing the hope that 'the various advances towards graduation made before the war will be sustained and developed after it' (1925, p. 350).[15]

It may be of some interest also to note that insofar as Mr Shehab's view is justified that Marshall only moved more explicitly in his later years towards advocating progression, it would mean that he made this move in spite of the fact that through the various editions of his *Principles* he seemed to put less and less weight and trust in the concept of utility or any possibility of its measurement. Marshall, at any rate, seems to have moved with the times, though there is not necessarily anything virtuous in doing that.

Marshall's most important and definitive discussion of policies against poverty comes in the last chapter of the *Principles* in a section added in the fifth edition (1907). Marshall writes:

> The inequalities of wealth though less than they are often represented to be, are a serious flaw in our economic organization. Any diminution of them which can be attained by means that would not sap the springs of free initiative and strength of character and would not therefore materially check the growth of the national dividend, would seem to be a clear social gain. Though arithmetic warns us that it is impossible to raise all earnings beyond the level already reached by specially well-to-do artisan families, it is certainly desirable that those who are below that level should be raised, even at the expense of lowering in some degree those who are above it. *Prompt action is needed in regard to the large, though it may be hoped, now steadily diminishing, 'Residuum' of persons who are physically, mentally, or morally incapable of doing a good day's work with which to earn a good day's wage*...The system of economic freedom is probably the best from both a moral and material point

---

[15] In a letter to *The Times* (16 November 1909) Marshall had given his blessing to Lloyd George's Budget of 1909 with its proposals for supertax and for taxing land values: 'In so far as the Budget proposes to check the appropriation of what is really public property by private persons, and in so far as it proposes to bring under taxation some income, which has escaped taxation merely because it does not appear above the surface in a money form, I regard it as sound finance. In so far as its proceeds are to be applied to social problems where a little money may do much towards raising the level of life of the people and increasing their happiness it seems to me a Social Welfare Budget. I do not profess to have mastered all its details; but on the whole I incline to think it merits that name.' See also the letter to Lord Reay of 12 November 1909 (1925, p. 464), in which Marshall strongly defended 'welfare spending: 'The notion that the investment of funds in the education of the workers, in sanitation, in providing open air play for all children etc. tends to diminish "capital" is abhorrent to me.'

of view for those who are in fairly good health of mind and body. But the Residuum cannot turn it to account.

Marshall is ready for vigorously paternalist measures. He holds: 'A beginning might be made with a broader, more educative and more generous administration of public aid to the helpless... *The expense would be great: but there is no other so urgent need for bold expenditure'* (1920, pp. 714–15, italics added).

I shall deal very briefly with the next main heading, Monopolies and Restrictive Practices. This again was a major concern of Marshall. It is one of the main themes of *Industry and Trade*. (Incidentally, it really is ludicrous to suggest that economists only got interested in monopolistic problems in the 1930s). In his paper of 1890, 'Some Aspects of Competition', Marshall wrote:

> It is clear that combinations and partial monopolies will play a great part in future economic history; that their effects contain much good as well as much evil, and that to denounce them without discrimination would be to repeat the error which our forefathers made with regard to protection... *It is a matter of pressing urgency that public opinion should accustom itself to deal with such questions* [1925, p. 289, italics added].

But Marshall has little to suggest in the way of remedies and countermeasures, most of his discussion being concerned with state regulation and nationalisation, to the second of which he was usually vigorously opposed. This is no criticism of Marshall. In the nearly eighty years that have passed since Marshall was examining the subject, it has hardly proved possible to propose systematic policies, based on tested coherent theories. Nor has price theory, including the analysis of imperfect and monopolistic competition developed in the 1930s, shown itself to be of great assistance in propounding answers to this problem.[16] The next major section for state action, although it really came to a head in the second quarter of this century, is that of the Monetary Framework, Aggregate Stabilisation, Employment or 'Macroeconomic' Policy, or the comprehensive process described by Sir John Hicks as 'the Nationalisation of Money'. Not that Marshall's proposals from the vantage, or disadvantage, point of the 1970s seem very extensive or relevant. Generally, for reasons examined by Professor R. C. O. Matthews (1968), Marshall in about 1900, unlike Foxwell and other contemporaries, did not consider that the problem of

[16] *Industry and Trade* is Marshall's longest work and is devoted to the theme of 'the limited tendencies of self-interest to direct each individual's action on those lines, in which it will be most beneficial to others'. This work has been almost completely neglected by Marshall's successors, some of whom have charged 'the neoclassicals' with concentrating on perfect competition. It was only with the supersession of the Ricardo–Mill value theory, and the use of the marginal concept by the neoclassicals, that the analysis of monopoly and monopolistic conditions could begin to develop.

unemployment was growing more serious. Marshall's various suggestions regarding these problems are scattered through half a century
of papers and memoranda. But perhaps the single most compact or
systematic treatment, on very simple lines, is in his short paper to the
Industrial Remuneration Conference of 1885, not collected in the
Memorials, of which some sentences were eventually quoted in *Money,
Credit and Commerce*, 1922. Marshall posed the question: 'How far do
remediable causes influence prejudicially (a) the continuity of employment, (b) the rates of wages?' He sees the main remediable causes
as 'chiefly connected in some way or other with the want of knowledge',
and proceeds to discuss nine remedies, some of which today certainly
seem of rather marginal relevance – such as avoiding vagaries
of fashion in dress, especially female dress, countering excessive
secrecy in traders by publishing income-tax returns in local newspapers, treating fraud more severely, and encouraging the growth
of moral feeling against gambling, especially among the young. More
significant seem his proposals for further research by economists
on short-term fluctuations and for the development of economic forecasting:

> I see no reason why a body of able disinterested men, with a wide range
> of business knowledge, should not be able to issue predictions of trade storms
> and of trade weather generally, that would have an appreciable effect in
> rendering the employment of industry more steady and continuous...
> though the time has not yet come for putting it [this proposal] into
> practice [1885, p. 181].

Undoubtedly Marshall's main suggestions were in the monetary
field, though they did not go far. First he proposed that: 'Arrangements must be made with the Bank of England, *or otherwise*, for raising
the normal limit of the ultimate cash reserve of the nation...It would
not do much, but it would do a little towards steadying the money
market directly and industry indirectly' (op. cit., p. 179).

Finally, Marshall made his proposal, which he elaborated on a
number of other occasions, that the government 'should publish tables
showing as closely as may be the changes in the purchasing power of
gold; and should facilitate contracts for payments to be made in terms
of units of fixed purchasing power'. He considered (1887) that this
would do something to reduce price fluctuations and therefore fluctuations in employment: 'The only effective remedy for them is to be
sought in relieving the currency of the duty, which it is not fitted to
perform, of acting as a standard of value; and by establishing, in
accordance with a plan that has long been familiar to economists, an
authoritative standard of purchasing power independent of the
currency' (1925, p. 188). However, in reviewing this list of Marshall's

remedies for aggregate fluctuations, or his proposals for macro-economic policy either through rules or authorities, we have perhaps merely made it plain how completely different a world Marshall was living in, as regards the objectives and techniques of economic policy, from the world of the second half of the twentieth century.[17]

When we came to our last heading, Britain's External Commercial Policy and her Relative Economic Position in the World, quite often in perusing Marshall's writings of about three quarters of a century ago we may feel how little has changed, and how similar are the problems, the warnings, and the admonitions, which Marshall handed out to those heard in Britain most days, and especially most weekends, in the 1950s and 1960s. Certainly Britain's economic position in the world and her slower rate of growth relative to other countries were of major concern to Marshall and an important theme in *Industry and Trade*.

Perhaps the most significant illustrations of this point are in two letters written at the end of 1897 to the Master of Balliol, concerning a strike in the engineering industry. The contrast with other optimistic expressions of Marshall about the rapidly increasing economic chivalry of unions and management in Britain is rather remarkable. Marshall writes of the strike: 'If the men should win, and I were an engineering employer, I would sell my works for anything I could get and emigrate to America. If I were a working man, I would wish for no better or more hopeful conditions of life than those which I understand to prevail at the Carnegie works now.' In his next letter (5 December 1897) Marshall summarises his views in the following paragraphs:

> (i) This is the crisis of our industry. For the last twenty years we have indeed been still progressing; but we have been retrograding relatively to the Americans and to the nations of central Europe (not France, I think) and to Eastern lands.
> (ii) The causes are partly natural, inevitable, and some are, from a cosmopolitan point of view, matters for satisfaction.
> (iii) But one is unmixed evil for all, and a threat to national well-being.

[17] In a letter to *The Times* (15 February 1886) Marshall expressed some sharply anti-Ricardian support for relief works: 'It is often said that political economy has proved that outdoor relief must do more harm than good: I venture to question this... Works that are not in themselves necessary, but are undertaken in order to give employment, should be such as can be suspended at any time. The pay should be enough to afford the necessaries of life, but so far below the ordinary wages of unskilled labour in ordinary trades that people will not be contented to take it for long, but will always be on the look-out for work elsewhere. I for one can see no economic objection to letting public money flow freely for relief works on this plan.' Later (1908) Marshall referred to unemployment as the symptom of a disease and went on: 'No doubt we ourselves, society at large, are responsible for the existence of this disease more than the victims of it are. And we ought not to be afraid of very large expenditure of public and private funds in removing or lessening the causes of the disease' (1925, p. 447, italics added). Thus Marshall ranged himself against the lingering Ricardian dogmas both regarding the Poor Laws and public relief works.

It is the dominance in some unions of the desire to 'make work' and an increase in their power to do so.

(iv) And there is another like it. It is the apathy of many employers and their contentment with inferior methods, until driven out of the field or threatened severely, at least, by more enterprising foreigners.

He goes on to speak of 'the laborious laziness' in many British workshops (1925, pp. 398–400).

Later Marshall makes the suggestion, as had Jevons in his *Coal Question* a generation before, of time running out for Britain: 'There is an urgent duty upon us to make even more rapid advance during this age of economic grace, for it may run out before the end of the century' (op. cit., p. 326). With the aid of two world wars it, of course, ran out before the end of the half-century.

Marshall returned to the theme, in quite vehement terms, in a letter of 20 January 1901:

> The Christian Socialists did, I believe, a great deal more good than harm: but they did harm. Their authority has been used with great effect by those mean, lazy and selfish men who since 1860 have done so much to undermine the vigour and honest work of English industry, and have removed her from the honourable leadership which she used to hold among the nations...
>
> Fifty years ago nine-tenths of those changes, which have enabled the working classes to have healthy homes and food, originated in England. But, speaking generally, anything which was not English was really dearer than the English, though bought at a lower price. We owed our leadership partly to accidental advantages, most of which have now passed away. But we owed it mainly to the fact that we worked much harder than any continental nation. Now, on the average, we work less long and not more vigorously than our fathers did: and, meanwhile, the average amount of thoughtful work done by the German has nearly doubled; and a similar though less marked improvement is to be seen in other countries. Americans and Germans jeer at the way in which many of our businessmen give their energies to pleasure, and play with their work; and they say, truly as I believe, '*unless you completely shake off the habits that have grown on you in the last thirty years, you will go to join Spain*'... It is, I believe, a fact that there is scarcely any industry, which has changed its form during the last ten years, in which we are not behind several countries; and that every Teutonic country, whether behind us or in front of us, is on the average growing in vigour of body and mind faster than we; and that, because there is none of them that is not less self-complacent than we are, less afraid to meet frankly and generously a new idea that is 'competing' for the field...
>
> Our real danger is that we shall be undersold in the product of high class industries, and have to turn more and more to low class industries. There is no fear of our going backwards absolutely, but only relatively. The danger is that our industries will become of a lower grade relatively to other countries: that those which are in front of us will run farther away from us, and those which are behind us will catch us up. This might be tolerable if peace were assured; but I fear it is not. Here I am very sad and anxious...
>
> I think therefore that the first step towards a right use of wealth within the country is the taking an [sic] unaggressive position among nations [op. cit., pp. 392–4].

Marshall considered the remedy of protective tariffs, then being energetically canvassed, in his 'Memorandum on Fiscal Policy' of 1903, surely one of the finest policy documents ever written by an academic economist, the publication of which apparently was only dragged out of him five years after it was written. Marshall regards 'the future of England with grave anxiety'. Though he had recognised the force of the infant industries argument for protection for less developed countries, Marshall comes out firmly and categorically against the senile industries argument for protection for Britain; nor is he enthusiastic about the imperialist element in the tariff programme, which might turn out to be too favourable to (what were to become) the white dominions. He emphasises the dangers of retaliation in view of the urgency of Britain's demands for imports, and the possibilities of political mismanagement. Free trade, Marshall says, 'diminishes the money value of political power'. He notes that Britain is falling behind in certain new industries such as electrical engineering and chemicals (1926, pp. 365ff).[18] Marshall, in this remarkable Memorandum, finally warned regarding 'the solid strength' of Britain's Trade Unions: 'Perhaps *her greatest danger* is, that they be tempted to use that strength for the promotion of the interests of particular groups of workers, at the expense of wider interests, as the landowning classes did when they had the power' (op. cit., p. 396, italics added).

Thus, though Marshall was keenly aware of the looming problem of the changing relative economic position of Britain, his influence, and that of other economists in the opening years of this century, probably helped to retain Britain's mainly free trade policy for another two to three decades. In fact, Marshall was certainly cautious about putting forward sweeping or drastic policy proposals. Although Keynes (of all people) has remarked that 'Marshall was too anxious to do good', he had strictly limited and disciplined ideas about the role of the academic economists as well as a conscientious grasp of that vital kind of knowledge which consists in an awareness and acceptance of the extent of one's ignorance. 'Why should I be ashamed to say that

---

[18] Though Marshall wrote this Memorandum in 1903 he did not publish it until pressed to do so in 1908. In his Prefatory Note Marshall explains that 'this Memorandum is written from the point of view of a student of economics rather than an advocate of any particular policy. I have not held back my own conclusion on the questions to which my attention was directed. But I have endeavoured to select for prominence those considerations which seem at once important and in some danger of being overlooked whether they tell for or against my conclusions.' On publication Marshall was attacked by Bonar Law for having adopted a 'frankly partisan' attitude to the issue. Marshall, with a kind of mild exasperation protested in a letter to *The Times* (23 November 1908): 'No one can be sure that he has acted up to his intentions and Mr. Bonar Law would have been within his rights if he had said that I had failed to act up to my purpose of preserving a non-partisan attitude. But he was not justified in the explicit statement that I had frankly adopted a partisan attitude.'

I know of no simple remedy?' (1925, p. 387) Marshall once exclaimed. Here is a notable contrast with the attitude of some of his classical predecessors as also with his successors in the half-century after his death.

Of Marshall's younger period Lord Annan has written:

> The seventies and eighties were years in which the prevailing political ethos, the system of duties and privileges on which institutions were built, and the economic structure, were all being criticised by the younger school of liberals, by the Fabians and the imperialists. Alfred Marshall did not abandon the moral sciences for economics by accident; economics became for him the study which bore most obviously on moral problems [1951, p. 243].

Though in his later years Marshall became very sceptical about state intervention (in the form, for example, of nationalisation) he moved with the times with regard to the great transition from classical proportionality to progressive taxation, expressing stronger support for the latter as he grew older, and urging that the proceeds be devoted to increasing social and educational expenditure on the poor.[19]

V

The move to progressive taxation in this country, which began very gradually to gather momentum from the 1890s onwards, has obviously led on to a transformation of economic policy in the twentieth century. Whatever one may think about the justice of this change, or the desirability of the distribution to which it has led, in order to assess it fairly a comparison must be drawn with the kind of distribution which would have obtained if the classical proportionality principle, and, for example, J. S. Mill's *dictum* that progressive taxation was 'a mild form of robbery', still dominated. In this change, the importance of Edgeworth's work must be emphasised. Edgeworth argued for the minimum sacrifice principle, that is, 'that *ceteris paribus* the sum of privation or sacrifice caused by taxation should be a minimum. Therefore, if a certain amount of taxation has to be raised...the *prima facie* best distribution is that the whole amount should be paid by the wealthiest citizens' (1925, vol. II, p. 130).

Certainly Edgeworth strenuously qualified this principle with regard

---

[19] Mrs R. McW.Tullberg (1975, p. 77) has stated that in an earlier version of this essay (1969), I had demonstrated that Marshall 'had little to contribute to this renewal of State concern with the alleviation of poverty'. I don't think my essay *did* demonstrate this (or tried, or *should* have tried, to demonstrate this). But certainly my emphasis on this subject has changed somewhat: partly from reading the distinguished work by José Harris quoted here; but also because of the realisation that the significant comparison with regard to Marshall's proposals for policy changes is *not* with the vast transformation that has come about *subsequently, following two world wars,* but with *the attitudes of Marshall's immediate predecessors.* Here they represent the insertion of the thin end of a massive wedge, or a vital first step.

to the danger of 'checking accumulation', and denied it any revolutionary significance. But he was justified in holding that his new principle marked 'an important theoretical difference', and, in fact, the thin end of the wedge of progressive taxation became firmly inserted in this country at the time Edgeworth was writing. As the most learned subsequent critic of progressive taxation has stated with regard to its introduction: 'The author who had in this connection the greatest influence in the English-speaking world was F. Y. Edgeworth.'[20] We are not, of course, concerned here either with the ethical and political evaluation, nor with the logical or empirical validity of the arguments from utility analysis of Edgeworth and other neoclassicals. Nor would we try to estimate the actual political weight and effect of these doctrines in gradually transforming taxation, relative to other political or electoral factors. We are simply concerned with them as evidence of the political intentions of the 'neoclassicals' who can be said to have first raised, fundamentally and effectively, basic questions of equity in taxation and distribution. Dr Shehab's conclusion is worth quoting:

> The development of this progressive distributional theory at the close of the last century and the beginning of the present one is particularly instructive. Whether we accept it in the form Edgeworth developed, or that of Cannan which attempts to associate welfare with equity, and interprets the latter in terms of the former, or in Professor Pigou's synthesis, we arrive at the same goal; namely the higher taxation of the rich in order to ameliorate the inequality of income distribution, and to procure optimum welfare. This end, it will be observed, is the same ultimate objective at which Socialists aim. Thus, for the first time, and after a whole century of *laissez-faire*, which the economists professed completely to support, the coalescence between academic discussion of tax distribution and popular demands was accomplished, a coalescence which the prominence of *laissez-faire* in English economic thought previously made inconceivable [1953, pp. 208–9].[21]

The new concern with the problem of poverty also led on to concern in the 1880s and 1890s with what was discerned as one of its main causes, that is 'irregularity of employment' and with relief works to counter this problem. These public works were supported by Marshall in 1886 and were to be defended in 1908 by Pigou who in his inaugural lecture challenged the Ricardian dogma by which they had been so effectively opposed for much of the nineteenth century. As José Harris, in her distinguished study of social policy from 1886 to 1914, points out:

---

[20] F. A. Hayek, 1960, p. 517. Dr Shehab in his scholarly monograph also ranks Edgeworth's paper 'The Pure Theory of Taxation' as the most important contribution by an economist to the introduction of progressive taxation (1953, p. 208). We cannot agree (nor, presumably could Professor Hayek and Dr Shehab) with Professor George Stigler's verdict that: 'After utility theory began to appear in the 1870s, it took no important part in any policy-oriented controversy up to World War I' (1973, p. 312).

[21] Dr Shehab is referring, of course, to *laissez-faire* in *distribution*, which was certainly upheld in a pretty thoroughgoing form by Ricardo.

The formation of new Liberal ideas on unemployment policy was merely an aspect of a much wider revolution in the Liberal attitude to social administration which occurred during the 1900s; a revolution in which many Liberals were consciously forced to abandon those principles of 1834 which have hitherto been the sheet-anchor of our social economics. This change in the Liberal approach to social problems had many origins, both intellectual and pragmatic. *Theoretically it was made possible by certain shifts of emphasis, in orthodox economics, particularly the teaching of Alfred Marshall* that gratuitous payments to persons in need did not necessarily depress wages, nor discourage thrift, nor act as an incentive to reckless procreation; they would instead raise wages, because the increased wealth of the working classes would lead to better livng, more vigorous and better educated people, with greater earning power, and so wages would rise [1972, p. 212, italics added].

In fact José Harris goes on to maintain: 'By 1914 fatalistic acceptance of the inevitability of the trade cycle and doctrinaire prejudice against the relief of unemployment seemed to have largely passed away' (op. cit., p. 5). Thus, after 1870 the leading economists in England, on questions of policy and the role of government in the economy, may be said, for better or for worse, to have moved with the times, in respect of the great changes which, at first gradually, but with gathering momentum, were to transform the role of government in the economy. These changes had already gone a considerable distance by 1914. Two major theoretical ideas, one negative and one positive, were basic to the new policy-doctrines as contrasted with those of their classical predecessors: the *first* was the complete abandonment, so far as Britain was concerned, of the natural wage doctrine and the rejection of any hard-line content in the Malthusian–Ricardian theory about population and wages. This opened up the problems of poverty and unemployment. The *second* idea was the introduction, or revival, of the utility concept, with the impetus it gave – justifiably or otherwise – towards the replacement of the classical principle of proportionality in taxation by progression. As Edwin Cannan justifiably claimed:

> The economist of to-day is far less hostile to socialism in general than his predecessors of the classical school...The doctrine of marginal utility stamps as economical many things which could formerly be recommended only on 'sentimental' or non-economic grounds...Assuming needs to be equal, modern economics certainly teaches that a given amount of produce or income will 'go further' the more equally it is divided. The inequality of the present distribution has no pretension to be in proportion to needs [1917, p. 319].

This survey breaks off rather unevenly around the turn of the century. But we cannot conclude without a brief reference to the work of Pigou which represents the peak, or climax, of the neoclassical discussion of economic policy in England. We can be very brief because we are citing later (Chapter 9, Section IV) Pigou's views in the 1930s on the economic role of government, which pointed ahead towards the mixed economy of the roughly two decades following the Second World War; and we have also reviewed elsewhere Pigou's earlier comprehensive treatment of economic policy in his *Economics of Welfare* (Hutchison, 1953, pp. 283–93).

The *Economics of Welfare* is built around the concept of the national income or dividend, and might be said, therefore, *in that respect*, to be 'the leading modern example of the approach to economics adopted in *The Wealth of Nations*' (Hutchison, 1953, p. 285).

However, Smith and his followers concentrated almost entirely on *production*. For Pigou, equally important with its production, or size, are the *distribution* of the national income, and its *stability* – and the stability of employment – through time.

On distribution, Pigou laid it down as:

> evident that any transference of income from a relatively rich man to a relatively poor man of similar temperament, since it enables more intense wants to be satisfied at the expense of less intense wants, must increase the aggregate sum of satisfaction. The old 'law of diminishing utility' thus leads securely to the proposition: Any cause which increases the absolute share of real income in the hands of the poor, provided that it does not lead to a contraction in the size of the national dividend from any point of view, will, in general, increase economic welfare [1929, p. 91].

Regarding stability of income and employment, it should be remembered that the *Economics of Welfare* originated in a study of the causes of unemployment, in which field Pigou was a pioneer, having attacked (1908) the Ricardo–Treasury view against public investment long before Keynes. Only subsequently (1924) was the treatment of stability of incomes and employment separated off by Pigou in a separate volume on 'Industrial Fluctuations'.

Concentrating, in its later editions, on production and distribution the *Economics of Welfare* comprehensively reviewed

> the main problems of economic policy arising in Britain in the first quarter of the twentieth century: the control of monopoly, cooperation, the public operation of industry, industrial peace, conciliation and arbitration, hours of labour, methods of wage payment, employment exchanges, interference to raise wages, minimum wages, sliding scales, rationing, subsidies, the redistribution of income, and a national minimum standard of real income [Hutchison, op. cit., pp. 285–6].

In subsequent years Pigou's views have been *extremely* differently described and criticised. It is easy to understand that modern libertarians regard his contribution to ideas on economic policy as a fatal step, breaking with the Smithian tradition, along the road to the bureaucratically dominated, interventionist economy – just as Professor Hayek has described Jevons's later views as constituting a fatal turning-point and compromise with the principles of the free economy. On the other hand, it is hardly reasonably comprehensible that, at the other extreme, Professor Joan Robinson should describe Pigou as – apart from a number of cases which he treated as exceptions – laying down *laissez-faire* as 'a rule, which, in general could not be questioned' (1973, p. 47).[22]

Pigou's general attitude to economic policy and the role of government, including policies against unemployment in the 1930s, was very near to that of Keynes – possibly, regarding many details, rather more interventionist than that of Keynes. This, of course, was fully acknowledged by Keynes who agreed (1937) that 'when it comes to practice, there is really extremely little between us' (1973, vol. xiv, p. 259).

But there were two important principles in respect of which Pigou (like Marshall and other neoclassicals) differed from Keynes, and still more from many of Keynes's followers.

Though Pigou, like Marshall, had started on the study of economics with glowing hopes of what this study could contribute to human betterment, social reform, and the relief of poverty, they both matured into a healthily sceptical attitude towards the ability and willingness of politicians to implement the policy proposals of economists with requisite ingenuity and integrity. As we have seen, Marshall had come to regard as a major virtue and advantage of free trade – whatever theoretical cases could be constructed against it – that it 'diminishes the money value of political power'.

As regards Pigou, certainly following the First World War, he became heavily sceptical regarding the motives and competence of politicians in all fields of policy, including the economic and financial field. This scepticism even went so far as to incline him to support returning to gold at the old parity, and to profound long-run apprehensions about monetary management, by politicians. In his Presidential address to the Royal Economic Society Pigou complained:

> The ambition, I have claimed elsewhere, of most economists is to help in some degree, directly or indirectly towards social betterment. Our study, we should like to think, of the principles of interaction among economic events provides for statesmen data, upon which, along with data of other kinds, they, philosopher kings, build up policies directed to the common good. How different from this dream is the actuality! [1939, pp. 220–1]

Of course, the expression of such uncompromising views about politicians, regardless of party and patronage, are hardly well calculated to forward one's name towards the Honours List or the House

---

[22] According to Professor Robinson: 'For fifty years before 1914 the established economists of various schools had *all* been preaching *one doctrine*, with great self-confidence and pomposity – the doctrine of *laissez-faire*' (1972, p. 2, italics added). See below Chapter 9, Section IV for further discussion of this Cambridge version of the history of modern economics.

of Lords. However, Pigou's political scepticism perhaps expresses a measure of realism often lacking in subsequent decades.

There is also a second point regarding the contribution of the leading English 'neoclassicals' on the subject of economic policy. They set, on the average, an admirably high standard of caution and modesty. Of course it was not that Jevons, Sidgwick, Wicksteed, Marshall, Pigou or even Edgeworth, upheld some kind of lofty intellectual unconcern with the economic problems of the real world, or were not sufficiently anxious 'to do good' (which Keynes, in fact, accused Marshall of being 'too anxious' to do). What the great English neoclassicals possessed was a degree of genuine awareness of the limitations of economic knowledge which has not generally been attained by economists of other periods and schools. Some 'classicals', some 'Keynesians', and most 'Marxists', naively unaware of the extent of their own ignorance, have entertained and encouraged quite presumptuous and exaggerated ideas about the extent of economic knowledge and the guidance which it can provide for policy. But Jevons (in his later years), Leslie, Bagehot, Sidgwick, Marshall, Pigou, and Edgeworth, possessed a realistic insight into the nature of economic knowledge and of its application to the problems of economic policy-making which has not been equalled by any other comparable group of economists, and was certainly far superior to that of their Ricardian predecessors with their comparisons with Newton and Euclid and the laws of physics.

5

The Keynesian revolution and the history of economic thought

I

The Keynesian revolution is the episode in the history of economic thought which is most widely acclaimed as fully deserving the description 'revolutionary'. Inverted commas are probably less needed in the case of the Keynesian 'revolution' than in the Smithian, Ricardian and Jevonian cases, though even here a few more extreme Marxists question the truly fundamental character of the Keynesian innovations. But it seems to have been very largely through the Keynesian case that the term 'revolution' has acquired such widespread currency among economists in the last few decades. Various other claimants to the title have mostly been put forward more or less as parallels to the archetypal Keynesian 'revolution'. Certainly the mountainous literature on Keynes's ideas for the most part explicitly treats them in terms of the revolution in theory and policy which they are held to have brought about.

Keynes launched his *General Theory* with a comprehensive and challenging generalisation about the history of economic thought which is set out in the opening paragraph of the book. The way in which this generalisation is developed and deployed may have aroused (and might still arouse, latent though controversy long has been) more and sharper disagreement than the various terminological, conceptual, and other propositions and arguments in the succeeding chapters. The manner in which this sweeping, arresting challenge was thrown down in the opening single-paragraph, half-page chapter, is obviously something of a polemical ploy. If one is to establish a claim to be initiating a revolution in ideas then one must first identify a formidable, established orthodoxy to be overthrown and superseded – as had Adam Smith with 'the mercantile system' and Jevons with 'the Ricardo–Mill Economics'.

Such a comprehensive challenge to academic orthodoxy was for Keynes something mainly new in 1936, unprecedented in his previous economic writings, such as *The Tract* or *The Treatise*. Previously Keynes had challenged much, including the Versailles treaty, the return to the gold standard, the doctrine of *laissez-faire*, and the Conservative and

Treasury opposition to public investment to reduce unemployment. But on economic issues he had usually claimed the agreement, or even the overwhelming support of university economists, or of the most advanced among them and, *on policy issues*, he continued to claim general support and agreement *throughout the 1930s*.[1] On the other hand, in his *General Theory* Keynes was concerned 'to contrast the character of my arguments and conclusions with those of the *classical theory* of the subject, on which I was brought up and which *dominates the economic thought, both practical and theoretical, of the governing and academic classes of this generation*, as it has for a hundred years past' (1936, p. 3).

Keynes sets out on page 1 the membership of 'the classical school' as including, after Ricardo and James Mill, 'the *followers* of Ricardo, those that is to say, who adopted and perfected the theory of the Ricardian economics, including (for example) J. S. Mill, Marshall, Edgeworth and Prof. Pigou'.[2]

As Edgeworth is never quoted, and J. S. Mill only briefly mentioned, 'classical' theory is mainly exemplified by Ricardo, Marshall and Pigou. Adam Smith is mentioned at the end of the book simply as 'the forerunner of the classical school' and is even commended for his favourable attitude to the usury laws (1936, p. 361n).

In this essay we are examining Keynes's comprehensive outline or sketch of an important aspect of the history of economic thought. We are attempting to assess how far it is valid or not. We shall try to suggest other examples and episodes which might fill in and strengthen Keynes's thesis, or which, at some points might alter or invalidate it. Altogether, Keynes sketched what amounts to an outline of over three hundred years of the history of economic thought or of a principal strand therein. For in the penultimate chapter of *The General Theory* Keynes went back to the early seventeenth-century writers (e.g. Malynes, 1622), while he brings his survey right down to 1933 with Pigou's *Theory of Unemployment* – 'the only detailed account of the

---

[1] For example, in 1924 Keynes had maintained: 'The almost revolutionary improvement in our understanding of the mechanism of money and credit and of the analysis of the trade cycle, recently effected by the united efforts of many thinkers, may prove to be one of the most important advances in economic thought ever made' (1924, p. 68). Again in 1929 when a Treasury document opposed, in terms closely resembling those of Ricardo, proposals for public investment as a remedy for unemployment, Keynes insisted: 'Not one of the leading economists of the country who has published his views, or with whose opinion I am otherwise familiar, would endorse the character of their argument.' The Treasury experts 'are not familiar with modern economic thought' (1929). Again, in 1931, Keynes asserted that 'scarcely one responsible person in Great Britain' disagreed with his opposition to wage cuts (1931). Finally, in December 1937 Keynes was maintaining that to dispute the view that public loan expenditure helps employment 'is running counter to the almost unanimous opinion of contemporary economists' (*The Times*, 28 December 1937).

[2] Incidentally, the very full and accurate index does not mention James Mill at all but does indicate that J. B. Say's name had been included in this footnote.

classical theory of employment which exists' (op. cit., p. 7). Obviously some parts of Keynes's more-than-300-year outline may be better founded than others.

II

The adjective 'classical' as applied to macroeconomic 'models' has come usually to possess little or no historical significance. Such 'models' are mostly simplified, streamlined, analytical stereotypes. No attempt is usually made to show that such a 'model', often extremely precisely formulated, was ever actually or consistently applied by any particular economist or group of economists. Indeed even so-called 'Keynesian' models sometimes seem to have only a somewhat tenuous relationship, if any, with what Keynes regularly asserted.

Insofar as we are actually quoting from or commenting on Keynes we can hardly avoid using his term 'classical' (though we shall spell it 'Klassical', when using it in Keynes's sense, to distinguish his from other usages of the word). The cumbersome term 'mercantilist' may similarly be to some extent unavoidable. But, insofar as we are putting forward an alternative version of the kind of historical outline Keynes suggested, we shall try to avoid the terms 'classical' and 'mercantilist' and develop an outline mainly in terms of 'Smithian' or 'pre-Smithian' theories or doctrines. That is, we shall take as a definite historical turning-point what was actually written by Smith in *The Wealth of Nations* (particularly in Book II, Chapter 3). We shall follow the Smithian doctrines through the nineteenth century, noting how precisely, consistently, and consequentially they were held to by leading writers in the earlier decades. We shall also see how, towards the end of the century, and after, they began, rather inexplicitly and untidily, to lose some, or much, but not all, of their hold in the half-century before *The General Theory*.

In the title of a wireless talk just over a year before he published *The General Theory* Keynes posed the question 'Is the Economic System Self-Adjusting?' He drew a crucial dividing line between those who answered 'Yes' to this question and those who answered 'No'. He described those who answered 'Yes', or 'the self-adjusting school', as:

> having behind it almost the whole body of organised economic thinking and doctrine of the last hundred years...It has vast prestige and a more far-reaching influence than is obvious. For it lies behind the education and the habitual modes of thought, not only of economists, but of bankers and business men and civil servants and politicians of all parties [1973, vol. XIII, p. 485].

Much of the history of economic thought, especially from the late seventeenth to the late nineteenth centuries, could be written round the theme of the development of theories of self-adjustment in one or other sector of economic activity, individual or allocational, aggregate or international. In fact sometimes 'progress' in political economy, or its emergence as a science, seems almost to have been equated with the development and the more and more unqualified assertion of the empirical validity of self-equilibrating models. Arguments over policy have very largely centred round the real-world applicability of such models.

When Keynes, however, answered his question with a challenging 'No' as to whether the economic system was self-adjusting, he was, of course, simply denying beneficent *macroeconomic* self-adjustment, in terms of the aggregate level of activity and employment. He did not deny completely, or anything like completely, the existence of beneficent self-adjusting forces in international trade and payments. Certainly, in *micro*economic terms, Keynes believed that the then system *was* more or less adequately self-adjusting, as he stressed in his Concluding Notes in *The General Theory*.[3] Correspondingly, he emphasised in this talk that 'a large part of the established body of economic doctrine I cannot but accept as broadly correct'.

However, with regard to macroeconomic self-adjustment Keynes 'ranged himself with the heretics', against what he called (apparently for the first time in print) 'the classical doctrine'.

He argued:

> The school which believes in self-adjustment is, in fact, assuming that the rate of interest adjusts itself more or less automatically, so as to encourage just the right amount of production of capital goods to keep our incomes at the maximum level which our energies and our organisation and our knowledge of how to produce are capable of providing [1973, vol. XIII, p. 490].

Though Keynes was apparently quite unaware of it, this description matches with remarkable accuracy the doctrine expounded with such originality, force, and consistency by Adam Smith. This doctrine of saving, investment, and the rate of interest is the central pillar of Smithian or 'Klassical' macro-economics. But the extensive, logically-

---

[3] 1936, p. 379: 'When 9,000,000 men are employed out of 10,000,000 willing and able to work, there is no evidence that the labour of these 9,000,000 men is misdirected.'

As regards self-adjusting forces in international trade and payments Keynes, in his last article, took an intermediate view. He maintained that: 'In the long run more fundamental forces may be at work, if all goes well, tending towards equilibrium...the classical teaching embodied some permanent truths of great significance...There are in these matters deep undercurrents at work, natural forces, one can call them, or even the invisible hand, which are operating towards equilibrium.' On the other hand, Keynes did 'not suppose that the classical medicine will work by itself or that we can depend on it.' The aim should be 'not to defeat, but to implement the wisdom of Adam Smith' (1946, pp. 185–6). *Mutatis mutandis* this view has some broad similarities with that of Cantillon and other great seventeenth and eighteenth century writers regarding self-adjusting processes.

related Klassical edifice comprises also a theory of money based on a denial or neglect of 'hoarding', as well as an ambiguous proposition, subsequently derived by J. B. Say, regarding the necessary adequacy of aggregate demand, accompanied by an emphasis on 'real', non-monetary analysis which was assumed to be applicable with little or no qualification to an actual monetary economy. Flowing straight from these propositions were, of course, highly negative, *laissez-faire* policy conclusions regarding government expenditure and borrowing, and the role of the state in maintaining employment. Subsequently Keynes discerned, as a fundamental assumption of the Klassical edifice, an extremely simplifying postulate regarding the transparent conditions of certainty, and correct knowledge and expectations, on the basis of which economic decisions were assumed to be taken (1937).

Let us, however, focus on Keynes's division between those who had, and those who had not, believed in the macroeconomically self-adjusting properties of the economic system. It must be noted first that the range of possible or actual beliefs or doctrines is by no means restricted simply to an either–or division between absolute believers and unbelievers. For Keynes allowed that the orthodox believers 'do not, of course, believe that the system is automatically or immediately self-adjusting. But they do believe that it has an inherent tendency towards self-adjustment if it is not interfered with and if the action of change and chance is not too rapid' (1973, vol. XIII, p. 487).

But just how long and painful may one consider the adjustment process to be while still being classifiable as an orthodox believer in the self-equilibrating properties of the system? It is clear that we are not confronted by a black and white dichotomy between doctrines asserting and doctrines denying self-adjustment, nor even with a single-dimensional range of possible doctrines. Within the field of possibilities may be distinguished:

(1) A range of doctrines or beliefs extending from those asserting very smooth and rapid self-adjustment up to very high, finely-tuned degrees of maximisation or optimality, at one extreme, and, at the other extreme, doctrines asserting that no self-adjusting processes are ever effective in the system at all.

(2) Secondly, the framework of institutions, rules, or policies required to maintain an effectively self-adjusting system may be regarded as extremely 'simple', 'natural', and easy to bring about and maintain (as Adam Smith seems, at some points, to have regarded his 'simple system of natural liberty') or as extremely complex and difficult, or as *practically* quite impossible to set up at all.

(3) Effectively self-adjusting processes, and the feasibility of the framework for their operation, may be regarded as generally or universally prevailing, or as much more nearly fulfilled at some times

and places than others, or, of course, as never realised, or realisable, at all. For example, Pigou regarded self-adjusting processes as having been generally operative in the labour market in Britain between 1850 and 1914, but not after 1919 because of the increased power of trade unions and the existence of general unemployment insurance.[4]

Any satisfactory survey or generalisation regarding economic doctrines and beliefs must take account of the full richness and complexity of this possible and actual variety. Moreover, it is sometimes difficult to locate an economist's precise position in this extensive and complex field of possibilities because he may not have been completely explicit or consistent, sometimes not even within one and the same work, let alone as between different works written at considerable intervals of time. However, several of the leading figures, notably Adam Smith and Ricardo, if not unquestionably and absolutely 100 per cent consistent, are so nearly and thoroughly explicit and consistent that they can be placed quite clearly and definitely in a pretty extreme position. Others, such as Marshall, are not quite so easily and definitely located, in some parts of their work taking up an almost purely Smithian position and in others appearing to veer more towards the other direction.

Furthermore, it is difficult in assessing economists' ideas not to get involved in historical judgments regarding their applicability, that is regarding the actual extent of self-adjustment in the economic system at different times – though often self-adjustment is asserted or denied in unqualified general terms. To take five leading names, Petty in the seventeenth, Steuart (1767) in the eighteenth, and Keynes in the twentieth century, all denied that the system was macroeconomically self-adjusting; whereas Smith (1776) in the late eighteenth century and Ricardo in the early nineteenth asserted comparatively easy and beneficent self-adjustment. Though a sudden wholesale change in the effectiveness of self-adjusting processes in the economy between 1767 and 1776 is hardly credible, it is conceivable, though perhaps not

---

[4] See Pigou, 1949, pp. 95ff. It is stated in a recent (1974) textbook: 'A market economy left to its own devices will settle into a full employment equilibrium. External shocks, of a variety of kinds, will dislodge it from equilibrium from time to time, but the economy's internal defences will speedily return it to equilibrium barring new shocks or actively destabilizing policies by government.' This statement, on the first page of the preface, may be elucidated as the book proceeds. It might be almost or completely tautological. As it stands it is not at all clear what are the precise requirements for the existence of 'a market economy left to its own devices' – in particular regarding monetary institutions and policy, and the foresight, wisdom and forbearance of those responsible for these institutions and policies. It is also not pointed out where such a market economy has (if ever) existed historically. If it was claimed that, say, the British economy in the middle decades of the nineteenth century fulfilled the requirements, it would have to be shown either (1) that full employment existed throughout; or (2) that such considerable instability and unemployment as might seem to have existed was entirely due to 'external shocks'. In neither case would such a demonstration be easy. (See M. H. Miller and C. W. Upton, 1974, p. vii. I am grateful to Professor Douglas Vickers for calling my attention to this passage.)

probable, that the views of four, if not all five, of these great economists were broadly valid, *for their own time and place.*

One criterion for locating and classifying economists' views regarding the effectiveness of self-adjustment is to consider what they said about economic policy – though obviously this does not settle whether or not their judgment was correct. Again, in terms of policy recommendations there is the same continuity in the range of possibilities from one extreme to the other. Actually, however, many economists have tended to polarise in terms of fairly general assertions or denials of the general desirability or undesirability of government policies to regulate the aggregate level of output and employment. However, Keynes himself, as we shall see below (Section IX), apparently did not accept a policy criterion in classifying his contemporaries as Klassical or not. He described, in some cases, as 'classical', writers who agreed with him on policy (e.g. Pigou), and as 'non-classical', a writer who opposed his policies (e.g. Hawtrey).

We now start our Keynesian review in the seventeenth century.

III

In discussing the writers of the seventeenth and eighteenth centuries we do not wish to get involved in generalisations or arguments about 'mercantilism', 'the mercantilists', or 'mercantilist thought'. These are concepts which involve generalising about both thought and policy, in different countries, over two or three centuries, lumping together the ideas and arguments of original and disciplined thinkers, such as Petty, Cantillon, or Steuart, with the outpourings of ephemeral special pleaders; as though the thoughts on economic policy of, say, Lord Keynes and Lord Beaverbrook were to be homogenised as examples of 'twentieth-century mercantilism', without any discrimination regarding the level and quality of their thinking.

Anyhow, Keynes's attempt at a new interpretation of pre-Smithian writings met with immediate condemnation even from his most enthusiastic disciples.[5] Furthermore, Heckscher, on whose work Keynes had copiously drawn, strongly rejected his attempt 'to rehabilitate' what they both called 'the mercantilist doctrine' (1955, vol. II, pp. 340ff).

Regarding Heckscher's strictures it should be noted that they are directed at both 'the mercantilist' and Keynes's own doctrines. Heckscher did not argue that the 'mercantilist' ideas and Keynes's were really quite dissimilar, as some subsequent critics of Keynes's interpretation of 'the mercantilists' have done. On the contrary, according

---

[5] Mr R. F. Harrod (as he then was) strongly objected to Keynes's penultimate chapter 'as a tendentious attempt to glorify imbeciles' (1951, p. 460).

to Heckscher, they resembled one another all too closely: 'Keynes's view of economic relationships is in many ways strikingly similar to that of the mercantilists' (op. cit., p. 340).[6]

Moreover, according to Heckscher, neither Keynes's theories, nor those of 'the mercantilists' (*nor, incidentally, the classical theories*) were founded on the facts of their own or any other period: 'There are no grounds whatsoever for supposing that the mercantilist writers constructed their system – with its frequent and marked theoretical orientation – out of any knowledge of reality however derived. There is nothing to indicate that they were any different in this respect from the classical economists' (op. cit., p. 347).[7]

Professor Mark Blaug has criticised Keynes's interpretation of 'mercantilism' in terms to some extent similar to Heckscher's, though more particularised. He agrees, apparently, that the seventeenth- and eighteenth-century writers were concerned with unemployment, but holds, like Heckscher, that they quite misconceived the problems of their day in advancing diagnoses and remedies similar to those of Keynes. For the kind of unemployment which they faced in the century or two before Adam Smith was – according to Professor Blaug – of a completely different nature from that with which Keynes was confronted:

> The kind of unemployment which caused greatest concern was either disguised under-employment or else voluntary unemployment in the sense of a marked preference for leisure over earnings... It may be conceded that a chronic shortage of currency impedes economic growth and that an increase in the stock of money can promote investment if it results in forced saving, but Keynesian remedies in a dominantly agrarian economy merely produce inflation without leading to full employment. If this be accepted, it follows that most of Adam Smith's predecessors were 'monetary cranks' not prescient Keynesians [1964, p. 115].[8]

[6] Other critics of Keynesian interpretations of seventeenth and eighteenth century economists have, on the contrary, denied any significant similarities or parallels between the views of Keynes and those of the earlier writers (see I. D. S. Ward, 1959, and also my article, 1953 *b*).

[7] On one quite vital and fundamental factual assumption Heckscher seems to confirm the views of 'the mercantilist writers' rather than 'the classical economists'. This relates to the existence and importance of 'hoarding', with which the former were much concerned (e.g. especially Boisguilbert) and which the classicals largely assumed out of existence. According to Heckscher (op. cit., p. 349), 'there is every reason to suppose that far into the nineteenth century people continued to hoard great quantities of money'. Presumably these hoards fluctuated. This is just what the seventeenth- and eighteenth-century writers were anxious about, and which Smithian doctrine emphatically denied.

[8] Elsewhere Professor Blaug has maintained: 'As for approval of public works, that was frequently based on nothing more than the typical mercantilist belief in the magical efficacy of state action simply because it is action undertaken in the public interest... There is very little in the literature to suggest that concern over employment-promoting schemes stemmed from a recognition that underemployment was due to a failure of effective demand' (1962, p. 15).

It is fortunately unnecessary to argue at length over what kind of unemployment caused, or should have caused, greatest concern in the seventeenth and eighteenth centuries. Perhaps 'voluntary unemployment', and unemployment due to shortages of capital, were relatively more important in the seventeenth and eighteenth centuries than in the twentieth century, and even conceivably were then the most important kind of unemployment. All we need to maintain is that involuntary industrial or manufacturing unemployment due to instabilities and deficiencies of aggregate demand was *a* major, serious problem, with which many of the writers of this time were justifiably concerned, in the context of which it was reasonable for them to have advocated government policies, such as public works, fiscal policies, and policies to maintain the money supply. Anyhow, hardly any of these writers are to be found asserting, like Smith and Ricardo later, that there was virtually no unemployment problem at all, or none with which government should attempt to deal. It also seems to be suggested that because 'Keynesian' policies cannot cure all, or nearly all, unemployment in some poorer, or 'less-developed' countries today (or in more developed either) therefore, writers of the seventeenth or eighteenth centuries, who suggested policies against unemployment in Britain, like those suggested by Keynes, must have failed to grasp correctly the problems of their time and place: for Britain at that time was also at a 'less-developed' stage. Such an argument seems unsatisfactory for two reasons: (1) it implies a crudely over-simplified, 'linear' conception of economic development, to suggest that all economies, in culturally quite different countries and continents, pass through the same stages, with processes and institutions working in the same way, only at different dates: that is, that the labour supply, labour market, and unemployment in India in 1970 can be assumed, in their institutions and processes, to be comparable or similar to those of a more 'developed' economy (e.g. that of Britain) at some earlier date, say 1670 or 1770.

(2) Even if unemployment at some times and places may not be completely or approximately curable by Keynesian policies, this certainly does not mean that it cannot be seriously reduced or increased by wise or unwise government stabilisation policies: in fact, when any sector of an economy has risen appreciably above a primitive agricultural level there may be a Keynesian problem of maintaining an appropriate level of aggregate demand and employment, even if a serious unemployment problem of a kind not curable by Keynesian methods may persist. It seems to involve considerable oversimplification to assume that at any one time and place *all*, or anything like all, unemployment must be of the same type. In fact, at most times and places, different types of unemployment will be existing side by side.

With regard to the 'voluntary' or 'involuntary' nature of the employment problem in the seventeenth and eighteenth centuries, it may be observed that one writer after another makes it abundantly clear that though sometimes *also* concerned with 'voluntary' unemployment, or laziness – which presumably exists in all times and places – the problem of involuntary unemployment was for them a major concern.[9] Of course, for Heckscher and those who agree with him, this means little because they hold that these writers had no knowledge of the realities of the economy which confronted them. However a number of more recent economic historians have maintained that involuntary industrial unemployment, due to instabilities of demand, which were to a serious extent of monetary origin, was a major problem in seventeenth-century England.

First, Mr R. W. K. Hinton has emphasised the extent to which many of the seventeenth-century English writers were concerned with *depression* (like Keynes, incidentally):

> The writings from which we infer the so-called mercantilist ideas at present under discussion were largely a product of economic depressions. Most of Thomas Mun's classic exposition was written apropos of the depression of 1620, like the famous tracts of Malynes and Misselden. Nearly all the works cited in Professor Viner's bibliography to *English Theories of Foreign Trade* and most of the English legislation cited in the index to Professor Heckscher's *Mercantilism* fall in or near the periods of bad trade identified by W. R. Scott. The seventeenth century commissions of trade, whose instructions embody mercantilist thought and whose enquiries encouraged it, were established in crises.
>
> In the seventy years of Mun's lifetime from 1571 to 1641 there were only thirty-six years of good trade, according to W. R. Scott; the rest he calls either depressed or bad; he counts seven severe crises of varying duration [1955, p. 284].

Professor B. E. Supple has also emphasised the extent to which seventeenth-century English writers were concerned with depression, and he strongly defends their realistic grasp of what were the significant problems of their day:

> There is incontestable evidence that it is impossible to dissociate some mercantilist writing from the problems of the day, and that it was usually a time of economic distress which provided an environment of urgency within which economic views first became fully articulate. Whatever the

---

[9] E.g. Petty, Davenant, Law, Berkeley, Massie and numerous lesser writers could all be cited: not that any clear-cut line between 'voluntary' and 'involuntary' unemployment was drawn by most writers, as this was, and is, a difficult line to draw in practice. The work of E. S. Furniss (1920) is rich in examples: see especially his discussion of 'the doctrine of *the right to employment*' (inevitably implying *in*voluntary unemployment) in Chapter IV. Keynes would have found a copious source of material for building up his thesis in this book, as he would also in the admirable study, published at almost the same time as that of Furniss, by B. Suviranta (1923), cited below.

theoretical shortcomings and blatant oversights of contemporary pamph-leteers, *their appreciation of the significant areas for economic investigation cannot be questioned.* If these men had their faults then they are largely those of any group desperately involved in an economic crisis. The whole tenor of what has come to be known as mercantilist literature owes not a little to this involvement [1959, p. 221, italics added].

Professor Supple also strongly defends the concern of these writers with 'the scarcity of money', implying that it was not they who were the 'monetary cranks', who completely misconceived the problems with which they were faced, but rather, perhaps, the classical 'cranks' of facile self-adjustment who assumed away 'hoarding' and the problems of securing a growing money supply:

> In large part the modern approach has been to discount contemporary theories of an independent shortage of currency on the grounds that they were products of a confused mercantilist view of the significance of treasure, and that any economic problems posed by a drain of specie would quite naturally be solved by the speedy readjustment deriving from deflationary pressures on prices, costs and the demand for imports.
>
> *But such analyses presuppose economic mechanisms quite remote from the reality of the early seventeenth century*...The operations of the seventeenth-century economy were not frictionless, and economic pressures which, in the perfect models of classical economics, lowered monetary values while maintaining full employment of resources, were likely, in Stuart society, to provoke chronic unemployment or underemployment as they met the relatively rigid line of prices and costs. *For an economy whose market values contained a significant traditional element and which depended so much on the availability of metallic coin for its continuing activity, fluctuations in the physical supply of liquid assets could impose long-term strains which cannot be measured by an exercise in formal logic.* For this reason it was quite possible, after 1611, for a shortage of money to be the cause of continuing dislocation and incipient deflation. It would therefore be misleading to claim that all such complaints of a shortage arose from a 'confused economic analysis' [op. cit., p. 177, italics added].

Finally, Professor Supple has emphasised the importance of the unemployment problem *and of the problem of industrial unemployment due to deficiency or instability of effective demand*:

> The most critical element of instability as far as the government was concerned was the possibility of chronic unemployment. And it has already been indicated that in this last respect the textile industry played an almost unique role at this time. Thus variations in the effective demand for cloth were the principal causes of outbreaks of unemployment for people who might, at such times, find few alternative sources of income...
> ...Since the prevention of social unrest by the maintenance of employ-ment in textiles was a major aim of policy, governments were clearly forced to consider the relationships between commercial crises and the structure of the cloth industry [op. cit., p. 234].

Unless Professor Supple can be shown to be very seriously wrong, we have here some quite massive support for the kind of interpretation of this literature which Keynes originated.

More recently (1969) this kind of interpretation has been supported in an article on Malynes – one of the writers cited by Keynes – who was much concerned with the instabilities of the money supply as a cause of unemployment:

It was because of the impact of a monetary drain on spending and demand that he feared a specie outflow. 'The want of money', he wrote, 'maketh a dead trade'. In fact, if sixteenth- and early seventeenth-century observers were correct, the money supply, rather than habits of saving or methods and intensity of investment, was a major source of economic fluctuations. The early Stuart economy rested upon a rather stolid agricultural base, and the visible origin of the economic growth urgently needed to absorb the troublesome body of unemployed was the foreign sector, or more specifically, the textile industry [Lynn Muchmore, 1969].

Professor Muchmore concludes that: 'The habit of continually assigning events a subordinate role has jeopardized the assessment of pre-Smithian economics. Malynes was immersed in the peculiar problems of his period.'

Certainly the 'assigning of a subordinate role' to a massive unemployment problem, and the over-simplification of the nature of that problem, will not conduce to a just interpretation of seventeenth- and eighteenth-century economists.

As regards the eighteenth century, the prevalence of instability and unemployment throughout a wide range of industries has been noted by Ashton (1959).[10] In fact, in marked contrast with Heckscher's attitude, a number of economic historians have more recently recognised Keynes's contribution. For example, Professor van Klaveren has written of the 'important steps' in the understanding of mercantilist theorising which 'have been properly acknowledged only since John Maynard Keynes' (1969, p. 141).

Professor C. H. Wilson has observed that 'it was John Maynard Keynes who first initiated a re-examination of orthodox attitudes here' (1967, p. IX).

Professor Wilson accuses Keynes of 'perpetrating an anachronism' in 'trying to isolate the purely economic element in "mercantilist" thought and policy'. But this must be an error perpetrated by many historians of economic thought. Professor Wilson himself has sought to defend and rationalise 'mercantilist' theories and policies with regard to the balance of trade, against their dismissal as the work of 'cranks' and 'ignoramuses'.[11]

[10] See also Ashton, 1955, p. 173 and p. 203, where 'the dearth of money of all kinds' and the extensive unemployment in manufacturing are emphasised.
[11] See 'Treasure and Trade Balances' (in 1967). Professor Wilson acknowledges the hint of G. N. Clark: 'The explanation of the mercantilist attitude seems to lie in the commercial conditions of the time, especially in the needs of traders for capital in a solid and ponderable form' (1947, p. 27).

It could certainly be argued that Keynes in his chapter in *The General Theory* concentrated rather too narrowly on theories about the rate of interest in the seventeenth- and eighteenth-century economists, and that he might have also given more attention to the direct concern of writers, from Petty to Steuart, with the problem of unemployment, as one which called for government policies and would not beneficently settle itself by a self-adjusting mechanism. In fact 'full employment' has been described as 'the economic objective of mercantilist policy, as distinct from its political objective which was national power'.[12]

Regarding the role of monetary theory in this period Professor Douglas Vickers concludes his very thorough study:

> Its relevance in particular was to the problems of growth or development on the one hand and to the level of employment and activity on the other. The strands of thought at these points are clearly intermixed – yet it is necessary to conclude that *the more important considerations for the development of the theory of money were those of employment rather than those of economic growth...*
>
> In moving, however, to the theory of employment, the theory of money here derives a clearer stimulus to analytical development, and it finds here its primary application. In the realm of policy again, the cause for concern was the chronic tendency to unemployment, poverty, and distress, and the social and human problems which these occasioned. Population, production, and activity were increasing during the eighteenth century, but the expansive trend was associated with a tendency to unemployment which was structural in part and which depended, moreover, on a dragging deficiency of the means of exchange. Employment, therefore, was itself a prerequisite of the healthy functioning and development of the economy and the objectives of monetary analysis became consistently those of the effects of the money flow on the level of employment and trade [1959, p. 294, italics added].[13]

In his discerning study of the balance of trade doctrine Suviranta emphasised how 'the question of employment came to be of paramount importance in economic policy' (1923, p. 136).

Suviranta, writing long before Keynes, went on:

[12] W. D. Grampp, 1952, p. 468. Professor Grampp has maintained: 'The unemployment of the sixteenth and seventeenth centuries was, in the language of today's economics, the result of (a) frequent deflations, some of them quite severe; (b) the long-run decline of particular industries...(c) the immobility of resources and especially labor; and (d) the wage and price rigidity caused mainly by the monopolistic practices of the guilds...It is interesting to note that Great Britain had a similar unemployment problem about 200 years after the close of the mercantilist period.' Grampp emphasises how Keynesian economics 'has an affinity to mercantilist doctrine' (1965, vol. I, pp. 92–3).

[13] Professor John Wood has concluded, regarding the history of monetary theory, 'Keynes was a better historian of economic thought than he has generally been given credit for. And if the great similarities between Keynes and the predecessors of Hume are not obvious to you, then we have all been wasting our time. An interest in periods of transition and a belief in the importance of money in the short-run was common to Keynes and the mercantilists' (1972, p. 12).

Much in the appreciation of money by mercantile writers does not, therefore, appear unreasonable...

As long as paper currency had not been introduced, there existed permanently, even at the time of the largest supply of money, a *potential* scarcity of money. A stoppage or even a substantial slackening in the supply of the precious metals would have, by the steadily growing demand for money, changed, sooner or later, the imminent danger of a scarcity into a painful reality. It is against this background that the mercantile psychology must be seen and that *the anxiety for a steady supply of money only becomes fully intelligible for us, who are living in greatly changed conditions*...

Instead of reproving them for a theory, fallacious, and insufficient, we may, on the contrary, grant that we find in their writings much common sense and also, often, fine theoretical judgment [op. cit., pp. 77, 95, and 166].[14]

It should be noted that Keynes claimed neither that the theories of the seventeenth- and eighteenth-century writers were devoid of errors and inadequacies, nor that they were identical in form and content with his own. Certainly economists in the seventeenth and eighteenth centuries had not developed the specialised, 'professional' terminology and the analytical and conceptual precision and refinement of the twentieth century. But they were able to discern the existence of unemployment, hoarding, and an erratic and often insufficient money supply as serious problems.

Moreover, those who deny significant parallels between the ideas of the seventeenth- and eighteenth-century writers and those of Keynes are apt to stress that the institutions of the two periods, and the nature of the important kinds of unemployment and of the labour market and the supply of labour, were completely different. But the most general economic theories – it is at once a source both of strength and weakness – apply in the most widely divergent institutional frameworks. Nevertheless, we are apparently to be prohibited from drawing parallels between, say, the supply and demand analysis of Smith (in Chapter VII of *The Wealth of Nations*) and the supply and demand analysis of twentieth-century economists, because the institutional framework today in which goods are supplied and demanded, and the goods themselves, are so extremely different – as are motor cars supplied and demanded on credit from hand-made horse-shoes supplied and demanded against metallic cash. If these vetoes are allowed, then any wide generality is denied to economic theories and the history of economic theory can hardly be written with significant continuity.

We are concerned with arguments which are apt to run in highly imprecise terms as to whether, or how far, the 'mercantilists', as some

---

[14] Mr R. W. K. Hinton has expressed the view that Suviranta's work 'remains the most useful study on this subject for the historian' (1955, p. 283). Certainly, together with the book of E. S. Furniss, that of Suviranta comes nearest, among the pre-Keynesian writers, to anticipating the interpretation given in *The General Theory*.

kind of generality, were 'precursors' or 'forerunners' of Keynes.[15] Keynes himself wished to claim that he had 'predecessors'. We would, however, claim that considerable evidence can be produced for the following propositions of Keynes:

(1) 'Mercantilist thought' (or, as we would prefer to say, the leading and more typical writers in the century and a half before *The Wealth of Nations*) 'never supposed that there was a self-adjusting tendency by which the rate of interest would be established at the appropriate level' (1936, p. 341).

(2) 'As a contribution to statecraft which is concerned with the economic system as a whole and with securing the optimum employment of the system's entire resources, the methods of the early pioneers of economic thinking in the sixteenth and seventeenth centuries may have attained to fragments of practical wisdom which the unrealistic abstractions of Ricardo first forgot and then obliterated' (op. cit., p. 340).

(3) Keynes was justified, in replying to the charge of 'glorifying imbeciles' in maintaining: 'What I want is to do justice to schools of thought which the classicals have treated as imbecile for the last hundred years, and, above all, to show that I am not really being so great an innovator, except as against the classical school, but have important predecessors and am returning to an age-long tradition of common sense' (1973, vol. XIII, p. 552).

IV

In the hundred years before *The Wealth of Nations* the idea was gradually gaining ground that self-adjusting processes of a more or less beneficent kind were operative in one sector or other of the economy, with regard, for example, to the balance of trade, the labour market, the rate of interest etc. At certain limited points some writers seemed to be prepared to rely on these 'natural' forces (e.g. Mandeville with regard to the labour market). But, for the most part, the major writers of the seventeenth and early eighteenth centuries, while recognising the existence of self-adjusting forces, were not prepared to place such exclusive reliance on them, as operating sufficiently smoothly, rapidly, and justly, as to exclude the need for a considerable measure of government intervention and responsibility. The major writers of this period (Petty, Locke, Boisguilbert, Cantillon, Galiani,

[15] Jacob Viner cited as an 'anticipation' of Keynes that 'from the seventeenth century on, there was an almost continuous stream of expositions of the view that unemployment and sluggish trade were the consequences of the failure of purchasing power to keep step with the expansion of productive power. Keynes found to his delight that the literature of mercantilism was saturated with this idea' (1964, p. 256).

Steuart and others)[16] might perhaps be described as supporters of a 'mixed economy'. They were far from being total planners and *dirigistes* in the style of Colbert. They recognised 'natural' forces of individual self-interest as operative in markets, and as, in some cases, or to some extent, working themselves out through competitive market mechanisms in a more-or-less beneficently self-adjusting way. But these writers were mostly not prepared to rely *solely* on these self-equilibrating mechanisms, with regard to the balance of trade and payments externally, or internally with regard to the level of activity and employment. Some of these writers urged monetary and fiscal policies on governments, as well as public works. They certainly held no such 'view' as that the government could not, and should not attempt to raise directly the level of investment and employment. It was with Adam Smith (and the Physiocrats and Turgot) that the balance shifted decisively and drastically towards the *general* recognition and advocacy of beneficent self-adjusting processes throughout the economic system, once 'the simple system of natural liberty' was allowed to assert itself, and towards a correspondingly radical general restriction on the economic functions of government.

Let us now look briefly at some distinguished writers of the late seventeenth and early eighteenth centuries who illustrate the tendencies we have just outlined, for example, Sir William Petty, J. J. Becher, Pierre de Boisguilbert, and Richard Cantillon.

Petty (described by Marx as 'the founder of modern political economy') made it quite clear that he was concerned with *in*voluntary unemployment, and his proposals for public works, as well as fiscal policy, are well known.[17] Regarding J. J. Becher (1635–82?), the German mercantilist, Schumpeter described the 'practically complete concordance' between his policy recommendations and those of Keynes, as well as Becher's emphasis on the fundamental importance of consumption as the prime mover of economic activity, expressed in 'Becher's principle' to the effect that 'one man's expenditure is another man's income'.[18] Schumpeter links with Becher the Rouen magistrate Pierre de Boisguilbert (1647–1714), with whom, alongside Petty, Marx held that the history of modern political economy begins (1973, p. 883). Boisguilbert was concerned with the profound de-

---

[16] Regarding Locke it has been maintained: 'Locke did not assume, as did his classical successors, that his system would gravitate toward a full-employment equilibrium' (A. H. Leigh, 1974, p. 218). For Galiani's view of self-equilibrating market mechanisms see 1959, p. 223.

[17] See 1899, pp. 29, 31, and 36. For example: 'When all helpless and impotent persons were thus provided for, and the lazy and thievish restrained and punished...it follows now, that we find out certain constant employments for all other indigent people'.

[18] See J. J. Becher, 1673, pp. 584–9; and J. Schumpeter, 1954, p. 283.

pression in the French economy towards the close of the seventeenth century and especially with the vicious circle which he called 'la misère moderne', that is 'an extreme of poverty in the midst of an abundance of all goods'.[19] Boisguilbert specially stressed the propensity to hoard and noted the different propensities to spend and consume between rich and poor.[20]

Most important is Richard Cantillon. Schumpeter has emphasised how 'few sequences in the history of economic analysis are so important...as is the sequence: Petty–Cantillon–Quesnay' (1954, p. 218).

All three have their places in an account of the pre-Smithian writers concerned with unemployment, or with the adequacy of effective demand and the possible effects of saving. Cantillon's concern with unemployment is expressed in passages like the following. Having estimated the labour force at 25 per cent of the population, he went on:

> If enough employment cannot be found to occupy the 25 persons in a hundred upon work useful and profitable to the estate, I see no objection to encouraging employment which serves only for ornament or amusement...How little soever the labour of a man supplies ornament or even amusement in a state it is worth while to encourage it unless the man find a way to employ himself usefully [1931, p. 91].

Cantillon more than once explains how different ways of increasing the money supply will, in the first instance, increase employment before, in due course, if continued, leading to price rises:

> If the increase of actual money comes from mines of gold or silver in the state the owner of these mines...and all the other workers will increase their expenses in proportion to their gains...They will consequently give employment to several mechanics who had not so much to do before and who for the same reason will increase their expenses.

Later Cantillon examines an increase in the amount of money brought about by investments by foreigners:

> These methods of increasing the money in the state make it more abundant there and diminish the rate of interest. By means of this money the entrepreneurs in the state find it possible to borrow more cheaply to set people on work and to establish manufactures in the hope of profit. The artisans and all those through whose hands this money passes, consume more than they would have done if they had not been employed by means of this money [op. cit., pp. 163 and 191].

For Cantillon (unlike Adam Smith) hoarding was a significant phenomenon: 'All the classes in a state who practice some economy,

---

[19] J. Schumpeter, 1954, p. 284. Hazel Roberts in her monograph holds that 'no modern writer adhering to the belief that economic ills spring in large part from underconsumption has put the case more strongly than Boisguilbert' (1935, p. 287). See also Stephen McDonald's article, 'Boisguilbert: A Neglected Precursor of Aggregate Demand Theories', 1954, pp. 401 and 413.

[20] See 1707, p. 419; and 1695, p. 199.

save and keep out of circulation small amounts of cash till they have enough to invest at interest or profit. Many miserly and timid people bury and hoard cash for considerable periods' (op. cit., p. 147).

The one point which Cantillon misses which would have completed his account would have been to link *variations* in the propensity to hoard with aggregate cyclical fluctuations to which he regarded the economy as subject.

Cantillon has frequently and authoritatively been mentioned as an anticipator of the 'classical' self-adjusting mechanism in international trade.[21] But though he emphasises the contracting and correcting forces set off by a payments surplus or deficit, Cantillon insists how these forces overshoot the mark, with the whole process working out as aggregate cyclical fluctuations rather than showing a tendency to equilibrium. Cantillon describes the process of such a 'circle', as he calls it, foreseeing rather the massive fluctuations of the nineteenth- and twentieth-century business cycle, in domestic and international terms, rather than the smoothly self-equilibrating 'model' of Smith and his followers.

V

The whole of the eighteenth century, in some ways the most important in the whole story, is very largely, though not completely, a blank in Keynes's outline. This may be partly because Heckscher's *Mercantilism*, on which Keynes drew, breaks off at about 1710. The only eighteenth-century writer who receives much more than incidental mention by Keynes in *The General Theory* is Mandeville, whom he cites as a successor of a number of seventeenth-century writers who held to what Heckscher described as 'the deep-rooted belief in the utility of luxury and the evil of thrift', or, as Keynes put it, ascribed 'the evils of unemployment to the insufficiency...of the propensity to consume' (1936, p. 358).

Certainly Mandeville lends no countenance to the supposition that unem-ployment was either entirely voluntary or non-existent, thanks to beneficent self-adjusting mechanisms. On the contrary: 'The labour of the poor, is so far from being a burthen and an imposition upon them; that to have employment is a blessing, which in their addresses to heaven they pray for, and to procure it for the generality of them is the greatest care of every legislature' (1970, pp. 250 and 360).

[21] 'In Richard Cantillon...the self-regulating mechanism is clearly and ably expounded' (J. Viner, 1937, p. 74). On the other hand, Douglas Vickers has noted how Cantillon argued for 'the threefold notion that the thing desired was a high level of economic activity at a high level of employment, that this depended on an appropriate level of monetary circulation, and that if left to itself the working of the monetary system would produce cyclical movements in the level of employment and prosperity' (1959, p. 191).

Keynes, however, very much underestimated Mandeville's influence throughout the eighteenth century, maintaining that his 'doctrine did not reappear in respectable circles for another century, until in the later phase of Malthus' (1936, p. 362).

On the contrary, Mandeville's ideas were highly influential, especially in France. In fact Keynes subsequently, in the foreword to the French edition of *The General Theory*, recognised Montesquieu's support for the kind of effective demand doctrine, which derived to some extent from Mandeville. As a consequence Keynes, rather extravagantly, ranks Montesquieu alongside Adam Smith as an economist.[22]

Furthermore, it can be said that the Smithian (or Klassical) doctrine of the unconditional beneficence of parsimony and frugality emerged to a considerable extent by way of a reaction against Mandeville. It was in reacting critically against Mandeville that Smith's teacher Francis Hutcheson developed 'the notion', as described by Keynes, 'that if people do not spend their money in one way they will spend it in another' (1936, p. 20), thus refuting the need for 'vicious' luxury spending, as argued by Mandeville, for the maintenance of effective demand. As Hutcheson put it: 'Unless therefore all mankind are fully provided not only with all necessaries, but all innocent conveniences and pleasures of life, it is still possible without any vice, by an honest care of families, relations, or some worthy persons in distress, to make the greatest consumption' (1727, p. 63).

If Hutcheson's critical reaction to Mandeville's eulogy of luxury foreshadows somewhat his pupil Adam Smith's doctrine of saving, David Hume, it may be noted, concedes Mandeville's essential economic point: 'By banishing vicious luxury, without curing sloth and an indifference to others, you only diminish industry in the state...Luxury, when excessive, is the source of many ills; but is in general preferable to sloth and idleness, which would commonly succeed in its place' (1955, pp. 31 and 39).[23]

[22] As has been emphasised: 'On n'a jamais assez insisté sur l'influence considérable de Mandeville au XVIII siècle. Pourtant, il est bien peu d'ouvrages sur la science économique ou sociale qui, directement ou indirectement ne lui doivent beaucoup.' Morize mentions Melon, Montesquieu, Voltaire, Diderot, d'Holbach and Helvetius. He continues: 'Son importance est capitale, car, dans cette féconde periode de préparation, il représente le moment décisif où le courant épicurien et sceptique français vient se fondre avec les conceptions économiques anglaises.' A. Morize, *L'Apologie du Luxe au XVIIIe Siècle*, 1909, pp. 68–9. In England Dr Samuel Johnson was an upholder of Mandeville's emphasis on consumption demand.

[23] Smith, on the other hand, criticised Mandeville in his Lectures of 1763 as a purveyor of the fallacy 'that national opulence consists in money', clearly anticipating his own 'real' analysis in *The Wealth of Nations*. (See A. Smith, 1896, pp. 207ff.) Professor Umberto Meoli notes Hume's support for Mandeville's treatment of luxury, as also that of Adam Ferguson in his *Essay on Civil Society* (1767). (See an unpublished paper on 'The Problem of Luxury in the Economic Thought of Condillac'.) It is also of interest that (as Mr M. A. Katouzian has pointed out to me) Smith himself in *The*

When therefore Keynes charged Hume with having 'a foot and a half in the classical world' (1936, p. 343) he seems to have got the proportion the wrong way round. Hume can be said to have more like a foot and a half in the pre-Smithian, pre-classical world. For, regarding luxury, he was rather on the side of Mandeville than that of his fellow Scotsmen, Hutcheson and Smith, while in monetary theory, like many pre-Smithian writers in the seventeenth and eighteenth century, Hume put great stress on the importance of an expanding money supply:

> From the whole of this reasoning we may conclude, that it is of no manner of consequence, with regard to the domestic happiness of a state, whether money be in a greater or less quantity. *The good policy of the magistrate consists only in keeping it, if possible, still increasing; because, by that means, he keeps alive a spirit of industry in the nation,* and increases the stock of labour, in which consists all real power and riches. *A nation, whose money decreases, is actually, at that time, weaker and more miserable than another nation, which possesses no more money, but is on the increasing hand...The worker has not the same employment from the manufacturer and merchant* [1955, p. 40, italics added].

Not only does Hume's concern with the money supply and fear of deflation place him on the side of the so-called 'mercantilist' monetary 'cranks' of the seventeenth and eighteenth centuries: such propositions asserted exactly what was denied and excluded by Smith and Ricardo.

As anticipators of Smithian doctrines we should mention briefly, in addition to Hutcheson, Josiah Tucker and Turgot. Tucker's advocacy of freer trade may have had a general influence on Smith, but he has a brief argument which is especially relevant to the question of an automatic or self-adjusting tendency in aggregate effective demand. In a pamphlet (1752) advocating freedom of immigration and denying that this will lead to unemployment, Tucker asks whether, in the nature of things it is possible for all economic activities and trades to be overstocked (1751, pp. 13–14).[24]

Tucker is suggesting here the proposition that *general* unemployment is impossible, anticipating the subsequent 'classical' slogan regarding 'the impossibility of general over-production'. Tucker is thus arguing that unemployment can only be partial or frictional and will cure itself in a free labour market.

Tucker's pamphlet, incidentally, was translated into French by Turgot, the co-founder, with Adam Smith, of the Klassical doctrine of the rate of interest – as Schumpeter has emphasised. Turgot does

---

Theory of Moral Sentiments (Part IV, Chapter 1) made considerable concessions to Mandeville's regard for the economic beneficence of luxury 'which rouses and keeps in continual motion the industry of mankind'.

[24] It was McCulloch who first called attention to Tucker as an originator of the 'Law of Markets'. (See P. Lambert, 1956, p. 14.)

not state the doctrine in quite the stark, dogmatic terms of Adam Smith ten years later. Nor does he draw out all the implications for government spending and monetary theory and policy to the full consequential extent that Smith does. But the essential points are all there: (1) that the rate of interest smoothly adjusts the supply of savings to the demand by borrowers; (2) that all savings pass '*immediately*' into investment; and (3) that 'economy' or frugality leads to the increase of capital in a nation and luxury to a decrease.[25]

It was this doctrine of Turgot's which, among other points, marked him off from the Physiocrats, to whom in several respects he was very close. For Quesnay emphasised the possibly harmful deflationary effects of hoarding and was not unconditionally, and in all circumstances, opposed to luxury spending. Regarding Quesnay's theory of saving Schumpeter emphasises how it had been 'adumbrated by Boisguilbert':

> In this analytic schema the prompt onward flow of purchasing power is everything. Saving is believed to interrupt it. Hence saving is a sort of public enemy. Quesnay makes it one of his *maximes*: que la totalité des sommes du revenue rentre dans la circulation annuelle et la parcoure dans toute son étendue (VII)...
>
> The similarity with Keynesian views is striking: in itself, saving is sterile and a disturber: it must always be 'offset', and this offsetting is a distinct act that may or may not succeed. A fairly strong anti-saving tradition thus acquired additional support shortly before it almost vanished into thin air [1954, p. 287].[26]

[25] 'It is, therefore, another mistake to suppose that the interest of money in commerce ought to be fixed by the laws of princes. It is a current price, fixed like that of all other merchandise...

It is, therefore, from money that they save, and the annual increase of capital takes place in money: but none of the entrepreneurs make any other use of it than to convert it *immediately* into the different kinds of effects upon which their undertaking depends; and thus this money returns to circulation...

The spirit of economy in a nation tends to augment incessantly the sum of its capitals, to increase the number of lenders, to diminish that of borrowers. The habit of luxury has precisely the contrary effect' (1898, pp. 74, 80, and 98, italics added).

[26] Quesnay's General Maxim VII, cited by Schumpeter is directed strongly against the danger of hoarding, or 'monetary fortunes' (the possibility of which was assumed out of existence by Smith and his followers): 'the whole of the sum of revenue should come back into the annual circulation and run through it to the full extent of its course...it should never be formed into monetary fortunes, or at least those which are formed should be counterbalanced by those which come back into circulation. For otherwise these monetary fortunes would check the distribution of a part of the annual revenue of the nation'. The same point is emphasised in General Maxims XXVII and XXVIII on government expenditure: 'That the government should trouble itself less with economizing than with the operations necessary for the prosperity of the kingdom; for very high expenditure may cease to be excessive by virtue of the increase of wealth...

That the administration of finance, whether in the collection of taxes or in the expenditure of the government should not bring about the formation of monetary fortunes, which steal a portion of the revenue away from circulation, distribution and reproduction.' (See R. L. Meek, 1962, pp. 233 and 237.)

VI

In Keynes's outline not only is the eighteenth century largely a blank: the two most important figures in the whole story are virtually omitted. These two come within nine years of one another, one from each side, at the crucial turning-point which we have been approaching in the previous section and have now reached. They are Sir James Steuart and his *Principles of Political Economy* (1767) and Adam Smith and his *The Wealth of Nations* (1776).

These two works, each to a remarkable extent consistent in itself, epitomise, from the opposite ends of the spectrum, the two contrasting macroeconomic viewpoints and doctrines with which this outline is concerned. If one tries to sum up the contrast in a single assumption or idea, one can find it in that of smooth, rapid, beneficent self-adjusting tendencies: its denial by one and its assertion by the other. It was this powerfully fascinating idea and assumption of general beneficent self-adjustment and self-equilibration which 'made' Smithian and classical political economy. Steuart would not and did not have it. He had, as his editor puts it, 'no very clear model'[27] – which was just what Smith not only had, but asserted as empirically valid for policy purposes. Perhaps we should make it clear that Sir James was not at all a total planner or *dirigiste*. He believed that in certain areas, to some extent, more or less beneficent self-adjusting processes existed. But he did not think that they worked sufficiently smoothly, swiftly, reliably, and justly – in particular, macro-economically, with regard to the level of employment. The government, therefore, 'must be continually in action'. None the less Steuart believed in relying on self-interest, and the value he placed on freedom is demonstrated in the sub-title of his work:

> The principle of self-interest will serve as a general key to this enquiry; and it may, in one sense, be considered as the ruling principle of my subject, and may therefore be traced throughout the whole. This is the main spring, and only motive which a statesman should make use of, to engage a free people to concur in the plans which he lays down in government...
>
> Public spirit, in my way of treating this subject, is as superfluous in the government as it ought to be all-powerful in the statesmen [1770, vol. I, pp. 162–4].

Such views are noteworthy in someone who has been dismissed as 'the last of the Mercantilists'. Steuart's doctrines about 'full employment', as well as his analysis of macroeconomic equilibrium and the use of public works and monetary and fiscal policies for raising the level of employment have, in recent decades, emerged from the

[27] A. S. Skinner, 1966, vol. I, p. lviii.

obscurity in which they languished for so long, and the close similarity with Keynes has been emphasised.[28]

Nine years after Steuart's *Principles* comes *The Wealth of Nations*. For the first time the assumption and assertion of beneficent self-adjustment is applied in general, more or less unqualified terms across most of the whole range of economic processes. Steuart's tiresome problems of the possible dangers of saving, of the money supply, of persistent unemployment, and of the balance of trade, fade away, 'like snow upon the desert's dusty face', before the radiant illumination of the self-adjusting model. Self-equilibration proved so powerfully attractive and fascinating a model and assumption that its general empirical validity came to be taken for granted. In fact, historians of economic thought of classical inclinations seem to have equated the progress of the 'science' of political economy in the eighteenth century (particularly insofar as this progress is represented by the great milestone of *The Wealth of Nations*) with the more and more confident and unqualified assumption, and assertion as empirically valid, of beneficent self-adjusting processes throughout the market system, macro-economically, micro-economically, and internationally. Beneficent self-equilibration provided the great systematising framework round which the 'science' – as it was soon claimed to be by James Mill and Ricardo – developed its 'Laws'. This model provided not only positive illumination but normative guidelines. The whole history of orthodox political economy and economics, in the nineteenth century, and after, depended on this fascinating systematising notion and on the confident qualitative, predictive, comparative-static judgments which could be so magisterially deduced from it. It is *possible* that from the later decades of the eighteenth century onwards the British economy, or important sectors of it, did actually become more self-adjusting, though such a proposition can amount to little more than a speculation very difficult to test. Anyhow, it seems impossible to believe that some dramatic transformation took place between 1767 and 1776.

The foundation of the Smithian model of *macroeconomic* self-adjustment is the saving and investing analysis.[29] This doctrine

---

[28] Professor Douglas Vickers emphasises how in Steuart's work 'is to be found the most complete anticipations of Keynes's general theory' and that 'both these authors fashioned their thought against a background of deflationary conditions' (1959, p. 268). Professor Paul Chamley cannot understand Keynes's omission of any reference to Steuart: 'Would it not constitute an insult to the author of *Essays in Biography* to suppose that he did not know Steuart? Can it be attributed to a maladroit pedantry that he quotes from a whole series of mercantilists but makes an exception precisely of the writer whose doctrine contains so many anticipations and in the footsteps of whom he follows with the greatest precision'? (1962, p. 311). See also S. R. Sen, 1947.

[29] Professor Haim Barkai has given a most interesting exposition of Smith's saving and investment analysis, describing it (rather anachronistically) as 'a specifically Smithian version of Say's Law' and as 'Say's Law with a vengeance' (see 1969, pp. 396 and 410).

constitutes the key to the whole Smithian or Klassical structure of theory and policy and is stated with immense and repetitive emphasis in Chapter 3 of Book II of *The Wealth of Nations*. The saving and investment analysis justifies the condemnation of luxury spending and the emphasis on the unconditional beneficence of 'frugality'. Given political security, hoarding is 'crazy' (Smith's adjective). This fits in logically with Smith's account of money, and, given a framework of banking legislation,[30] justifies what might be called monetary, or macroeconomic *laissez-faire*, as well as the Ricardo (or 'Treasury') view against public investment.

It should, however, perhaps be emphasised that Smith's macroeconomic doctrines relate primarily to saving and investment, money, public expenditure and borrowing. They do not contain any complete, direct, or precise theory of *employment*. Smith's doctrines simply imply that unemployment cannot arise from deficiencies or instabilities of effective demand which the state can do anything to alleviate. Smith does refer to 'the competition for employment' reducing wages but he does not argue that all unemployment will be completely or immediately removed by this process, which he refers to as operative mainly in the stationary and regressive states where the demand for labour is constant or declining. In the stationary economy: 'There could seldom be any scarcity of hands . . . The hands, on the contrary, would, in this case, naturally multiply beyond their employment, and the labourers would be obliged to bid against one another in order to get it.'

In the regressive state where the demand for labour was declining, 'many would not be able to find employment even upon these hard terms' (1937, pp. 71 and 73).

In this Smithian model, with a fixed wages fund, flexible wages must increase the amount of employment. But if the fund is stationary or declining some unemployment may persist until overtaken by the harsh adjustments of population reduction.

As Schumpeter has emphasised, Smith's monetary and macroeco-

[30] For Smith's optimism regarding the monetary and banking framework see Professor S. G. Checkland's article on 'Adam Smith and the Bankers', 1976, pp. 504ff. Smith was confident that the banking system was maintaining, and would maintain, the money supply. As Professor C. H. Wilson comments regarding the mercantilists: 'Much thought and policy was devoted to ensuring that a supply of precious metal was maintained adequate for a sound and plentiful currency. The anxiety lest "a scarcity of coin" should slow down the volume of trade and bring about an economic depression affected writers repeatedly every time a crisis threatened. To Adam Smith such anxieties were absurd. Yet his sense of historical change was not strong and his own chapter on Metallic and Paper Money contained implications which he does not fully consider. If the growth of new methods of payment had been of such significance in the century before 1776, how had Mun and his contemporaries fared without these later devices of paper money, bank credit, etc., whose effects Adam Smith found so beneficial?' (1958, p. 17). See also above Chapter I, Section VI.

nomic model in *The Wealth of Nations* represents the victory of 'real' analysis and a pro-saving theory for 150 years to come. He goes on to support Keynes's generalisation regarding nineteenth-century orthodoxy and emphasises the long supremacy of the Turgot–Smith saving and investment theory which

> proved almost unbelievably hardy. It is doubtful whether Alfred Marshall had advanced beyond it, certain that J. S. Mill had not. Böhm-Bawerk no doubt added a new branch to it but substantially he subscribed to Turgot's propositions. Secondly, the theory was not only swallowed by the large majority of economists: it was swallowed hook, line and sinker. As if Law – and others – had never existed, one economist after another kept on repeating that only (voluntary) saving was capital creating. And one economist after another failed to look askance at that word 'immediately'. But in effect...this came to mean that every decision to save coincides with a corresponding decision to invest so that saving is transformed into (real) capital practically without hitch and as a matter of course [1954, p. 325].

Sir John Hicks, noting the significance of the Smithian revolution, explains its triumph in terms of the power of the self-adjusting model. Seeking an explanation, Sir John enquires:

> How is it to be explained? It is not simply the reaction against Mercantilism; Hume was equally against Mercantilism, but Hume's Essay on Money is not 'anti-Keynesian' in the way that Smith is...
>
> I believe that it is to be explained – that the whole change is to be explained – if we attribute it to the power of a model...
>
> ...It was because the model paid no attention to plans and expectations that it neglected uncertainty and liquidity; so that the bridge between real theory and monetary theory, of the possibility of which Hume had had some inkling, remained unbuilt. The only monetary theory which could match the static real theory was one which concentrated upon the more mechanical aspects of the monetary system; this is just what the 'classical' Quantity Theory was. The responsibility for all this goes back to Adam Smith; it is the reverse side of his great achievement [1965, p. 41].

VII

We now come to much the most discussed part of the story. The classical period proper (in the non-Keynesian sense) has always been the most cultivated phase in the history of economic thought. Keynes himself devoted much attention to Malthus and Ricardo and included the two Mills in his original list of Klassicals.

Let us note, first, that the supremacy of the Smithian doctrines was not achieved without much dissent and resistance, especially in the opening decades of the nineteenth century. It might, in any case, seem improbable that war and post-war conditions would be conducive to the rise to dominance of the idea of smooth and beneficent macro-economic self-equilibration. It may well, for a time, have been touch and go as to what kind of orthodoxy, if any, was going to dominate monetary and macroeconomic theorising – the views of Smith, revised and developed, or views fundamentally critical of Smith. In the opening decade of the nineteenth century the explicit or implicit critics of the Smithian doctrine included some highly important figures such as Bentham, Malthus, and Lauderdale, as well as lesser writers such as Spence and Blake. Thornton's great work, though not explicitly critical of the Smithian doctrine, is not strictly compatible with it at some points and opened up a superior alternative analysis. Sismondi[31] and Torrens, and later on towards the middle of the century, Attwood, Chalmers, Wakefield, Scrope, Cayley, Cazenove, Lalor, Sleeman, and Pettman could also be mentioned as having to some extent diverged from, or rebelled, in one way or another, against the Smithian–Ricardian orthodoxy.[32] It is impossible to say whether, purely numerically, if some poll of 'economists' had been taken, a majority would have followed or rejected orthodoxy. (Anyhow, the orthodox, if James Mill had had his way, would have been bound to win an overwhelming majority by defining the term 'economist' so as to require agreement with their doctrines (1966, p. 382).) But there can be no doubt as to which side of the debate achieved the prestige of orthodoxy and dominated policy. That the Smithian doctrine won through at this juncture and attained its long-dominant position may be traced to two initial factors, in addition to the fascination of the self-adjusting model.

(1) Though the dissenters rejected the general conclusion that the economic system was adequately, and sufficiently smoothly, self-adjusting in macro-economic terms, several of them – as we shall briefly notice – involved themselves in a logically damaging acceptance of the basic Turgot–Smith saving-is-investment doctrine, together with the assumption that hoarding does not exist. The one major figure who at this stage explicitly went to the root of the Smithian analysis of saving is Bentham, with his excellent and original analysis of inflation in *The True Alarm* (1804) which was, of course, suppressed through the efforts of James Mill and Ricardo.[33]

(2) The second reason for the triumph of the Smithian doctrines, and for their achieving the hold of a dominant orthodoxy, was the powerful and dogmatic advocacy and influence of James Mill and Ricardo, and later J. S. Mill. J. B. Say has also been assigned a

---

[31] For the important contribution of Sismondi see T. Sowell, 1972, Chapter 2. Professor Sowell holds that the basic features of Malthus's analysis are present in Sismondi's *Nouveaux Principes*. I have also learned very much from a paper on Sismondi by Professor Piero Barucci (1975).

[32] On these writers see B. A. Corry, 1962 (for Attwood, Chalmers, Lalor and others); G. S. L. Tucker, 1960 (for Cayley and Lalor); R. D. C. Black, 1967 (for Sleeman and Pettman); and B. J. Gordon, 1967 (for Cayley, Cazenove, Sleeman and Pettman).

[33] On Bentham's trenchant criticism of the Smithian analysis of saving, on his distinction between conditions of full employment and of some unemployment, and for the role of government in the latter case, see my article 'Bentham as an Economist', 1956.

prominent part here in later accounts, but we would argue that his writings were, in fact, much more ambiguous and inconsistent than those of Mill and Ricardo.

James Mill: The role of James Mill was absolutely vital – as it was more generally in the instigation and promotion of Ricardian political economy. In *Commerce Defended* (1808) Mill drew on the authority of Adam Smith and his saving-is-investing doctrine, and elaborated this in terms of the ambiguous rigmarole about the equality of supply and demand, which he repeated, just as dogmatically in his *Elements* (1820).[34]

J. B. Say: The contribution of J. B. Say, on the other hand, though his name and his alleged 'Law' have loomed large in subsequent debate, seems to have been highly ambiguous and overrated. To start with, 'Say's Law' so glibly and frequently cited and defined, is an unhistorical construct. J. B. Say never set down any single clearly defined proposition as his 'Law'. He himself refers to his 'theory', and Ricardo calls it 'M. Say's doctrine'. In his *Traité* he simply had a chapter 'Des Debouches', which was expanded from three to a dozen pages through successive editions (1803–41), 'growing more woolly all the time', as Schumpeter observes (1954, p. 615).[35] The main purpose

---

[34] See James Mill, 1966, pp. 326 and 329: 'It is undeniable, that the demand, which every man brings, is equal to the supply which he brings...It makes no difference to say, that perhaps he only wanted money; for money is itself goods; and besides, no man wants money but in order to lay it out, either in articles of productive, or articles of unproductive consumption.

'Every man having a demand and a supply, both equal; if any commodity be in greater quantity than the demand, some other commodity must be in less.

'If every man has a demand and supply both equal, the demand and supply in the aggregate are always equal.'

Let us contrast what became an 'underground' or 'underworld' view as expounded by an anonymous reviewer of Mill's *Elements*. After a discussion of 'the propensity of man to lay up in store or to consume' the anonymous critic goes on: 'Savings do not become capital, unless they are employed reproductively; and it is the difficulty of finding modes of so applying them, not the strong inclination of man to spend all that he can obtain, that opposes a bar to the rapid accumulation of capital. Any plan, therefore, of increasing the capital of the country by an artificial diminution of consumption, proceeds upon a supposition of very dubious truth. You may, by such means diminish the amount of the unproductive consumption of the country, but you will not necessarily increase its productive consumption. The more probable result will be, either that the amount of annual production will be lessened, or that a proportion of the unproductive consumption will be shifted from one class of commodities to another' (Anon., 1822, p. 158, quoted by J. Viner, 1964, p. 257). Professor B. J. Gordon has called attention to the volume of often anonymous but 'vigorous and not unintelligent criticism; in influential journals, directed against Say's Law and Smithian–Ricardian orthodoxy': 'see Say's Law, Effective Demand and the Contemporary British Periodicals', 1965, pp. 435ff.

[35] It would be interesting to know who first used the term 'Say's *Law*'. As Professor T. Sowell has observed, those supporting 'Say's Law' 'did not clearly distinguish an identity from a behavioral equation, and drifted unconsciously back and forth between the two concepts, tending under polemical pressure to adopt the impregnable tautology'. As Say wrote to Malthus in 1827: 'Our discussion on markets begins to be no more than a dispute over words' (see T. Sowell, 1972, p. 121).

of the chapter seems to have been to extol the smooth-working harmonies of the market mechanism, domestically and internationally, while echoing the then fashionable denunciations of the alleged 'mercantilist' fallacies about the money supply. In the course of Say's chapter, definitions and equilibrium conditions, short and long run, with assertions or assumptions about self-equilibrating tendencies, get conflated together.

Moreover, Say himself did not uphold the Smithian doctrines consistently. At one point he even rejects the vital assumption of no hoarding and attacks Ricardo for holding to it:

> Mr. Ricardo insists that, notwithstanding taxes and other charges, there is always as much industry as capital employed: and that all capital saved is always employed, because the interest is not suffered to be lost. *On the contrary, many savings are not invested, when it is difficult to find employment for them*...Besides, Mr. Ricardo is completely refuted...by our present circumstances, when capitals are quietly sleeping in the coffers of their proprietors [1841, p. 45n].[36]

Secondly, Say was not consistent in placing a complete reliance on self-adjusting processes. He was prepared to recommend public works to counter technological unemployment – a proposal which Smith and Ricardo would presumably have regarded as a wasteful diversion of resources: 'Une administration bienveillante peut préparer, d'avance de l'occupation pour les bras inoccupés, soit en formant, a ses frais, des entreprises d'utilité publique, comme un canal, une route, un grand édifice; soit en provoquant une colonisation, une translation d'un lieu dans un autre' (1841, p. 86n).[37]

D. Ricardo: As Keynes recognised, the most logical and influential upholder of Smithian or Klassical doctrines, and of what he first called 'Mr. Mill's idea' (1814) and later 'M. Say's doctrine' (1820), was, of course, David Ricardo. In his *Principles* Ricardo restates the Smithian doctrine, as verbally reformulated by Mill and Say as follows:

> No man produces, but with a view to consume or sell, and he never sells, but with an intention to purchase some other commodity, which may be immediately useful to him, or which may contribute to future production. By producing, then, he necessarily becomes either the consumer of his own goods, or the purchaser and consumer of the goods of some other person. *It is not to be supposed that he should, for any length of time, be ill-informed of the commodities which he can most advantageously produce*, to attain the object which he has in view, namely, the possession of other goods; and, therefore, it is not probable that he will continually produce a commodity for which there is no demand [1951, vol. I, p. 290, italics added].

Here is the logic of complete, easy self-adjustment, *with perfect knowledge, and therefore smooth and rapid equilibration confidently assumed.*

---

[36] Quoted by S. Hollander, 1969, p. 318, italics added.
[37] See also D. H. Macgregor, 1949, p. 113.

But Ricardo's great achievement and contribution was to carry the logic of this doctrine over into the policy arena, driving home inexorably the implications regarding current policy issues for the enlightenment of MPs and Committees of the Lords and Commons. Not only can employment not be reduced by credit expansion: it cannot be reduced directly by public works as, later in the year (1821), Ricardo reminded the Commons: 'When he heard the honourable members talk of employing capital in the formation of roads and canals, they appeared to overlook the fact that the capital thus employed must be withdrawn from some other quarter' (1952, vol. v, p. 32).

This is the doctrine regarding public investment which when repeated to the House of Commons 110 years later, by (strangely enough) Winston Churchill, came to be known as 'the Treasury view'. Ricardo, therefore, draws out certain policy implications a little further, or at any rate rather more explicitly than Adam Smith.

Ricardo certainly sustains as rigorously as Smith, and no less consistently, the various implications and ramifications of the Smithian doctrine. It is simply on the same particular point as Smith that Ricardo seems to be rather less than fully consistent, that is, regarding the advantages of paper money in flexibility, and in stabilising the value of money.[38]

Finally, regarding the implications for the employment of labour, Ricardo spelt these out rather more explicitly than had Smith (in spite of 'neo-Ricardian' claims to the contrary). Professor Garegnani has written: 'Ricardo saw no inconsistency between free competition and unemployment of labour. In his view lower wages could eliminate unemployment only by decreasing the growth of population or by favouring accumulation' (1972, p. 278).

This may be 'neo-Ricardian' doctrine, but it happens to contradict what *Ricardo* actually said, and it is more like what Malthus maintained and Ricardo explicitly denied. Writing to Malthus, Ricardo argued:

> You say 'we know from repeated experience that the money price of labour never falls till many workmen have been for some time out of work'. I know no such thing, and if wages were previously high, I can see no reason whatever why they should not fall *before* many labourers are thrown out of work. All general reasoning I apprehend is in favour of my view of this question, for *why should some agree to go without any wages while others were most liberally rewarded?* Once more I must say that *a sudden and diminished demand for labour in this case must mean a diminished reward to the labourer and*

---

[38] See his plan for an 'Economical and Secure Currency', 1951, vol. IV, pp. 55–8. See also L. Robbins, 1968, pp. 138–9 and J. R. Hicks, 1969, p. 259. Sir John suggests that the classical economists had also 'at the back of their minds' a short-period theory in which expansions and contractions of the money supply will stimulate or depress output. It was certainly a remarkable feat of Ricardian abstraction to have kept this 'short-period' (i.e. realistic) theory so far to 'the back of his mind' in the years 1815–20.

not a diminished employment of him . . . and this will be so in order that his employer may have an adequate motive for employing him at all, which he certainly would not have if his share of the produce were reduced so low as to make increased production an evil rather than a benefit to him [1952, vol. IX, p. 25, italics added].

Ricardo is dealing here with a case where wages are 'high', but his insistence on how competition and wage-flexibility reduce unemployment applies whatever the initial level of wages. Of course this argument does not deny the further effect of a wage-cut in the form of a reduction of population. But wage flexibility will help to maintain employment while lower wages force a contraction of numbers on larger families.

T. R. Malthus: In his outline of the history of thought Keynes devoted more attention to Malthus than to any other economist on either side of the controversy (with the possible exception of Pigou). It was in his additions of 1933 to his essay on Malthus, with his account of the then recently discovered epistolary debate with Ricardo on effective demand, that Keynes developed the notion of a dominant, Ricardian orthodoxy winning out over, and driving 'underground', the ideas rather unsatisfactorily represented by Malthus.[39]

It is hardly surprising that the combination of Keynes's bold challenge and Malthus's intriguing and inspissated ambiguity has generated an extensive controversial literature, of international dimensions, arguing over such questions as 'Were Keynes's claims about Malthus justified?', and 'What did Malthus really mean?'. But the concepts involved in such arguments are so imprecise that it is also hardly surprising that in due course it was being observed that 'the question "Was Malthus an anticipator of Keynes?" seems to have received every possible answer' (Black, 1967, p. 59).

For there is room for disagreement not only as to what Malthus's answers were, but as to what questions he was trying to answer. Like most economists, until comparatively very recently, Malthus often did not sharply or regularly distinguish between the long-run growth of capacity and shorter-run variations in the employment of resources. But the most important difficulty arises from the extent to which Malthus committed himself to the Smithian saving-is-investing doctrine. For on this point, as on others, over his long career, Malthus changed his ideas without explicitly recognising or recording his changes, which have not been sufficiently noted by some modern commentators. In his *Essay* of 1798 Malthus strongly endorsed not only the saving-is-investing proposition but also the unqualified Smithian

[39] 'With *The Means to Prosperity*, the essay on Malthus marks an important stage on the way to the *General Theory*' (D. Moggridge, 1973, vol. XIII, p. 419). But the Keynesian use of the adjective 'classical' does not appear in this essay.

emphasis on the benefits, social and individual, of parsimony: 'Dr. Adam Smith has very justly observed, that nations, as well as individuals, grow rich by parsimony and poor by profusion; and that, therefore, *every frugal man was a friend and every spendthrift an enemy to his country*' (1798, p. 282, italics added).

By the time of the first edition of his *Principles* (1820) Malthus, without explicitly mentioning any change of view, had completely abandoned his endorsement of Smith's doctrines of the general benefits of parsimony. But he still endorsed Smith's saving-is-investment doctrine: 'It is stated by Adam Smith, *and it must be allowed to be stated justly*, that the produce which is annually saved is as regularly consumed as that which is annually spent, but that it is consumed by a different set of people.'[40]

However, in the posthumously published second edition, the emphatic endorsement (in the words italicised above) of the Smithian proposition is removed. Again there is no explicit recognition of the change, the logic of which is not completely carried through elsewhere in the *Principles*, though much of Malthus's argument therein is inconsistent with the Smithian saving-is-investing proposition, which he had endorsed in the first edition. Perhaps Torrens was going rather far when he observed that: 'In the leading questions of economic science, Mr. Malthus scarcely ever embraced a principle, which he did not subsequently abandon.'[41]

But this complaint is not entirely devoid of justification, as also is Ricardo's at the end of his *Notes on Malthus*: '*Mr. Malthus never appears to remember* that to save is to spend, as surely, as what he exclusively calls spending.'[42]

In other words Malthus was constantly, though usually unconsciously or inexplicitly, trying to break out, or actually breaking out, of his original Smithian assumptions. It does not seem that even Malthus should be charged with assigning a very fundamental role in his argument to a proposition which he '*never*' appeared to remember.[43]

---

[40] Ricardo took this as 'an important admission from Mr. Malthus...at variance with some of the doctrines which he afterwards maintains' (see 1951, vol. II, p. 15, italics added).

[41] *Essay on the External Corn Trade*, 1815, p. ix, quoted by M. Paglin, 1961, p. 157 (where there is an excellent discussion of this subject in Chapter V). Nor was the inconsistency only on Malthus's side. In a letter to Ricardo, Malthus notes J. B. Say's admission 'qu'il y a beaucoup d'épargnes qui ne se placent pas lorsque les emplois sont difficiles'. Malthus claims that here Say '*fully concedes all that I contend for*' (Ricardo, 1952, vol. VIII, p. 260, cited by S. Hollander, 1969, p. 319 (italics added)).

[42] See 1952, vol. II, p. 449 (italics added). As R. G. Link has put it: 'Malthus made a logical jump and wrote as if an increase in saving involved a reduction in spending' (1959, p. 70).

[43] For example, Malthus writes of 'redundant capital'; of how 'it is no contradiction in terms to say that both labour and capital may be redundant, compared with the means of employing them profitably'; of how 'capital would be seeking employment

To the numerous quotations bandied about in support of opposing interpretations of Malthus we shall venture to add simply the final paragraph of the second edition of Malthus's *Principles*. Malthus is writing of the distress caused by recurring depressions:

> Theoretical writers are too apt, in their calculations, to overlook these intervals; but eight or ten years, recurring, not unfrequently, are serious spaces in human life. They amount to a serious sum of happiness or misery, according as they are prosperous or adverse, and leave the country in a very different state at their termination. In prosperous times the mercantile classes often realize fortunes, which go far towards securing them against the future; but unfortunately the working classes, though they share in the general prosperity, do not share in it so largely as in the general adversity. They may suffer the greater distress in a period of low wages, but cannot be adequately compensated by a period of high wages. To them fluctuations must always bring more evil than good; and, with a view to the happiness of the great mass of society, it should be our object, as far as possible to maintain peace, and an equable expenditure [1836, p. 437].

These last words have an element of the prophetic. In fact, Malthus is rejecting here the treatment of aggregate fluctuations as mere 'frictions' and the dismissal of stabilisation measures as impossible, unnecessary, or undesirable. *Historically, it was on just this point that English economists, oblivious of Malthus's final message, belatedly took up the problem of macroeconomic stability and the business cycle a half to three quarters of a century later, and began to put forward public works policies in defiance of the Smithian–Ricardian doctrine that government could only divert, not add to, investment and employment.* A recent thorough study of the treatment of the problem of unemployment has justifiably observed:

> For fifty years after the Poor Law reform of 1834 unemployment as a serious theoretical and practical question was virtually ignored by English economic theorists and social reformers...
> In the mid-1880s, however, social investigators began to observe that irregular employment could have a chronically depressive effect upon the living standards of a whole community [J. Harris, 1972, pp. 1 and 35].

These many decades of neglect by economists would not have happened if Malthus's closing words rather than the dominant Smithian–Ricardian orthodoxy had prevailed.

It might be noted that Keynes himself did not use such terms as 'precursor' or 'anticipator'. Nor did he claim that Malthus produced a clear and satisfactory argument or a theory precisely resembling his

but would not easily find it...under these circumstances, the saving from revenue to add to capital...would only aggravate the distresses of the capitalist'; and of how increased 'saving...contributes to explain the cause of the diminished demand for commodities' (1836, pp. 349, 414–15, and 421). One difficulty in understanding Malthus may be that – as Dr Pullen has pointed out – he does not use the term 'investment' in either of the two editions of his *Principles* (see J. Pullen, 1974, p. 575).

own.[44] Though it may be slightly exaggerated, there is much justification for Keynes's complaint: 'The almost total obliteration of Malthus's line of approach and the complete domination of Ricardo's for a period of a hundred years has been a disaster to the progress of economics' (1933, p. 141).

Though the 'domination' was not quite complete, it was considerable, and very consequential both for policy and the analysis of saving and investment.

Here again Schumpeter comes down broadly in support of the Keynesian view. Malthus, Schumpeter claims,

> treated total output (Marshall's 'national dividend') not, like Ricardo, as a datum, but as the chief variable to be explained: Therefore Malthus should indeed, though for a reason that does not coincide with that which induced Lord Keynes to arrive at a similar result, stand in the history of analysis not only as the author of a valid alternative to Ricardo's theory but as the sponsor (or rather as one of the sponsors) of the victorious one. This is much. At the same time, it is not all. It is perfectly compatible with recognition of these facts that much less ingenuity went into Malthus's than into Ricardo's analytic schema, and that the former was throughout in the most unenviable position an economist can be in, namely, in the position of having to defend plain sense against another man's futile but clever pirouettes [1954, p. 483].[45]

Regarding Malthus, we shall not venture to describe him as a 'precursor' or 'forerunner', or as a 'Keynesian'. It is not clear enough what the precise qualifications are for these appellations. But, in any case, Malthus rebelled against doctrines of macroeconomic self-adjustment and self-equilibration and if the similarities between his and Keynes's ideas have been exaggerated by some, *so have the dissimilarities by others.* We would accept the conclusion of Professor Samuel Hollander's thorough study: 'We must take issue with those who see no Keynesian affinity – because 'savings are invested' – in their interpretations of Malthus. This approach fails to consider the entire analysis of the post-war crisis and the recognition of involuntary unemployment which may not be amenable to correction by money-wage reductions.'[46]

[44] 'Since Malthus *was unable to explain clearly* (apart from an appeal to the facts of common observation) how and why effective demand could be deficient or excessive, *he failed to furnish an alternative construction*' (Keynes, 1936, p. 32, italics added).

[45] We can only express a *most emphatic support* for the philosophical preference for 'plain sense' as against 'clever pirouettes' indicated by Schumpeter, as contrasted with Professor G. J. Stigler's judgment: 'The triumph of Ricardo over Malthus cannot be regretted by the modern economist; it is more important that good logic win over bad than good insight win over poor' (1965, p. 324). Insight *ought* to win every time.

[46] 1969, pp. 306ff. As R. G. Link has put it regarding Malthus and Keynes: 'The great similarity lies in the discussion of aggregate demand, with the description of the way in which the level of demand is connected with the distribution of property, and with the incomes of the main classes of society' (1959, p. 71). Mr Andrew Skinner also after a thorough and discerning survey concludes that 'in Malthus and Keynes we have two recognisably similar critics of two recognisably similar systems' (1969, p. 195).

We would simply emphasise further (1) Malthus's concept of aggregate effective demand; and (2) his concern with the instability of employment.

J. S. Mill: With J. S. Mill the Smithian macroeconomic and monetary doctrines begin to lose some of the pristine firmness and consistency of outline displayed in *The Wealth of Nations* and in the statements of James Mill and Ricardo. At one or two points important ambivalences and contrasts began to open up, though the preponderant impression remains of the Smithian doctrines being as dogmatically asserted as ever. We shall not quote further from the various passages in the *Principles* and other writings where Mill powerfully reasserts the doctrines of Adam Smith, Ricardo, and his father. However, Ricardian economic orthodoxy succeeded in turning even J. S. Mill into a dogmatist. Remarkably uncharacteristic in its intolerance is Mill's castigation of earlier economists and of 'the shallowness of the political reasonings of the last two centuries'. Mill goes on to explain: 'In opposition to these palpable absurdities, it was triumphantly established by political economists, that consumption never needs encouragement. All which is produced is already consumed, either for the purpose of reproduction or enjoyment. The person who saves his income is no less a consumer than he who spends it' (1844, pp. 47–8).

The two contrasting lines of thought, which, if he had followed them through further than he did, would have led Mill into opposition to the Smithian doctrines of self-adjustment, consisted (1) of his analysis of the demand for cash in his essay 'Of the Influence of Consumption on Production' (1829–30); and (2) his revised attitude to government spending in an economy approaching the stationary state (*Principles*, IV.V.I).

As regards (1), Mill seems to treat as a minor emendation what, in fact, is a very major limitation, or even refutation of his father's version of the Smithian doctrine, that is, that it only applies to a barter economy and not to actual monetary economies. Anyhow, J. S. Mill holds that the appropriate policy conclusions, to the effect that there is nothing government should attempt with regard to aggregate stabilisation, need no revision in the light of the crucial qualification which he introduced. Although he attempted a considerable revision and extension of classical doctrines on economic policy, as Professor Schwartz has shown, Mill's analysis of fluctuations in the demand for money and of crises left him rigidly orthodox in the 'assumption underlying all his work, namely the impossibility of prolonged involuntary unemployment' (1972, p. 38).[47]

---

[47] R. G. Link has also emphasised how Mill regarded 'the problem of cyclical unemployment' as 'unimportant'; also his 'neglect of depression as a social problem'; and how Mill believed that 'the normal state of affairs was a state of full employment' (1959, pp. 168, 177 and 179).

Mill's influence was throughout on the side of the orthodoxy which pursued 'the will of the wisp of an automatic monetary policy...The currency system could be designed so that it managed itself; and the recommendation of any cure for social evils based on the manipulation of the monetary system could be left to cranks' (op. cit., pp. 40–1).[48]

In fact there was no need for the government to be responsible for a steadily increasing money supply.

(2) The second element which Mill introduces which contrasts with, though does not logically contradict, the Smithian doctrines, consists of his treatment of the 'Consequences of the Tendency of Profits to a Minimum'. Mill held that as profits decline to a minimum with the approach of the stationary state – from which, according to Mill, the British economy was only 'a hand's breadth' away – this 'greatly weakens, in a wealthy and industrious country, the force of the economical argument against the expenditure of public money for really valuable, even though industriously unproductive purposes' (1909, IV.V.I).

This might be taken as suggesting a revision of the Ricardian view of public expenditure as deployed in Mill's early criticism of Blake. But this seems rather to be another case where Mill suggests, or points towards, new vistas in economic policy-making, or political economy, conflicting with the views of Smith, Ricardo, and his father, but where he himself fears to tread or follow up. Mill is not here necessarily abandoning the full employment assumption. For government expenditure to be increased the resources will always *have* to be withdrawn from other employments, but not necessarily from *productive* employments, as the stationary state is approached.[49]

There seems, therefore, to be little doubt that, in spite of the contrasting possibilities which he seemed very tentatively to open up, the great influence of Mill worked, on balance, strongly towards sustaining Smithian orthodoxy. That also was the direction taken by his two later disciples, Fawcett and Cairnes.

[48] See also Mill's article of 1844 on 'The Currency Question' (quoted by F. W. Fetter, 1965, p. 187): 'There are at this day numerous persons who can read and write, and some who think themselves oracles of wisdom, who can see no harm in emancipating a paper currency from the restraint of convertibility...There are writers of pretension, not only out of Bedlam, but even, we can assure Sir Robert Peel, out of Birmingham, who think it the duty of the legislature periodically to degrade the standard (*or to authorize an issue of inconvertible paper exactly equivalent*) *in proportion as the progress of industry creates an increase of production and a multiplication of pecuniary transactions*. But it is not against these extreme aberrations that it is now necessary to contend.' A hundred years later Mill would, of course, have found the leaders among such 'writers of pretension' coming from Chicago rather than Bedlam or Birmingham.

[49] My account of Mill's views on crises (1953a, pp. 346–56) seems to exaggerate somewhat the extent to which J. S. Mill diverged from the Smithian doctrines of his father and Ricardo, and the significance of these divergences.

VIII

We have cited earlier Schumpeter's emphasis on the durability of the Smithian, or Turgot–Smith, saving and investment doctrine, and on how it is doubtful whether Marshall had advanced beyond it, and how Böhm-Bawerk substantially subscribed to it. Allied with this saving and investment doctrine, and developing from the related Smithian doctrine of the fallacy of 'mercantilist' worries about the money supply, was the nineteenth-century gold standard dogma. This, from soon after the Napoleonic wars onwards, took on in established circles, according to Professor F. W. Fetter, much of the authority of an article of religious faith. The gold standard dogma became the main form in which Smithian, *laissez-faire*, monetary and macro-economics justified itself, in terms of public policy, in the century down to 1914. According to Professor Fetter's account: 'Among economists from the 1820s on the gold standard was a matter of economic theology rather than economic analysis. Other aspects of monetary and banking policy might be treated in analytical terms, but *questioning the standard was not a proper subject for discussion for a man who called himself an economist*' (1965, p. 142, italics added).

Professor Fetter's explanation of this phenomenon runs partly in terms of profound distrust and scepticism regarding the policies of Government, or of a private monopoly like the Bank of England, which, it was strongly felt, should on no account be allowed the slightest discretion in 'managing' the currency. But the economic theory which supported this attitude predicted that monetary policies had little effect on aggregate income and employment. This theory derived from the Ricardian full employment assumption and hence the Smithian saving and investing doctrine. In fact, in the nineteenth century Professor Fetter even assigns a primary role to the monetary ideas:

> The strength of Say's Law, with its assumption of full employment, probably was the result rather than the cause of monetary thinking. Instead of being responsible for the monetary ideas of the economists of the period, it appears to have been accepted by them as a means of bolstering monetary thinking that had emerged out of their observance of recent history and out of their distrust of discretion by a Government dominated by an aristocracy and by a Bank run by a 'company of traders' [op. cit., p. 143].

Surely historically there can be no doubt that in the beginning was the Smith–Turgot saving and investment doctrine, and that this in turn had been elaborated and propagated by James Mill and Ricardo *before* the rise of the orthodox gold standard ideas of the nineteenth century. Moreover the gold standard orthodoxy was able to take over because it was based on the Smithian flexibility assumption that the economic system would in fact adjust smoothly, or, by allowing the simple system of natural liberty to operate, could easily be rendered effectively adjustable, to whatever changes in the money supply were necessary for maintaining, *or returning to*, the gold standard parities. Smith's flexibility assumption was taken especially far in the two serious contractions involved in Britain's return to gold parities in 1819 and 1925.[50] It was on the basis of this Smithian–Ricardian assumption that the gold standard orthodoxy developed a certain power of its own in shaping the City of London's largely *laissez-faire* attitude to macroeconomic policy.

Anyhow, the rapid and extensive loss of credibility and influence undergone around 1870 by classical orthodoxy, in the form of the Ricardo–Mill theories of value and wages, left, *for the moment*, unscathed the doctrines of Smithian–Ricardian macro-economics – in spite of the temporary waverings earlier detectable in parts of J. S. Mill's writings. The increased emphasis on the demand side in the theory of value, or micro-economics, was not at once accompanied by any renewal of interest in the *aggregate* demand concept. However, certain seeds had been sown, though when they began to germinate the growth was at first patchy and untidy.[51]

Jevons: Meanwhile, Jevons, the leading rebel against the orthodox theories of wages and value maintained by 'the Ricardo–Mill economics', as he called it, was in close and full agreement with Cairnes – sometimes called 'the last of the classicals' – with regard to aggregate demand and supply. In an elementary textbook he reproduced the Turgot–Smith saving-is-investing doctrine.[52] It is paradoxical that

[50] As Lord Robbins has put it, in 1819 Ricardo 'supported the recommendation then made...for a return to the old parity. Moreover it must be admitted that, during the crushing deflation of 1815 onwards, the Classical writers and those under their influence, exhibited no real awareness of the cause of the contemporary troubles alleging all sorts of explanations other than the obvious one of contraction of the circulation. It is not to the Classical Economists but to those who subsequently – partly by their own fault – became regarded as currency-cranks, like the Attwoods, that we have to turn for the true explanation of what happened in those disastrous years' (1976, p. 72).The 'Classical Economists' were, of course, those who were broadly accepting and applying the Smithian flexibility assumption. Ricardo applied it in specially drastic and extreme terms.

[51] What may be called the Jevonian and the Keynesian 'revolutions' may well be seen as the two legs or halves of an anti-classical or anti-Ricardian counter-revolution, which restored demand to its rightful place, first micro-economically and then macro-economically: i.e. to the place which it had generally held before Smith and Ricardo, and which it had mostly retained outside Britain (which had been dominated for a century or more by its peculiar classical exaggerations). It is of some historical interest to seek to explain why the first Jevonian leg of the counter-revolution came a half to three quarters of a century before the second, Keynesian leg, and not the other way round.

[52] See 1878, p. 22: 'If every person were to save his money instead of spending it, trade, they think, would languish and workmen would be out of employment... *The argument is a bad fallacy*. The fact is that a person who has riches cannot help employing labour of some kind or other.'

Jevons was, nevertheless, a great pioneer in trade cycle research, as well as in the construction of index-numbers. But he seems to have pursued these studies quite separately, without relating them to his doctrines of money, saving and aggregate demand. All the same, this specialist study of cyclical fluctuations by a leading academic theorist marks a recognition of the significance of problems of macroeconomic instability which goes at least a step or two beyond J. S. Mill's treatment in his *Principles*, though Jevons was for two or three decades very little followed in his field by other leading neoclassicals.

Marshall: Marshall is, of course, one of the great arch-Klassicals in Keynes's account and there are, indeed, in his early writings one or two brief restatements of the Smithian saving and investment doctrine. Keynes justifiably quotes, for example, from Marshall's *Pure Theory of Domestic Values*: 'It is a familiar economic axiom that a man purchases labour and commodities with that portion of his income which he saves just as much as he does with what he is said to spend' (1879a, p. 34).[53]

Keynes's rather sharp criticism is not unjustifiable, and Schumpeter was entitled to express doubts as to whether Marshall had advanced beyond the Smithian saving and investment analysis. There is a certain ambiguity which pervades Marshall's *Principles* and its composition, which had started as 'Volume 1' of a multi-volume treatise planned to cover all the main branches of the subject. But the *Principles* ended up as a single volume, more or less on its own, not clearly related to the further volumes on industry and money published decades later in Marshall's old age. The story of Walras' *Elements* and Menger's *Grundsätze* is somewhat similar. They were both also originally planned as first volumes to be followed by others much extending the scope and range of the subject. What remained as the *Principles of Economics* was centred round a rather simplified mainly, or 'normally', competitive and largely non-monetary microeconomic 'model', smoothly self-equilibrating, because decisions were tacitly assumed to be based on certainty and adequate knowledge. It was made by no means as clear as it might have been whether such processes as were left for examination in the *Principles of Economics* were to be regarded as what 'normally' happens, or 'tends to' happen, or as a consciously very simplified picture, somehow justifiable heuristically or pedagogically

[53] Another quotation from the same year is from *The Economics of Industry*, p. 17 (written with Mrs Marshall): 'It is not good for trade to have dresses made of material which wears out quickly. For if people did not spend their means on buying new dresses they would spend them on giving employment to labour in some other way'. This is very reminiscent of Francis Hutcheson's criticism, about a century and a half before, of Mandeville's advocacy of luxury, which heralded the great Smithian emphasis on the frugal man as a public benefactor. The Smithian doctrine reappears in one of Marshall's last publications (on taxation, 1917): 'That part of an income which is "saved" is spent, if not by the person who saves, yet by those to whom he hands over its use in return for promised income. Thus all is spent' (1925, p. 351n).

as an 'introductory' treatment, or 'first approximation', or as largely consisting of a kind of auxiliary scaffolding to be removed from the structure at some later stage. Marshall certainly did not assert the Smithian saving and investment doctrine with the same forthrightness as J. S. Mill, but he retained it behind a screen of simplifying assumptions, which were plausibly claimed by Pigou to have had some empirical validity down to 1914, but which were obviously of increasingly questionable relevance as the twentieth century wore on.

However, Marshall did recognise the existence of aggregate fluctuations and of problems of stabilisation, though holding that 'the function of a legislator as regards currency is to do as little as possible' (1926, p. 292).

But he was in favour of attempts to improve short-term forecasting, and recommended that the government should publish index-numbers facilitating the making of contracts in terms of units of fixed purchasing power. He also expressed support for relief works in times of depression (1886). By these short first steps Marshall did, like Jevons, advance significantly beyond Mill – and first steps count.

Cyclical fluctuations and unemployment: In the closing decades of the nineteenth century, perhaps as far back as the late 1860s or early 1870s, the beginnings of fundamental changes can be discerned which, in the twentieth century, were completely to transform economic policy. One might start with the abandonment of the hard-line version of the Malthusian doctrine, as upheld in the wage theories of Ricardo and Mill, which had long largely shut out a more active concern with problems of poverty and the distribution of income. Another profound factor for change in economic policy, which worked itself out very slowly and uncertainly over the ensuing half-century, was the extension of the franchise down the wealth scale to a majority who were bound to be more concerned with measures to reduce economic insecurity than had been the *comparatively* wealthy and secure electorate between 1832 and 1867. Thirdly, at a profound level, communication, or social self-consciousness, internally within Britain, was awakening, expanding, and intensifying the awareness of social problems, and, in particular, of the problem of poverty. One English economist who saw economic insecurity, or irregularity of employment and income, as the major problem of the time (1886) was Foxwell. He quoted the labour writer George Howell: 'If the science of political economy is to be of any practical value, its expounders ought to try and find out some means whereby these frequent fluctuations can be avoided, instead of which they only teach men how to increase them by declaring that wages must be dependent on the variations of "the market".'[54]

---

[54] 1878, p. 228. The passage is quoted by H. S. Foxwell in his lecture 'Irregularity of Employment and Fluctuations of Prices', 1886. (See T. W. Hutchison, 1953, p. 411.)

Such words summoned economists to start again precisely at the point where Malthus had left off in the final paragraph of his *Principles*, a point which had been almost completely disregarded for more than half a century by the dominant Ricardian–Mill orthodoxy. As we have already cited, Malthus's last words, in his *Principles*, had been to deplore the overlooking, by 'theoretical writers', of economic fluctuations and of the 'serious sum of human misery' which they involved, especially for the working classes, in whose interests, particularly, 'it should be our object, as far as possible, to maintain...an equable expenditure'.

At the same time, in the 1880s, during a period of heavily falling prices, there was much debate regarding the monetary standard and the desirability of price-stability as a means towards greater general economic stability.

Certainly there was no break-through in fundamental economic theorising. But actual policies against unemployment made considerable advances in response to the discovery of social need or political demand. Chamberlain's circular of 1886 regarding relief works to be started by local authorities during depressions, did not, of itself, amount to much, but can be seen as something of a landmark. In the decade before 1914 the Liberal Government, besides setting up labour exchanges, and starting unemployment insurance, launched plans for 'National Development', including public investment and works projects against unemployment in Lloyd George's budget of 1909. In the same year there were also proposals for counter-cyclical public works in the Minority Report of the Royal Commission on the Poor Law – the Majority went almost as far – as well as Beveridge's monograph on unemployment. Winston Churchill, in some contrast with his attitude of twenty years later, was entertaining visions of 'a scientific remedy for unemployment' in the form of a 'shelf' of public works held ready for operations during depressions. As a recent study has gone so far as to conclude: 'By 1914 fatalistic acceptance of the inevitability of the trade cycle and doctrinaire prejudice against the relief of unemployment seemed to have largely passed away.'[55]

Largely, perhaps, but not completely. In 1929 Ricardian dogmas still survived in the Treasury.

When the unemployment problem emerged in a much more massive and obstinate form in Britain after the First World War, Lloyd George and the Liberal Party in 1924 resumed their thinking on the subject at this point. And this, so to speak, was where Keynes came

[55] J. Harris, 1972, p. 5. Developments seem to have been somewhat similar in Sweden, though the theorists were probably rather closer to policy developments and proposals against unemployment than they were in England until the middle 1920s (see O. Steiger, 1971, pp. 45ff).

in.[56] These policy developments, up to this point, had mostly not been opposed, and had in part been supported, by leading economists, though they could not be said to have been impelled by developments in economic theorising.

A picture of the state of monetary and macroeconomic theorising, at any time in the half-century before *The General Theory*, is difficult to bring into focus and an account of its development over the period is very difficult to summarise. There are too many different points of departure and too many contrasting aspects each to be given its due place: the gold standard, cyclical fluctuations, unemployment, and theories of interest and money. The fundamental assumptions are seldom very clear, nor the relation between the treatment of these problems and what was then the main body of economic theory of value and distribution. Elements in the Smithian–Ricardian dogmas continued to appear,[57] but not the original full, comprehensive theoretical and policy doctrine. Moreover, the basic theoretical component regarding saving, investment, and interest underwent an often inexplicit transformation, from being asserted as what actually happened, as by Smith and Ricardo, into a hypothetical abstraction or simplification, claiming justification on heuristic or pedagogic grounds, though not necessarily on any clear grounds of empirical relevance.

The serious real-world problem of the business cycle, or the problem of cyclical fluctuations, was only admitted to a primary place among the problems of economics, so far as English academic economists were concerned, in the years just before 1914. However, regarding monetary theory, the broad optimistic notion of monetary management was certainly gaining ground, that, as Wicksell had put it: 'It is part of man to be master, not slave of nature, and not least in a sphere of such an extraordinary significance as that of monetary influences' (1936, p. 4).

However, Wicksell's main ideas aroused very little attention in England. Among the characteristics of the dominant English school of economic thinking at this time there was, perhaps, a certain rather complacent unwillingness to re-examine fundamental assumptions, in

---

[56] It is not accurate to maintain that Keynes 'helped to persuade Lloyd George...to support a major programme of public works'. It was Lloyd George who put forward the idea in 1924 which was then taken up by Keynes (see J. K. Galbraith, 1976, p. 229).

[57] See Hutchison, 1953, p. 355. Böhm-Bawerk, for example, repeated the Smithian denial of hoarding: 'An economically educated people does not hoard, but applies what is saved' (1921, p. 149). J. B. Clark repeated 'the unquestionable fact that saving is in reality demanding and getting productive instruments as part of an income' (1898, p. 14). According to G. Cassel: 'In modern society, however, the person who saves money generally invests it' (1903, p. 132). From the underground J. A. Hobson maintained that 'saving means buying productive goods with income' (1910, p. 50). We shall be citing below Edwin Cannan's concept of saving.

particular regarding knowledge, uncertainty, and money. As Sir Dennis Robertson later said of Cambridge in 1910: 'We thought we knew pretty well what sort of things we wanted to know about.'[58]

The rather stuffy, uncritical 'loyalty' to the Marshallian scriptures, cultivated by some of his leading disciples, may explain, and even possibly to some extent justify, some of the Keynesian 'revolutionary' vehemence. But it must emphatically be recognised that it was Marshall's pupil and grand-pupil, Pigou (1908), and Robertson (1915), who were the first English academics – long before Keynes – to attack the Smithian–Ricardian–'Treasury' view opposing public works against unemployment, which had been the main policy conclusion of Klassical economics with its doctrine of macroeconomic self-adjustment.

The underworld at home and abroad: We have seen that at least up to the middle of the nineteenth century what Keynes called the 'underworld', or 'underground', was, in the form of rebels against, or critics of, the orthodox macroeconomic doctrines of Smith and Ricardo, rather more vociferous and numerous than he (or Schumpeter) seems to have suggested. Any glance at the 'underground' later in the century, however brief, must make mention of Karl Marx. Keynes's treatment of Marx in relation to the Klassical school seems more than usually paradoxical or even contradictory. In a wireless talk, just over a year before the publication of *The General Theory*, Keynes discerned a very close relationship between Marxian economic theory and the orthodox 'self-adjusting school', or the 'classical doctrine'. In fact, Keynes maintained that 'the essential elements' in the theories of macroeconomic self-adjustment

> are fervently accepted by Marxists. Indeed, Marxism is a highly plausible inference from the Ricardian economics, that capitalistic individualism cannot possibly work in practice. So much so, that, if Ricardian economics were to fall, an essential prop to the intellectual foundations of Marxism would fall with it.
>
> Thus, if the heretics on the other side of the gulf are to demolish the forces of nineteenth-century orthodoxy – and *I include Marxism in orthodoxy equally with laissez-faire*, these two being the nineteenth-century twins of Say and Ricardo – they must attack them in their citadel.

Shortly after, Keynes predicted to Bernard Shaw that, as a result of his book, 'the Ricardian foundations of Marxism will be knocked away' (1973, vol. XIII, pp. 488 and 493, italics added).

On the other hand, in *The General Theory* itself Keynes includes Marx among the heroes of the opposition or 'underworld': 'The great puzzle of Effective Demand with which Malthus has wrestled vanished

---

[58] 1952, p. 14. However, Robertson's subsequent complaint (1936) does not seem unjustified: 'To exaggerate differences and represent all knowledge as brand new… doesn't breed a scientific spirit but the reverse – a blind scramble to acquire the new orthodoxies for fear of being out of fashion' (see Keynes, 1973, vol. XIII, p. 96).

from economic literature...It could only live on furtively, below the surface, in the underworlds of Karl Marx, Silvio Gesell or Major Douglas.'[59]

If these two views of Marx's macro-economics seem rather sharply contrasting – even for Keynes – there is some justification or excuse. Quite contradictory views can be found in the writings of the critics and expositors of Marx,[60] the truth seeming to be regarding the Prophet that, very conveniently, as Professor Joan Robinson put it, 'part of the time he is accepting Say's Law and part rejecting it' (1966, p. 86).

However, whatever one's assessment of this part, or other parts, of Marx's economic teachings, there can be little doubt that as one of his main contributions – perhaps his main one to economic theorising – he gave a valuable stimulus to theorising about aggregate fluctuations (notably though the work of Tugan-Baranovsky).

We need not say much about Keynes's other denizens of the 'underworld' in the late nineteenth and early twentieth century. Indeed, of C. H. Douglas perhaps the less said the better. Silvio Gesell is altogether a more respectable, if crankish, figure, and J. A. Hobson, again, was a very different kind of case. His treatment by his orthodox contemporaries, including apparently Edgeworth, and his loss of lecturing jobs owing to his heretical views, taken to be 'equivalent in rationality to an attempt to prove the flatness of the earth', were symptomatic of the kind of domination exercised by the established Smithian–Ricardian ideas. Admittedly there was a certain flaw in his theorising, to some extent similar to that which had weakened Malthus's case. Though setting out to overturn the basic Smithian doctrines of macroeconomic self-equilibration, Hobson unfortunately to some extent adopts one of Smith's central, basic assumptions to the effect that saving is investing and hoarding is 'abnormal' (though he explicitly made an exception of commercial depressions) (Hobson, 1910, p. 50).

Easily the most distinguished and penetrating of the underworld theorists, to whom Keynes had referred in *The Treatise*, but of whom

[59] 1936, p. 32. Earlier, in 1925, Keynes had delivered his famous verdict on '*Das Kapital*' as 'an obsolete economic textbook which I know to be not only scientifically erroneous but without interest or application for the modern world' (1931a, p. 300).

[60] Fashions in Marxmanship change, of course. In the 1930s and 1940s it was depression and unemployment to which Marx had propounded the infallible and comprehensive solution. In the 1960s and 1970s the Marxist intellectual panacea was held to answer all the problems of inflation and the tensions of more rapid growth. Whatever the current problems of 'capitalism', omniscient Marxists possess the infallible key to their explanation. Anyhow, according to Professor Tsuru, Marx, like Keynes, 'repudiated Say's Law though for slightly different reasons' (1968, p. 177). But according to Professor W. J. Barber, Marx 'was too closely wedded to the classical tradition of Say's Law to provide a systematic demonstration of cyclical fluctuations' (1967, p. 149).

he made no mention in *The General Theory*, was N. Johannsen, who considerably advanced the analysis of saving and who also developed what he called 'The Multiplying Principle'. The inclusion of Johannsen would have lent real originality and distinction to Keynes's army of underworld heretics.[61]

In the second half of the nineteenth century, and on into the twentieth, for the insular English believer in the orthodoxies of English classical political economy and later of Marshallian economics, 'foreign' economists and their ideas could be, and were often, treated like the rebels and 'cranks' of the domestic underworld, that is as outsiders beyond the pale. Anyhow, outside Britain, fundamental criticism and rejection of the Smithian–Ricardian 'macro' and monetary doctrines, and of the derived ideas known as 'Say's Law', had certainly not been driven underground, or dismissed from serious consideration, to the extent that they had been in Britain. In Germany and Austria many, or most, of the major nineteenth-century figures were explicit critics of Say's Law, following K. H. Rau's discussion (1821) of the controversy between Say and Malthus in which he sided with the latter. For example, the leading historical economist Wilhelm Roscher, also roundly condemned Ricardian orthodoxy, and Mangoldt followed Roscher in criticising the idea of 'Say's Law', as did Carl Menger.[62] Perhaps the Smithian macroeconomic doctrines and the idea of 'Say's Law' had a rather larger proportion of support in France, Italy, and the United States, than in Germany and Austria, but they certainly did not achieve the kind of domination, in driving criticism and alternatives underground, which they did in Britain. Moreover, in both France and the United States there appeared major pioneer studies of aggregate fluctuations, notably those of Juglar (1862–9) and Wesley Mitchell (1913), which stand out far above anything achieved before 1914 in the home of classical orthodoxy.

IX

We now come to Keynes's contemporaries regarding whose 'classical' or 'non-classical' characteristics he enlarged in his correspondence. Writing to Sir Ralph Hawtrey (24 March and 15 April 1936) Keynes

---

[61] Johannsen's most important work was probably *A Neglected Point in Connection with Crises*, 1908. On Johannsen see H. W. Schnack, 1951. As H. Hegeland has shown, other pioneers of the multiplier concept were two Danes, J. Wulff (1896) and J. Warming (1928) (1954, pp. 14–19).

[62] According to Roscher: 'The mere introduction of money is quite sufficient to rule out Say's theory in the strict sense. As Lord Lauderdale has very rightly remarked, savings are only truly useful so long as they run parallel with a real demand for labour' (1849, p. 287). See also T. W. Hutchison, 1953, pp. 356–7; and on Menger, E. Kauder, 1962.

remarked: 'You have never been a classical economist.' Keynes went on: 'I mean by the classical school, as I have repeatedly explained, not merely Ricardo and Mill, but Marshall and Pigou and Henderson and myself until quite recently, and in fact every teacher of the subject in this country with the exception of yourself and a few recent figures like Hayek whom I could call "neo-classicals"' (1973, vol. XIV, pp. 15 and 24).

It may be noted at this point that Keynes's 'classical' and 'non-classical' categories, and his attack on 'the classical school', had, with regard to his contemporaries, hardly any implications for policy. This seems clear in spite of Keynes's insistence that in *The General Theory* he was 'putting all the driving force I know how behind arguments which for me are of painfully practical importance'.[63]

In the early 1930s it seems that a considerable majority of university economists – and, in Britain, *very* few of any other kind then existed – broadly agreed with Keynes on policies against unemployment. Keynes, however, accused them – including, for example, Pigou and Robertson, with whom he broadly agreed on policy, but disagreed on 'theory' – of profound intellectual inconsistency. He claimed that 'they insist on maintaining theories from which their own practical conclusions cannot possibly follow' (1973, vol. XIV, p. 259).

Let us now very briefly examine the cases of four of Keynes's distinguished contemporaries explicitly designated as 'classical' or 'non-classical' by Keynes: namely Pigou, Henderson, Hawtrey, and Robertson. The two former were Klassical, the two latter *not* Klassical.

(a) *Pigou* was, of course, the arch-Klassical: 'from whose hands the classical theory has received its most mature embodiment', and who in 1933 in his *Theory of Unemployment* had given 'the only detailed account of the classical theory of employment which exists'.[64]

This, however, must not be taken to imply that Keynes regarded Pigou as in any way typical of 'Klassicism' (or of anything else): 'The

---

[63] 1936, p. 88. Subsequent 'Keynesians' have tried strenuously, but quite misleadingly, to pretend that the 'theoretical', analytical or verbal controversies aroused by *The General Theory* had some vast and vital practical or policy significance. As Professor D. Patinkin has said, neither *The General Theory* nor *The Treatise on Money* 'made any basic, new contribution to policy' (June 1975, p. 261). Keynes's last peace-time proposals in 1937 against a prospective slump were on substantially the same lines as his first policy proposals against unemployment when he turned to the problem at the instigation of Lloyd George in 1924; and these in their turn were based on the counter-cyclical proposals from the Minority Report of the Royal Commission on the Poor Law (1908) and other similar proposals circulating before the First World War. A considerable majority of academic economists supported Keynesian policies in the early 1930s while by 1935, a year before the publication of *The General Theory*, such policies had the support of the top officials in the Treasury and the Governor of the Bank of England.

[64] 1936, pp. 7 and 32. For a fuller discussion of Pigou's views on wage-cuts and policies against unemployment, see the next chapter.

stuff he writes seems to me the most extraordinary in the history of the subject' (1973, vol. XIII, p. 525).

Regarding policy, Pigou had been probably the first English academic economist (apart, possibly, from Malthus), or the first in the twentieth century, explicitly to refute the key policy conclusion of Klassical economics, that is, the Smithian–Ricardian–Treasury view opposing public spending to relieve unemployment. In his inaugural lecture in 1908 Pigou had concluded that, on the contrary, 'the true result of relief works and so on is not to leave the unemployment in the country unaltered, but to diminish that amount' (see Hutchison, 1953a, p. 416).

We shall show in the next chapter how, a quarter of a century later, in the early 1930s, Pigou and Keynes were in very close agreement on policies, signing the same memoranda and letters to the press. Like a considerable majority of English economists, they both opposed wage-cuts and advocated public works against unemployment; indeed, in 1937 Keynes himself is remarking how '*when it comes to practice, there is really extremely little between us*'.[65]

Pigou made repeated and profound studies of aggregate fluctuations and unemployment, which subjects had originally comprised an integral part of his economics of welfare. He can also be said to have contributed to the development of 'multiplier' analysis (Hegeland, 1954, pp. 19–23). Pigou certainly did not hold to the Smithian savings and investment doctrine and its implications, and *he substantially agreed with Keynes on policies against unemployment.* There was also a political difference between Pigou and Keynes in respect of which the former was much nearer to the classical liberal viewpoint: Pigou was much more sceptical, pessimistic, and mistrustful of the discretionary management of comparatively sophisticated economic policies by politicians, than was Keynes. This partly explains their differences with regard to Britain's return to the Gold Standard and Pigou's doubts about Keynes's advocacy of tariffs against unemployment in 1930–1, regarding which their disagreements over economic theory were minimal. However, these characteristics of Pigou hardly add up to a significant kind of 'Klassicality'.[66]

(b) *H. D. Henderson* was another contemporary described by Keynes

---

[65] 1973, vol. XIII, p. 259 (italics added). Keynes went on to ask why Pigou (and Robertson) 'insist on maintaining theories from which their own practical conclusions cannot possibly follow'. But no one has spelt out this failure in logic on the part of Pigou and Robertson with actual quotations from their writings.

[66] One might quote, at this point, the conclusion of Professor R. L. Meek: 'So far as Keynes's immediate predecessors are concerned the notion that their work was invalidated by the presence of an all-pervasive "Say's Law", which it was Keynes's historical mission to exorcize, is so misleading as to be almost laughable. Nothing is easier than to show that Keynes's characterization of neo-classical economics was an Aunt Sally' (1967, p. 184).

as a 'classical' economist, although he had opposed the Smithian–Ricardian–Treasury doctrines on public investment and had actually collaborated with Keynes on the famous pamphlet of 1929 'Can Lloyd George Do It?', which proposed public works against unemployment. Keynes described Henderson as 'classical' because he was alleged to be one of 'those who believe that the existing economic system is, in the long run, a self-adjusting system, though with creaks and groans and jerks'.[67]

Henderson himself had certainly proclaimed (October 1934) that he was 'convinced that the world will recover sooner or later from the present depression, as it has recovered from depressions in the past' (1934, p. 647).

However, like Keynes at that time, Henderson was very concerned at the effects of declining population while productivity was rising appreciably: 'So a condition of over-production, once established, may last a very long time, and it may be a very painful matter to correct it... Increasing productivity and declining numbers, taken together, will make an economic world in many ways more unstable than that of prewar days' (op. cit., pp. 646–7).

So it is far from clear what was the crucial degree of belief in the self-adjusting properties of the economy which made Henderson a Klassical. Obviously in 'Can Lloyd George Do It?' Henderson did *not* hold that the British economy was, macro-economically, *so smoothly and rapidly self-adjusting* that massive government investment and intervention against unemployment should be dispensed with. In 1935, with the depression lifting, Henderson advocated 'a policy of fairly considerable public works over the next ten years' (1955, p. 160).

He certainly played a considerable part in the conversion of the top Treasury officials from their Ricardian dogma against public works of 1929 to the support of public investment to reduce unemployment by early 1935.[68] At the same time, Henderson expressed extreme scepticism about many of the more novel elements and revolutionary claims in *The General Theory*. But he tended to be highly sceptical of all 'general theories', including, or in particular, those of easy and rapid self-adjustment.[69] Paradoxically, during and after the Second World

---

[67] *The Listener*, 21 November 1934 (reprinted in 1973, vol. XIII, p. 486). Certainly, in the crisis year of 1931 Henderson sharply attacked Keynes on his lax attitude to public expenditure – while, at the same time condemning, at the other extreme, the May Committee. (See the remarkable quotation from Henderson's letter to Keynes on p. 87 of S. Howson and D. Winch, 1977.) But subsequently, after 1931, on the Committee on Economic Information, Henderson and Keynes were for the most part in close agreement and together converted the top Treasury officials.

[68] See S. Howson and D. Winch, 1977, p. 130. The frequently shifting doctrinal relationships between Henderson and Keynes during the 1930s are interestingly portrayed in this volume.

[69] See, for example, his papers on 'The Uses and Abuses of Economic Planning' (1947) and on 'The Price System' (1948), in (1955).

War, Henderson's ideas about international economic policy *were distinctly more sceptical regarding classical liberal doctrines of self-adjustment than were those of Keynes.* Sir Roy Harrod has written of Henderson, during the Second World War, being 'absolutely convinced that, as a matter of hard fact, we should have to resort to every conceivable device after the war to protect our balance of trade'. Keynes, on the other hand, was 'somewhat rueful at the lapse of an old disciple' (1951, p. 530).

So there was apparently quite a reversal of roles for the 'Klassical' on the one hand and the 'Revolutionary' on the other – a reversal which might lead one to question how much validity or significance Keynes's original designation of Henderson as a 'Klassical' ever possessed.

(c) *Sir Ralph Hawtrey* was, as we have seen, recognised by Keynes as having 'never been a classical economist'.

But from his first book Hawtrey had been a strong and leading opponent of public investment policies against unemployment, such as, for example, the counter-cyclical public works proposed in the Minority Report of the Royal Commission on the Poor Laws (1909): 'The writers of the Minority Report appear to have overlooked the fact that the Government by the very fact of borrowing for this expenditure is withdrawing from the investment market savings which would otherwise be applied to the creation of capital' (1913, p. 260).

Of course we have here the essential policy conclusion of Smithian and Ricardian macro-economics in almost verbally similar terms to those Ricardo had used nearly a hundred years earlier; and Sir Ralph remained for decades much the most persistent and influential exponent in Britain of the Ricardo–Treasury view. However, Hawtrey's theorising also possessed some strongly non- or anti-Klassical features, which may explain Keynes's designation. Hawtrey started from a concept of 'total effective demand' and attacked the limitations of Smithian, anti-mercantilist, 'real' analysis in terms rather like those of Malthus: 'At one time economists were so anxious to guard themselves from the fallacy of identifying money and wealth that they slipped into an almost pedantic disregard of the influence of money in economic phenomena.'[70]

But it must be noted that what Keynes claimed to be the inconsis-

---

[70] Op. cit., p. 5. See also T. W. Hutchison, 1953a, pp. 396–7. Compare the often-quoted footnote in the second edition of Malthus's *Principles* (p. 324): 'Theoretical writers in Political Economy, from the fear of appearing to attach too much importance to money, have perhaps been too apt to throw it out of their consideration in their reasonings... The circulating medium bears so important a part in the distribution of Wealth, and the encouragement of industry, that it is hardly ever safe to set it aside in our reasonings.'

tencies of his contemporaries worked both ways. If there were those like Pigou and Henderson who supported the same policies as Keynes 'inconsistently' with their Klassical theories – whatever these were – there was on the other side Sir Ralph Hawtrey who had, over decades, most influentially and consistently opposed the policies which Keynes – and Pigou and Henderson – had long advocated, while on theoretical or conceptual grounds he had, apparently, '*never*' been 'a Klassical economist'.

(d) Fourthly, among Keynes's leading contemporaries, we come to *Sir Dennis Robertson*, who, like Hawtrey, was also designated by Keynes as not a 'classical' economist in spite of his holding a 'radically opposed' theory of the rate of interest in terms of 'loanable funds'. In fact Keynes maintained that Robertson had abandoned classical ideas before he had himself, and told him that 'the last thing I should accuse you of is being classical'.[71] On nearly all, and on all the major policy issues of the 1930s Robertson's views were closely similar to those of Keynes (as, of course, Keynes acknowledged). There was a certain *hypothetical* difference of emphasis in the boom of 1937 when Robertson was prepared to advocate a rise in the rate of interest, if necessary 'to prevent a boom getting out of hand' (Howson and Winch, 1977, p. 143). But with unemployment never falling below about 12 per cent, this eventuality never occurred. Generally Robertson seems to have been less optimistic than Keynes at this time about the possibility of smoothing out aggregate fluctuations either by monetary policy or by public works. But certainly Keynes did not think that there were any major differences between himself and Robertson on policy or practical issues since he maintained (10 November 1937) that 'when it comes to practice, there is really extremely little between us'. (But, of course, Keynes was not a 'Keynesian'.)

Thus although certain Smithian–Ricardian ideas can still be found here and there in the writings of Keynes's contemporaries, by the 1920s and 1930s the complete, closely-knit pattern of Smithian–Ricardian doctrine had largely disintegrated and faded away: that is, the combination of the saving and investment theory, the 'real' barter analysis, the anti-'mercantilist' dismissal of a money-supply problem, and the denial that public works could raise investment and employment, had largely disappeared as a coherent whole.

Where some traces of the key Smithian saving and investment theory, together with the anti-public-works policy-conclusions, were still to be found in the 1920s and 1930s was in some of the Austrian and London writings, though in a much qualified form. Edwin Cannan

---

[71] 1973, vol. XIV, p. 94. When in July 1937 Robertson surveyed the current situation in a broadcast talk entitled 'Is Another Slump Coming?' Keynes wrote: 'I doubt if there was a sentence from which I disagreed' (op. cit., p. 250).

had held to a modified but robust form of the Smithian saving doctrine. While objecting strongly to Smith's maintaining that 'what is
saved is spent or consumed', Cannan insisted that 'saving' meant producing a surplus of goods over what was consumed: 'If he "saves
£500" it simply means that he decides that he will take £500 worth of
goods, not in the form of commodities for his personal consumption,
but in some form, say, for example, a cycle factory or telephone wires'
(1901, vol. III, p. 356).[72]

Thirty years later, also in an encyclopedia article on 'Saving',
Professor Hayek – as we have seen, described as a 'neo-classical'
by Keynes, whatever, precisely, he meant – maintained that only in
'special cases' would the saving and investment mechanism fail to adjust smoothly and beneficently, self-equilibration being, apparently,
the *general* case. Referring to theories descending from Malthus and
Lauderdale arguing the need to maintain consumers' purchasing
power during depressions, Hayek maintained: 'It is becoming increasingly clear, however, that these theories are false and that there
are only the three special cases – hoarding, violent fluctuations in the
rate of saving, and forced saving through credit expansion – in which
excessive saving may be said to cause depression' (1939, p. 167).

Certainly the Smithian doctrine, in its pristine vigour and purity,
did not recognise these vital 'special cases'. But in terms of what it takes
to be the *general* case this statement is clearly of Smithian descent.
Moreover, this treatment of saving was combined with an opposition
to government spending and any increase in the money supply at
the bottom of the slump, with unemployment over twenty per cent.

X

We may conclude this review of Keynes's version of the history of
economics by expressing broad agreement with his favourable and
enlightening treatment of 'the mercantilists', Mandeville, and Malthus, and, on the other side, with his criticisms of Ricardo and the Mills.
There are, however, huge gaps in Keynes's outline, which, if filled in,
would render his version still more impressive. Especially is this the
case with regard to the eighteenth century. He omits completely the
two most important champions on either side, the two contemporaries
Sir James Steuart and Adam Smith.

However, with regard to about the last fifty years of Keynes's story,
that is from around the 1880s onwards, the *comparatively* simple pattern
breaks up, and the story becomes much too complex and variegated
for a simplified, black-and-white account in terms of 'Klassical' and
'Keynesian' theories and policies.

[72] See also F. A. Hayek, 1941, p. 272 for a discussion of the Smithian doctrine.

At first the comparatively sudden and extensive loss of credibility suffered in the late 1860s and early 1870s by the dominant Ricardo–Mill theories of distribution and value was not accompanied by any significant questioning of the Smithian macroeconomic doctrines. But the deeper forces which had been at work in bringing about the decline of the Ricardian distribution and value theories were in due course, over the next two decades, to lead on to the disintegration of the Klassical Smithian–Ricardian macroeconomic doctrines. It was the loss of credibility, and the abandonment, of the hard-line version of the Malthusian doctrine of natural wages, the *empirical* core of the theory and policy-doctrines of the Ricardo–Mill economics, which, as well as calling for a fundamental reconsideration of distribution and value theory, in due course opened up the poverty question – as Marshall recognised – and through the poverty question led on to the recognition of an unemployment problem and to the discussion of public relief works as a remedy. The recognition of unemployment and economic insecurity as serious questions was initially largely the work of social investigators of the poverty question, and of less orthodox economists such as Foxwell or Hobson. But the policies against poverty and unemployment which began to emerge, some fifty years before *The General Theory*, were certainly not opposed by Marshall, who, on the whole, went along with them. Certainly, in his inaugural lecture of 1908, and in his first major work on *Wealth and Welfare*, Pigou took unemployment to be one of the main socio-economic problems – perhaps the main one. Also in the decade before the First World War, when Keynes was beginning his work as an economist, the problem of aggregate stability, in the form of the business cycle, was being given serious attention as a major economic problem by leading orthodox British theoretical economists.

It is impossible to treat unemployment and aggregate fluctuations as serious problems, not mere 'frictions', and remain within the confines of the self-adjusting Smithian–Ricardian macroeconomic theory and policy doctrines. However, these Smithian–Ricardian doctrines were not often, or fully, fundamentally and explicitly repudiated. The doctrines of smooth self-adjustment lingered on, more particularly in what are euphemistically called the more 'long-term' models – i.e. the more extremely over-simplified and unrealistic 'models'. In one or two cases, representing only a minority of economists since about the beginning of the century, the Smithian–Ricardian *policy* doctrines found expression – notably in the famous Treasury White Paper of 1929. But it was certainly justifiable to protest – as Keynes later did – about the undue complacency and obscurity regarding the simplified and unrealistic assumptions underlying important parts of economic theory, especially with regard to the absence of ignorance, uncertainty, and volatile expectations. But for some decades before *The General Theory* the adjective 'classical' had ceased to be applicable, in any very significant sense, to the majority of leading economists. Of course it might be possible to discover a sense in which Pigou and Henderson were 'classical', and Hawtrey and Robertson were not 'classical', but it can be nothing remotely resembling the full-blooded theoretical and policy sense in which, say, Smith and Ricardo were 'classical' (or Klassical) and Steuart and Petty were not. As the framework for an historical generalisation covering a very long and important period, of about 250 years, in the history of economic thought, Keynes's 'classical' or 'non-classical' concept had a rich and significant content: as a polemical weapon against contemporaries it was neither sharp nor accurate.[73] In general, the intellectual situation in economics that confronted Keynes – and which, as such, he was thoroughly justified in criticising – was one of rather complacent, intellectually messy, confusion, not some rigid, consistent, logically clear-cut, and widely-held 'classical' orthodoxy.

In fact, Keynes himself seems to have described the intellectual situation in somewhat similar terms when he wrote to J. R. Hicks (31 March 1937) about

> a period when economists had slipped away from the pure classical doctrine without knowing it...But if you were to go further back, how far back I am not quite sure, you would have found a school of thought which would have considered this an inconsistent hotch-potch. The inconsistency creeps in, I suggest, as soon as it comes to be generally agreed that the increase in the quantity of money is capable of increasing employment. A strictly brought-up classical economist would not, I should say admit that [1973, vol. xiv, p. 79].

[73] If one attempts to apply the Keynesian 'classical' and 'non-classical' dichotomy to the macroeconomic theorising and theorists of the 1970s, obviously the first candidate for consideration as a 'classical' is Professor Milton Friedman. He certainly believes that the economic system is broadly and beneficently self-adjusting, macroeconomically as well as in other respects, *given* a *fairly* simple framework of rules. But the framework for Friedman's 'simple system of natural liberty' includes a steadily growing money supply for a growing economy, a stipulation *pretty* completely missing from the Smithian doctrines. In fact, Professor Friedman's ideas would not have the originality they in fact can claim – we are not discussing validity – if this stipulation about a steadily growing money supply had been clearly laid down by earlier 'classical' writers. But, in fact, and on the contrary, it can fairly be said that a steadily increasing money supply was just what the better *pre*-Smithian writers were especially concerned about. And for being concerned about it they have been described as 'monetary cranks', concerned only with accumulating gold for its own sake, by Smithian and subsequent writers on the history of economic thought. In his concern about a steadily growing money supply Professor Milton Friedman *could* be said to be more 'mercantilist' than Smithian (however much he might detest such a categorisation in view of the usual associations of these terms). But extremes meet. There is both a Smithian and an extreme pseudo-Keynesian sense in which 'money doesn't matter' – though these senses differ widely.

Certainly Ricardo would not have readily admitted that an increase in the quantity of money could increase employment. But the precise nature of the subsequent 'inconsistency' is not at all clear. Perhaps, in fact, there is greater 'inconsistency' in Keynes's own historical generalisations. In the opening pages of *The General Theory* we hear of economists 'strongly wedded' to 'the classical theory', of 'deep divergencies' which have 'almost destroyed the practical influence of economic theory', and of how the 'classical' theory 'dominates' economic thought 'both *practical* and theoretical'. But, as we have seen, Keynes also claimed, in 1929, that 'not one' leading economist endorsed the Ricardo–Treasury view; that, in 1931, 'scarcely one responsible person' supported wage-cuts; that, in 1937, public loan expenditure against unemployment was supported 'almost unani-mously' by economists (as well as, incidentally, by the top Treasury officials who, *by 1935*, had been converted from their Ricardian 'view' of 1929, not to mention the Governor and senior officials of the Bank of England). Finally, by 1937, Keynes was agreeing that on policy, or 'practical matters', there was '*really extremely little*' between himself, Pigou and Robertson. Unfortunately, while the highly questionable statements in the opening pages of *The General Theory* have been widely known and quoted, and a highly influential revolutionary mythology has been built upon them, Keynes's contrasting, and much more accurate, pronouncements, before and after 1936, which would have undermined this mythology, have been far less widely available.

Professor Jacob Viner pronounced on Keynes as follows:

> As a historian of thought in areas in which he was emotionally involved as a protagonist and prophet, Keynes seemed to me to be seriously lacking in the unexciting but essential qualities for the intellectual historian of objectivity and of judiciousness. Even when he was engaged in selecting those upon whom to bestow laurels for having in some degree anticipated his discoveries, his selection seemed to me then, and still seems to me now that I have acquired more knowledge of the older literature, often to have been random when not eccentric.

One can, on the whole, agree with this as a just verdict, though it certainly does not err on the side of excessive generosity. However, Viner goes on to concede what might be regarded as the main point when he concludes: '*I would nevertheless have agreed with him on what I take to be his major complaint against the main line of 'orthodox' English economics*' (1964, p. 254, italics added). An accurate and balanced writing of the history of economic thought was not Keynes's primary nor even his secondary purpose. He was concerned to devise a per-suasive, 'revolutionary' setting for his own ideas, an enterprise liable to serious abuse. In doing this it was not popular myths or amateur misconceptions which Keynes was concerned to combat, but the comparatively sophisticated orthodoxy of Smith, James Mill and Ricardo. Nevertheless, Keynes produced a new and illuminating interpretation of, or insight regarding, a considerable period of, or element in, the history of economic thought, and this had much validity for about 250 out of the roughly 300 years about which he so audaciously generalised.

6

Demythologising the Keynesian revolution:
Pigou, wage-cuts, and *The General Theory*

I

Revolutions depend upon and create their own myths. Sometimes the leader is responsible, or partly so, for starting such myths, and sometimes the followers build them up further in order to maintain revolutionary momentum and exclusiveness. An important part of revolutionary myths is the unmasking and condemnation of heinous fallacies perpetrated by the 'old' regime, and the demonstration that before the revolution all had been darkness and error. The young J. S. Mill, for example, maintained that before Adam Smith 'the ideas universally entertained both by theorists and by practical men, on the causes of national wealth' had been 'completely erroneous' (1844, p. 47). To its credit, the Jevonian revolution did not generate so much in the way of myth-making. But the Keynesian revolution has been, and still is, fertile in the creation of myth and *mystique*. One of its typical myths, for which Keynes himself bears *some* measure of responsibility, but which was largely blown up by followers and PROs, concerns the subject of Pigou and wage-cuts. According to this myth Pigou's one definite policy proposal during the slump of 1929–33 was that of wage reductions. But this particular myth was simply part of a comprehensive revolutionary *mystique* regarding the publication of Keynes's *General Theory*, which is held to have exercised a major or revolutionary influence in transforming economic *policies*. Although initially Keynes himself may have had some slight responsibility for inspiring these myths, already by October 1937 he had admitted that they were hollow by asserting that, regarding policy or 'practical matters', there was '*really extremely little*' between himself and those cast as the leading anti-revolutionary defenders of orthodoxy (1973, vol. XIV, p. 259). But these myths have maintained their hold and have been propagated for decades by economists and historians.

II

A survey, down to the fateful year of 1929, of economists' views on the unemployment problem, concluded:

A majority of economists in Britain supported the general case for public works to combat unemployment (e.g. Keynes, Henderson, Pigou, Robertson, Clay, etc.). Public works policies were opposed by Hawtrey and later by supporters of the Austrian monetary theory of over-investment. At the same time a considerable body, probably a large majority, of economists held that general wage reductions would, *in the then existing circumstances,* diminish unemployment (e.g. Pigou, Clay, Beveridge, and perhaps Keynes) [Hutchison, 1953, p. 422, italics added].

There does not seem to be anything seriously wrong with this description as far as it goes. But the treatment of the question of wage reductions, and economists' views thereon, after 1929, could certainly do with more detailed explanation and documentation.

As regards the views of Pigou – and others, for example, Clay – it is worth recalling that the suggestion that high and rigid wages had some responsibility for unemployment in Britain, was originally developed not so much as a deduction from some abstract model of competitive flexibility, but as a simple historical argument of the *post hoc ergo propter hoc* type, which may have been right or wrong but which is not easy to refute. It was natural enough in the 1920s to start a diagnosis of unemployment in Britain with a comparison with pre-1914 conditions when unemployment had averaged less than half the post-war figures. It was observed, surely accurately, that wages had been much more rigid since the war, and that this was presumably connected with more powerful trade union policies and with the development of comprehensive unemployment insurance. As Pigou put it (1927):

> If it is correct – if, that is to say, post-war policy is in fact responsible for adding some 5 per cent to the volume of unemployment which is normally brought about by other factors – *the country is confronted with a problem of a type which pre-war economics never found itself called upon to study.* An extra 5 per cent of unemployment – I do not, of course, stress the precise figure – is an extremely serious matter.[1]

Pigou then considered the remedies of import restrictions and subsidies to wages which he considered might conceivably be effective in reducing unemployment without reducing money wages. But he judged that both of these devices would in practice be 'bungled' by the politicians and so in the long run would work out harmfully. Like Keynes three years later, as we shall see, Pigou did not on this occasion mention public works policies. But he insisted that he was not implying that any decline in working class incomes was in any way desirable or, indeed, 'any reduction in the general level of real wages below which it is now' (1927, p. 366).

[1] 1927, p. 359 (italics added). H. Clay argued two years later: 'A great change has taken place during the last twenty years in the methods of negotiating wages...Before the war the policy of maintaining wage-rates in spite of unemployment could be practised only by the organized minority of wage-earners. The majority were unable to resist reductions that were needed to maintain employment' (1929, pp. 323 and 332).

In a lecture published in January 1930, Keynes developed a closely similar argument by calling attention to the rise in real wages in Britain 'of some 10 per cent' since the return to the gold standard in 1925. Sceptical about governmental wages policies, he expressed:

> *grave doubts whether an indiscriminate public opinion, reinforced by the votes of wage earners, in favour of raising wages, whenever possible, is really the best means open to us, within the existing framework of society, for attaining what is presumably the object, namely, the betterment of the material conditions of the working class.* For the High-Wage Party forget that we belong not to a closed system, but to an international system [1930, p. 115, italics added].

Keynes emphasised that what he called the High-Wage Movement 'has consequently provoked an almost chronic tendency in the direction of dear money', and that the result of the rise in real wages since 1925 had been a fall of profits, 'a fall so severe as to make many branches of English business definitely unprofitable' (op. cit., p. 118). Keynes continued:

> What has happened, should, I suggest, be a warning to us for the future. If we want to better the condition of the working class, it is inexpedient to attempt to do it by the method which reduces the rewards of capital below what is obtainable in other countries. Or, at any rate, if we do adopt this method, we must supplement it by abandoning or diminishing the existing freedom of foreign investment. *For it never pays to render the entrepreneur poor and seedy. It is impossible in the present order of society to secure the optimum level of output and employment by any other way than by paying the capitalist his full rate, and, if anything, a little over...* If we decide that the interests of justice and charity require that the income of the working class should be higher than that which they receive from the economic machine, then we must, so to speak, subscribe to that end. Taxation is a measure of compulsory subscription, and the subscription must be spread over the whole community. But if the subscription is made to fall solely on a particular body of employers then we must not be surprised if the level of employment and output is below what it should be.

These views on wages and employment relate, of course, to the period before the onset of the Great Depression at the end of 1929, that is, to an unemployment problem which was regarded as primarily structural rather than cyclical. For some conditions or periods – before and since – these closely similar views of Pigou and Keynes may well have had validity. But in the year 1930 conditions were to change at an almost unprecedentedly rapid rate, with unemployment rising in Britain more rapidly than in any year before or since, that is, from about 10.4 per cent to about 16 per cent.

III

It is about Pigou's views on policy in this critical year 1930 that certain myths have developed. Since in these myths Pigou's views are presented by way of a black-and-white contrast with Keynes's views, any errors may also involve getting Keynes's views and achievements seriously out of perspective.

Before we proceed to discuss these myths it might be of interest for any readers not recently in touch with the literature to indulge in a couple of preliminary exercises. Most of the leading economists, either as members or as witnesses, contributed to the work of the Macmillan Committee, that is, either to its Report and Addenda (published July 1931), or to the various Memoranda and Evidence (taken mostly in 1930):

I. Here are two pieces of dialogue from the Macmillan 'hearings':

(1) W: If there is a general stage of stagnancy, it might really be impossible for the banks to do anything.
X: Does not this depend on the rate of interest?
W: Undoubtedly in part.
X: Is not that fundamental?
W: There is the state of mind of the business man. The business man might be in such a state that he would not borrow money or use money at o per cent.
X: That is an extremely abnormal state of things? [Macmillan, Evidence, 1931, vol. II, p. 89]

(2) Y: ...I should have thought it was more plausible to suppose that that high rate of interest was much more responsible for the lack of investment than anything else.
Z: I feel that you may want a frightfully low rate of interest, even a negative one, in certain circumstances, to overcome the lack of confidence.
Y: It is rather premature to suggest that [op. cit., vol. I, p. 335].

Who were, or was, X and Y with their rather optimistic and classically inclined regard for the effectiveness of flexibility in the interest-rate mechanism? And who were, or was, W and Z with the rather pessimistic and non-classical scepticism? X and Y were, of course, Keynes, and W and Z were Pigou and Robertson respectively.

II. If Pigou and Keynes were responsible for one each of the following two passages, who was responsible for which passage?

(a) I would favour large Government expenditure on really useful public goods...The Government should put in hand and should encourage local authorities and public utility companies to put in hand enterprises of a useful character, even though they are likely to yield a return substantially below current rates, and even though guarantees of interest involving a cost to the Treasury are necessary [op. cit., vol. II, pp. 92–3].

(*b*) If money incomes have been established at a level appropriate to a certain purchasing power of money and if purchasing power then undergoes a large increase, the fortuitous advantage which will then accrue to those whose money incomes are unchanged may be quite inappropriate to the new situation and without substantial justification. Great evils must needs result, and have resulted, from the excessive rigidity of various types of money-income in such circumstances . . . A readiness to accept the fact that the value of incomes is something which must be accommodated to changing circumstances is, indeed, an essential, condition of the sound working of our economic system [Macmillan, *Report* 1931, pp. 193–4].

Passage (a) is from Pigou's evidence and his additional Note on policy. Passage (b), stressing the importance of income flexibility, is from Addendum 1 to the Report in which, as Sir Roy Harrod puts it, 'the more progressive members of the committee' joined with Keynes (1951, p. 424).

It would of course be fantastically misleading to quote this passage from Addendum 1 on income flexibility without explaining that the signatories went on to advocate not, of course, wage-cuts, but, on the contrary, import restrictions and a programme of public works.

But this is precisely how certain myths have treated Pigou's evidence to the Macmillan Committee. Just as there are some significant parallels between Pigou's article on wages (1927) and Keynes's article of 1930, so Addendum 1, signed by Keynes, proceeds on a pattern that has some similarities in principle and outline with Pigou's evidence, though of course there are many differences of emphasis and terminology. But Pigou in his evidence proceeded first to examine wage flexibility and concluded that, in the then circumstances, this was impracticable and undesirable – as did Keynes and the other signatories of Addendum 1. Then, at the end of his evidence, Pigou made positive proposals for increased public expenditure, as well as for international monetary action and other measures. It would be similarly fantastic to conclude that Pigou had no clear lead other than wage reduction to offer the Macmillan Committee, or that he could only suggest that if unemployment was to be reduced it was up to the workers to shift jobs and locations.

IV

We now come to these myths regarding Pigou's views on employment policy in 1930, in particular as expressed to the Macmillan Committee.

Professor Lekachman writes of Pigou's evidence to this Committee:

When he was asked to explain why unemployment was so high, Cambridge's distinguished professor of political economy could extend no aid more useful to his fellow citizens than a diagnosis that 'the relative demand for labour in different occupations has altered, and the transfers of labour appropriate to those alterations have not taken place'. There was little hint in Pigou's remarks of any novel solution. *If unemployment existed the efficacious remedies were in the hands of ordinary workers and their trade unions. All that workers needed to do was shift jobs and locations judiciously and accept lower wages if necessary, and unemployment would disappear.* The point was made explicitly in the following dialogue:

Chairman: Would you necessarily create vacancies. . .by the reduction of wages?

Pigou: I think you would to some extent.

Chairman: If wage rates were reduced, you think there would be an increased demand for labour?

Pigou: Then, I think there would be an increased demand for labour.[2]

One of the editors of the *Economic Journal*, Sir Austin Robinson, in a review on many points highly critical of Professor Lekachman's book agrees with him, or perhaps echoes his conclusions, regarding Pigou's contribution: 'Pigou had no clear lead other than wage reduction to offer to our Macmillan Committee' (1967, p. 650).

It is necessary first to point out that the omission actually indicated by Professor Lekachman in his quotation of the Chairman's first question consists of the words 'in these other industries'. Again, the words 'in those industries' are omitted (after 'rates') from the Chairman's second question without any indication that the question as quoted is incomplete. Moreover, and again without any indication that an omission is being made, the bulk of Pigou's first answer is also omitted, which actually continues at some length as follows: 'Of course, I am not saying that in some industries there are not vacancies as it is, but you have industries in which the wage rates are now so adjusted that there are no vacancies. It is no use sending coal miners into those industries, because they would not find work' (Macmillan, *Evidence*, 1931, vol. II, p. 48).

Having repaired the quotation it is possible to see something of its immediate context. Pigou was not here discussing general wage-cuts but the effect of wage reductions 'in those industries' *not* subject to serious structural unemployment, as contrasted with the coal industry which notably was so subject. Having been interrupted in mid-sentence by Keynes, Pigou, later in his evidence, went to special pains to emphasise this point:

This does not, of course, imply that, relatively to the existing conditions, the rates of real wages are too high in the sense I have defined it in the

---

[2] 1967, p. 51 (italics added). Possibly this myth has its ancestry in the statement of L. R. Klein that when Pigou 'was called upon to give testimony before the Macmillan Committee...he supported a policy of wage cuts' (1st ed., 1947 and 2nd ed., 1966, p. 46). This is a highly misleading statement. But unlike subsequent writers Professor Klein does not say that wage reduction was *all* that Pigou had to suggest.

depressed industries. I did not intend to suggest, as any form of remedy, lowering the real wages in the depressed industries. There is no way of saying whether the wages there are too high or not. So, when I came to my division of possible methods of remedy, assuming you can get people transferred, one may assert that unemployment would be diminished if the rate of real wages in the undepressed industries were lowered. *Secondly it would also be diminished if the conditions of demand could be so altered that there should be a higher demand. Thus, either by reducing real wages or by raising the demand, you would employ more people.*[3]

Immediately before Professor Lekachman's quotation Pigou had explained:

> If you have got unemployment, one can say that the cause of the unemployment is either that the real rate of wages is all right, but there is not enough demand; or if one takes the demand as given one can say that the real rate of wages is too high...*So I do not want to say that unduly high wages are the cause* [op. cit., p. 48, italics added].

Again a little later Pigou repudiated the suggestion that his analysis implied that he was recommending wage-cuts to eliminate unemployment: 'There may be other means of doing that' (op. cit., p. 50).

Yet again Pigou emphasises this point. When asked whether it was his conclusion that in the existing state of demand for labour the rates of wages in the non-depressed industries were too high, Pigou answered: 'Yes in the existing state of demand. I do not want at this stage to beg the question whether you could not improve the state of demand' (op. cit., p. 52).

Again Pigou repeated: 'I am not advocating a reduction of real wages' (op. cit., p. 52).

When a member of the Committee suggested that economists did not make enough allowance for the practical impossibility of moving men from one type of industry to another, Pigou replied 'I agree' (op. cit., p. 49).

Pigou's evidence, not unbefittingly for a university economist, was primarily concerned with analysis and diagnosis rather than with policy proposals. But he could hardly have repeated more frequently than he did that he did *not* advocate cuts in wages. The closing passages in his evidence are concerned with his policy proposals. It may be noted that he did not envisage devaluation (May 1930). *But neither did Keynes* nor any member of the Committee in the Report and Addenda (published in July 1931 – two months before the actual

---

[3] Op. cit., vol. II, p. 78, para. 6432 (italics added). Pigou developed this point in his *Aspects of British Economic History 1918–1925*, 1947, p. 55: 'Had it been feasible to reduce wage rates in the sheltered industries, larger quantities of labour would have been demanded there, so making it more apparent to people in the over-crowded industries where work was to be found. More of them, we may presume, would have moved across; and employment in the two sets of industries together would have been larger than it was.'

devaluation).[4] Pigou agreed with the theoretical arguments that tariff measures could conceivably reduce unemployment but was opposed on grounds of probable political mismanagement. He advocated international monetary measures to stabilise prices. He recommended serious efforts to check the flow of new recruits into abnormally depressed industries. And he favoured, as we have seen, 'large Government expenditure' and a programme of public works by the government, local authorities, and public utilities – adding that 'the Bank of England and the banking system should not hesitate to allow the volume of bank deposits to expand so that the money needed to finance these undertakings will not need to be withdrawn from other forms of expenditure' (Macmillan Committee, vol. II, p. 93). Finally, once again, in the very last sentence of his Note on policy Pigou emphasised that his wide range of constructive proposals *was designed to enable present real wage-rates to be maintained* (italics added).

In fact, in their contributions to the Macmillan Committee, Pigou and Keynes were involved in virtually no fundamental or far-reaching differences regarding current policy. Though there were a number of disputes on emphasis, terminology, and abstract assumption, the most important clash between the two was over the historical question of the return to the gold standard. Here again the difference turned largely not on theoretical principles, but on Pigou's severe pessimism, as contrasted with Keynes's comparative optimism, regarding the probable management by the politicians and bankers of alternative monetary policies to that which was adopted of returning to gold at the pre-war parity.

Barely one week after Pigou's evidence to the Macmillan Committee, given on 28 and 29 May 1930, a leader in *The Times* criticised public works proposals, on the lines of the Treasury view. Pigou wrote in as follows (6 June 1930):

> When industry is in equilibrium, the conditions of demand and the rates of wages being so adjusted to one another that, apart from people in process of movement from one place or occupation to another, everybody seeking work can find it, there is a presumption that state action designed to stimulate employment in any particular field will be injurious. It will, in general, merely divert labour from more productive to less productive occupations. This presumption is capable of being stated in a great variety of forms, and is frequently to be found in current discussions of the unemployment problem. There is also a presumption that men set to work in 'artificially created' occupations will not be worth their wage...and that the 'artificial creation' of employment is a waste of national resources...Both these presumptions, whether in pure form or wrapped

---

[4] See Addendum I (p. 199): 'We have already agreed, however, that for a country in the special circumstances of Great Britain the disadvantages would greatly outweigh the advantages.' In 1931, at any rate, with unemployment over 20 per cent and still rising, Keynes was *not* prepared to put employment before the exchange rate.

in the customary wrappings, would provide good reasons for deprecating State action designed to reduce unemployment, whether by Governmental programmes of national development or in other ways – provided that there were no unemployment to reduce! When, however, as at the present time, there is an enormous mass of unemployment their virtue and their relevance are lost. If employment is 'artificially created' in these conditions, men are available to come into it, not merely from more useful occupations elsewhere, but from soul-destroying idleness...It is important to be sure that our presuppositions are adjusted not to imaginary but to actual conditions.

One could hardly ask for a more fundamental and reasoned refutation of the 'classical' fallacy that had come down from Smith, Ricardo, and James Mill. It follows the lines of similar refutations which Pigou had been making since 1908.[5] So much for wage reductions being Pigou's only suggestion in 1930.

Professor Lekachman also maintains that Mr D. H. Robertson 'allied himself' with Pigou in that he also 'committed himself to the conclusion that the route to full employment in 1939 (1930?) ran through a series of wage reductions terminating in a lower average level of wages'.[6]

V

Only about two months later a committee of the Economic Advisory Council was set up consisting of Keynes (Chairman), Pigou, Henderson, Stamp, and Robbins to consider the unemployment problem and suggest remedies. At its first meeting (10 August 1930) Keynes asked Pigou 'to prepare a memorandum outlining briefly the heads of evidence for subsequent discussion'. Pigou's memorandum was ready by 6 September and the sub-committee reported on 24 October.

These interesting and important documents were first reported on by Mr R. Skidelsky in his scholarly and instructive study *Politicians and the Slump* (1967). Mr Skidelsky describes Pigou's memorandum as an 'extremely lucid and interesting statement of the economic malaise and of the various alternative remedies'.[7] Mr Skidelsky's account makes it clear that Pigou's memorandum followed very closely, as one would expect, the lines of his evidence to the Macmillan Committee which he had given in May. In fact, Mr Skidelsky's only considerable

[5] See for example his inaugural lecture, 1908, pp. 27–8, and 1913, Chapter XI (quoted in Hutchison, 1953, p. 416). See also Pigou's lecture on 'Economy and Waste' in 1935, pp. 26ff.

[6] 1967, p. 51. Professor Lekachman quotes Robertson as saying that he considered wages to be in excess 'of what the economic value of the work would be if there were full employment' – a view presumably shared by Keynes. (See Macmillan, *Evidence*, vol. I, p. 339.)

[7] 1967, p. 207. The Committee's report (without Pigou's memorandum) has been reprinted in S. Howson and D. Winch, 1977, pp. 180–243.

quotation can be found verbatim in the Macmillan evidence. This is Pigou's 'second best' argument. According to Mr Skidelsky, Pigou and Keynes both:

> sought the most direct means of producing employment. Their philosophy was very much as Pigou described it in the following analogy: 'A man ordered to walk a tight rope carrying a bag in one hand would be better off if he were allowed to carry a second bag in the other hand, though of course if he started bagless to add a bag would handicap him.'[8]

The Committee produced a majority report signed, with some reservations, by Keynes, Pigou, Henderson, and Stamp, who all agreed in calling for an increase in home investment on a large scale. Professor Robbins wrote a dissenting minority report. Mr Skidelsky concludes that 'despite some confusion in analysis and remedy, the economists' report was a radical document with a comprehensive programme of action' (1967, p. 215). He maintains with regard to economists generally that 'most of them gave the right advice...The "wrong" advice was given much more frequently by the business community, the City and the Bank of England than by the professional economists.'[9]

VI

Continuing evidence of a fairly close compatibility of views on current policy between Pigou and Keynes in 1932 and 1933 may be glimpsed from letters and articles in *The Times*. At the bottom of the slump (17 October 1932), with unemployment over 20 per cent, there was a letter in *The Times* attacking the orthodox classical maxims of saving and economy in the following terms:

> One thing is, in our opinion, clear. The public interest in present conditions does not point towards private economy; to spend less money than we should like to do is not patriotic.
>   Moreover, what is true of individuals acting singly is equally true of groups of individuals acting through local authorities. If the citizens of a town wish to build a swimming bath, or a library, or a museum, they will not, by refraining from doing this promote a wider national interest...Through their misdirected goodwill the mounting wave of unemployment will be lifted still higher.

This letter was signed by Keynes together with Professors Pigou and Macgregor, Sir Walter Layton, Sir Arthur Salter, and Sir Josiah Stamp. The above letter was answered, two days later, by four London

---

[8] Op. cit., p. 213. See also *Committee on Finance and Industry, Evidence*, vol. II, 1931, p. 80.

[9] Op. cit., p. 209. Reviewing Mr Skidelsky's account *The Economist* concluded regarding the committee of economists, 'all except one gave broadly the right advice' (27 January 1968, p. 38). But it would probably be incorrect to suggest that the Bank of England was frequently giving the 'wrong' advice on public works, at any rate by 1935.

University economists (Professors Gregory, Hayek, Plant and Robbins). They argued in thoroughly Klassical terms:

We are of the opinion that many of the troubles of the world at the present time are due to improvident borrowing and spending on the part of the public authorities...the depression has abundantly shown that the existence of public debt on a large scale imposes frictions and obstacles to readjustment very much greater than the frictions and obstacles imposed by the existence of private debts. Hence we cannot agree with the signatories of the letter that this is a time for new municipal swimming baths, etc., merely because people 'feel they want' such amenities.

If the Government wish to help revival, the right way for them to proceed is, not to revert to their old habits of lavish expenditure, but to abolish those restrictions on trade and the movement of capital (including restrictions on new issues) which are at present impeding even the beginning of recovery.

As regards Pigou, previously on 7 June he had claimed – perhaps with some slight, but not much, exaggeration – that '*economic opinion is practically unanimous*' in holding that 'where there are no good personal reasons for private economy, there are, in present conditions, no good patriotic ones; and that the same principle is true of institutions' (italics added).

On 6 January 1933, Pigou contributed an article to *The Times* calling for a policy of expansion. He argued: 'For prosperity to be restored either money costs must fall or money prices must rise. The practical difficulties in the way of the former solution have proved so serious and the friction to be overcome so great that the *main body of instructed opinion has turned towards the latter*' (italics added).

With the forthcoming World Economic Conference in view he called for 'a general step-for-step movement towards monetary reflation... It is imperative for the Government to act'. Certainly he was cautious with regard to public investment policies. He was not prepared to suggest 'that the National Government should float a spectacular loan and devote the proceeds to *ad hoc* public works. But it is suggested that the pressure hitherto exerted in favour of policies of contraction should be lifted; the engines have been reversed long enough; it is time to move cautiously forward.' Subsequently Pigou added the message: 'When in doubt, expand.'[10]

---

[10] In a letter to *The Times* of 21 February 1933. According to Professor Dudley Dillard, in a milder version of the wage-cut myth: 'In his *Lapses from Full Employment*, published in 1945, Professor Pigou says he is in favour of attacking the problem of unemployment by manipulating demand rather than by manipulating wages. *This involves a major departure from the classical position* and a major triumph for Keynes.' In fact Pigou made it quite clear to the Macmillan Committee (1930), and again in the above article, and yet again in 1933 (p. 250), that he was in favour of operating on the side of demand (or 'prices') and not on that of costs or wages. (See Dillard, 1948, p. 24 and p. 220, italics added.) Keynes had many great and well-deserved 'triumphs' but not this one. Moreover, Pigou's position had represented '*a major departure from the classical position*' since his first writings on the subject in 1908

Far from Keynes fighting single-handed for the policies he advocated, by the time of the great depression a very large majority of the university economists who publicly expressed their opinion were supporting policies identical with or closely similar to those of Keynes. On 5 July 1932 a letter drafted by Mr R. F. Harrod (as he then was) appeared over the signature of 41 university economists, a considerable percentage of the total in those days. The signatories, who included Keynes himself and economists from a number of universities, argued for tax cuts and increased government expenditure financed by borrowing from the banks. Again, early in March 1933, a further letter, also drafted by Harrod, appeared over the signatures of 37 economists from a wide range of universities in England, Scotland, and Wales. Many names subsequently more famous were among the signatories, including those of Hall, Harrod, Helsby, Gaitskell, Meade, Carr-Saunders, and Robinson (J. and E. A. G.). They called on the Government for a programme of expansion, holding that 'the Government is singularly well placed to assist in raising demand', which it should do out of borrowing on capital account. This borrowing should be separated from the current account items in the budget to be balanced out of taxation. Thus quite a large percentage of the university economists in the country at that time were advocating publicly a policy of government spending and expansion and suggesting a means by which it should be organised by 'deficit finance'. They were opposing the Treasury view on the one hand and the principle of economy in Government spending on the other.[11]

Later in the month (March 1933) Keynes published his own expansionist proposals in his articles on *The Means to Prosperity*. As regards the internal measures, these were essentially the same mixture as before, that is the kind of proposals he had been advocating for almost a decade. As Sir Roy Harrod puts it: 'On the domestic side he was still pressing those remedies which he had begun to urge in 1924 – large-scale public works on loan account' (1951, p. 441). Sir Roy points out that in *The Means to Prosperity* the multiplier concept was much

– long before Keynes. Similar myths seem to be current among economic historians. Professor E. J. Hobsbawn maintains that during the great slump, 'the economists, with what can only be described as a quiet heroism worthy of Don Quixote, nailed their flag to the mast of Say's Law which proved that slumps could not actually occur' (1969, p. 212). In a volume 'prepared for the Economic History Society' (1972) Mr B. W. E. Alford writes that Pigou believed 'that cuts in wages would provide an important part of the solution'. According to Mr Alford 'the Government preferred to be guided by "conventional wisdom"; and insofar as the views of such economists as Cannan, Gregory, Hawtrey, Hayek, Pigou and Robbins accorded with this they found favour in official circles' (p. 68 and p. 72). This is totally incorrect regarding Pigou and 'conventional wisdom', or, at any rate, majority views.

[11] According to Lord Balogh: 'Keynes fought single-handed against all his learned colleagues who wanted to cure the great deflationary crisis with more deflation' (*Listener*, 19 August 1948). This is sheer fantasy.

more precisely developed than previously. He adds that 'the first inkling' of the idea of deficit finance was introduced. But as regards deficit finance, there had been at least quite clear 'first inklings' in, for example, Keynes's criticism of the May Committee's Economy Report in August 1931. He writes there of governments being forced to borrow as 'nature's remedy' against an indefinite downward spiralling of the slump (1931, pp. 161–2).

VII

As a further indication of the close agreement between Keynes and Pigou on current policy issues at this time there is Keynes's letter to *The Times* of 28 July 1933. A *Times* leader had rather rashly attempted to suggest a distinction or divergence between the views of Pigou and Keynes with regard to the monetary processes involved in an increase of public investment. Keynes promptly replied:

> Your leading article today suggests *a difference of opinion between myself and Professor Pigou which does not, I think, exist.* Like him, I contemplate that public works would be paid for out of loans. How far the 'creation of new money' would be necessary as a complement of this policy depends on the meaning of these words... The main point, however, is that which has been emphasized by Professor Pigou – namely, whether there are not many enterprises which would pay for themselves if we were to credit to their cost what they would save the Treasury in unemployment relief, and, I should add, what they would earn for the Treasury in the increased yield of taxation.

A few months after this, towards the end of 1933, Pigou's *Theory of Unemployment* was published, which was described by Keynes in *The General Theory* as 'the only detailed account of the classical theory of employment which exists'.[12]

Much of Pigou's argument in *The Theory of Unemployment* proceeds, as is emphasised in the Preface, at a high level of abstraction in terms of 'a simplified model of the economic world rather than that world itself in its full completeness' (1933, p. vi). But when, at one point, Pigou discusses questions of current policy he expresses support for the range of measures which he had recently been advocating together with Keynes, that is: 'Not only the undertaking of large-scale public works, but bounties, guarantees of interest, and if successful in their purpose, protective duties' (1933, p. 250).

Certainly Pigou only recommended such policies for an 'exceptional depression'. But he made it clear that this covered not only the depression phase of 'a normal trade cycle' but the structural mal-

---

[12] 1936, p. 7. See also p. 279 where *The Theory of Unemployment* is described as 'the only attempt with which I am acquainted to write down the classical theory of unemployment precisely'.

adjustment from which Britain had been suffering 'for the decade following the post-Armistice boom'.

It should be noted that these policies, almost precisely those that Keynes himself was recommending, are those which are supported in this sole 'detailed account of the classical theory of employment', and that Keynes's use of the term 'classical' is therefore quite compatible with support for the same policies which he himself supported in the 1930s: that is, the adjective 'classical', and presumably its obverse 'Keynesian', *have no coherent implications with regard to policies, but only with regard to theories or models.*[13] On the other hand, it may be emphasised that Smith and Ricardo, for example, never advocated, and were generally strongly opposed to, the policies supported by Pigou in *The Theory of Unemployment* and elsewhere, and by Keynes. However, we would note Professor Dudley Dillard's view that it 'involved a major departure from the classical position' to be in favour of attacking unemployment from the side of demand rather than wages, *as Pigou had, of course, long favoured.*

Attempts from the Keynesian side to resolve what might seem to be something of a paradox have been of two contradictory kinds:

Either (a) it is alleged – as we have seen above – that Pigou supported crucially different policies from Keynes, in particular, with respect to wage reductions.

Or (b) it is suggested that somehow Pigou was inconsistent as between his theory and the policies he recommended.

Neither of these arguments is well founded in logic or fact; and although Keynes might be said to have toyed with each of them, *he himself never seriously developed or persisted with either.*

[13] Professor D. Patinkin has emphasised the point that monetary theory and monetary policy 'represent two different spheres of discourse. And whatever the relationship between the two, it is clearly not a one-to-one correspondence: different policy recommendations can emanate from the same conceptual theoretical framework; and different frameworks can lead to the same policy conclusions.' Professor Patinkin then contrasts the 'conceptual frameworks' of Pigou and Henry Simons with that of Keynes and concludes: 'Thus both quantity theorists and Keynesians – each from their own conceptual framework – advocated policies of combating unemployment by public-works expenditure and/or deficit financing.' We would only comment that this could very easily be the case with regard to differing *'conceptual frameworks'* – whatever exactly these are – which are presumably empirically unfalsifiable and without empirical content. But 'monetary theory' should surely constitute something more than simply a 'conceptual framework'. So contrasting *theories*, presumably, often may not be compatible with the same policy-recommendations – (even assuming, of course, the same value-judgments). (See Patinkin's article, 1972, pp. 140–1.) Subsequently Professor Patinkin has concluded that 'the major revolution affected by *The General Theory* was in the field of theory and not of policy'; and that 'the difference between Keynes' policy views in the *Treatise* and in *The General Theory* stems less from the theoretical differences between these two books than from the experience of five additional years of unprecedented depression in England during which the long-term rate of interest had continued unavailingly to decline' (see Patinkin, 1975, p. 261, and 1976, p. 137).

As regards (a), Keynes himself could hardly seriously pursue the allegation that Pigou supported direct cuts in money wages – that fantastic distortion has been left for a subsequent generation. *First*, Keynes knew that Pigou had been signing the same reports and letters on policy as himself. *Secondly*, Keynes himself had stated (1930–1) that with regard to the policy of cutting wages 'there is scarcely one responsible person in Great Britain prepared to recommend it openly', and that: 'the unwillingness of employers and associations of employers who have appeared before the Macmillan Committee to recommend this solution has been truly remarkable.'[14]

Obviously there was nothing very novel or 'revolutionary' in the 1930s in opposing wage-cuts. However, in *The General Theory*, in criticising Pigou's *The Theory of Unemployment*, Keynes did rather vaguely and misleadingly accuse Pigou of believing 'that in the long run employment can be cured by wage adjustments' (1936, p. 278, italics added).[15]

But one of Keynes's own most celebrated dicta emphasises the practical irrelevance for mortals of propositions about 'the long run' and this applies to Keynes's criticism of Pigou. Nevertheless, Keynes's criticism of *The Theory of Unemployment* has been seized upon in order to charge Pigou with 'the sheer indecency of calling for wage cuts at a time when many of even those in employment were finding it a struggle to make ends meet'.[16]

[14] See S. Howson and D. Winch, 1977, p. 55; and Keynes, 1931, p. 31. Keynes was giving one of the Harris Foundation lectures in Chicago. An interesting account of the discussions at the 1931–2 meetings of the Harris Foundation has been given by Professor J. R. Davis who makes clear that most of the leading American economists who expressed views on the point *were opposed to wage-cuts* (e.g. H. L. Schultz, Hansen, Schlichter). See Professor Davis's paper of 1972, and his book (1971). Dr G. Myrdal has maintained that 'before the Great Depression in America economists in general actually believed in Say's Law of the equality, or even identity of aggregate supply and demand...The inherited and still prevalent theory was that unemployment should be cured by pressing down wages.' Similarly Professor J. K. Galbraith writes of 'the rigid and enduring commitment to Say's Law' of the economics profession during the early years of the Great Depression. Neither Dr Myrdal nor Professor Galbraith cite any evidence for these generalisations (except that the former recounts an anecdote of a conversation in the 1920s with a single, unnamed American economist). There seems to be plenty of evidence refuting the propositions of Dr Myrdal and Professor Galbraith. (See Myrdal, 1973, p. 4; and Galbraith, 1971, pp. 63–4.)

[15] Susan Howson and Donald Winch agree that: 'It should be clear...that Pigou was not a simple-minded and fatalistic advocate of wage-cuts.' It certainly should. Howson and Winch continue: 'Nevertheless, it is not difficult to see how such a misconception could arise, and why Keynes should succumb to the temptation of treating Pigou's *Theory of Unemployment* as a repository of "classical" ideas' (1977, p. 66n). It is not difficult to see this if one bears in mind the powerful desire on the part of Keynes (and his followers for decades afterwards) to create and believe in a revolutionary mythology.

[16] M. Stewart, 1967, p. 68. Mr Stewart also claimed that in the early 1930s the 'view was almost unanimous' among economists that wages and government expenditure should be cut in the depression while 'most economists' supported the Treasury view

As regards (b) the suggestion that Pigou and others were not *logically* entitled to have joined with Keynes, as they had, in opposing the 'Treasury' view and in advocating public investment: neither Keynes nor his followers have ever spelt out, with the relevant texts, just what Pigou's logical failure amounted to. Keynes confined himself to his commendation of Professor Robbins as 'almost alone' among 'post-war economists' in that he continued 'to maintain a consistent scheme of thought, his practical recommendations belonging to the same system as his theory'.[17] Pigou's answer was to maintain that according to Keynes: '*Logically* "the classical school" are bound to reject Government attempts to alleviate a slump by means of public works and to welcome economy campaigns in times of depression... This, of course, is a travesty. The classical view is not one which either asserts or implies that full employment always exists.'[18] One can only comment that what can be described as a 'travesty' of the views of 'the classical school' depends on what you mean by 'the classical school'. In so far as Pigou himself is being described as a representative of 'the classical school', this, of course, *is* a 'travesty'. But not much of a 'travesty' is involved in attributing such doctrines to Adam Smith, James Mill, Ricardo, and others.

However, although there was 'really extremely little' disagreement between Pigou and Keynes as to what should be done to counter depression and unemployment in the early 1930s, it seems that there might have been serious *hypothetical* disagreement regarding what *would have been* the right policies, or about what forces were at work, in the somewhat milder cyclical depressions of the half century or so before 1914. In *Employment and Equilibrium* Pigou claimed that significant wage flexibility had existed before 1914 and that this explained a fairly stable average level of unemployment, over the cycle, of about 4–5 per cent over the latter part of the nineteenth century, during a period when very large changes in the size and nature of the labour force were taking place. He concluded that the statistical

(op. cit., p. 66). However, these historical observations were replaced by a less imaginative version of the record in the second edition of Mr Stewart's book (1972).

[17] 1936, p. 20n. Professor D. E. Moggridge (1976, p. 30) emphasises that Keynes believed in 'this inconsistency between premises and conclusions'. But no attempt is made to explain just what this alleged 'inconsistency' amounted to in, for example, the writings of Pigou. The charge seems to be unfounded.

[18] 1949, p. 96. In his review of *The General Theory* Pigou complained: 'When one of the arraigned persons had palpably not made a particular mistake, the method of lumping enables Mr. Keynes to say that he ought to have made it, and that, in making it, he was false to the "logic" of his own school – has allowed his "good commonsense to overbear his bad theory"' (1936, p. 116). However, Pigou was historically and tactically mistaken in accepting the label of 'classical' and therefore his being 'lumped' together with Smith, James Mill, and Ricardo, who never countenanced the kind of public works policies which Pigou advocated, and who were originally responsible for the opposition to such policies which he repeatedly attacked from 1908 onwards.

evidence which he presented showed that 'the classical view', on his definition of it, had 'not done badly'.[19] Presumably the Keynesian interpretation of the history of unemployment in Britain in the nineteenth century would have been entirely different, as would views on the policies which were then appropriate. But the Keynesian side in this case never seems to have been elaborated with the same degree of explicitness *and empirical evidence* which Pigou had brought to bear on the side of what he called 'the classical view'.

VIII

The broad measure of agreement on employment policy between Pigou and Keynes thus continued on through the bottom of the slump. From 1934 the economy was slowly moving out of the depths of depression and the level of unemployment was falling. Whether for this reason, or because of the ferocious and apparently fundamental disputes that broke out with the publication of *The General Theory* in January 1936, Pigou seems to have contributed little or nothing further to current policy discussions by way of letters and articles in *The Times* or elsewhere.

In *The General Theory* Keynes was concerned to emphasise to the full what he considered to be fundamental disagreements on terminology, assumptions, and historical criticisms. This represented a complete and sudden *volte-face* compared with his policy writings for the past decade, *which had repeatedly and strongly emphasised agreement.* Now, however, in *The General Theory* Keynes saw himself as having to convince 'my fellow economists' of fundamental errors 'in orthodox economics', as represented particularly by Pigou. He maintained that he was attempting 'to bring to an issue the deep divergences of opinion between economists which have for the time being almost destroyed the practical influence of economic theory, and will, until they are resolved, continue to do so' (1936, p. vi).

But on policy issues only a fairly small minority of university

[19] 1949, p. 98. Pigou developed this point in an article of 1944 arguing that before 1914 it was often taken for granted that you could reduce wage rates while leaving total outlay, and so the demand for labour, or wages bill, intact. Pigou maintained that this view was not then wrong, but goes on to recognise Keynes's 'very important contribution to clear thinking' when he challenged this during the 1930s. However, Pigou then makes plain that he does *not* accept the view advanced by 'certain priests' of 'the new economics' that general wage-cuts are *necessarily* foredoomed to failure in reducing unemployment. Incidentally, Pigou goes on to warn of the danger of progressive inflation resulting from high levels of employment: 'The danger is a real one. For with wage rates settled by negotiations conducted independently in separate industries without much regard for the economic situation of the country as a whole, the tendency for these rates to be pushed upwards as the employment situation improves will be very strong' (1944, pp. 18ff).

economists, in particular at the London School of Economics, disagreed at all significantly with Keynes's policy proposals (though Mr
R. G. Hawtrey at the Treasury was also opposed on rather different
grounds). There was probably then far less disagreement and divergence among university economists on the main policy issues than
in the 1950s and 1960s. Again, at the beginning of the century, on the
tariff reform issue, the minority of university economists in favour of
tariffs was relatively much weightier, and had much more to say for
itself, than the minority in the early 1930s. The massive obstacles to
the adoption of expansionist policies in the *early* 1930s lay not with
academic opinion, but in Whitehall, the City, and Westminster – to
whom of course *The General Theory* was not addressed and on whom
it could have had little or no *direct* impact. *Shelves-full of often extremely
abstract literature, with volumes of high-priori 'theorising' and 'model'-
building, have been devoted to the differences between Keynes and 'the classics'
(with whom Pigou is, we would suggest, quite misleadingly included) with
regard to analysis, abstract models, 'conceptual frameworks', terminology, and
critical–historical judgments. Perhaps it signifies something about what
economists often miscall 'theory' that whether all these 'fundamental' differences had any implications for policy or for policy-relevant predictions – and
if so precisely what – seems to have been very little investigated.* Again, there
has been much expert study of the changes in terminology and
abstract model-building between the *Treatise on Money* and *The General
Theory*. But again, whether these changes had any significant implications for policy, and if so precisely what were the corresponding
shifts in Keynes's predictions and policy proposals, does not seem to
have received much attention.[20] The question therefore arises as to
the significance for policy of *The General Theory* and as to the changes
in policy based on such new predictions as it provided, as contrasted
with the predictions and policies on which Keynes had been in broad,
fundamental agreement with Pigou.

In fact, the onset of war forced macroeconomic policy problems
towards a much more practical and operational framework (one in fact
which was eventually to prove useful in peace as well as war). Here
undoubtedly Keynes was the leader. But if peace had continued it is
difficult to see just in what way the onslaughts in *The General Theory*
on 'orthodoxy' and the 'classicals', would have hastened the relief of
unemployment. For these attacks were in large part on those *who agreed
with Keynes regarding policy.* The conflicts which broke out *might*
therefore have had the effect of concealing rather than strengthening

[20] According to Mr Lauchlin Currie, one of the doyens of 'the fiscal revolution' in
America: 'Although I considered myself a Keynesian from way back, I felt (and still
feel) that *we had little to learn for policy purposes from The General Theory*' (1972, p. 141,
italics added).

and making more impressive the considerable range of agreement in the 1930s among economists regarding policies against unemployment; and this could hardly have helped in the conversion of hesitant politicians and civil servants.

In fact, Keynes's policy proposals, though varying in emphasis and priorities from time to time, remained, with regard to the unemployment problem under peacetime conditions, broadly the same from 1924 onwards. In what was virtually his last policy proposals under more-or-less peacetime conditions in December 1937 he was proposing the preparation of plans by local authorities, the railways, port and river authorities, etc., etc., to counter the next slump. These plans were essentially and substantially on the same lines as those he had been putting forward for the previous thirteen years, and indeed on not dissimilar lines to those of the Minority Report of the Royal Commission on the Poor Laws of 1909. As Herbert Stein has observed:

> The fact is that the theoretical framework Keynes was later to construct was not necessary to the policies he was recommending, which later came to be known as Keynesian policies. The old theory – the standard Cambridge (England) 'classical' economics – was sufficient to support these policies.
>
> *Keynes's economic policy views of the 1920s were unorthodox with respect to what was being done, but not with respect to British academic economics of the time* [1969, p. 135, italics added].

Keynes had started to advocate public investment policies against unemployment in 1924 at the instigation of Lloyd George, who in turn was reviving the ideas of the pre-war years developed by the Webbs and others, which, as we have seen, had even then influenced Churchill – who, paradoxically, was now to switch round to the other side.[21] Now, of course, after the war, the unemployment problem was a much more serious one. But at no stage was it a case of the sophisticated analysis of those who advocated public investment against unemployment, confronting the primitive 'common-sense' of those who opposed government action on the basis of what came to be known as 'The Treasury View'. Quite the opposite: the robust common-sense was with those who maintained that government spending could and should do something to alleviate massive unemployment: the sophisticated analysis, deriving especially from Ricardo, was deployed by those who maintained that government investment and public works would not, and/or could not, reduce unemployment.

[21] According to an anecdote of Professor W. A. Robson, at a party in the early 1930s, 'when Keynes came up to greet Mrs. Webb...she said, "Ah, Mr. Keynes, we are awaiting with great interest your economic theory to cure unemployment." To which Keynes replied, "Oh, it's all in the Minority Report, Mrs. Webb"' (W. A. Robson, 1963, p. xii). This is quoted by Otto Steiger (1971). Dr Steiger gives a valuable account of the Swedish contributions to employment theory and policy which went back to before the First World War.

Anyhow, regarding not *hypothetical* differences, but actual current policy problems, Keynes, by 1937, is admitting and agreeing that 'when it comes to practice, there is *really extremely little*' between himself, on the one hand, and Pigou and Robertson on the other.[22] It must also be noted how the majority view of economists, aided perhaps by the grim demonstration by Nazi Germany of how a government then could spend its way out of unemployment, began to sway a wider body of opinion as the 1930s wore on. The majority view of economists, in favour of public spending, was brought to bear on the top Treasury officials through the Economic Advisory Council and its offspring the Committee on Economic Information, which was regularly expressing Keynes's views, or near equivalents thereof.[23] In fact, by early 1935 the top experts in the Treasury had abandoned their notorious Ricardian 'view' expressed in 1929 that public works could not or would not alleviate unemployment, and such key Treasury eminences as Sir Frederick Phillips and Sir Richard Hopkins were urging public works and investment as a stimulus to economic revival.[24] *It is clear, therefore, that a decisive phase in the conversion of the Treasury to 'Keynesian' ideas had taken place one year before the publication of The General Theory.* Moreover, not only among a considerable majority of academic economists, not only among the top Treasury officials, but *at the top of the Bank of England*, the conversion to Keynesian ideas had taken place *well before the publication of The General Theory in 1936*. As Professsor Sayers has revealed, with the appointment as

[22] When Susan Howson and Donald Winch, as loyal 'Keynesians', maintain that there were 'major differences of emphasis' on policy questions between Keynes, on the one hand, and Pigou and Robertson on the other, they are contradicting Keynes's own statement that the differences were 'really extremely little'. But this simply exemplifies that, as he himself is reported as stating, Keynes was not a 'Keynesian'. (See Keynes, 1973, vol. XIV, p. 259; and S. Howson and D. Winch, 1977, p. 163.)

[23] See S. Howson and D. Winch, 1977, especially p. 130.

[24] It was in 1929 in his Budget speech that Winston Churchill made his often-quoted statement of what he called the Treasury 'dogma', repeating what Ricardo had proclaimed in Parliament in 1819 to the effect that: 'Very little additional employment, can, in fact, and as a general rule, be created by State borrowing and State expenditure.' It is paradoxical that Churchill should have associated himself with this 'dogma' because in 1908 – the first year in which Pigou had launched what seems to have been the first modern attack on it – Churchill himself, somewhat like the Webbs in their Minority Report of the Poor Law Commission a year later, had spoken of the 'paramount necessity to make scientific provision against the fluctuations and setbacks which are inevitable in world commerce and in national industry'. Churchill had deplored 'the lack of any central organisation of industry, or any general concerted control either of ordinary government work, or of any extraordinary relief works', and adopting what his son described as 'an almost Keynesian position', had emphasised the need to have 'in permanent existence certain recognised industries of a useful, but uncompetitive character, like afforestation, managed by public departments and capable of being expanded or contracted according to the needs of the labour market, just as easily as you can pull out the stops or work the pedals of an organ' (see Randolph Churchill, 1967, p. 292, quoted by H. Stein, 1969, p. 512).

an Economic Adviser to the Governor of Henry Clay in 1933 – and even from 1931 before his formal appointment – he 'was the evangelist of a Keynesian approach to the problem of unemployment'. By *early 1935* the Governor himself was maintaining that a policy of expansion was 'his well-established position' and that it was 'ridiculous', and unfair, to suggest 'that if the Chancellor could be persuaded into a public-works attack on unemployment, "the whole thing would be stopped by Norman at the Bank of England"' (R. S. Sayers, 1976, vol. 2, pp. 472–3).

IX

In his work *The Years of High Theory* Professor Shackle has argued for the 'clearer vision', at some points, of *The Treatise on Money* as compared with *The General Theory*, with its 'many pages of irrelevant, confused and fallacious argument' (1967, p. 143).

Professor Shackle even asks regarding *The General Theory*:

Was it necessary or worthwhile? *The Treatise* had efficient machinery, easier, indeed, to grasp than that of the *General Theory*. This was not altogether an advantage, in the circumstances of the time and for the purpose in hand. *The mystique, the ascendancy of the later book arose partly from its seeming so difficult, and that difficulty arose partly from faults of exposition* [op. cit., p. 162, italics added].

The relative merits of *The Treatise on Money* and *The General Theory* are involved with obviously highly controversial points of interpretation and intellectual taste as to which Professor Patinkin (1976) takes an almost opposite view to that of Professor Shackle. But Professor Shackle is surely justified with regard to the yearning for a revolutionary *mystique*, which has remained so powerful as to fashion history in terms of myths rather than facts.

In fact it seems that a 'mystique' is what 'High Theory' is mainly there to produce. As Professor Galbraith has cogently explained:

Prior to the publication of the immensely difficult *General Theory*, he had advocated its principal conclusion...in clear English in both the United States and Great Britain. He had not been greatly influential. Then in *The General Theory* he involved economists in a highly professional debate on technical concepts and their interpretation. His practical recommendations were not central to this discussion. But the participants carried his practical program to Washington and Whitehall. *Would a simple clearly argued book ...have been as influential? My reluctant inclination is to doubt it.*[25]

[25] 1971, p. 36 (italics added). Professor H. G. Johnson, in his trenchantly cynical account, also emphasises that 'the new theory had to have the appropriate degree of difficulty to understand'. This was in order to recruit on its side a new cohort of Young Turks eager for an academic generation-war which would leave their seniors' intellectual equipment devalued (1975, p. 95). See our concluding chapter.

So 'High Theory' *can* be fruitful for policy-making, but not exactly by the rational processes its devotees would like to claim. Technical jargon, or a '*mystique*', heighten the confidence of academics who are then more successful in impressing bewildered civil servants and politicians. It was certainly not *logically or intellectually* essential that before government spending could be increased to employ some of the 10–23 per cent of the labour force who were unemployed between 1924 and 1939, volumes – however, 'professional' and full of 'theory', or rather of analysis, or of conceptual-frameworks – had to be produced arguing over such issues as whether 'savings' and 'investment' were necessarily equal or not, or as to what 'really determines' the rate of interest. The controversies stirred up might rather have had the effect of encouraging the excuses of politicians for their inactivity on the grounds of the disagreements between economists. Moreover, as Mr Robert Skidelsky has rightly observed: 'The emergence of social science as a modern growth industry has reinforced the tendency of social scientists to emphasise the theoretical requirements for social action in order to justify the heavy investment of public funds in their activities' (1975, p. 91).

This questionable intellectual tendency would seem to account, to a large extent, for subsequent attempts to exalt the contribution to policy-making of *The General Theory*. It does seem to amount to sheer pedantry to insist that before *The General Theory* in 1936 Keynes, and all the other economists who had already done so, 'could not really answer' the Treasury view against public investment.[26] The Treasury view, or rather the Ricardo view, had been answered as long previously as Bentham. In fact, though there were one or two exceptions, Mr Skidelsky is pretty well justified in maintaining that it was 'rejected by all the leading economists, quite apart from Keynes' (1967, p. 40) and that *certainly* included Pigou.[27]

---

[26] Mr Stewart, for example, has taken 'the Treasury view' extremely seriously, in order, apparently, to highlight the achievement of *The General Theory*: 'Keynes could not really answer this theoretical case, and although he continued to advocate public works in the early 1930s, he was in the position of a man calling on emotional grounds for a course of action that the intellect showed was wrong. The subordination of emotion to reason represented by government policy in the early 1930s is a sufficiently rare phenomenon in politics to call for encouragement and praise; it must have been particularly galling to an arch-intellectual like Keynes that it should happen in a case where he was stubbornly convinced that reason had got it wrong' (1967, p. 67). According, therefore, to Mr Stewart, in the early 1930s almost all economists were subordinating reason to emotion, while the great champions of reason as against emotion, such as Ramsay MacDonald, Snowden, Jimmy Thomas, Neville Chamberlain etc., were defending the Ricardo–Treasury view that – with unemployment well over 20 % – public works could not, or should not be used to reduce unemployment.

[27] In 1976 Professor D. E. Moggridge remarks how, in the early 1930s at the University of Chicago, 'economists working in the classical tradition had reached Keynes's policy conclusions through commonsense observation while continuing to hold to traditional theory' (p. 107). The logic of the Chicago economists is (rightly) not questioned. Also a most welcome recognition is forthcoming from Professor Moggridge

The General Theory, therefore, appeared one year before the launching of the rearmament programme, which marked the beginning of the end of chronic mass unemployment. One can only speculate as to what would have happened regarding Keynesian policies and the level of unemployment had the Second World War not occurred when it did. But it is clear that the conversion of public opinion, including Treasury opinion, was well advanced before the onset of war or even of the rearmament of 1937.[28] Certainly Keynes's great leap forward in applying his analysis, or 'theory', to policy-making came with the transition to the war economy, notably in his articles 'The Income and Fiscal Potential of Great Britain' (December 1939), 'The Concept of National Income' (March 1940), and parts of 'How to Pay for the War' (1940). These were, of course, among Keynes's greatest constructive achievements and one of the most effective practical applications of an appropriate 'conceptual framework' to government policies – though hardly of 'laws', functional relationships, or 'theories' in an authentic empirical sense. It might be claimed that the development of the national income framework stems in part from *The General Theory*. But it could also be claimed that the rather dogmatic discussion of national income concepts such as 'saving' and 'investment' was among the most unsatisfactory parts of that book.[29] The pioneer attempt to quantify Keynesian concepts in terms of a national income framework seems to have been Mr Colin Clark's treatment based on the 'Fundamental Equations' in *The Treatise on Money*. It might well be questioned whether, in this respect, there was an advance rather than the reverse as between the *Treatise* and *The General Theory*, which simply as far as policy guidance is concerned might well have been largely by-passed.

of the prevalence of 'strong myths' regarding Keynesian economics, notably of a myth which 'sees pre-1936 depression policies and policy advice as concentrating on wage cuts and rejecting counter-cyclical public works policy' (p. 183). Professor Moggridge rightly noted that – as late as 1976 – the myth 'is far from dead' – at any rate in Cambridge, England. It seems, therefore, rather a non-sequitur for S. Howson and D. Winch to argue (1977, p. 162) that: 'Since the Treasury officials were to some extent "monetarists", partly because of Hawtrey but also because the quantity theory of money was an integral part of "classical" economic theory, Keynes could not produce a really satisfactory alternative to the orthodox views until he had abandoned that theory. Keynes's ability to provide an alternative...only became really forceful when he argued on the basis provided by his *General Theory*.' But the top Treasury officials had abandoned their classical 'view' of 1929 and had been converted to Keynesian policies by early 1935, a year before the publication of *The General Theory* – as Howson and Winch show (p. 130).

[28] Keynes himself maintained that 'the weight both of authority and of public opinion in favour of meeting a recession in employment by organized loan expenditure is now so great that this policy is practically certain to be adopted when the time comes' (*The Times*, 3 January 1938).

[29] It is interesting to note such a dyed-in-the-wool 'Keynesian' as Sir Roy Harrod maintaining that the *Treatise* 'is a much richer store of Keynesian thinking' than *The General Theory* (see R. Lekachman, ed., 1964, p. 141).

If one can imagine that Keynes had been less intellectually energetic then he might have produced in 1936, not *The General Theory*, but a second, revised edition of *The Treatise on Money*. Among such revisions or extensions, Keynes might well have produced the elaboration of the operational national income concepts, and the beginnings of the regular statistical measurements involved, which he and others developed in 1939–40. Certainly the academic world would have been deprived of a huge intellectual–argumentative bonanza. But it seems doubtful whether, in the longer or shorter run, *the development of policies against unemployment and instability* would have been less effective – in the longer run perhaps more effective. Of course *The General Theory* introduced challenging insights about the history of economics, as well as considerable changes in definitions, terminology, and in his 'conceptual framework'. But such *empirical* and *predictional* changes as were introduced by Keynes between 1930 and 1936 naturally reflected the very special deflationary conditions of the greatest depression in history, and as such would be unlikely to provide sound *empirical* foundations for a *general* theory.

X

There were three main policy doctrines regarding unemployment which Keynes called 'classical', and certainly the first two of them may suitably be so described. These were (i) that public investment could not raise the level of employment and investment but only divert part of an apparently fixed fund of investment resources; and (ii) that governments should practise economy and cut down spending especially in depressions – the classical built-in destabiliser. These doctrines were both well rooted in the Turgot–Smith theory of saving and investment to the effect that all savings pass smoothly and 'immediately' into investment, a theory which may well be called 'classical' since it was above all propagated by Smith, James Mill and Ricardo, the latter expressly applying it in Parliament to employment policy in the post-war depression after the Napoleonic wars. These doctrines remained influential right down to the early 1930s, and, of course, had been trenchantly restated by the Treasury in opposing proposals for public works in 1929. By this time, however, the Klassical doctrines had lost most of their grip on academic circles, except in London. Though they were still influential in Whitehall, the City, and Westminster, *even there they were soon to fade*. But in *The General Theory* Keynes concentrated not so much on these two doctrines – on which of course Pigou, some time before Keynes, was emphatically anti-classical – as on a *third* doctrine to the effect that general wage-cuts would relieve unemployment – though he had claimed in 1931 that 'scarcely one responsible person' was actually advocating this policy. The wage-cuts doctrine involved assumptions, as Pigou explicitly recognised, of perfectly free competition and perfect mobility in the labour market. Pigou also recognised, of course, that these assumptions were completely unrealistic, though it is true that a few other English economists, notably at the London School of Economics, urged wage 'flexibility' as a cure for unemployment (without apparently taking account of the unreality of the assumptions needed). Certainly Pigou made some use of the flexible, perfectly competitive model simply as a reference model. But he repeatedly made it clear that this model differed crucially from the real-world economy of Britain in the inter-war years and he repeatedly and emphatically rejected policy conclusions drawn from such a flexible, competitive model.

Anyhow, whether or not Pigou is to be described as 'classical' in a Keynesian sense – a term which can indeed historically be given a very valid and weighty content – we have seen that in his day Pigou, in 1930, gave what nearly forty years later can be recognised as thoroughly sound and relevant policy advice, in broad agreement, of course, with Keynes. Sir Austin Robinson (1967) – after claiming that 'Pigou had no clear lead other than wage reduction to offer' in 1930–1 – invited us to 'contrast today'.[30] There was indeed a contrast, but unfortunately it seems to work in the opposite direction to that which he implies. One may venture the judgment that if English 'Keynesian' – or Pseudo-Keynesian – economists in the 1960s and 1970s had been giving nearly as well-founded and widely-agreed advice as Pigou contributed in 1930 – and if indeed this advice had been acted upon – British economic policy would have been considerably less unsuccessful at the latter date than it actually was.

However, in the two to three decades following Keynes's death, in spite of the declining relevance of key assumptions in *The General Theory*, 'Keynesian' or Pseudo-Keynesian policy-doctrines exercised great influence, though these doctrines were crucially exaggerated or distorted as compared with those to which the Master had actually committed himself.[31] But this is another story.

[30] 1967, p. 650. Anyhow, even having 'no clear lead' other than wage reductions in 1930–1, may not, perhaps have been *quite* so harmful or useless as having 'no clear lead' other than an 'incomes policy' in 1974–5.

[31] One of these policy-doctrines related to the vital question of the unemployment target. In 1937 in his last current proposals under actual mainly peace-time conditions, Keynes advocated the cutting back of public investment expenditure when unemployment *was still at* 12–13%, because 'we cannot safely regard even half of these unemployed insured persons as being available to satisfy home demand'. This indicates that Keynes held *very* different conceptions of the employment targets which could wisely be aimed at from those of pseudo-Keynesians in the decades after his death. (See Keynes's articles in *The Times*, 12, 13, and 14 January 1937, and Hutchison, 1977.)

7

The Keynesian revolution, uncertainty, and deductive general theory

I

The view has been maintained, with some justification, that, ever since its emergence in the late seventeenth and the early eighteenth century, orthodox modern economic theorising has been built around, or has mainly consisted of, one central model of maximisation and self-equilibration. It has been claimed regarding modern political economy and economics that though there have been 'unsuccessful rebellions ...its basic maximising model has never been replaced',[1] that is, neither its maximising statics nor its self-adjusting dynamics.

The self-adjusting, self-equilibrating model, or 'system', was generalised and consummated in *The Wealth of Nations*. But by Adam Smith the model was not carried to extremes of unrealistic abstraction, and was based on historical and psychological evidence and analysis, including a view of man. Ricardo, however, reduced self-adjustment and self-equilibration to one of his extreme abstractions, or 'strong cases', by explicitly and precisely introducing the critical fundamental assumption which is essential for this 'model'. For the keystone of the whole orthodox, post-Ricardian structure, in terms of 'explaining' how individuals might come to be acting, or might *be able* to act, in the way prescribed by the model, was an assumption about knowledge, certainty, and expectations. This keystone has, ever since Ricardo, retained its essential role in the central body of orthodox theorising, and also in some theorising claimed to be anti-, or contra-orthodox. I would like to quote an earlier account of this 'fundamental assumption', which included examples from Bentham to Professor Joan Robinson, and which was written when the Keynesian 'revolution' was at its height (Hutchison, 1937 and 1938):

> There is one remarkable characteristic common to nearly all formulations of the 'Fundamental Principle' from its origins in Utilitarian doctrines down to the present time. One of Bentham's formulations was: 'Nature has placed mankind under the governance of two sovereign masters, pain and pleasure. It is for them alone to point out what we ought to do, as well as to determine what we shall do' [1859, vol. I, p. 1].

[1] D. F. Gordon, 1965, p. 124. See below Chapter 11, Section 1.

Ricardo expressed the principle, in a particular connection, thus: 'Whilst every man is free to employ his capital where he pleases, he will naturally seek for it that employment which is most advantageous; he will naturally be dissatisfied with a profit of 10 per cent, if by removing his capital he can obtain a profit of 15 per cent' [1951, vol. 1, p. 88].

J. S. Mill speaks of the fundamental assumption 'that man is a being who is determined, by the necessity of his nature, to prefer a greater portion of wealth to a smaller in all cases' [1844, p. 138].

Finally, a modern formulation: 'The fundamental assumption of economic analysis is that every individual acts in a sensible manner, and it is sensible for the individual to balance marginal cost against marginal gain...sensible conduct leads to the maximisation of money gains' [J. Robinson, 1933, pp. 211–12].

The common characteristic of all these different formulations – chosen quite at random – of the Fundamental Assumption, is that as they stand they appear further to postulate, and only are applicable if the further postulate is made, that all expectations are perfectly correct. They therefore involve passing over all the problems of economy in the world as it is which may be said to arise from precisely this factor of uncertainty and imperfect foresight. They all make no mention of the question *how* one is to maximise one's profits. They simply say that it is 'rational', 'sensible', or 'natural' to do this assuming, presumably, that one *knows* how this can be done. To decisions which are not of this certain, automatic kind they have no applicability. The absence of uncertainty in the conditions analysed emerges clearly from the formulae themselves [Hutchison, 1937, p. 637; 1938 and 1960, p. 84].

II

Essentially interconnected with 'the fundamental assumption' of full or adequate knowledge and correct expectations have been the two central concepts of competition and equilibrium. Competition, with heightened 'rigour', became *perfect* competition, while market equilibrium requiring correct, and therefore compatible, expectations, introduced the 'dynamic' element. The competitive concept with its essential characteristic of large numbers of decision-makers, each too 'small' to impinge on one another's decisions, is logically interlocked with the perfect knowledge concept so as to secure the compatible and correct expectations required for equilibrium. Oligopoly and monopoly – beyond a single isolated monopolist – cannot be accommodated in the general model. The existence of oligopolists and monopolists (if not arbitrarily isolated) would introduce contradictions with regard to the fundamental assumption of adequate knowledge, which would have to be specifically and arbitrarily 'squared', or lifted *ad hoc*.[2] To quote again:

[2] As Professor Herbert Simon has observed: 'More than a century ago, Cournot identified a problem that has become the permanent and ineradicable scandal of economic theory. He observed that where a market is supplied by only a few producers, the notion of profit-maximisation is ill-defined. The choice that would be substantively

A game of chess or bridge with all players having perfect expectations of one another's play, and then adjusting their own, could not be played. The example might be put forward of two duopolists both of whom foresaw that the other possessed full knowledge of the theory of duopoly and was going to fix his price at the monopoly price, fixed *their own* prices at the monopoly price, and thus, in a certain sense, maximised their profits. But this is not really a case of perfect expectation and consequent adjustment of conduct in accordance with the maximum principle... Perfect expectation is only compatible with 'competitive' conditions [Hutchison, 1937, pp. 643–4].

In fact what the 'fundamental assumption' of adequate knowledge does is to set up the central model, and its various offshoots, as what Dr Latsis has illuminatingly described as a 'single-exit', or 'strait-jacket' model (1972, p. 211). It is the adequate knowledge postulate which closes off all the exits except one, and which tells consumers and firms which exit to take, as well as telling economists which exits they *should*, or logically *must* take. But, as Professor Shackle has empha-sised, nothing describable as acts of 'choice' or 'decisions' can be said to take place under such an assumption. Thus the 'model' para-doxically renders purely mechanical what it is purporting to describe and explain as the actions of competitive individuals:

> With uncertainty absent economic life is 'problemless' and automatic, and people would become more or less automata. As Professor Knight has pointed out: 'With uncertainty absent man's energies are devoted altogether in doing things; it is doubtful whether intelligence itself would exist in such a situation; in a world so built, it seems likely that all organic readjustment would become mechanical, all organisms automata' [Hutchison, 1937, p. 638, and Knight, 1921, p. 268].

With regard to the equilibrium concept: 'The position of equilib-rium has always been the very central concept of economic analysis. The only justification for the special concern with this position and the treatment of disequilibrium as simply a temporary aberration from the normal, can be that, in fact, the economic conditions under which we live in some sense 'tend' towards it' (Hutchison, 1937, p. 646).

The implications of the equilibrium concept are all-pervasive throughout the central body of economic theorising, entering into such other concepts as 'normal' rates of profit and into the treatment (or non-treatment) of money:

> The assumption of a tendency towards equilibrium implies, on the usual definition, the assumption of a tendency towards perfect expectations, competitive conditions, and the disappearance of money. To get anything like a precise answer to the question as to what extent this assumption is true or untrue would require vastly complicated empirical investigations. Possibly it was nearer the truth in the 19th century than it is to-day. In some

rational for each actor depends on the choices made by the other actors; none can choose without making assumptions about how others will choose' (1976, p. 140).

markets, obviously, expectations are more nearly perfect than in others. Probably the more 'oligopolistic' markets become the less perfect expectations become, for then there is an important addition to the number of factors about which, up till now, at any rate, only fairly uncertain expectations can be formed – the behaviour of rival oligopolists. The lengthening of the processes of production would also probably increase uncertainty and disequilibrium [op. cit., p. 648].

III

Since Ricardo first inserted this decisive element into the central model of so much of orthodox economic theorising, it is remarkable how far economists have managed to avert their gaze from the extreme unrealities of the abstractions involved in the adequate knowledge assumption. Until very recently, those who have paid any significant attention to this decisive assumption have been very few and far between. In fact, excluding living writers, perhaps only four names need mentioning in this connection: Cliffe Leslie (1879), Carl Menger (1883), F. H. Knight (1921), and Keynes (1910 and 1936–7), to which might be added the Swedish contribution, notably from Myrdal, regarding 'anticipations' and the ex-ante and ex-post distinction (see *Monetary Equilibrium*, first published in Swedish in 1931). Of these, Leslie's criticisms were much the most radical methodologically.

In his brilliant essay of 1879, 'The Known and the Unknown in the Economic World', Cliffe Leslie anticipated the famous Preface of Keynes's *General Theory*: 'It is a curious characteristic of the deductive political economy that, in spite of its show of logic, its followers have never firmly grasped either their own premises or their conclusions.'

Leslie emphasised that 'the orthodox, a priori, or deductive system' postulates '*full knowledge*'. He explicitly castigated Ricardian theory and in particular '*the main postulates of the Ricardian theory*, that the advantages of all the different occupations are known' (n.d. pp. 227–9 and 231).

Unlike Leslie, on the other hand, Menger and Knight, though recognising that the perfect knowledge assumption imposed limitations, did not, as vigorous upholders of neoclassical method and theory, see it as representing a fundamental methodological inadequacy. Menger, in fact, in a brief reference in the course of his attack on the historical school, offered the point to his opponents, the historical critics of general economic theorising, who – Menger suggested – had been too lenient in passing it over as a limitation of orthodox theorising.[3]

[3] 'The circumstances that people are not guided exclusively by self-interest prohibits ...the strict regularity of human action in general, and of economic action in particular and thereby eliminates the possibility of a rigorous economic theory. But there is another factor, equally important, that does the same thing. I mean *error*,

F. H. Knight set out much more clearly than anyone before him the full implications of the fundamental, adequate knowledge assumption, but recognised that it was inevitably involved in the construction of abstract models of microeconomic behaviour, if any degree of generality was to be claimed. The absence of ignorance and uncertainty is, Knight maintained, 'the most important underlying difference between the conditions *which theory is compelled to assume* and those which exist in fact' (1921, p. 51, italics added).

IV

In his very first published paper on economics, on Great Britain's Foreign Investments (1910), Keynes emphasised the significance of expectations in investment decisions: 'The investor... will be affected, as is obvious, not by the net income which he will actually receive from his investment in the long run, but by his expectations' (1971, vol. xv, p. 46).

Significantly Keynes added that, 'no mathematical rule can be laid down respecting the exact compromise which will be struck between the fear of loss and the desire for a high rate of interest'.

More than a quarter of a century later, in his *General Theory*, Keynes returned to this theme of expectations and uncertainty with regard to investment decisions. In doing so he undoubtedly suggested a fundamental methodological criticism of Ricardian orthodoxy, such as Cliffe Leslie had pressed home. But Keynes was not prepared to take on board the methodological implications for his own mode of theorising. In *The General Theory* Keynes emphasised, 'that human decisions affecting the future, whether personal or political or economic, cannot depend on strict mathematical expectation, since the basis for making such calculations does not exist' (1936, p. 162). Then, in an article published a year after *The General Theory*, Keynes broadened out his argument into a comprehensive attack on 'orthodox theory':

> I accuse the classical economic theory of being itself one of those pretty, polite techniques which tries to deal with the present by abstracting from the fact that we know very little about the future...

> a factor which surely can be separated still less from human action than custom, public spirit, feeling for justice, and love of one's fellow man can be separated from economy. Even if economic men always and everywhere let themselves be guided exclusively by their self-interest, the strict regularity of economic phenomena would nonetheless have to be considered impossible because of the fact given by experience that in innumerable cases they are in error about their economic interest, or in ignorance of the economic state of affairs. Our historians are too considerate of their scholarly opponents. The presupposition of a strict regularity of economic phenomena, and with this of a theoretical economics in the multiple meaning of the word, is not only the dogma of ever constant self-interest, but also the dogma of the "infallibility" and "omniscience" of human-beings in economic matters' (1963, p. 84).

The orthodox theory assumes that we have a knowledge of the future of a kind quite different from that which we actually possess. This false realisation follows the lines of the Benthamite calculus. The hypothesis of a calculable future leads to a wrong interpretation of the principles of behaviour which the need for action compels us to adopt [1937, p. 192].

These criticisms were indeed fundamental and revolutionary. But in fact they played very little part in the process, or episode, known as 'the Keynesian revolution'. Few of the early – or subsequent – expositors of the revolution gave to this argument regarding uncertainty and expectations an important role, and most of them hardly even mentioned it.[4] For over three decades Keynes's treatment of expectations and uncertainty, and especially its significance as a fundamental criticism of much orthodox theorising, received – with only one or two notable exceptions – almost no attention from economists.[5] The reason for the thoroughgoing neglect of this absolutely fundamental criticism, so plainly and bluntly developed by Keynes himself, is perfectly obvious. For Keynes's description of 'a pretty, polite technique' was, and is, applicable not simply to the orthodox classical, or neoclassical theory of investment; it is equally applicable and destructive across most of the whole range of orthodox economic model-building since Ricardo. Not only the targets which the revolutionaries wished to attack, but other intellectual investments were exposed, which they were by no means willing to abandon (for example, imperfect competition analysis, growth-modelling, the concept of the 'normal' rate of profit, etc.). In fact, a full recognition of the attack Keynes was making on what we have called the fundamental assumption of adequate knowledge would have called in question the whole method of theorising of 'orthodox' and 'revolutionaries' alike – *as Cliffe Leslie who launched the attack over sixty years before clearly recognised and insisted. In any case, Keynes himself never pressed home this fundamental point regarding ignorance and uncertainty, and their methodological implications, with regard to his own methods.*

Three points may be noted in relation to this conclusion. In the *first* place, Keynes did not go to extremes in generalising the argument, or at any rate in drawing general conclusions about the non-self-adjusting nature of the economy, or parts of it, implied by a full recognition of ignorance and uncertainty. For Keynes, self-adjusting forces, though they might need supplementing by government action,

---

[4] It is, for example, hardly ever mentioned in Professor Joan Robinson's *Introduction to the Theory of Employment*, 1937, or her *Essays in the Theory of Employment*, 1936 and 1947; or in L. R. Klein's *The Keynesian Revolution*, 1947.

[5] Professor E. Roy Weintraub in his article on 'Uncertainty and the Keynesian Revolution', very rightly refers to Keynes's treatment of uncertainty as 'an innovation of sublime importance *ignored for almost thirty years by most economists and still ignored by many*' (1975, p. 530, italics added).

played quite an important part in various sectors of the economy, in allocating resources and internationally in the balance of payments.[6]

Secondly, neither in his macroeconomic theory of employment, nor in his criticism of 'classical orthodoxy', did Keynes put his main thrust behind the criticism of the assumption of certainty and adequate knowledge. In spite of its quite fundamental character, Keynes's introduction of ignorance and uncertainty was almost something of an *obiter dictum*. As an expositor of what is described as 'neo-', or 'post-Keynesian' theorising (forty years after *The General Theory*) has quite rightly pointed out:

> In Keynes's surviving written work there is no indication that he considered expectations as the distinguishing feature of his approach. Pride of place was instead reserved for the principle of 'effective demand'...Indeed, expectations and disappointment are consciously made to take second place in relation to the exposition of this principle...
>
> The emphasis that is commonly placed on the possible divergence of *ex-ante* and *ex-post* values and on the possible disappointment of expectations as *the* crucial factors in Keynes's contribution seems both misplaced and historically inaccurate.[7]

Thirdly, Keynes himself adopted no clearly stated or satisfactory procedure for meeting the fundamental methodological problem to which he had called attention. As Professor Patinkin has observed: 'In neither *The General Theory* nor the 1937 article in *The Quarterly Journal of Economics* ...does Keynes develop a theory of economic behaviour under uncertainty' (1976, p. 142). But it must be added that 'a theory of economic behaviour under uncertainty', if it were to be useful, would *have* to be founded and constructed by a quite different *method* from that which Keynes called the 'pretty, polite technique' of deducing conclusions about maximisation under certainty from a fundamental assumption of adequate knowledge. Of course, Keynes could not continue with the fundamental assumption of adequate knowledge; so he proceeded to reach the conclusions he wanted by thinking up *ad hoc*, or 'plucking from the air',[8] the suitable assumptions about expectations and ignorance. To serve the purpose – as Keynes explicitly acknowledged – of 'reducing to a minimum the necessary degree of adaptation' of the 'orthodox' theory (1936, p. 146) he, at some points, assumed that expectations remained constant in

---

[6] See, for example, the conclusion in *The General Theory* (p. 379) that 'when 9,000,000 men are employed out of 10,000,000 willing and able to work, there is no evidence that the labour of these 9,000,000 men is misdirected'; also the references in his posthumously published article ('On the Balance of Payments of the United States') to 'deep undercurrents at work, natural forces, one can call them, or even the invisible hand, which are operating towards equilibrium' (1946, p. 185).

[7] J. A. Kregel, 1976, pp. 210–14.

[8] The phrase is Sir Henry Phelps Brown's. See his condemnation of arbitrary abstraction in his presidential address 'The Under-development of Economics', 1972, p. 3.

the long run, though they nevertheless might meanwhile have been disappointed. As Mr Kregel has agreed: 'Unfortunately, Keynes often changed what he was assuming about expectations to suit a particular purpose.'[9]

For example, the dogmatic Keynesian conclusion about the impossibility of bringing about a general cut in real wages by means of a general cut in money wages was obtained by assuming a particular kind of expectations, which may well have represented an important *possibility*, unjustifiably excluded by 'orthodoxy', but one which it was arbitrarily dogmatic to insist upon in general terms as *the only* possibility.

Keynes's cavalier, casual empiricism with regard to expectations, or his plucking of assumptions about them out of the air, may have been partially justifiable for a major pioneer, on the frontiers of the subject, gifted with Keynes's own outstanding 'flair and genius'. It is hardly justifiable as a 'normal', or routine method.

V

In the decades following the publication of the *General Theory* there was one economist who continued to insist that what was so thoroughly neglected by most of Keynes's followers was indeed of quite central and fundamental significance. As Professor G. L. S. Shackle has summarised the significance of ignorance and uncertainty:

> Unemployment is the consequence and reflection of disorder. A theory of unemployment is, necessarily, inescapably, a theory of disorder. The disorder in question is the basic disorder of uncertain expectation... It is the disorder of adventurous decision, of 'enterprise'. The world in which *enterprise* is necessary and possible is a world of uncertainty. The notion of enterprise, so central in Marshall, the realist, had no proper or legitimate place in the conception of a *general equilibrium*, the equivalent of a general agreement on what is to be done... Enterprise is risk, risk is ignorance, and equilibrium, by contrast, is the effective banishment of ignorance. It is not surprising that an *Economics of Disorder* was not intellectually acceptable to those trained in the Economics of Order, viz. in Value Theory... In perceiving and in stating this ultimate ground of the possibility of massive general unemployment, Keynes, we may claim, had no predecessors. To state this ground was to deny the orderliness of economic society and economic life, and to deny this life the attribute of orderliness was to seem to deny the study of it the attributes of science [1967, pp. 133–4].

We would only add that (1) Keynes did not press his reliance on this particular, quite fundamental element in the diagnosis of unemployment; and that (2) there are various other important and profound manifestations of economic 'disorder', apart from unemployment. For

---

[9] 1976, p. 215. As Professor A. Leijonhufvud writes: 'Keynes's theory of expectations was sketchy at best' (1968, p. 178).

we have already emphasised how the concepts of competitive equilibration and adequate knowledge are interlocked, and how the vital
role of the adequate knowledge assumption has, until recently, received very little explicit recognition. On the other hand, the complementary, and equally vital role of the assumption of competition
has been repeatedly proclaimed on the highest authority.

In turn, J. S. Mill, F. Y. Edgeworth, and Sir John Hicks, have held
that the absence of competition would imply an absence of what
Professor Shackle calls 'the orderliness of economic life and society',
which in turn would deny to economics 'the attributes of a science'.
Presumably with Ricardo in mind – for his comments certainly do not
apply to Adam Smith – J. S. Mill maintained, regarding Competition
and Custom:

> Political economists generally, and English political economists above others,
> have been accustomed to lay almost exclusive stress upon the first of these
> agencies; to exaggerate the effect of competition, and to take into little
> account the other and conflicting principle. They are apt to express them-
> selves as if they thought that competition actually does, in all cases, whatever
> it can be shown to be the tendency of competition to do. This is partly
> intelligible, if we consider that *only through the principle of competition has
> political economy any pretension to the character of a science.* So far as rents,
> profits, wages, prices, are determined by competition, laws may be assigned
> for them. Assume competition to be their exclusive regulator, and principles
> of broad generality and scientific precision may be laid down, according to
> which they will be regulated. The political economist justly deems this his
> proper business; and as an abstract or hypothetical science, *political economy
> cannot be required to do, and indeed cannot do anything more* [1909, II.IV.I, italics
> added].

In similar terms Edgeworth, in his paper on Monopoly in the
Economic Journal (1897), emphasised how if, and insofar as, monopoly
replaced competition: 'Among those who would suffer by the new
regime there would be one class which particularly interests the
readers of this Journal, namely the abstract economists, who would
be deprived of their occupation, the investigation of the conditions
which determine value. There would survive only the empirical
school, flourishing in a chaos congenial to their mentality' (1925, vol. I,
pp. 138–9).

Finally, the point made by Mill and Edgeworth was rubbed in by
Sir John Hicks:

> It has to be recognized that a general abandonment of the assumption of
> perfect competition, a universal adoption of the assumption of monopoly,
> must have very destructive consequences for economic theory. Under
> monopoly the stability conditions become indeterminate; *and the basis on
> which economic laws can be constructed is therefore shorn away...*
>   It is, I believe, only possible to save anything from this wreck – and it must
> be remembered that the threatened wreckage is that of the greater part of

general equilibrium theory – if we can assume that the markets confronting most of the firms with which we shall be dealing do not differ very greatly from perfectly competitive markets.[10]

And with the assumption of perfectly competitive markets is inter-locked the assumption of perfect or adequate knowledge and correct expectations.

VI

There is no single, general fundamental assumption, either normative or positive, regarding objectives and decisions under uncertainty as there is for the standard or traditional maximisation-under-certainty model. Therefore:

> So long as one is concerned with a world where the choice is always an automatic one between a return which is *certainly* maximum and others which are *certainly* smaller, the assumption that people expect to maximise their returns and the assumption that they *actually do* maximise them come to the same thing. But where the consequences of all decisions can be perfectly foreseen, the maximum principle clearly works itself out in a very special way...An analysis of a world with any uncertainty in it, and particularly an analysis which takes into account the factor of money (which can be construed as a sign that uncertainty is present, or even as a measure of its amount), cannot start from the same assumption of 'sensible' or 'rational' conduct as that applicable in a world without uncertainty – the kind of world with which, consciously and explicitly or not, the bulk of pure economic theory from Ricardo onwards appears to have been concerned [Hutchison, 1937, pp. 648–9].

The fundamental assumption of maximisation under certainty has sometimes been explained as 'a first approximation', or as a piece of auxiliary 'scaffolding', which will in due course, 'at the end of the day', be removed. *But there is no second approximation*, or rather there is an infinite number of logically possible 'second approximations' from which it may be highly arbitrary to pick out one as a *general* assumption, to replace the oversimplification of maximisation under certainty. Hence the 'scaffolding' is very difficult to remove without arbitrariness, or so as to leave intact a valid general model. Correct expectations can only be correct by corresponding with events, and there is only one set of correct expectations in each situation, or for each decision. But incorrect expectations can be incorrect or inadequate in an infinite

---

[10] 1946, pp. 83–4 (italics added). See also T. W. Hutchison, *A Review of Economic Doctrines 1870–1929*, 1953, pp. 112–13.

It is interesting to note that Marshall was strongly opposed to the doctrine of Mill and Edgeworth as to the essential role of the competitive assumption. He urged that: 'We must throw overboard the most mischievous and untrue statement that...it was only on the assumption of free competition that...any economic science was possible' (1961, vol. II, p. 151).

variety of different ways: too optimistic, too pessimistic, too adaptive, too unadaptive, too elastic, too inelastic, and so on. Professor Herbert Simon after reviewing the growing body of experimental evidence regarding decision-making under uncertainty and ignorance, concludes:

> It appears, then, that humans can either over-respond to new evidence or ignore it, depending upon the precise experimental circumstances. If these differences in behaviour manifest themselves even in laboratory situations so simple that it would be possible for subjects to carry out the actual Bayes calculations, we should be prepared to find variety at least as great when people are required to face the complexities of the real world [1976, p. 135].

Of course, a more or less infinite variety of 'models' can be set up on assumptions 'plucked out of the air' or devised to suit a particular argument. This is the procedure adopted by, and since, Keynes. Certainly particular assumptions, regarding particular kinds of incorrect expectations, might well be shown as applicable to particular historical cases, types, or episodes, by assembling the appropriate evidence. But little *general* validity could be claimed for 'models' based on assumptions produced in this way.

The first critic of orthodoxy to emphasise the limitations of the adequate knowledge assumption, Cliffe Leslie, drove home some major implications regarding method. These have been summarised as follows:

> A broader methodological conclusion would appear to follow...In so far as one is dissatisfied with 'static', a-monetary analysis, omitting the uncertainty factor – which alone may be said to create any problems of conduct, economic or otherwise – the method of deduction from some 'Fundamental Assumption' or 'principle' concerning economic conduct is more or less useless, because no relevant 'Fundamental Assumption' can, on our present knowledge, be made. The use of such a method as the deduction of chains of 'conclusions' from some 'Fundamental Assumption', only seemed applicable so long as a more or less tacit assumption as to expectations was being made. When assumptions as to expectations are more or less explicitly introduced there come the accusations of 'circularity', 'begging the question', and 'assuming what one requires to prove'....
> ...According to Professor Hayek, the immediately pressing questions in this field are how entrepreneurs react to the expectations of particular price-changes, how the expectations of entrepreneurs are formed, and how given price-changes in the present affect entrepreneurs' expectations. Clearly the answers to such questions cannot be deduced from some 'Fundamental Assumption' or conjectured at all accurately *a priori*...If one wants to find out the answer to such questions one must admit with Richard Jones: 'I really know of but one way to obtain our object, and that is to look and see'....unless deductive theorists are simply going to continue building up their analysis on any assumptions which appeal to them vaguely *a priori*, or which make possible a fascinating display of mathematical or geometrical ingenuity, or which merely fit in with their political views [Hutchison, 1937, pp. 652–3].

Professor Simon states very incisively the methodological implications of attempting to advance from the extremely simplified model based on certainty and knowledge, towards accounting for, or explaining, real-world decisions taken in conditions of ignorance and uncertainty. As Professor Simon insists: 'There seems to be no escape. If economics is to deal with uncertainty, it will have to understand how human beings in fact behave in the face of uncertainty, and by what limits of information and computability they are bound.'

This shift to the study of real-world decision-making, Professor Simon continues:

> *requires a basic shift in scientific style, from an emphasis on deductive reasoning within a tight system of axioms to an emphasis on detailed empirical exploration of complex algorithms of thought.* Undoubtedly the uncongeniality of the latter style to economists has slowed down the transition, and accounts in part for the very limited success of economic behavioralism in the past. . .
>
> As economics becomes more and more involved in the study of uncertainty, more and more concerned with the complex actuality of business decision-making, *the shift in program will become inevitable. Wider and wider areas of economics will replace the over-simplified assumptions of the situationally constrained omniscient decision-maker with a realistic (and psychological) characterization of the limits on Man's rationality, and consequences of those limits for his economic behaviour* [1976, pp. 147–8, italics added].

VII

Of course, to qualify or replace the fundamental assumption of adequate knowledge and, consequentially, of the general existence of equilibrium, is *not* to assert that complete ignorance generally prevails, or that *no* self-equilibrating forces are to any extent operative, or could not easily be made operative. Nor is it necessary, or just, to regard as a total waste of effort the elaboration of the long dominant model based on adequate knowledge, when this model is interpreted and applied – as it frequently has not been – with judgment and tact. The questions are: just when, and in what circumstances, what kinds of ignorance and incorrect expectations occur; and just when, on the other hand, more-or-less adequate knowledge, and equilibrating tendencies, are likely to be operative. The existence and operation of equilibrating tendencies in the real world may then be shown, in particular types, or historical cases, to be supported by psychological and institutional factors, as extensively set out in *The Wealth of Nations*, and not assumed as an abstract, and irrelevantly 'rigorous', and completely general, 'strong case', as by Ricardo.

Meanwhile, nothing in the nature of a fundamental methodological 'revolution' can be said to be involved in simply replacing the traditional, fundamental, adequate knowledge assumption by arbitrarily and casually postulated ignorance, and incorrect expectations, of one particular kind or another, or in this or that particular case (or 'to suit a particular purpose' as Dr Kregel describes Keynes's choice of assumptions about expectations) *without any systematic evidence provided in support.* This is certainly 'casual empiricism' at its most casual.

It could well be claimed, however, that, as suggested by Professor Simon, the shift in programme from the elaboration of 'models' based on the general assumption of adequate knowledge, to the study of real-world decisions under ignorance and uncertainty, would demand, or amount to, a methodological 'revolution'. A programme centred round the traditional type of 'model', based on certainty, would be replaced by empirical and historical studies of particular cases and types of ignorance and incorrect expectations, as described by Professor Simon, with the results applied to the explanation of particular historical episodes. There has been, from critics of what is called 'neoclassical economics' a certain amount of rather opaque verbiage about the need to reintroduce 'historical time' into economic theorising or model-building. 'Historical time' was clearly present in *The Wealth of Nations* and was extruded by Ricardo: there is not *very* much of it in Keynes's *General Theory*, though he complained of its exclusion by 'orthodox theory'. We have attempted to indicate in this chapter what such a reintroduction of 'historical time' might mean and require *in terms of method.*

In fact, there could come about by this reintroduction, the anti-Ricardian methodological revolution which Cliffe Leslie explicitly called for in his essay of 1879 on the Known and the Unknown in the Economic World, and which subsequent critics of orthodox theory have also indicated. As a consequence of such a 'revolution', the existence, or possibility, of equilibrating tendencies would not be sweepingly denied, but would not simply be generally and casually assumed. In the same way, decisions based on ignorance and uncertainty would be studied empirically in the manner described by Professor Simon, and not be dealt with simply by casual, convenient assumptions.

Some of Keynes's *obiter dicta* pointed towards this kind of methodological revolution. But the Keynesian revolution with its claim to provide a *General Theory*, tended also to a large extent in the opposite, Ricardian direction.

8

Economists and the history of economics: revolutionary and traditional versions

I

J. B. Say, the close associate of the English classicals, once wrote about the study of the history of economic thought:

> What useful purpose can be served by the study of absurd opinions and doctrines that have long ago been exploded, and deserved to be? It is mere useless pedantry to attempt to revive them. The more perfect a science becomes the shorter becomes its history. Alembert truly remarks that the more light we have on any subject the less need is there to occupy ourselves with the false or doubtful opinions to which it may have given rise. Our duty with regard to errors is not to revive them, but simply to forget them.[1]

These views of Say found confident and enthusiastic echoes in the 1950s and 1960s in Britain and America, when a 'quantitative revolution' was taking place which led to imaginative comparisons between economics and the natural sciences, somewhat similar to those drawn by James Mill, Ricardo and McCulloch, nearly a century and a half before, when they had claimed a kind of authority for the laws of their new science similar to that generally ascribed to the laws of Newton. Thanks to the new quantitative 'revolution', economics had apparently become more and more a 'science' like physics or chemistry, in its methods and criteria, as well as, *apparently*, in its simple technical applicability and its promised achievements. It was, therefore, as unnecessary and even demeaning for students of economics to study the history of the subject as it was for physicists and chemists to study the history of physics and chemistry. As J. B. Say had long ago explained such a study would simply be concerned with false or dubious doctrines long ago deservedly 'exploded' (like, for example, the quantity theory of money). Admitting a role for the history of economics would have damaged the 'image' of economics which the ambitious PROs of 'the quantitative revolution' were seeking to build up.[2]

---

[1] J. B. Say, 1828–9, vol. II, p. 540, quoted by C. Gide and C. Rist, 1948, p. 10. Gide and Rist aptly countered Say's claim with an admirable suggestion from Condillac: 'It is essential that every one who wishes to make some progress in the search for truth should know something of the mistakes committed by people like himself who thought they were extending the boundaries of knowledge.'

[2] In 1962, even so accomplished a historian of economic thought as Mr Donald Winch was accepting the updated J. B. Say line, holding that historians of economics should

Though the disciplined and systematic study of the history of economics may often have been dismissed or denounced in the manner of J. B. Say, in fact economists – including Say's own fellow-classicals – can often be found invoking or inventing their own versions of it, especially at the major turning-points, and in most of the major broad controversies in the history of economics and political economy. Economists, who have no use for a systematic and disciplined study of the history of their subject, in fact resort to concocting their own version of it, especially in times of fundamental debate when a painful realisation fleetingly breaks in that there is something gapingly inadequate about the clothing of one or another of the leading kings or queens parading about the economic stage. For many of the broad issues in economic theory and policy do not get settled with sufficient definiteness and conclusiveness, because the requisite evidence cannot be obtained and the relevant tests cannot be set up.[3] So the exponents of particular ideas or theories, revolutionary or otherwise, which cannot win through decisively by evidence and testing, try to gain credibility for their case by the persuasive presentation of a favourable framework in terms of the history of thought and theory.[4] On the other

not imagine that their subject had any more significance for, or claims on, economists and students of economics, than the history of physics has for physicists and students of physics. In fact, historians of economic thought should get together with historians of the natural sciences in a separate department (in some ways a very promising idea). Mr Winch then maintained: 'At present the economics profession appears to be confident that the powerful techniques which it is learning to use will yield worthwhile results; this confidence is supported by the many demands made by public and private bodies for the services of economists... In my view, economics at present shows evidence of a blend of confidence without complacency which is least conducive to an interest in ancestry' (1962, p. 194).

[3] Wicksell long ago complained: 'Within the whole of his science, or what he insists on calling science, no generally recognised result is to be found, as is also the case with theology, and for roughly the same reasons; there is no single doctrine taken to be a scientific truth without the diametrically opposed view being similarly upheld by authors of high repute. Of course, it is true that conflicts of opinion take place in other sciences, and indeed to some extent they constitute a real part of scientific life and research; but there is this great difference, that in other fields of science these conflicts usually come to an end, the defenders of the false opinion are defeated and admit themselves beaten; or, as more frequently occurs perhaps, they withdraw from the struggle and no new defenders come forward to take their places' ('Ends and Means in Economics', 1958, p. 51). Wicksell's lament of 1904 may seem *slightly* exaggerated seventy years later – but only slightly.

[4] Not only is the more distant past history of economic thought made use of, or made up, by economists for purposes of argument, polemic and persuasion, the *very recent or contemporary* history of economic theories or opinions is invoked, or invented, sometimes even more imaginatively. One of the oldest argumentative or persuasive ploys in the world, especially beloved by newspaper editors, is, when commending a particular doctrine, theory, sentiment, or point of view, to begin by claiming that all qualified, right-minded, knowledgeable, 'experts', or otherwise trustworthy authorities subscribe to it. Economists, classical and contemporary, can be found making use of the same formula in propagating particular economic theories and policies. Of course, if reasonably conclusive tests and evidence were at hand regarding, for example, the economic effects of devaluation, or of Britain joining the European

hand, the existing orthodoxy, 'theory', or 'paradigm', which revolutionaries hope to dislodge, may be presented unfavourably, if necessary by slight, or more than slight, over-simplification or distortion; or, by an exaggeration of the importance of the errors to be eradicated or of the extent and the influence of such errors. Thus the significance of their 'revolutionary' overthrow is magnified.[5]

In fact, the history of economic thought was first developed, at least insofar as its best-known, early pioneers were concerned, in order to provide an impressive, prestigious setting, or a legitimately authoritative intellectual–historical framework, for a particular would-be influential school, body of doctrine, or orthodoxy: for a 'classical', or Smithian–Ricardian body of doctrine in the case of John Ramsay McCulloch, and for his own massive corpus in the case of Karl Marx. The distinctive and very scholarly contribution to the history of economic thought made later by Jevons had, to some extent, a similar purpose or function with regard to his own 'revolution' in the theories of value and wages. The Keynesian version, extending over about 300 years of the history of economic thought, was an outstanding example of a largely successful 'revolutionary' version of the history of the subject, or of an important part of it. Indeed, a great deal of the Keynesian version, in spite of some gaping omissions, provided new, valid and illuminating insights (though it was also disfigured by grotesque distortions and exaggerations, partly by Keynes, but predominantly, subsequently, on the part of 'Keynesians'). *We would emphasise, therefore, that these persuasive and justificatory 'scenarios', devised as a kind of prestigeful framework for the advancing of their theories and ideas, may, in some cases, have had a valuable contribution to make to the history of the subject.*

In accordance with the manner in which it is intended that a version of history should justify the historian's own contribution, approach, or school of thought, the historical setting, or scenario, may be revolutionary or conservative. A mainly revolutionary scenario – like that of Keynes – will set out the previous history of the subject,

'common market', it would be more or less otiose to invoke the contemporary history of economic thought or opinion as being heavily, or even unanimously, of one mind on the subject (in the particular favoured direction, of course). See the Appendix on 'Economic Knowledge and Ignorance in Action' to my 1977. These claims for overwhelming majorities, or unanimity, in favour of particular measures seem to express a kind of striving for authority and certainty which ends up in fantasy, or in a pretence that a kind of scientific consensus exists which simply is not there.

[5] 'Revolutions close with a total victory for one of the two opposing camps. Will that group ever say that the result of its victory has been something less than progress? That would be rather like admitting that they had been wrong and their opponents right' (T. S. Kuhn, 1970, p. 166). Of course in the social sciences, unlike the natural sciences about which Kuhn is generalising, 'victories' are seldom total and permanent. But the revolutionaries *want to think* they are and draft their versions of the history of the subject on this assumption.

or some major phase thereof, as dominated by some fatal, all-pervasive error or misunderstanding now triumphantly swept away by the new enlightenment. On the other hand, a conservative version will have more the function of an ancestral portrait gallery (all warts painted out) designed to impress the world with the distinction of one's ancestry or pedigree. Sometimes the focus may be on just one or two illustrious ancestors, Ricardo or Marx, Marshall or Keynes, as the supreme embodiment of the wisdom of the ages, of which the historian himself, and his school or party, are now the exclusive descendants and interpreters, on whose shoulders alone the mantle of the prophet now reposes. The English classicals, and more recently Keynes, have been used from time to time in a kind of self-satisfied, 'conservative', ancestral-portrait-gallery, historical role.

We repeat that this kind of history, revolutionary or conservative–traditional, resorted to by economists as a persuasive weapon in fundamental controversies, is not to be dismissed or denounced out of hand. Some such versions have been on a much higher level than others and have contributed valuable insights. But the limitations and dangers of this kind of history are obvious, especially when it amounts to the propaganda of the victors, or would-be victors, in some 'revolutionary' movement. It may become too much like a 1984 attempt to control the past in order to dictate the future. An initial justification, or *raison d'être*, or at least some scope, is therefore provided for specialist, *critical* historians who can explore the history of the subject from some different, less exclusivist viewpoint detached from the party-warfare of economists. At least a specialist historian of economics can seek to set the record straight, if not with some absolute ideal 'straightness' at least with some reasonable degree of freedom from the outright falsifications and factual errors introduced by propagandists for the various brands of 'establishment' and 'revolutionary' history.[6] From an early date such more detached histories were

---

[6] Doubtless the rather bathetic interjection may be heard that *any* version of the history of economics, including the versions of those I have described as 'specialist' historians of the subject (assumed to be uncommitted to any particular 'revolutionary' or 'traditional' version) *must* be based on valuations or 'biases' of some kind, and cannot be absolutely 'neutral'. Of course. But it is permissible to suggest as valuable (as we have above) an approach to the history of economics *not* based on the valuations or preconceptions of some particular 'revolutionary' or 'traditional' approach (just as one might suggest the value of writing the history of Europe not from the valuations or biases of some particular nationalist–chauvinist historian, but with valuations *critical* of all particular nationalist–chauvinist versions). Moreover, as Barrington Moore has said: 'The thesis that neutrality is impossible is a powerful one...But I do not think that it leads to a denial that objective social and historical analysis is possible. Different perspectives on the same set of events should lead to complementary and congruent interpretations, not to contradictory ones. Furthermore the denial that objective truth is possible in principle flings open the door to the worst forms of intellectual dishonesty' (1960, p. 522, quoted by M. Bronfenbrenner, 1974, p. 483).

being attempted in France and Italy.[7] But in Britain they only began to emerge to a significant extent during the much-maligned 'neo-classical' period.

We shall now survey the version of the history of political economy and economics propagated by some of the leading English classicals (notably J. R. McCulloch and the Mills) and then those by Marx (and/or 'Marxists'), Jevons, Marshall, and Keynes. The most recent version of this kind seeking to justify what is claimed or proclaimed as the latest 'revolution' in the history of the subject ('the Sraffa revolution') is left for separate treatment.

II

There can hardly be said to have been a Smithian version of the history of political economy. But his treatment of his predecessors may well have encouraged somewhat the version subsequently created by some of his classical successors. Smith condemned, of course, the prevailing policies of what he calls 'the mercantile system', and mentioned the wide prevalence of the idea that 'wealth consists in money, or in gold and silver'. But in *The Wealth of Nations* there are few or no references to many or most of those who had been building up the subject in the previous hundred years. (Such names, for example, as Petty, Barbon, North, Mandeville, Steuart, Pufendorf, Boisguilbert, Galiani, Turgot, Beccaria, Verri, and others, hardly appear at all, while Cantillon's appears only once). We are not bringing any complaints or charges against Smith, who may, to some extent, simply have been following the scholarly practices of his day.[8] But the foundation or starting-point was thus more or less innocently and unintentionally provided for what might perhaps be called the English Classical view of the history of political economy – (though it was not uniformly and universally held by all the 'classicals' and never propounded by Smith himself). According to this view, Adam Smith created, or 'founded', the subject almost single-handed: that is, before Smith there had been very little written on political economy which was not gravely or fundamentally erroneous and confused. It was implied that no, or only intellectually negligible, alternatives to the Smithian doctrines existed,

[7] I am indebted to Professor Piero Barucci for information regarding the writings of Carlo Bosellini (1825–7), G. Pecchio (1829) and A. Blanqui (1837). Blanqui's work, subsequently translated into English, devotes much space to the centuries before Adam Smith.

[8] According, however, to McCulloch: 'The want of notes, and the fewness of references to authorities, may be mentioned as a peculiarity of Smith's writings: and one in which they differ very widely from those of his contemporaries, Hume and Robertson, especially the last. Stewart says that "Smith considered every species of note as a blemish or imperfection, indicating either an idle accumulation of superfluous particulars, or a want of skill and comprehension in the general design"' (1863, p. xvii).

or had ever existed.[9] But on the foundations laid by Smith – so his classical successors in the early nineteenth century proclaimed – a new Science had very rapidly been constructed, regarding nearly all the important conclusions of which all people qualified to hold an opinion were in agreement.

But the adjective 'classical' is a dangerous one with which to generalise. So it would be considerably safer and more accurate to refer to 'the McCulloch–Mill (J. and J.S.) version' of the history of political economy. Adam Smith might be said innocently and unintentionally to have prepared the way for it, while not actively contributing much to it. Ricardo was almost completely non-historical and non-historiate beyond echoing Smith's generalisations and condemnations regarding 'the mercantile system'. Malthus and Senior were doubtful about this version, certainly not sharing in the extreme confidence with which it was put forward by McCulloch and the Mills. Nevertheless, though far from universally shared, this version of the history of the subject became a dominant one in Britain in the middle decades of the nineteenth century when 'classical' political economy, or 'the Ricardo–Mills economics', attained a unique authority and prestige in this country.

The pioneer 'classical' historian of political economy (to whom we are, of course, indebted for some most solid, scholarly contributions) was J. R. McCulloch. For McCulloch: 'Political Economy is of a very recent origin' (1824, p. 20),[10] dating only from the middle of the eighteenth century. McCulloch hails Adam Smith as possessing 'an undoubted claim to be regarded as the founder of the modern system' (1845, p. 12).

Previously 'the *absolutely* false and erroneous' principles of the Mercantile System had largely dominated policy and thought, except for a few isolated individuals such as Sir Dudley North, who 'exposes the folly of thinking that any trade advantageous to the merchant can be injurious to the public' (1856, p. xiii).

Indeed McCulloch was highly optimistic that false and biased doctrines had been finally vanquished in the light of the new science, for which he claimed the most remarkable progress in the mere half century or so of its existence, especially regarding the subject of distribution: 'The relation between rent and profit – between profit and wages, and the various *general laws* which regulate and connect the apparently clashing, but really harmonious interests of every

---

[9] As J. B. Say put it: 'When one reads Smith as he deserves to be read, one perceives that before him there was no political economy' (1841, p. 29, quoted by H. M. Robertson, 1976, p. 399).

[10] Much of *The Discourse* survived into the later editions of McCulloch's *Principles*, *including* the quotations from it which we make here, and also into the Introductory Discourse in his new edition of *The Wealth of Nations* (1863).

different order in society, have been discovered, *and established with all the certainty of demonstrative evidence.*[11]

McCulloch boldly compared Political Economy with Physics and Chemistry regarding the 'certainty' of its conclusions. Admittedly there had been, in the past, some differences of view. But the significance of these had been misinterpreted and, anyhow, they had now nearly disappeared:

> Since it has become an object of more general attention and inquiry, the differences which have subsisted among the most eminent of its professors, have proved exceedingly unfavourable to its progress, and have generated a disposition to distrust its best established conclusions.
>
> It is clear, however, that those who distrust the conclusions of Political Economy, because of the variety of systems that have been advanced to explain the phenomena about which it is conversant, might, on the same ground, distrust the conclusions of almost every other science... We do not refuse our assent to the demonstrations of Newton and Laplace, because they are subversive of the hypotheses of Ptolemy, Tycho Brahe, and Descartes; and why should we refuse our assent to the demonstrations of Smith and Ricardo, because they have subverted the false theories that were previously advanced respecting the sources and the distribution of wealth?... *The errors with which Political Economy was formerly infected have now nearly disappeared, and a very few observations will suffice to show that it really admits of as much certainty in its conclusions as any science founded on fact and experiment can possibly do.*[12]

Similarly, in 1821 Robert Torrens had announced: 'In the progress of the human mind, a period of controversy must necessarily precede the period of unanimity. With respect to political economy the period of controversy is passing away and that of unanimity rapidly approaching... Twenty years hence there will scarcely exist a doubt respecting any of its more fundamental principles' (1821, p. xiii).

---

[11] 1824, p. 75 (italics added). It may be noted that this is how the Ricardian theory of 'distribution' was interpreted by a leading disciple, that is as propounding laws of *real* 'harmony' and only *apparent* 'clashes'. There seems to be little doubt that Ricardo himself would have *mainly* agreed with McCulloch on this question.

[12] 1824, pp. 8–9 (italics added). It is possible that McCulloch's glowing confidence faded in later years. As Professor O'Brien has pointed out, in 1845 (p. 18) McCulloch remarked regarding James Mill's *Elements* that 'the science is very far from having arrived at the perfection Mr Mill supposed'. Nevertheless McCulloch continued to propagate the belief that (as Professor O'Brien puts it in a distinguished and illuminating lecture) 'the millennium of economic thought was at hand'. For in 1863, in the last year of his life, *he was still reprinting his Discourse of nearly forty years before, including the words quoted and italicised above* (see McCulloch, 1863, p. xvii). As between the 1824 and 1863 versions of the above quotations there are *one or two extremely trivial*, verbal changes. This would seem to suggest that McCulloch must have re-read and reconsidered the above quotation and must have *approved its substance*. As Professor O'Brien also interestingly points out this was not the first time that a 'millennium of economic thought' had been proclaimed. The first millennium in political economy was proclaimed by the first 'school' in the subject, the Physiocrats, at the first attempt at a bold systematisation. Quesnay's *Tableau Economique* was proclaimed as, after the invention of writing and money, the third great discovery in world history (see D. P. O'Brien, 1974, p. 6).

Even more exuberantly confident than Torrens or McCulloch was James Mill, the tutor and mentor of Ricardo, who played such a vital, key role in promoting the Ricardian version of English classical political economy. Mill maintained in a paper of 1836 entitled 'Whether Political Economy is Useful':

> Among those who have so much knowledge on the subject as to entitle their opinions to any weight, there is a wonderful agreement, greater than on almost any other moral or political subject. On the great points, with hardly any exception, there is general concord... *In the great doctrines concerning production, distribution, exchange and consumption, you find perfect concurrence*; it is only as to some of the minor questions involved in these great doctrines that there is any dispute; and I might undertake to show that in few instances is even that dispute other than verbal. There is no branch of human knowledge more entitled to respect [1966, p. 382, italics added].[13]

When we come to J. S. Mill it seems remarkable how, with his broad intellectual sympathies and extensive understanding, he was prepared to lend his immense influence and prestige to this view of the subject. But, as Schumpeter has discerned: 'Mill, however modest on his own behalf, was not at all modest on behalf of his time. "This enlightened age" had solved all problems. And if you knew what its "best thinkers" thought, you were in a position to answer all questions.'[14]

In his earlier essays (1829–30) Mill had emphasised the great recent progress in political economy, and 'the comparatively precise and scientific character which it at present bears'.

This was thanks to his father, J. B. Say, and Ricardo, before whom complete error had reigned:

> Before the appearance of those great writers whose discoveries have given to political economy *its present comparatively scientific character*, the ideas *universally* entertained both by theorists and by practical men, on the causes of national wealth, were grounded upon certain general views, which *almost all who have given any considerable attention to the subject* now justly hold to be *completely* erroneous [1844, pp. 1 and 47, italics added].

Later in his career, in the Preface to his *Principles*, Mill emphasised the tremendous progress in the preceding seventy years. As compared with Mill's own day, with its 'extended knowledge and improved ideas', Mill observes: '*The Wealth of Nations* is in many parts obsolete, and in all, imperfect, *Political Economy, properly so called, has grown up almost from infancy since the time of Adam Smith*' (1909, p. xxviii).

Moreover, 'the philosophy of society', as Mill calls it 'has advanced many steps beyond the point at which he [Smith] left it'.

[13] See above the essay: James Mill and Ricardian economics: a methodological revolution (Chapter 2).

[14] 1954, p. 530. More recently in the 1960s, economists, or some of them, would have upheld sentiments such as Mill's in terms of 'the profession', or 'professional experts', rather than in terms of 'this enlightened age'.

As regards economic theory, Mill maintained that there only remained for political economists the task of applying and interpreting the principles of the science to changes in society. Later in his *Principles* (III.I.2) he put forward his famous claim that: 'Happily, there is nothing in the laws of value which remains for the present or any future writer to clear up; the theory of the subject is complete.'

Again, in the last year of his life, as it seemed to Mill: 'The investigations of pure economics are almost completed.'[15]

However, in his very last years Mill certainly became sceptical regarding some of the current *applications* of classical political economy (especially to Irish land policy) and this forced him back to the methodological assumptions of such 'orthodox' economists as Robert Lowe. But this belated scepticism on Mill's part did not find much expression outside letters and speeches.[16]

At the popularising or text-book level, Henry Fawcett, in his *Manual*, expounded the McCulloch–Mill version. *The Wealth of Nations* had been: 'the first great work on political economy'.

Before this the subject had been dominated by an 'erroneous conception of wealth, *which was universal... The error once exposed may appear incapable of misleading a child, yet no error was ever more tenaciously clung to*; it not only corrupted speculative science, but it infected the whole commercial policy of every European nation... The essence of the mercantile system was to identify wealth with money' (1863, pp. 3, 4, and 8, italics added).

However, the science of Political Economy, according to Fawcett, was, by his day, comparable with mathematics and Euclid as 'an exact science'.

In a manner sometimes to be resorted to by subsequent textbook-writers Fawcett encouraged his beginner-readers to throw aside pedantic philosophical or methodological doubts and queries:

All who have studied an exact science must have experienced the formidable difficulties which elementary chapters invariably present...

A definition of political economy, and an inquiry into the method of investigation that ought to be pursued in this science, involve considerations which are sure to perplex the beginner; but the young mathematician need not be driven away from his Euclid because philosophy has not decided

[15] See P. Schwartz, 1972, p. 237. This belief of J. S. Mill, though clearly deriving from his confident youthful opinions is somewhat similar to that of Marshall, a quarter to half a century later, to the effect that the abstract 'organon' of economic analysis was more or less adequately completed; or, as Sir Roy Harrod puts it: 'Marshall thought that the fundamental principles of the subject were now fixed beyond dispute, and that the next generation of economists would be free to concern themselves mainly with the application of these principles to all the bewildering variety of institutions and practices in the real world' (1951, p. 143).

[16] But see Mill's review 'Leslie on the Land Question' (1870) (in 1967, vol. II, pp. 671ff). See also above the essay: The decline and fall of English classical political economy and the Jevonian revolution (Chapter 3).

whether axioms are intuitive truths, or truths learnt from experience; in a similar way, the student in political economy ought not to have his faith shaken in the truths of this science, because he has learnt beforehand that political economists still dispute upon questions of philosophic method [1883, p. 3].

III

The remarkably confident McCulloch–Mill version, or view, of the development of the subject, was prominent, or dominant, from the 1820s to the 1860s. But especially in the 1820s and 1830s very different views had been held by a considerable number of other economists. For example, it is surely very much to the credit of Malthus that he explicitly rejected the claims to certainty and agreement and the comparisons with mathematics indulged in by James Mill and McCulloch. Malthus, in fact, was far ahead of Ricardo in awareness of the extent of ignorance, as he showed in the Introduction to his *Principles*, where he maintains that: 'The principal cause of error, and of the differences which prevail at present among the scientific writers on political economy, appears to me to be a precipitate attempt to simplify and generalise.'

This has led to 'crude and premature theories' (1836, p. 4).

Indeed, while McCulloch and James Mill were proclaiming the remarkable extent of agreement among competent economists Malthus was maintaining: 'The differences of opinion among political economists have of late been a frequent subject of complaint' (1827, p. vii).

Senior, also, in his lectures at Oxford, both in 1826 and again in 1852 emphasised that the subject was 'in a state of imperfect development'.[17]

He discerned also the difficulties with regard to progress in the social sciences as contrasted with the natural sciences:

> One of the great obstacles to the progress of the moral sciences is the tendency of doctrines, supposed to have been refuted, to reappear. In the pure and in the physical sciences, each generation inherits the conquests made by its predecessors... In the moral sciences the ground seems never to be incontestably won; and this is peculiarly the case with respect to the sciences which are subsidiary to the arts of administration and legislation [1928, vol. II, p. 154].

In fact, at the very time when McCulloch and James Mill in the 1820s and 1830s were expressing such confidence there was probably an

---

[17] However, Senior was quite prepared to claim, on behalf of the British political economists and theorists of his time, responsibility for his country's prosperity and economic leadership as 'the triumph of theory'; see below Chapter 10. A century later British economists, oddly enough, were rather less ready to accept a positive relationship between a country's relative, or absolute, economic performance and the quality of its economists.

above-average diversity of views on fundamental theoretical questions among writers on political economy. The Ricardian-type doctrines, which Mill and McCulloch upheld as beyond dispute, were probably rejected, as a whole or in large part, by a majority of 'economists', almost certainly if 'economists' outside Britain were included, or regarded as existing.[18] In Britain the Ricardian doctrines were being challenged, at this time, from at least three different directions. There was (1) the theoretical challenge regarding value (and wages) from Bailey, Senior, Longfield and Lloyd; (2) the fundamental historical challenge to the Ricardian method from Richard Jones (as well as to the Ricardian treatments of population and rent); and (3) there was the 'socialist', political challenge from Hodgskin, Thompson and others. In addition there were other, not easily classifiable, critics such as Read and Ravenstone. Now from the point of view of such critics, instead of the wonderful 'certainty' and 'perfect concurrence' discerned by McCulloch and Mill, there was, on the contrary, widespread disagreement, confusion, and a proliferation of sects. According to William Thompson (1827): 'We shall find as many sects in the schools of political economy as in the schools of religion, each of them relying on his own peculiar doctrines as the exclusive means of salvation for the operative or industrious classes.'

Two years later (1829) Samuel Read maintained:

By all who are acquainted with the most recent and most noted works on Political Economy, it will be readily admitted that the science is at present in a very unsettled and unsatisfactory state. There is indeed scarcely a single doctrine – if we except that of *commercial* freedom, as expressed long since by the French economists – upon which there is a perfect and uniform, or even a general agreement, among the various sects and schools, into which the science is now divided.[19]

Which of the two diametrically contradictory views of the recent history and condition of political economy in the 1820s was nearer the mark? That of the, in important respects, unorthodox Malthus, together with such little-known 'outsiders' as Thompson and Read? Or the opposite views of the Ricardians, McCulloch and the Mills, which were to acquire such almost unparalleled prestige and dominance in Britain in the middle decades of the century? According to James Mill, of course, such questions are absurd. In today's parlance men like Thompson and Read were not 'professionals' and did not possess sufficient 'knowledge on the subject as to entitle their opinions to any weight'.

[18] 'English economists can hardly fail to be proud of Ricardo; and whether their pride takes the form of treating him as an Angel of Light or as the Prince of Darkness, they will probably all assign to him much greater influence than foreign economists allow' (W. J. Ashley, 1891, p. 475).

[19] I am indebted for these quotations to F. W. Fetter, 1969, p. 69. See W. Thompson, 1827, p. 39, and S. Read, 1829, p. v.

To some extent, J. E. Cairnes, known as 'the last of the classical economists' shared some of the doubts and uncertainties of the critics of orthodoxy in his *Character and Logical Method of Political Economy* (1875). Cairnes explicitly rejected the over-confidence of Torrens of thirty-five years previously, as well as the robust claims of McCulloch and James Mill. He conceded that much was still open and unsettled and he protested especially against the acceptance of the *laissez-faire* doctrine as part of the orthodox teachings of the 'science'. But he claimed that 'Political Economy is a science in the same sense in which Astronomy, Dynamics, Chemistry, Physiology, are Sciences' (op. cit., p. 18). However, he added the further extraordinary claim that, thanks to introspection, as contrasted with the physicist, '*the economist starts with a knowledge of ultimate causes*. He is, already, at the outset of his enterprise, in the position which the physicist only attains after ages of laborious research' (1875, p. 75). (Similar claims, derived from that of Cairnes, for the great advantages or superior reliability of economists, or their generalisations, as compared with the natural sciences, were developed by Friedrich Wieser, and in the nineteen thirties by Professors Hayek and Robbins.)

While, however, recognising criticisms and weaknesses, Cairnes held to the orthodox doctrines and methods. In fact, thanks to J. S. Mill, his populariser Fawcett, and others, the confident McCulloch–Mill version of the development of political economy had a strong and influential hold as late as the early 1860s. This version asserted, in short, that *the subject was virtually created by Smith, before whom it had been sunk in total, or almost total, error; and that, thanks almost entirely to British writers, political economy by about 1823, or 1848 at the latest, had reached a very highly advanced state, comparable in the certainty and authority of its conclusions with the most advanced natural sciences, with a very high measure of agreement among those intellectually or professionally qualified to pronounce on the subject, or among those possessed of sufficient knowledge as to entitle their opinions to any weight.* This perhaps slightly optimistic view of their subject – that, as Professor Denis O'Brien has put it, 'the millennium of economic thought was at hand' – has bequeathed a heritage of rather complacent Anglican confidence, regarding the extent of economic knowledge, to subsequent generations, including those who may have thought themselves to have advanced far beyond the 'classical' doctrines.

However, when Jevons challenged what he called 'the Ricardo–Mill economics' he challenged also its version of the history of the subject. But before we come to Jevons we must consider the version of another great pioneer historian of political economy, namely, Karl Marx.

IV

Marx is often regarded as a kind of 'classical' economist. But, except for his considerable regard for Smith and Ricardo, Marx's version of the history of political economy was very different, at some points though not others, from that of McCulloch and the Mills. In the first place Marx estimated very highly some of the leading economists of the seventeenth and eighteenth centuries in the hundred years before *The Wealth of Nations*. In fact for Marx, *not* Adam Smith but Sir William Petty was not only the first 'classical' economist, but 'the founder of modern political economy...one of the most gifted and original economic investigators' (1951, p. 15).

The contributions of Davenant, Locke, and especially Steuart, as well as Boisguilbert and others, are very seriously and respectfully treated by Marx who emphasised that: 'one must not think of these mercantilists as so stupid as they were subsequently made out to be by the vulgar free traders' (op. cit., p. 24).

In fact Marx's treatment of 'the mercantilists' is much closer to that of Keynes and far removed from the McCulloch–Mill version of pre-Smithian political economy.

Furthermore, again in complete contrast with the McCulloch–Mill version, for Marx, classical political economy had ended with Ricardo. After prodigious studies in the literature of the subject Marx concluded in 1851 (in the sharpest contrast with J. S. Mill in 1848): '*Basically, this science has made no further progress since A. Smith and D. Ricardo.*'[20]

Certainly, whatever one may or may not think about Marx as an economist, one must recognise that he was a great pioneer student of the history of the subject, with a relatively wider and deeper knowledge of the economic writings of his predecessors than that of most other leading figures in the history of political economy. Moreover, Marx worked out his own doctrines, in political economy as in philosophy, as the end-product of his vast researches in the history of the subject. As Mr McLellan has noted: 'Marx evolved his own ideas by a critique and elaboration of his predecessors' (1973, p. 336).

Nevertheless, Marx's version of the history of economic thought was even more drastically shaped and explicitly tailored for the

[20] See D. McLellan, 1973, p. 283 (italics added). Of course anyone but an almost uncriticisable Prophet who, at the age of 33, proclaims that there is nothing more worth reading on his subject, in any language, *might* be suspected of premature hardening of the intellectual arteries. Marx shows no knowledge of, or interest in, the work of such fundamentally original economists of the 1830s and 1840s as Hermann, Thünen, Mangoldt, A. Walras, Dupuit, Lloyd and Longfield. He is also completely contemptuous of Roscher, the founder of the German historical school. Surprisingly, Marx *does* refer to Cournot's *Recherches*, though with his own theorising concentrated so narrowly on competition he shows no constructive interest in Cournot's pioneering analysis of monopoly. (See 1962, Bd. 19, p. 383.)

favourable presentation or justification of his own ideas, than, for example, the versions of Jevons and Keynes. For Jevons and Keynes, as partial instigators of major transformations in the subject, the previous theories or doctrines, in the areas with which they were concerned, were inadequate or fallacious. This was not at all how Marx treated his predecessors. Marx was considerably and obviously indebted to Ricardo and to some extent to Smith. In fact, Marx seems to have regarded the history of economic theory as developing in a way parallel to that of the 'capitalist' economy itself; that is, as passing through creative and constructive phases, before moving into decline, crisis, and an inevitable revolution. Correspondingly, Adam Smith, and still more Ricardo, represented for Marx the valid, constructive phase in the history of political economy, with the despicable re-presentatives of decline and crisis, that is his own contemporaries, swept magisterially aside by his own revolutionary fulfilment and consummation of the subject. A, or the, key passage in Marx's – or Marxists' – interpretation, or presentation, of the history of economic thought comes in the '*Nachwort*', or 'Afterword' (of 1873) to the second German edition of vol. 1 of 'Capital'. Here Marx argues:

> Political Economy can remain a science only so long as the class-struggle is latent or manifests itself only in isolated and sporadic phenomena.
>
> Let us take England. Its Political Economy belongs to the period in which the class-struggle was as yet undeveloped. Its last great representative, Ricardo, in the end, consciously makes the antagonism of class-interests, of wages and profits, of profits and rent, the starting-point of his investigations, naively taking this antagonism for a social Law of Nature. But by this start the science of bourgeois economy had reached the limits beyond which it could not pass...
>
> The succeeding period, from 1820 to 1830 was notable in England for scientific activity in the domain of Political Economy. It was the time as well of the vulgarising and extending of Ricardo's theory, as of the contest of that theory with the old school. Splendid tournaments were held...The unprejudiced character of this polemic...is explained by the circumstances of the time [1961, p. 14].

Marx proceeded to compare these years of the 1820s with the decade or so before the French revolution, 'after Dr. Quesnay's death'. He then seizes on the particular year 1830 as marking the decisive 'crisis' or turning-point:

> With the year 1830 came the decisive crisis.
>
> In France and in England the bourgeoisie had conquered political power. Thenceforth, the class-struggle, practically as well as theoretically, took on more and more outspoken and threatening forms. It sounded the knell of scientific bourgeois economy. It was thenceforth no longer a question, whether this theorem or that was true, but whether it was useful to capital or harmful, expedient or inexpedient, politically dangerous or not. In

place of disinterested inquirers there were hired prize-fighters; in place of genuine scientific research, the bad conscience and the evil intent of apologetic [op. cit., p. 15].

Even J. S. Mill is included by Marx in this process of degeneration and decay: though he is admittedly not placed in the 'hired prize-fighter' class, the 'shallow syncretism' of which he is 'the best representative' represents 'a declaration of bankruptcy by bourgeois economy'.[21]

We must pause for a moment at this stage to consider the status of this *Nachwort* of 1873 from which the foregoing often-quoted words are taken. It has been claimed by some Marxologists that the *Nachwort* does not do justice to Marx, or is not a definitive exposition of his views. (This is about as near to 'criticism' as Marxologists can come regarding the Prophet, though on this point they should be commended for recognising very serious faults in the 1873 *Nachwort*.) These deviationist Marxists maintain that Marx's treatment of the history of economic thought is much more representatively displayed in the *Theories of Surplus Value*.[22] But the *Nachwort* of 1873 was a

[21] It is true that Marx had at one point observed regarding 'men like J. S. Mill', that 'it would be very wrong to class them with the herd of vulgar economic apologists'. But this is hardly sufficient to justify Mr M. H. Dobb's assertion that Marx 'was careful to discriminate and by no means treated all economists as "hired prize-fighters"' – even those writing after 1830. The writings of very few economists after 1830, and almost none after 1840, receive any reasonable treatment from Marx. Jones and Ramsay in the 1830s, Cherbuliez (1840), and *The History of Prices* by Thomas Tooke seem to be the only exceptions. Tooke (1774–1858) is referred to as 'the last English economist of any value'. In the *Grundrisse* (Pelican ed., 1973, p. 883) Marx states: 'The history of modern political economy ends with Ricardo and Sismondi.' (See also M. H. Dobb, 1973, p. 29; K. Marx, 1961, p. 611; and 1962, Bd. 19, pp. 380 and 648.)

[22] J. E. King, op. cit., p. 3. It may be noted that Mr King, for the purpose of trying to ward off criticisms of the Prophet in a comparatively sophisticated Discussion Paper, alleges that the *Nachwort* 'does not do justice' to, or 'is not representative' of Marx. But in a textbook purveying 'the Political Economy of Marx' to elementary students, Mr King (and his co-author) produced a thoroughly uncritical and commendatory summary of Marx's aspersions regarding the intellectual dishonesty and dubious motives of economists after 1830, *from the Nachwort* – while adding their own elaborations in terms of Jevons and marginal analysis. The following is Messrs Howard and King's accurate summary of the *Nachwort*: 'He distinguished very clearly between what he termed the "scientific" and the "vulgar" economists. The former correspond to classical political economy... The latter were seen by Marx as essentially *a product of heightened class tension after 1830, and as mere apologists for capitalism*; neither he nor Engels paid very much attention to developments in economic theory which took place after this date. *For Marx, then, a decisive break in the history of economic thought occurred in the 1830s, a decade in which methodological rigour and scientific honesty, characteristic of classical political economy, began to succumb to a superficial and trivial apologetic.* Though the culmination of this trend may be seen in the so-called "marginalist revolution" of the 1870s, Marx placed the fundamental watershed some forty years earlier' (1975, p. 62, italics added). It seems to amount to a rather rapid and drastic – though welcome – revisionism, that the following year Mr King conceded, in the above-cited Discussion Paper, that (1) the *Nachwort* 'distorts and exaggerates the role of motivation as opposed to questions of methodology and theoretical profundity', and that (2) 1830 did *not*, in fact, mark 'a decisive break'. This is a most emphatic rejection of what

deliberate, mature, and concise statement, apparently intended as a kind of intellectual manifesto, and placed in a very important and prominent position in a new edition of the one outstanding, major volume on political economy which Karl Marx himself prepared for publication – and published – in his lifetime. On the other hand the so-called *Theories of Surplus Value* were left by Marx as a vast collection of notes, and how these should be edited or written up has been a matter of sharp controversy.[23]

In any case, whether or not the *Nachwort* does justice to Marx, *it is certainly thoroughly and validly representative of much or most subsequent 'Marxist' criticism of the history of economic thought.* For it is agreed, even by those seeking to dismiss the *Nachwort* as unrepresentative of Marx, that the passages cited above, with their wholesale accusations of dishonest motives against his economist contemporaries, must be among the most frequently quoted of Marx's writings.[24]

So it is along these lines of the Nachwort, as quoted above, that the history of economic thought has been set up by Marxists as a process culminating in the Prophet's own unique, supreme, and hardly criticisable contribution. Marx could not, like Jevons or Keynes, sweepingly declare his predecessors completely in error, or hopelessly blinded by prejudice and illusion. He had himself clearly drawn too deeply from the work of Ricardo to wish, or to be able, to turn round and declare his source fundamentally fallacious or polluted. So immediately after Ricardo, Marx invents and declares a decisive cut-off point, after which all economic

has been the main theme of the Marxist version of the history of economic thought. If taken on board by other Marxist historians this rejection necessitates profound revisions.

[23] According to the editors of the Moscow edition, the *Theories of Surplus Value* was misrepresented and bowdlerised in the Kautsky edition: 'In "editing" Marx's manuscript, Kautsky tried to tone down the annihilating criticism to which Marx subjected the views of the bourgeois economists, and to substitute "decorous" sleek expressions for the angry, passionate, caustic language used by Marx in his merciless criticism of the apologists for the bourgeoisie.' Thus Kautsky in all passages removed from Marx's characterisation of bourgeois economists such epithets as "asses", "dogs", "canaille"' (op. cit., vol. i, p. 23). Certainly, though he was a pioneer scholar of the history of economic thought, the author of the extraordinary *Herr Vogt* (1860) was also a frenzied and almost pathological polemicist. Attempts to rig out the Prophet in academic gown and mortar-board – while sweeping discreetly under the carpet much-quoted items like the *Nachwort* – seem completely unconvincing.

[24] J. E. King, op. cit., p. i. The famous passages from the *Nachwort* above have certainly been repeatedly invoked and commended by Marxist historians of economic thought. For M. H. Dobb, long the *doyen* of English Marxist economists, the *Nachwort* obviously possessed Scriptural significance. For he not only quoted it at length in his 1937 (p. 138), but he quoted it three times in his 1973 (pp. 28–9, 96n, and 110). Dobb's quotation is reproduced in the Marxist anthology of E. K. Hunt and J. G. Schwartz, 1972, p. 45. Professor R. L. Meek also approvingly quotes the *Nachwort* on the subject of 'scientific' economics and 'hired prize-fighters'. So does the party luminary Emile Burns (1951, p. 10). M. de Vroey also quotes approvingly and at length from the passage in the 1873 *Nachwort* regarding the 1830 cut-off point in his Marxist article, 1975, pp. 433–4.

thought – except, of course, his own – is liable to condemnation as prejudiced or subject to 'the evil intent of apologetic'.[25] According to Marx, during the period in which he was writing almost the only genuinely disinterested or scientific writer on political economy was Marx himself.

We would comment here on Marx's assumption that 'class antag-onism' was latent while Ricardo was writing and suddenly burst out in the 'crisis' year of 1830. (It may, incidentally, be worth emphasising that Marx *does* hold that 'scientific' and 'unprejudiced' political economy is quite possible.) For it seems clear that 'class antagonism' must, in fact, have been at least as acute during the years in which Ricardo was writing as in any other decade and perhaps more so. For example, the Marxist historian Professor Hobsbawm writes of 'the sense of imminent social explosion, which had been present in Britain almost without interruption since the end of the Napoleonic wars (except in most of the 1820s)...Waves of desperation broke time and again over the country: in 1811–13 in 1815–17, in 1819' (1969, p. 94).

Thus it might well be argued that it was *just when Ricardo was writing* that the ferocity of class antagonism would most certainly have, *on Marx's own theory*, ruled out any 'scientific', or disinterested, political economy.

We are concerned here to emphasise how Marx's selection of the year 1830 as a 'crisis', or turning-point, was perfectly suited for the purpose of putting his great source Ricardo in the clear, while sweepingly dismissing, or bringing under the deepest suspicion, all Marx's own 'bourgeois' contemporaries and successors as beyond the pale of serious scientific discussion, unless specially and graciously exempted by the Prophet.[26] This device sets up the development of economic thought as a process uniquely culminating in, and consum-

[25] It must be noted that *Marx is hardly prepared to show any approval or recognition to any economist, in any country, born after 1800, or within decades of himself. He was only prepared to be generous to older writers such as Petty, Steuart, Smith, Ricardo, Tooke, Jones, and Hodgskin – all born long before himself.*

It is, however, also noteworthy how completely and contentedly Marx relies on government sources such as the Reports of the Factory Inspectors and Public Medical Officers all through the 1840s, 1850s and 1860s, long after, apparently, the sharpening 'class-struggle' might presumably have rendered such sources hopelessly suspect as mere propaganda of the increasingly ruthless governing class (as, of course, government reports in communist Russia should have been regarded). Marx writes of 'men as competent, as free from partisanship and respect of persons as the English factory-inspectors, her medical reporters on public health, her commissioners of inquiry into the exploitation of women and children, into housing and food' (1961, p. 9).

[26] Marx's cut-off date of 1830 was presumably derived from French political history and the 'bourgeois' revolution of the year. But Marx proceeds to make this date in French political history decisive for the history of English economic thought.

mated by, the writings of Marx himself. What must be emphasised is that there is no historical justification whatsoever, so far as Britain is concerned, for selecting 1830, rather than 1800, 1810, or 1820, or 1850, or 1860, as some absolutely crucial turning-point, both in the history of the 'class struggle', and, therefore, also in the history of economic thought. Insofar as such a proposition can be tested by any historical evidence, the 'class-struggle' was quite as acute in 1815–23, when Ricardo and Malthus were writing, as it was in 1830, or 1848, or 1871. A sharpening of 'class-antagonism' in 1830 is simply plucked out of the air to legitimise sweeping attacks on the biases and motives of particular economists who have advanced theories which do not fit in with Ricardian–Marxist preconceptions and cannot be refuted by citing logical errors or empirical counter-evidence. Presumably after the revolution, when the Utopian, millennial conditions of communist society are realised, with all class struggles finally liquidated, economists would cast off all tendencies to 'prejudice' and 'apologetic' and would devote themselves to purely 'scientific' political economy.[27]

In the meantime, pending the revolution, Marxist historians of economic thought have devoted themselves, like Marx – but unlike Jevons or Keynes – to their accusations regarding motives and bias. Jevons and Keynes in their 'revolutionary' claims were concerned not only with conceptual or analytical innovations, but with empirical propositions and predictions, and the evidence for them, which, they claimed, refuted or contradicted previous empirical propositions and which had important new implications for policy. For Marx, and certainly for many of his followers, it seems sometimes to be enough, or a main component in their arguments, to impugn motives, without ever following out precisely where these motives and bias have led to particular empirically invalid or logically faulty propositions. The condemnation of motives is simply switched on and off with a sweeping generalisation, too vague to be refuted, when convenient for polemical purposes and when adequate logical and empirical arguments are not available.

Now undoubtedly bias has constantly been at work in economic argument, sometimes very seriously. In the nineteenth century this bias was often in defence or approval of the prevailing market or 'capitalist' economy. More recently, though no statistics are available, one might guess that there has been, probably, much more bias present

[27] 'In communist society, where nobody has one exclusive sphere of activity but each can become accomplished in any branch he wishes, society regulates the general production and thus makes it possible for me to do one thing today and another tomorrow, to hunt in the morning, fish in the afternoon, rear cattle in the evening, criticize after dinner, just as I have a mind. Without ever becoming hunter, fisherman, shepherd, or critic' (see 'The German Ideology', 1953, p. 361).

in economists' writings in favour of various kinds of bureaucratic planning (sometimes in defence of the most totalitarian, terroristic, and genocidal methods of 'planning') than there has been in favour of the market or 'capitalist' economy. However that may be, attempts to trace the operation of bias in economics obviously cannot be confined simply to one particular political direction. Surely 'the evil intent of apologetic' can be, and has been, exercised by economists in various directions, as well as in defence of capitalism. Moreover, this bias can be shown to have had the effect of distorting the basic treatment of the theory of value and distribution just as seriously and fundamentally as has the alleged desire to cover or hush up 'class-antagonism' under 'capitalism'. For example, the emphasis in much 'neoclassical' theorising based on the assumption of freedom of individual choice of jobs and consumer goods, with the separable implication – which need not be accepted – of its normative desirability, is bound to be furiously attacked by apologists for Stalinist and similar methods of planning and the direction of labour. Such economists will, of course, be moved to the most extreme intellectual efforts and antics to devise 'models' of price-and-value-formation from which all elements of individual demand, with its possible repugnant implications regarding individual freedom, are completely purged, while they will welcome the labour-value ideology with its obscuring of human differences and its dehumanising reduction of individual people to homogeneous, 'socially necessary' labour-units. For, in recent decades, this kind of 'model' has found its fullest application and fulfilment in Stalinist-type labour camps, where the rations of 'subsistence' – at, above, or below starvation level – are calculated in accordance with the productive and political objectives of the management.

V

Though the most incisive statement of his version of the history of economic thought was written in 1873, Marx never seems to have shown much interest in the upheaval in the subject which took place in England in the late 1860s and early 1870s, or in the new utility and marginal analysis. So from about the middle of the nineteenth century onwards Marxistic versions of the history of economics have to be based on extrapolation rather than on the Prophet's own words. This seems to have made for some uncertainty in Marxist circles regarding what has been called the 'Jevonian' or 'Marginal' Revolution.

It might be reasonable to begin by asking how far, if at all, there was really anything 'revolutionary', in any genuine sense of that much-overworked term, in what happened to political economy in the late 1860s and early 1870s. We have dealt elsewhere with this question and will confine our answer here to three fairly concise propositions:[28]

(1) Nothing fundamentally 'revolutionary' happened *outside* Britain in the early 1870s, though the long, gradual build-up of an eventually massive structure of 'theory' can be dated from the works of Menger and Walras, as can the rise of their important 'schools'.

(2) In Britain there was no sudden, extensive, or rapid swing to a new theory of value or distribution.

(3) But there was in Britain in the late 1860s and early 1870s a relatively rapid and widespread collapse in the dominance and credibility of most, but not all, of the central theories and doctrines of the most influential and celebrated school in the whole history of the subject, the, in Britain, long-dominant 'classical' school.

The Jevonian version of the history of economic thought is given in the prefaces to his *Theory of Political Economy*, especially in that to the second edition (1879). He opens his first preface by describing and rejecting what we have just called the classical, or McCulloch–Mill, version of the history of the subject. His own work, Jevons challengingly maintains,

> can hardly meet with ready acceptance among those who regard the Science of Political Economy as having already acquired a nearly perfect form. I believe it is generally supposed that Adam Smith laid the foundations of this science; that Malthus, Anderson and Senior added important doctrines; that Ricardo systematised the whole; and, finally, that Mr. J. S. Mill filled in the details and completely expounded this branch of knowledge. Mr. Mill appears to have had a similar notion [1931, p. v].

In the preface to the second edition Jevons complains of the narrow insularity of the subject in Britain: 'The exclusive importance attributed in England to the Ricardian School of Economists, has prevented almost all English readers from learning the existence of a series of French, as well as a few English, German, or Italian economists' (op. cit., p. xviii).

Jevons was not, as he claimed, the first Englishman to have discovered the value of Cournot's work. But it was, in fact, in his Preface of 1879 that Dupuit and Cournot were for the first time given adequate and generous recognition by a leading English economist: 'It is the French engineer Dupuit who must probably be credited with the earliest perfect comprehension of the theory of utility.'

Cournot's *Recherches*, Jevons states, 'contains a wonderful analysis of the laws of supply and demand, and of the relations of prices, production, consumption, expenses and profits' (op. cit., pp. xxviii and xxix).

[28] See above the essay on 'The decline and fall of English classical political economy and the Jevonian revolution' (Chapter 3).

Leon Walras' work, as well as that of his father Auguste, is generously recognised by Jevons. Attention is also called to Gossen and, briefly, to von Thünen. The only major names missing are those of Mangoldt and Menger.

Jevons goes on to announce:

> The conclusion to which I am ever more clearly coming is that the only hope of attaining a true system of Economics is to fling aside, once and for ever, the mazy and preposterous assumptions of the Ricardian School. Our English Economists have been living in a fool's paradise. The truth is with the French School, and the sooner we recognise the fact, the better it will be for all the world, except perhaps the few writers who are too far committed to the old erroneous doctrines to allow of renunciation [op. cit., p. xiv].

Jevons was optimistic, indeed rather over-optimistic, regarding the working out of a new theory of wages: 'I feel sure that when, casting ourselves free from the Wage-Fund Theory, the Cost of Production doctrine of Value, the Natural Rate of Wages, and other misleading or false Ricardian doctrines, we begin to trace out clearly and simply the results of a correct theory, it will not be difficult to arrive at a true doctrine of wages' (op. cit., p. xvi).

On the constructive side Jevons's Preface is a notable historical contribution which, in its day, set new standards of scholarship in political economy. Jevons set out for the first time what must be some of the major components in any history of modern price theory and was the first to give something like their just due to the leading French and German pioneers.

On the critical side Jevons's rejection of the natural wage doctrine was timely and valid as, to a lesser extent, were his criticisms of the cost-of-production theory of value. Also, his attacks on Ricardo's assumptions as 'preposterous', if not 'mazy', had considerable justification, especially with regard to those concerned with population, wages, the labour market, technology, land, 'corn', and the speed and smoothness of equilibrating processes.[29] But the attack on the wages-fund doctrine was too sweeping and categorical, though this came not only from Jevons, but from one economist after another (including Marx) in the late 1860s and throughout the 1870s. In fact, Alfred

---

[29] In denouncing what he describes as Jevons's 'hostility to the workers' wages struggle', Mr I. Steedman (1972, pp. 49–50) tries to counter Jevons's criticism of Ricardo's oversimplified assumptions regarding a stable occupational and relative wage structure, by observing that the wage of each different grade of labour 'may be taken as given'. Of course, one may 'take as given' anything one is unable or unwilling to try to explain – just as Ricardo also took aggregate demand as 'given'. But in this case an important problem of wages is left out which Jevons was entitled to demand that a theory of wages should seek to explain. Followers of Ricardo today, with even less justification than Ricardo himself, seek to retreat into a fantasy world from which all intellectually or politically uncongenial features are banished by arbitrary assumption, or by 'taking as given' whatever it might be awkward to have to explain or recognise as important.

Marshall, wishing as he did to stress evolutionary continuity, and to deflate the revolutionary emphasis in Jevons's version of the recent history of the subject, might more suitably have chosen to defend the classical wages-fund doctrine, rather than the Ricardian 'theory' of value, by portraying the latter as so little open to criticism as closely to resemble Marshall's own teaching.

Anyhow, from a Marshallian point of view, or from that of establishing a façade of professional prestige and respectability, extreme and comprehensive revolutionary claims and denunciations are not helpful. To attain influence and recognition the practitioners in a field of study must be ready to claim important and striking advances and to give the impression that their subject is on the march. Of course ideally these advances should have some significant empirical, and perhaps policy-relevant content, though an appearance of 'dynamism' can be attempted simply by some conceptual, terminological, or taxonomic novelties, or some scene-shifting with regard to 'models' or abstractions. The more established and cautious professional operators, however, though eager to proclaim 'progress', and 'exciting break-throughs', will not wish to see the preceding orthodoxy or authorities revealed as too suddenly and thoroughly immersed in error. Outsiders might then wonder, if a previous orthodoxy or 'consensus' in the subject can be exposed so soon and so completely, whether the present approved or authoritative doctrines may not in their turn, shortly be shown up in a similar light.

In Jevons's day there was no youth-movement at hand, or younger generation of 'professionals', eager to swing the trend of fashion towards a devaluation of their seniors' intellectual equipment. It was not difficult, therefore, for Sidgwick and Marshall to bring about a deflation of Jevons's revolutionary claims. Marshall's version of the history of the subject is unfortunately best known for, or at any rate characterised by, his defence of Ricardo's theory of value (though it should be emphasised that he withdrew his earlier, more extreme claims in the later editions of his *Principles*). But Marshall, in what became Appendix B of his *Principles*, did, nevertheless, present a learned and justly balanced version of the history of economics. Unlike McCulloch and the Mills, Marshall was at least fair to 'the Mercantilists' maintaining that: 'many of the changes which they set themselves to bring about were in the direction of the freedom of enterprise... The tendency to exaggerate the importance of gold and silver as elements of national wealth was carried further by their opponents than by them.'[30]

---

[30] 1961, vol. I, p. 755 and vol. II, p. 752. Mr Guillebaud reported Marshall as saying: 'There is a tendency amongst some economists to urge that we should now go behind Ricardo to Adam Smith. I would agree, but I would go further and say "Back to before Adam Smith"' (1971, p. 7).

Secondly, Marshall, in his own way, was quite prepared to be almost as weightily critical of his classical predecessors as had been Jevons and the historical critics, especially with regard to their doctrines on labour and wages:

> For the sake of simplicity of argument, Ricardo and his followers often spoke as though they regarded man as a constant quantity, and they never gave themselves enough trouble to study his variations...
>
> The same bent of mind, that led our lawyers to impose English Civil law on the Hindoos, led our economists to work out their theories on the tacit supposition that the world was made up of city men...
>
> *Ricardo and his followers neglected a large group of facts, and a method of studying facts which we now see to be of primary importance...*
>
> It caused them to speak of labour as a commodity without staying to throw themselves into the point of view of the workman...
>
> *They therefore attributed to the forces of supply and demand a much more mechanical and regular action than is to be found in real life: and they laid down laws with regard to profits and wages that did not really hold even for England in their own time.* But their most vital fault was that they did not see how liable to change are the habits and institutions of industry. In particular they did not see that the poverty of the poor is the chief cause of that weakness and inefficiency which are the causes of their poverty: *they had not the faith, that modern economists have, in the possibility of a vast improvement in the condition of the working classes* [1961, vol. I, pp. 762–4, and 1925, p. 155, italics added].

Thirdly, Marshall, *at least in his earlier approach, though not in his later attitudes,* did much to further what Cannan (1903) described as 'the loss of insularity which English political economy has undergone' (1917, p. 331).

There may be a touch of condescension in Marshall's treatment of 'the French school', but he recognises that it 'has had a continuous development from its own great thinkers in the eighteenth century, and has avoided many errors and confusions, particularly with regard to wages, which have been common among the second rank of English economists'.

Marshall recognised also 'that America is on the way to take the same leading position in economic thought, that she has already taken in economic practice'.

Perhaps his most glowing tribute, however, is that to the German historical school: 'It would be difficult to overrate the value of the work which they and their fellow-workers in other countries have done in tracing and explaining the history of economic habits and institutions. It is one of the great achievements of our age; and an important addition to our real wealth' (1961, vol. I, pp. 766–8).

However, as the régime of Marshall and his *Principles* began, in the opening decades of the twentieth century, to take on a similarly authoritative, dominating role to that of Mill's *Principles* half a century before, there was, unfortunately, something of a reversion, so far as Marshall's school was concerned, to a kind of rather blinkered, chauvinist complacency such as had existed earlier among supporters of English classical orthodoxy.

Apart, however, from the Marshallian school, it was in the closing decades of the nineteenth, and the opening decades of the twentieth century, that the history of economic thought began, in Britain, to develop as a serious field of study in its own right, that is as an academic discipline, rather than simply, as with McCulloch and Marx, as a means of providing an impressive historical background and pedigree for some particular 'school' or body of doctrine, classical or Marxian. The works, in Britain, of Ingram, Ashley, Cannan, Bonar, and Scott, together with those of a number of German, Italian and French historians were based, especially in the cases of Ingram and Ashley, on a historical scepticism regarding the rival theoretical claims of the classicals and their post-1870 critics. For Marshall the attacks of Jevons on the Ricardo–Mill economics had gone too far. But for the historical critics and sceptics the Jevonian revolution had not gone nearly far enough, or methodologically deep enough. For them the common methodological features and assumptions of economic theorising, before and after 1870, were much more important than the contrasts. In fact the new post-Jevons theories, as they gradually developed, were seen more as a renewal of classical theories, methods, and assumptions (such as Ricardo's omniscient economic man) in opposition to the fundamental historical critics, such as the German school, and Leslie and Toynbee in Britain.[31] The term 'neoclassical', in fact seems to have originated in this way with historical economists.[32] Their approach to the history of political economy and economics did much to raise scholarly and intellectual standards by inculcating a realisation that political economy or economics is a house of many mansions, or a subject to which there are many different approaches, a number of which possess both validity and interest as well as weaknesses and defects; and that economic truth is not the monopoly of some one particular school or method, or of some one

[31] The first historical economist of note in Britain was Richard Jones, considerably admired by both Marx and Marshall, who sharply attacked Ricardo and his method.

[32] It is not clear when, or by whom, the term 'neoclassical' was first used. What is at least an early use occurs in Gide and Rist's *History* of 1909. They wrote of Walras as 'the doyen of the new school', which 'is essentially Neo-classical and pretends nothing more than to give a fuller demonstration of the theories originally taught by the old masters... The *homo economicus* of the Classicals which has been the object of so much derision has been replaced on its pedestal... It would be futile to deny that the new school has undertaken the task of carrying out the work of the Classical writers' (C. Gide and C. Rist, 1948, pp. 489 and 507–9). Some time before, W. J. Ashley had written of Jevons as 'the re-creator of abstract economics in England' (1891, p. 474).

particular academic or political group.[33] Such an approach promotes the idea of synthesis and compromise rather than the lasting confrontations of revolutionary extremes.

It has been suggested that neoclassical historians have sought to promote their own particular, blinkered version of the history of the subject, which to some extent may well be true. But it is surely not true to anything like the extent that it is of the 'classical' or McCulloch–Mill version, or the Marxist version, or the Keynesian version. Schumpeter has sometimes been described as above all a neoclassical historian. But this is how Schumpeter summed up the central achievement of the neoclassicals:

> They naturally exaggerated the importance of their central achievement. They saw more in it than do we, that is, more than a logical schema that is useful for clearing up certain equilibrium relations but is not in itself directly applicable to the given processes of real life. They did not realize how many and how important the phenomena are that escape this logical schema and loved to believe that they had got hold of all that was essential and 'normal'.[34]

Would that 'classical', Marxist, and Keynesian historians took, or had taken, such a modest and critical view of their heroes' achievements.

Finally, there was certainly another sense, apart from the methodological one, in which 'the Jevonian revolution' had been insufficiently radical. There had been no, or very little, questioning or criticism of the Smith–Ricardo–Mill macroeconomic and monetary doctrines and preconceptions. Changes in this part of the subject were gradual and insufficiently explicit. But the trade cycle began to be studied (e.g. by Jevons himself) much more seriously than before 1870. Moreover, the demise of the natural wage doctrine and a changed attitude to poverty led on to questions about unemployment and the relief thereof by public works. The next revolution in economics, in due course and after a world war, started here.

[33] In his Preface to a new edition (1907) of J. K. Ingram's *History* (1888), E. J. James described this work as 'the first serious attempt by a properly qualified English writer to present a view of the progress of economic thought' (p. x). He goes on to maintain that from the history of economic thought, 'the student becomes aware that every one of the great systems possessed some truth, and no one has been elaborated which contains the whole truth. He becomes aware of a still more important fact, and that is, that owing to the continual changes in the nature of the elements with which he has to deal, no universal system, no system which shall be valid in all time and place, can at present, if indeed it ever can, be formulated.'

[34] 1954, p. 1132. Schumpeter is described as a neoclassical historian by Sir John Hicks (1975, p. 325n).

VI

The Keynesian revolution was not a revolution in the whole of economic theory, as was, virtually, the Smithian or classical 'revolution', and as, more nearly, though not entirely, the Jevonian 'revolution' was. The Keynesian revolution left price theory mainly unaffected. But it could nevertheless be said to have altered sufficiently the scope and shape of economics as a whole to be describable as a 'revolution' in the subject. Indeed, perhaps more economists today would be prepared to grant revolutionary significance or status to the Keynesian revolution than to any other claimant. It is interesting, therefore, to find the view being maintained that:

> The 'Keynesian Revolution' can scarcely be put on a level with the Jevonian, despite the author's statement that 'the matters at issue are of an importance that cannot be exaggerated'. For one thing, its effects upon the general conceptual framework of economic theory went less deep, whatever the significance of its policy-implications for the conduct of a modern capitalist economy may have been [Dobb, 1973, p. 214].

Whatever the effects of 'the Keynesian revolution' may have been on 'the general conceptual framework of economic theory', certainly it considerably extended the range of economic theorising. Admittedly, also, there was a fair component of dubious conceptual analysis and logomachy (regarding such non-problems as whether 'saving' was really equal to 'investment' or not, or as to what 'really determined' the rate of interest). But many would be inclined to hold that the Keynesian revolution gained in depth and genuine revolutionary character just because, like the Jevonian and Smithian revolutions, it contained *some* significant empirical content and policy-implications – however blindingly obvious these may seem today – in addition to purely conceptual and terminological changes, or changes in abstract assumptions or ideological prejudices – unlike the more recent so-called, or would-be, 'Sraffa revolution'.

Anyhow, Keynes's version of the history of economic thought, which he outlined as a framework for the presentation of his own macroeconomic theory, and in order to help to undermine, or demolish, the prevailing orthodoxy, or what he took to be the prevailing orthodoxy, is more sweeping and ambitious than the versions of history put forward by the classical economists and by Jevons.[35] Where, however, the Keynesian version became most seriously inadequate was (like Marx's version, though in a different manner) with regard to contemporary developments. It was in attempts to sort the sheep from the goats, or the 'classicals' from the 'revolutionaries' among

[35] The essay above on 'The Keynesian revolution and the history of economic thought' (Chapter 5) gives a much fuller account of what is summarised in this paragraph.

his contemporaries, that the over-simplified Keynesian categories emerged as over-strained and inadequate (as in Marx's attempt to separate the 'scientific' economists from the *bourgeois* apologists of his own day).

VII

The question might now arise as to whether there can be said to have taken place any further 'revolution', turning-point, or watershed, in economics since the Keynesian one of some decades ago. There might be several claimants, such as, for example, what has been called the Monetary Counter-Revolution, on behalf of which some inventive historical accompaniment has certainly been attempted (Patinkin, 1969, pp. 46–70). Then there has been the mathematical, or 'quantitative', revolution, a comprehensive phenomenon, but one involving criteria, form, or style, rather than substance or scope. Even here, where anything in the way of historiate virtuosity, or even historical interest, can hardly be expected, it has been found difficult to escape from history altogether and one or two gems have been forthcoming.[36]

Certainly of the recent claims to new revolutionary status the most elaborate *historical* accompaniment and interpretation has been forthcoming on behalf of the Cambridge 'neo-Ricardian', or neo-Marxistic, or 'neo-' or 'post-Keynesian' critique and analysis. In fact, it may seem that the historical scenario for the antecedents, or setting, of this would-be 'revolution' is much the most *empirically* substantial element about this rather peculiar intellectual phenomenon, to which we turn in the next chapter.

[36] For example: 'In the sixties the character of the subject changed from being an art to an applied science.' Professor A. G. Hines, quoted in *Times Higher Educational Supplement*, 30 March 1973.

9

On recent revolutionary versions of the history of economics

I

Recently certain 'radical' versions of the history of economics have been formulated as historical settings or scenarios for a new would-be 'revolution' in economics. We are concerned here primarily with historical questions, with questions of historical fact and explanation involved in these radical versions. But we cannot entirely avoid questions of substance regarding the content (if there is any) of the new 'theories', or 'paradigms', as compared with the orthodoxy which it is claimed is being overthrown or superseded. We are examining two main texts proclaiming these new versions of the history of the subject: M. H. Dobb's *Theories of Value and Distribution since Adam Smith* (1973), and Book 1 on 'Economic Doctrines' of *An Introduction to Modern Economics* (1973) by Professor Joan Robinson and Mr J. Eatwell. We shall also refer to other writings by Dobb and Professor Robinson as well as to a contribution on 'Value in the History of Economic Thought' by Professor R. L. Meek (1974). We would emphasise that these works are on very different intellectual levels. But they all draw on, or extrapolate, Marx's special version of the history of political economy, and are also centrally concerned with the supersession, *in Britain*, around 1870, of 'classical', or 'Ricardian', theories of value and distribution by 'neoclassical' theories (discussed above in the chapters on 'The decline and fall of English classical political economy and the Jevonian revolution', and 'The Jevonian revolution and economic policy in Britain'). They are also concerned to provide a historical setting, or framework, for a new 'revolution' in the subject in the 1970s.

II

In his survey of theories of value and distribution Dobb seeks to maintain, as far as he can, Marx's doctrine that some crucial cut-off point in the history of political economy occurred in 1830, after which, with the increasing intensity of the 'class-struggle', the 'scientific' political economy of Ricardo was inevitably supplanted by the 'apologetics' of 'hired prize-fighters'. Dobb cites as evidence the volume of criticism directed at Ricardo's theories and concepts around, or soon after, 1830, especially from 'economists of gentry-breed in Dublin or Oxford...from the cloisters of ancient universities' (which seems to be Dobb's way of describing Whateley, Senior, Lloyd and Longfield).

Apart from criticising or abandoning Ricardian ideas and concepts, some of these economists, together with other critics such as Scrope or Read, had developed the concept of 'abstinence'. So Dobb enquires: 'Was Marx's bad conscience and evil intent of apologetic too strong a characterisation of such as these?'[1]

We are faced at once with the Marxist practice of condemnation by the imputing of political motives. That criticism and rejection of Ricardian theories might have been based on any unrealism or inadequacy, theoretical or practical, in these 'theories' (e.g. in the assumptions of homogeneous labour-units, absence of increasing returns, 'corn', the 'original and indestructible powers of the soil', the 'laws' of natural wages, and rapid adjustments to equilibrium) Dobb seems unprepared to envisage. Nor does Dobb explain that some of those whom he cites as 'forerunners of Marx's *Das Kapital*', such as Richard Jones,[2] and Thomas Hodgskin,[3] who were approvingly 'singled out'

---

[1] 1973, pp. 110 and 137. Dobb describes W. F. Lloyd as belonging to 'the anti-Ricardian reaction who anticipated some of the main ideas of the "Jevonian Revolution" of some forty years later', that is, as one of the 'gentry-breed' from 'the cloisters of ancient universities', for whom, presumably, Marx's 'bad conscience and evil intent of apologetic' was not 'too strong a characterisation'. This, of course, flies in the face of the facts regarding Lloyd, who, in spite of being a pioneer of marginal utility, might well be described as the English economist who came nearer than any other to anticipating some of Marx's economic doctrines, including immiserisation, concentration, and the reserve army of unemployed. In fact, it is fair to say that there was much more of the substantial elements of Marxian political economy in the ideas of the Oxfordian, 'gentry-bred', marginal utility theorist, than in those of Ricardo. Lloyd looked forward to the prospect 'when accumulated experience of the results of unlimited competition, operating to the degradation and misery of a large portion of the working class, shall have dissipated the prejudices which now exist, in favour of a pernicious freedom' (1835, p. 126. See also 1836). This is *not* to say that Lloyd was a 'socialist'. I am indebted regarding Lloyd to Professor Barry Gordon and Chapter VII of his thesis, 1967. See also R. M. Romano, 1971, pp. 285ff.

[2] Richard Jones was the most fundamental historical critic of the Ricardian method. But he was highly regarded by the Prophet himself and is praised by Dobb (op. cit., p. 139) for expressing 'a not dissimilar emphasis anticipating Marx's'. The arbitrary and rather topsy-turvy nature of Marxist historical judgments is displayed by the fact that no one could have emphasised more profoundly *the harmony of class interests* than Jones, and thus exposed himself to the Marxist charge of 'bad conscience and the evil intent of apologetic'. Jones concludes his *Essay on the Distribution of Wealth* (1831, p. 328) as follows: 'All systems are essentially false and delusive, which suppose that the permanent gain and advantage of any one class of the community, can be founded on the loss of another class: because the same providence which has knit together the affections and sympathies of mankind, by so many common principles of action, and sources of happiness, has in perfect consistency with its own purposes, so arranged the economical laws which determine the social condition of the various classes of communities of men, as to make the permanent and progressive prosperity of each, essentially dependent on the common advance of all.'

as such by the Prophet himself, were extremely severe and fundamental critics of Ricardo. In fact, the Marxist pattern of an anti-
Ricardian, anti-working-class 'reaction' of 'gentry-breed' economists
'in the cloisters of ancient universities', gallantly opposed by faithfully 'Ricardian' socialists, to be found 'in Mechanics Institutes and
among incipient trades unions and radical fraternities' (Dobb, 1973,
p. 137), breaks down against the simple facts regarding the critic
of the market economy Lloyd, and the virulently anti-Ricardian
Hodgskin.[3]

More seriously, Dobb's survey of theories of value and distribution
is provincially Anglo-centric, taking no account of the fact that
Ricardian doctrines had, for the most part, very little vogue or influence outside Britain in the nineteenth century. Dobb does not attempt
to explain why such economists as Cournot, Dupuit, Hermann, von
Thünen, and Mangoldt (most of whom he never even mentions, but
on whom Menger and Walras were to build) preferred to develop
value theories with a significant role for demand and/or utility, or
distribution theories with an emphasis on productive contribution.
Presumably this was because all these writers, also, were 'economists
of gentry-breed', imbued with 'the evil intent of apologetic'. In fact,
apart from rejecting the grotesque over-simplifications of the main
Ricardian assumptions, some of these writers were seriously trying to
get to grips with increasingly important real-world problems of
monopolies and public utilities in face of which the Ricardian labour-
cost theory was completely useless.

However, while attempting to protect the significance of Marx's

---

[3] In the Marxian version of the history of political economy an important niche is
assigned to Thomas Hodgskin on the basis of a quite erroneous view of his doctrines.
Hodgskin was much admired and quoted by Marx, who seems to have launched the
error that he was a follower of Ricardo, marking a kind of halfway stage between
Ricardo and Marx himself. In his *Theories of Surplus Value* (especially vol. III, Chapter
21) Marx includes Hodgskin with 'the proletarian opposition based on Ricardo'. In
fact, Hodgskin would much more accurately be described as a 'Smithian anarchist'
than as a 'Ricardian socialist'. Certainly there were economists – of 'gentry-breed' or
otherwise – who criticised both Ricardo and Hodgskin. *But there was no stronger or more
comprehensive critic of Ricardo than Hodgskin.* An early paper of his denounces Ricardo
on value, rent, wages and distribution and proclaims: 'I dislike Mr. Ricardo's opinions
because they go to justify the present political situation of society and to set bounds
to our hopes of future improvement...Mr. Ricardo's doctrines are the strongest
support I know, as far as reasoning goes, to aristocracy...I think I never saw a book
more destitute of facts than Mr. Ricardo's...To me it appears to rest entirely on
arbitrary definitions and strange assumptions...It does appear to be built on no sort
of facts, to contradict many and to have little more merit than a "bewildering
subtlety"' (see E. Halévy, 1956, pp. 67 and 77–8; and also my review, 1957, p. 89).
Admittedly it has been pointed out that Hodgskin, a friend of Herbert Spencer, stands
'for the extreme statement of the individualist platform: self-interest, competition,
laissez-faire', etc. – which might point to Ricardian influence. But the conclusion stands
that Ricardo, in fact, had no significant influence on Hodgskin (E. Lowenthal, 1911,
pp. 82 and 103).

quite arbitrarily selected cut-off year of 1830, as the date when scientific political economy – apart, of course, from Marx's own works – came to an end, Dobb now feels bound to recognise the importance of another turning point or 'revolution' in 1870 or 1871.[4]

In an earlier work, Dobb, in line with much Marxist teaching, had severely belittled the significance of 'the Jevonian revolution':

> Of that new departure in economic thought which marked the last quarter of the century neither Marx nor Engels seems to have made more than cursory mention or to have taken much notice. If they had done so, it seems probable that they would have regarded it as a continuation of tendencies already latent in the 'vulgar economists', rather than as the revolutionary novelty in economic thought which it has generally been regarded as being [1937, p. 139].[5]

But in this latest survey 'the Jevonian revolution' is now treated as a major turning-point, with a 'deep' effect on 'the general conceptual framework' on a much more profound level than the Keynesian revolution. One may well applaud this change of view and welcome Dobb's conversion to an appreciation of the importance of Jevons, Menger and Walras. It has to be recognised that such a change of view does tend to heighten the 'revolutionary' significance of what Dobb calls 'the Sraffa System and Critique', which he writes of as a 'true watershed in critical discussion'.[6]

A 'true watershed' cannot be defended as very 'true' so long as one of the rivers flowing down from it is being dismissed as merely a 'vulgar', derivative trickle, worth no more than 'cursory mention'.

[4] This leaves J. S. Mill in an ambiguous, twilight position, and Dobb seems to stretch himself rather far on the admittedly difficult issue of the extent of Mill's 'Ricardianism'. He ends up with a view, similar to Schumpeter's, that the economics of Mill's *Principles* is 'no longer Ricardian', and 'much nearer to Marshall than it was to Ricardo'. Previously, however, Dobb had expressed the doubt, regarding Ricardo, 'whether respect for his doctrines would have continued to be anything like so great as it was in the middle of the nineteenth century without the loyal championship (as well as popularisation), of his main doctrines by John Stuart Mill'. *This seems to contain a historically very important part of the truth.* Ricardo's doctrines of value and distribution were rightly attacked root and branch, from all directions, as soon as they appeared. They were only kept alive by the charisma of Mill. In particular, *what Mill kept alive was the proposition, fundamental for both theory and policy, of the Law of Population and the natural wage theory derived from it,* as well as the James Mill–J. B. Say doctrine of markets, and a cost-of-production approach to value (see Dobb, op. cit., pp. 96–122). A strong case for the specifically and centrally Ricardian influences traceable in J. S. Mill's economic theorising has been made by S. Hollander, in his 1976, pp. 67ff.

[5] Still in a later essay (1949) 'the Jevonian revolution' was regularly described as 'so-called' – a qualification which only, at last, disappeared in 1973. (See also 1955, pp. 104 and 111.)

[6] 1973, p. 249. Writing on 'The Sraffa System and Critique' Dobb maintains: 'What is at stake here is the logical tenability of the whole line of theoretical doctrine dating back to Jevons and the Austrians – to what has been called the Jevonian Revolution (itself a conscious counter-revolution against the classical school and against Ricardo and Marx in particular)' (1972, p. 205).

Like Keynes who, by no means unjustifiably, though at some points with serious distortions and exaggerations, built up the enormity of 'classical' theory, so a spokesman for the latest would-be 'revolution' finds it timely to recognise the significance of what, it is claimed, is being overthrown.

Dobb is especially concerned to emphasise the limitations of the 'neoclassical', or 'modern', theory of 'distribution', which he describes as follows:

> What the 'modern' theory (as I shall call it) in its several variants since Jevons and the Austrians essentially does is to locate a theory of distribution *entirely* within the circle of market relations or the sphere of exchange: to derive the price of what Walras called the productive services of factors (and hence income distribution) as part of the general pricing process of commodities; and this without introducing any sociological *datum* [1972, p. 205].

This description is seriously false with regard to Walras and several other leading neoclassicals. It should be realised that Walras regarded Political Economy as consisting of three parts, to each of which he planned to devote a book in his comprehensive treatise of the subject. Book I 'Elements of Pure Economics' includes no Theory of Distribution in its table of contents. There is the 'Theory of Production', which includes, of course, the pricing of productive services. The Theory of Distribution is the main subject of Book III: 'Elements of Social Economics or The Theory of the Distribution of Wealth via Property and Taxation' (Walras, 1954, pp. 35 and 73–80).

In fact, Walras' whole approach to Political Economy, as he inherited it from his father, started from the analysis of *property*. Unfortunately, like Marshall and Menger, Walras never completed the multi-volume treatise as he originally planned it. But, instead of a fully finished Book III, he did publish a large volume, *Etudes d'économie sociale* (1896, 488 pp.). This makes it clear that the distinction between what may be called the analysis of the pricing of the factors of production, and the theory of distribution proper was quite basic to Walras' whole conception of Political Economy.

Walras' *Etudes d'économie sociale*, which bears the sub-title 'Théorie de la Répartition de la Richesse Sociale', is not a finished, unified work, but a collection of essays. It indicates clearly Walras' leading ideas regarding distribution, including his plan for the nationalisation of land. We cannot attempt a summary here, though a quotation may be given which sets out the basic approach of Walras:

> Nous avons toujours considéré jusqu'ici l'économie politique et sociale comme composée de trois parties: l'étude de la richesse sociale dans sa nature, sa cause et ses lois, ou *économie politique pure*, l'étude de la production de la richesse, ou *économie politique appliquée*, et l'étude de la répartition de la richesse sociale, ou *économie sociale*. Ainsi l'étude de la répartition de la richesse sociale entre les hommes en société, ou théorie de la *propriété* et de

l'*impôt*, trouve assez naturellement sa place à côté des deux autres catégories économiques, en raison de ce qu'elle porte, elle aussi, sur la *richesse sociale*.[7]

Of the other leading first (or second) generation neoclassicals, Jevons never completed any systematic new theory of distribution, while Marshall denied that the marginal productivity analysis provided a 'theory' of wages. As for Walras' successor Pareto, he believed that if one aspired to pushing beyond static formulae into real-world problems of economic dynamics one would inevitably have to take into account social factors, and the social framework, so that any purely economic analysis would be incapable of yielding significant conclusions. Pareto, therefore, advanced boldly into the field of sociology.[8]

The one leading neoclassical who it is not completely impossible to fit into a Marxist stereotype of 'neoclassicism' is Carl Menger – though, of course, unlike Jevons and Walras he is hardly ever cited in this connection. Certainly Menger cannot possibly be accused of devising his analysis to counter Marxian ideas. As he himself insists, he was following the main lines of German theorising on value and distribution, which had long differed fundamentally from English 'classical', or Ricardian doctrines, and he shows hardly any signs at all of any acquaintance with Marx's writings. But in his discussion of rent, interest, and distribution, Menger did, quite explicitly, counter the socialist ideas of Rodbertus,[9] who, Menger maintains:

> argues that our social institutions make it possible for the owners of capital and land to take part of the product of labor away from the laborers, and thereby live without working. His argument is based on the erroneous assumption that the entire result of a production process must be regarded as the product of labor. Labor services are only one of the factors of the production process, however, and are not economic goods in any higher degree than the other factors of production including the services of land and capital [1950, p. 168].

Menger goes on sharply to distinguish between the economic aspects of distribution and the legal or moral aspects:

[7] 1896, p. 51. Walras explains: 'Je crois que c'est peu que la richesse sociale soit produite abondamment, si elle n'est équitablement répartie entre tous les membres de la société' (p. 31). Of course, Walras completely dismisses Ricardian notions of *laissez-faire* in the field of distribution as well as production.

[8] As Pareto put it in *The Mind and Society*: 'Until economic science is much farther advanced, "economic principles" are less important than the reciprocal bearings of economics and the results of other social sciences. Many economists are paying no attention to such inter-relations, for mastering them is a long and fatiguing task requiring an extensive knowledge of facts; whereas anyone with a little imagination, a pen, and a few reams of paper can relieve himself of a chat on "principles"' (quoted in Hutchison, 1938, p. 160).

[9] In Wieser's *Natural Value* Rodbertus is also very briefly criticised. Of the 252 pages of this book, eight contain mild and partly sympathetic criticisms of socialist ideas (without mention of Marx). According to Professor Meek, however: 'Wieser's *Natural Value*, for example, was in intention and effect a sustained polemic against the Marxian and Rodbertian systems' (1973b, p. 237).

One of the strangest questions ever made the subject of scientific debate is whether rent and interest are justified from an ethical point of view or whether they are 'immoral'. Among other things, our science has the task of exploring why and under what conditions the services of land and capital display economic character, attain value, and can be exchanged for quantities of other economic goods (prices). But it seems to me that the question of the legal or moral character of these facts is beyond our science...

It may well appear deplorable to a lover of mankind that possession of capital or a piece of land often provides the owner a higher income for a given period of time than the income received by a laborer for the most strenuous activity during the same period. Yet the cause of this is not immoral [op. cit., p. 173].

However, at least Marxists can firmly agree with Menger's final conclusion:

If the demand for higher wages is not coupled with a program for the more thorough training of workers...it requires that workers be paid not in accordance with the value of their services to society, but rather with a view to providing them with a more comfortable standard of living, and achieving a more equal distribution of consumption goods and of the burdens of life. *A solution of the problem on this basis, however, would undoubtedly require a complete transformation of our social order* [op. cit., p. 174, italics added].

The other two leading Austrians fail completely to fit into the stereotype of 'neoclassical' theorising on value and distribution suggested by Dobb. Wieser took the same road into sociology as Pareto, in his *Theorie der gesellschaftlichen Wirschaft* (1914) and *Das Gesetz der Macht* (1926).[10]

In the same year as Wieser's *Social Economics* his brother-in-law Böhm-Bawerk published his essay *Control or Economic Law*. In contrast with Dobb's account of the treatment of value and distribution by 'the whole line of theoretical doctrine dating back to Jevons and the Austrians', what Böhm-Bawerk maintained was:

It would be idiotic to try to deny the influence of institutions and regulations of social origin in the distribution of goods...

[10] The following passages may give a faint indication of the tendency of Wieser's views on distribution and *laissez-faire*, which are fairly near the social reformist and interventionist views of the *Verein für Sozialpolitik*. Wieser (1) clearly rejected the classical doctrine of proportionality in taxation in favour of progression. (2) He accused the classicals of examining 'only the pure forms of monopoly and of competition', and went on: 'The modern trend to production on a large scale has called into being numerous, novel, intermediate, monopoloid forms, which today are far more important than either of the pure forms. The classical formula, unconditional approval of social competition and absolute repudiation of anti-social monopoly, can no longer do justice to the institutions of to-day.' (3) Wieser held that the growth of capitalist power 'has cut the ground from under the classical doctrine of freedom ...Every power, even the merely personal superiority of the more gifted or the more active individual, restrains the freedom of choice for the less gifted, the less active.' (4) Wieser held that the modern theory of economic policy 'has decisively repudiated the doctrine of non-intervention', which 'the classical theorists thought ...applied for all succeeding periods' (see Wieser, 1927, pp. 217, 405–10, 433).

The marginal value school had furnished only an incomplete skeleton of the theory of distribution as a whole, and it was well aware of this shortcoming. It never pretended fully to have covered the complex reality with that concept; on the contrary, it never failed to emphasise, again and again, that its past findings had to be supplemented by a second series of investigations, whose task it would be to inquire into the changes that would be produced in this fundamental concept by the advent of changed conditions, particularly those of 'social' origin...

In our modern economic progress the intervention of social means of control is continuously gaining in importance. Everywhere trusts, pools and monopolies of all kinds interfere with the formation of prices and with distribution. On the other hand, there are the labor organisations with their strikes and boycotts, not to mention the equally rapid growth of artificial interference emanating from the economic policies of governments. *In the eyes of the classical economists, the theory of free competition could claim to be the systematic foundation of the entire problem, as well as the theory of the most important normal case. But at present, the number and importance of those phenomena which no longer find an adequate explanation in the theory of free competition already exceed the number of those cases which may still be explained by that one formula...*

There literally exists no price nor any form of 'distribution' (except perhaps highway robbery and the like) without containing at least some legalistic–historical aspect [1962, pp. 149–51 and 160, italics added].

Again, Philip Wicksteed might well be regarded as the leading exponent among English economists of 'neoclassical' distribution analysis in its purest form. But Wicksteed concluded his major pronouncement on the subject as follows:

The more we analyse the life of society the less can we rest upon the 'economic harmonies'; and the better we understand the true function of the 'market', in its widest sense, the more fully shall we realise that it never has been left to itself, and the more deeply shall we feel that it never must be. Economics must be the handmaid of sociology [1933, vol. II, p. 784].

Certainly few subsequent economists have been so bold as to follow Pareto and Wieser along the road to economic sociology, though this arduous road has always been open. So it might, perhaps, seem that there is some justification for the rather different account of the 'modern' treatment of distribution given earlier by Dobb:

Most obvious of the difficulties under which it has always laboured is that it has virtually to take the distribution of income as given, since this affects not only the supply of productive agents but also the pattern of demand. Yet the prices of factors of production, and hence the incomes of those who supply them, are among the dependent variables of the pricing problem. It is hardly surprising in the circumstances that modern economic theory should have abandoned the attempt to provide a theory of distribution: a problem which Ricardo had regarded as central to economic enquiry. The omission has been justified on the ground that the assumption of income distribution as an independently determined datum is not more drastic than the assumptions which any alternative type of theory would have to make; and that all abstraction which cuts off a slice or aspect of the real world for the purpose of analysis must ignore certain types of interaction [1955, p. 108].

But if all that Dobb wishes to say is that 'modern' economic theorising suffers seriously, and recently increasingly seriously, from arbitrary and over-simplified abstraction, including, in particular, abstraction from all kinds of 'social' forces and factors, this is undoubtedly true and important. But it is far from new, having been argued, for example, over a century and a quarter ago by German historical critics of the English classicals, and has been repeated, on and off, ever since by critics of 'orthodoxy'. Moreover the charge applies comprehensively over much of the range of economic theorising, for example to theories of inflation just as much as to theories of distribution;[11] *and it applies even more comprehensively and fatally to the would-be 'revolutionary' constructions of Dobb's Cambridge colleagues.*

Anyhow, from Ricardo to contemporary Cambridge, no one ever has produced a satisfactory general theory of class distribution, or anything approaching such a theory, by abstract Ricardian methods and 'model' building. In fact, although the subject of distribution can be said to have been unduly neglected, there is a tradition in English empirical, social economics which *has* contributed valuably and significantly to the knowledge of distribution. In England alone there is a line of investigation from Booth and Rowntree, through Bowley and others, which is very much alive today and which has considerably illuminated problems of poverty. It is certainly reasonable to hope for progress from this line of basic empirical, statistical and factual research – though certainly not from the endless elaboration of over-simplified 'models' in the Ricardian tradition, filled out, if at all, with some crude, early nineteenth-century theory of 'classes'. Dobb's diagnosis, in which he denounces excessive abstraction one moment, and then, in the next moment, calls for a return to Ricardian procedures, presents a very bizarre *volte face*.

We cannot, however, end this section without welcoming the

---

[11] I can claim, for what it is worth, to have long ago interpreted marginal productivity analysis in strictly microeconomic terms: 'The unassailable...core of the marginal productivity analysis lay in the maximization formula for the individual producing unit in a factor market, the total turnover of which involved a very small proportion of the national income...Perhaps it was not sufficiently clear, to what very different and much more limited questions the marginal productivity analysis was a kind of answer, as compared with the Ricardian analysis of relative aggregate shares combined with a somewhat wavering application of the Malthusian principle...It is extremely doubtful whether the marginal productivity analysis should be ascribed any significance for the determination of wages "as a whole"' (1953, pp. 317–19).

An earlier version of recent controversies about marginal productivity analysis, covering much the same ground in a much more illuminating and penetrating way, was given in Tugan-Baranovsky's Marxist essay, *Die Soziale Theorie der Verteilung* (1913), and in Schumpeter's masterly reply, 'Das Grundprinzip der Verteilungstheorie' (1917).

cautious and modest conclusion of Dobb's survey, which is in very striking contrast with the attitudes of some of his Cambridge colleagues: 'One can only conclude, at the time of writing, that such alternative explanations of distribution are *sub judice* in current economic discussion, and that discussion (or even elaboration) of them has proceeded insufficiently far as yet to make final judgment possible, still less to speak of a *consensus*' (1973, p. 272).

One must point out, however, that it is quite unreasonable to hope for, or even 'speak of', a consensus in any 'scientific' sense, except regarding issues on which logical or empirical testing and criteria can be brought to bear, and are generally accepted. Admittedly there can be waves of fashion, but fashions don't last. Thus insofar as recent debates – strongly laced with propaganda[12] – turn on the political overtones and innuendos in alternative terminologies, or on which of contrasting preposterously over-simplified abstractions is the less arbitrary and preposterous, these can only be expected to peter out in exhaustion and boredom – as with previous such controversies – unless, of course, the 'consensus' which Dobb was envisaging is to be of the kind maintained by Stalin's regime in Russia or Mao's in China.

III

In the Robinson–Eatwell volume, the treatment of 'The Neo-Classical Era' is fundamental. In this chapter the authors try to set out the last hundred years of the history of economics as – in the main, insofar as what they call 'orthodoxy' is concerned – a record of bias, deception, delusion and error, almost unbroken except for the Keynesian interlude and one or two isolated outsiders like Veblen. This chapter, therefore, is really intended to supply the starting-point and *raison d'être* for a 'revolution', by providing a fresh, new, 'modern' introduction free from the 'fudge', and covering up, of the 'old' orthodoxy of the last hundred years. This treatment of the 'neoclassicals', and of the last hundred years of economic thought, has the function of demonstrating why some 'new start' is necessary. In fact, although many neoclassical concepts and assumptions are employed throughout the volume, the closing words of Book I are: 'It is time to go back to the beginning and start again.'

Professor Robinson and Mr Eatwell have not much use for Marx's 1830 'cut-off' point, nor any space to castigate Dobb's 'economists of

[12] See, for example, E. K. Hunt and J. G. Schwartz, eds., 1972. The editors inform us (p. 32): 'The entire school of economic theory *going back to the 1870s* is now under attack...'Severely rational modern economics", the austere science, is being seen to function essentially as a pseudo-sophistication proclaiming the greatest beneficence, while the wretched of the earth are starved, clubbed, gassed and bombed into submission' (as in Cambodia, of course).

gentry-breed', who so brazenly paraded their class-prejudices by actually making so bold as to criticise some of Ricardo's preposterous abstractions and over-simplifications. While assigning a highly dubious role to J. S. Mill's *Principles*, the authors take 1871 as a decisive turning-point and the beginning of what they call 'the new economics'.

In explaining the supersession of 'classical' or Ricardian doctrines in England, the authors, like Dobb, will, of course, allow only an insignificant role to actual errors or defects in these doctrines and their increasing inadequacies in the face of serious real-world problems. Professor Robinson and Mr Eatwell base their explanation on im-puting political motives: 'The change in the political and ideological climate...made classical ideas appear not so much irrelevant as dangerous...*It was not so much a weakness in pure theory as a change in the political climate, that brought the reign of the classics to an end*' (1973, italics added).

Four points should be made:

(1) Regarding 'pure theory', the weaknesses in the prevailing Ricardo–Mill economics were not simply difficulties with the water and diamonds paradox – as alleged by Professor Robinson and Mr Eatwell. They were serious and fundamental, and provided quite sufficient grounds for rejecting the Ricardo–Mill theories of value and wages, apart from any alleged 'change in the political and ideological climate'. These basic theoretical difficulties, which were becoming more and more serious as the British economy developed, stemmed, in particular (a) from the over-simplifications regarding homogeneous units of labour; (b) from the Ricardo–Mill subsistence or natural wage theory; and (c) from the failure to deal with falling costs and monopoly which were clearly of growing importance. In fact, the generalisation might be sustained that as standards of living rise above subsistence, and techniques of production become more complex, 'labour' theories of value and distribution become increasingly inadequate and useless, while marginal analysis is inevitably required for the more complex allocation problems which arise – whether in a 'capitalist' or in a 'socialist' economy. A further illustration of this same generalisation might be discerned in the rather pathetic, and apparently hardly successful attempts to apply marginal analysis in Soviet Russia, about a hundred years after its systematic development in Western Europe. (But, of course, those kinds of complex allocation problems do not, or cannot, arise in as acute a form so long as free consumers' choice is ruthlessly suppressed by political authority.)

(2) But although basic theoretical weaknesses are sufficiently abun-dant and obvious to explain the rejection of the Ricardo–Mill theories of value and wages, there were serious practical inadequacies which would also have provided ample grounds for supersession. These

included the practical impotence of the Ricardo–Mill theories in the face of the problems of public utilities, which were growing rapidly in importance in the middle of the nineteenth century, and which provided the starting-point of one or two of the 'neoclassical' pioneers, such as Dupuit (naturally never mentioned either by Dobb or by Professor Robinson and Mr Eatwell). Today, indeed, its contribution to the problems of public utilities and nationalised industries is, perhaps, one of the major credit items to the account of 'neoclassical' economics.

(3) Thirdly, an accompanying role, by itself nothing like sufficient, and not even necessary, may well have been played by what may be described as 'changes in the political and ideological climate', especially insofar as these were relevant in changing the demands on economic policy. But the changes in the political climate *were of a totally different character from those indicated by Professor Robinson and Mr Eatwell.*

(4) Fourthly, it should be noted that the revolt against 'classical' political economy, or 'the Ricardo–Mill economics', began well before Marx's main writings were at all widely known to English readers, and also well before the onset of the Great Depression, and that the initial collapse of credibility in England was with regard to the subject of distribution rather than value,[13] and in particular regarding the wages-fund doctrine. With regard to the political or ideological implications of the widespread revolt against the wages-fund doctrine, it should be noted that this doctrine had been associated with an allegedly strong anti-trade-union and anti-working-class bias on the part of orthodox, or Ricardian economists (unfairly so associated in the case of J. S. Mill). The attacks on, and the withdrawal of the wages-fund doctrine, a central pillar of classical and Ricardian distribution analysis, in the late 1860s and early 1870s, took place in the context of a wider recognition of the power and position of trade unions – not conceded by most earlier classicals – following the Electoral Reform of 1867 and soon to become acknowledged by the Trade Union legislation of 1871 and 1875. In fact this anti-wages-fund element in the neoclassical revolt against Ricardian economics was strongly endorsed, at its outset in the middle and late 1860s, by Karl Marx himself.[14]

It may well be that the mounting attacks on the *laissez-faire* maxim, which was widely regarded – and quite rightly so in the case of Ricardo – as the central policy conclusion of 'classical' political economy, interacted with the political and constitutional changes then

[13] See above Chapter 4: 'The Jevonian revolution and economic policy in Britain.'
[14] In *Wages, Price and Profit* (1865) and in *Capital* (1867) the attack on the wages fund is launched on the same lines as were followed by the leading 'neoclassical' critics from F. D. Longe (1866) onwards.

going forward in Britain, such as the extension of the franchise in 1867 (and 1884), and the political and legal recognition and establishment of Trade Unions (1871 and 1875). Attacks on what was regarded as its main policy principle certainly had a part in the declining influence and credibility of classical political economy, *and such criticisms were logically and closely linked with its theoretical weaknesses*:

(a) The rejection of the 'natural' wage doctrine led to the attack on Ricardian *laissez-faire* in distribution, social reform and education.

(b) The new emphasis on the utility concept in value theory (with the rejection of the concept of homogeneous labour units) promoted the abandonment of the classical proportionality principle in taxation, and led on to support for financing social reform by progressive taxation – to become increasingly popular with the new electorate. But the authors of this textbook seem to be suggesting quite a different, almost an opposite, kind of 'change in the political climate' as the *main factor* in the transformation of economics.

As a kind of framework for their version of history, Professor Robinson and Mr Eatwell start from a *simpliste* Marxistic 'reflection' theory of economic thought. For example, we are told that J. S. Mill's *Principles* '*reflects* the increasing self-confidence of mid-nineteenth century Britain...Mill's analysis derives from a prosperous age' (1973, pp. 12 and 27, italics added).

This Robinson–Eatwell 'reflection' theory is also applied to the writings of Marx, as follows: 'It might be said that Volume I of *Capital reflects* the ferocious conditions of the eighteen forties, when the Communist Manifesto challenged the world, and that Volume III *reflects* the milder situation at the end of the eighteen fifties' (op. cit., p. 188, italics added).

It may first be noted that parts of Volume I of *Capital* may actually have been written *after* parts of Volume III, in the 1860s. It seems, furthermore, that the historical fact may have failed to remain uppermost in the minds of the authors that J. S. Mill's *Principles* and *The Communist Manifesto* were published *in the same year*. In fact, Mill and Marx must have finished holding up their two mirrors to English economic reality, or completed their two 'reflections', within a few months of one another around the end of 1847. One mirror, however, 'reflected', apparently, 'the ferocious conditions of the eighteen forties', at almost exactly the same moment as the other mirror was 'reflecting' what is described as a 'prosperous age', in which the 'antagonism of capitalist and worker was not emphasised' – as in *The Communist Manifesto*. What such a 'reflection' theory amounts to, if anything; whether this is the History of Political Economy Through the Looking-Glass, or whether it's all done by mirrors, only Professor Robinson and Mr Eatwell can explain to their beginner audience.

As regards what Jevons was 'reflecting' in 1871, Professor Robinson and Mr Eatwell simply move forward Marx's cut-off point for 'scientific political economy' by forty years. By the time of Jevons: 'Fear and horror aroused by the work of Marx were exacerbated by the impact throughout Europe of the Paris Commune of 1870. Doctrines which suggested conflict were no longer desirable. Theories which diverted attention from the antagonism of social classes met a ready welcome' (op. cit., p. 35).

To substantiate such a striking explanation as this would require evidence, in the form of passages from, say, Jevons and Marshall, Menger and Walras, expressing 'fear and horror' of Marx and of the Paris Commune. Moreover, it would be necessary to show how this 'fear and horror' led such economists to indulge in the elaborate deception of inventing fundamental new theories of value and distribution so as to 'divert attention from the antagonism of social classes'. But the authors do not consider any evidence to be necessary.[15]

[15] Mr G. Routh (after the stock citation of Marx's *Nachwort* applied to 1871 instead of 1830) goes on to produce a paler version of the Robinson–Eatwell account by claiming that Jevons was 'apprehensive' about the 'threat' of democracy. Mr Routh writes: 'Jevons viewed the demands for reform with apprehension. "It is very difficult to know what view to take of the Reform Agitation", he wrote to his brother in 1866. "I am not a democrat, as perhaps you know, and don't much care to adopt popular views to please the mob."' *But Mr Routh demonstrates how 'apprehensive' Jevons was by neatly cutting off the next and concluding sentence in which Jevons himself explains how unapprehensive he was, i.e.: 'However, I don't think any Reform Bill that is likely to pass will really upset our system here, while it may lead to many real improvements'* (italics added). However, Mr Routh is a distinctive and genuine kind of radical critic in that he is non-Marxist and non-Keynesian, wishing to base a new 'paradigm' on the historical tradition. In fact Mr Routh asks about the revolution of 1871: 'Why was the line of Jevons, Menger and Walras chosen rather than that of Sismondi, Richard Jones, Cliffe Leslie and their friends?' But in Germany, *the latter choice was, or had been, made by the historical economists and the Verein für Sozialpolitik.* Mr Routh fails to explain why we should be impressed by the consequences of his 'choice', as actually followed in Imperial Germany (though we agree with much of his position).

But the most piquant irony in Mr Routh's account is that it was precisely his historical heroes (whom we join in admiring) who, perfectly justifiably, attacked most trenchantly ideas about class conflict. We have cited Jones above (section II). Cliffe Leslie attacked Ricardo as follows in what may be one of the first references (1879) to Marx by an important writer on economics in English: 'Ricardo's theory, that no improvement or economy in production can augment profit unless it lowers wages, has in like manner done incalculable harm... Had he been an English Lassalle or Karl Marx, and his main object to sow enmity between capital and labour, he could not have devised a doctrine better adapted to the purpose. The notion, too, which his language did much to establish, that all wealth, including capital itself, is the produce of labour, in the sense of manual labour, exclusive of the capitalist's enterprise, invention, trouble, and abstinence, is actually the corner-stone of the creed of the German "social democrat".' It is thus from Leslie, *who rejected Jevons's marginal utility analysis as well as Ricardo's abstractions,* that just the kind of quotation can be obtained which Mr Routh, together with Marxist critics, would so dearly like to pin upon Jevons, Walras, or Marshall, but which just isn't there to find in the 'neoclassicals'. Mr Routh can hardly maintain, of the historical critic of Ricardo, Cliffe Leslie (as he does of Jevons), that his work is distorted and vitiated by political apprehensions, or even

It is interesting to note that other Marxist explanations of the transition in economic thought around 1870 are based on a *quite opposite* account of the facts. Other Marxist authors have held that by 1870 the 'capitalist' order, far from suffering from more severe tension and insecurity, was now soundly established, while the working class, with higher standards of living and the extension of the franchise, was beginning, in England, to lose revolutionary potential. Mr Easlea, for example, maintains that not 'fear and horror' but *complacency* was what Jevons's new departure would have 'reflected' (if it 'reflected' anything).[16] Another Marxistic explanation likewise rejects the notion of Professor Robinson and Mr Eatwell that 1870–1 may be regarded as simply Marx's own cut-off date of 1830 (for 'scientific' economics being replaced by political propaganda and apologetics) being moved forty years forward. On the contrary, with the increasingly secure position of 'capitalism' in Britain this kind of intellectual support was unnecessary (as it had been, according to the Prophet himself, before his cut-off date of 1830): 'During the classical period, the capitalist class was still emerging as the new ruling class and needed intellectual support to back its ascent. At the time of neo-classical economics, its power position already was well established, and this support was no longer needed that much' (de Vroey, 1975, p. 437).[17]

There is probably very little mileage in *any* of the explanations of this kind, either in those of Mr Easlea and Mr de Vroey, or in that of Professor Robinson and Mr Eatwell. But since the Prophet himself never pronounced on the issue it cannot be assumed that he would have interpreted 1870–1 as a kind of repeat of his own cut-off date of 1830. So it is impossible to decide the issue by reference to Holy Writ.[18]

'fear and horror' of the 'subversive' Ricardian–Marxist labour 'theory' of value. For Mr Routh maintains that Leslie's critical 'line' *ought to have been chosen by economists*, since it '*led towards the complexities of the real world*'. See G. Routh, 1975, pp. 204–6, and T. E. C. Leslie, n.d., p. 193.

[16] 'By the latter half of the nineteenth century the new social order in England appeared to have triumphed' (B. Easlea, 1973, pp. 112–13).

[17] As Professor Hobsbawm has observed regarding Victorian critics of Marx: 'No anti-capitalist movements challenged them, few doubts about the permanence of capitalism nagged them, and between 1850 and 1880 it would have been hard to find a British-born citizen who called himself a socialist in our sense, let alone a Marxist. *The task of disproving Marx was therefore neither urgent nor of great practical importance*' (Dr Marx and his Victorian Critics, in *Labouring Men*, 1964, p. 240, italics added).

[18] Throughout most of his life Marx believed that the great revolution was imminent in Europe or just round the next corner. When he came to London in 1849 'for years he shared the view of most of his fellow refugees that a new round of revolutions would soon break out on the Continent'. Later 'his predictions in this field caused amusement to his friends'. By the late 1860s he was urging that 'the next revolution...is perhaps nearer than it seems'. However, although Marx in 1870–1, for almost a year after the Commune, 'was imbued with a thoroughgoing revolutionary optimism', from about 1871 he 'gradually gave up expecting a quick revolution'. So perhaps the Prophet would not have regarded 1871 as a repeat of 1830 (see D. McLellan, 1973, pp. 226, 282, 378, and 404).

One might well go on to question how far what Professor Robinson and Mr Eatwell call 'doctrines which suggested conflict' were really predominant in Ricardo's thought, taken as a whole. Since Marx, elements of 'conflict' have, to a large extent, been read into Ricardo's writings and blown up for propaganda purposes. But even if it is assumed |– not admitted – that some such intimations of class antagonism can be extricated from Ricardo's writings, by 1870 the dominant authority had long been J. S. Mill's *Principles*. Although Mill did preserve some vital elements in the Ricardian doctrines – and notably a pretty hard-line form of the Law of Population and the natural wage doctrine – he certainly cannot be said to have held aloft the torch of class-antagonism, though in spite of his adherence to the Law of Population and the natural wage doctrine, he did open up new vistas with his famous distinction between the laws of production and the laws of distribution. Mill could be said to have thus pointed forward to the awakening of interest in the poverty question and progressive taxation in the 'neoclassical' period later in the century, though he himself was held back by his continuing belief in 'the Law of Population' and what his disciple Cairnes called 'the great Malthusian difficulty'.

However, according to Professor Robinson and Mr Eatwell, Mill's *Principles*,

> which was the basic textbook on political economy until the rise of the neo-classicals, reflects the increasing self-confidence of mid-nineteenth century Britain, and, in the process, *often obscures the clarity of Ricardian thought.*
> *The conclusions that Mill drew from classical analysis were diametrically opposite to those drawn by Karl Marx...* Mill's analysis derives from a prosperous age in which the conflict between capitalist and landlord had diminished, *and the growing antagonism of capitalist and worker was not emphasized.*[19]

[19] Op. cit., pp. 12 and 27 (italics added). With regard to Professor Robinson and Mr Eatwell's treatment of J. S. Mill, while summarising very briefly several hundred years of the history of economics, the authors, à propos of nothing in particular, find space to introduce the following rather succulent anti-American quotation from J. S. Mill, to the effect that despite many favourable circumstances, in America 'all that these advantages seem to have done for them is that the life of the whole of one sex is devoted to dollar-hunting, and of the other to breeding dollar-hunters'. Professor Robinson and Mr Eatwell do not make clear to their beginner-audience that (1) this sentence only appeared in the first (1848) edition of Mill's *Principles*; (2) was considerably qualified in the second (1849); and (3) was completely removed by Mill in the 1865 and subsequent editions. *In the edition which they profess to be using,* the sentence produced by the authors only appears in quotations in a footnote, in brackets, *by the editor.* In the actual text the following glowingly pro-American statement appears regarding the competitive society: 'It is an incident of growth, not a mark of decline, for it is not necessarily destructive of the highest aspirations and the heroic virtues; as America in her great civil war, has proved to the world, both by her conduct as a people and by numerous splendid individual examples' (see J. Robinson and J. Eatwell, op. cit., p. 28, and J. S. Mill, 1909, p. 748).

So, even on the grotesque assumption that economists around 1870 were pressured by political changes to 'divert attention from the antagonism of social classes', why on earth was it necessary or desirable to go to the length of reconstructing fundamentally their basic theories, and, in particular, to attack and reject Mill's *Principles,* as Jevons so ferociously did? Why were Mill's doctrines 'no longer desirable' – as they certainly were not for Jevons and others – if they so effectively 'obscured the clarity of Ricardian thought' and carefully hushed up the alleged 'antagonism of capitalist and worker'? Above all, what was the political and ideological *need* for 'the new economics' – the main factor in bringing it into being, according to this textbook – if the dominant authority was putting forward conclusions 'diametrically opposite to those drawn by Karl Marx'? How much more 'opposite' can one get than 'diametrically'? On the contrary, the alleged requirements of 'the political and ideological climate' *should* have driven economists to uphold Mill's *Principles,* to redouble their regard for his doctrines, and do everything possible to reinforce their credibility and prestige, rather than fanatically and fundamentally attacking and rejecting them, as Jevons did.

So the interpretation of the history of the neoclassical revolution presented by Robinson and Eatwell is hard to relate to the chronology and writings of the main contributors to the development of economic thought at that period. Especially as Robinson and Eatwell do not present adequate evidence for their viewpoint.

IV

Dobb's variant of the Cambridge version does not pay much attention to ideas and proposals about policies. But Professor Robinson and Mr Eatwell link the changes in economic theorising, which may be dated from around 1870, with a more intensified application of the *laissez-faire* dogma: 'For Adam Smith, *laissez-faire* was a programme...For the neo-classicals *laissez-faire* became a dogma...The moral to be drawn from it was that free enterprise will allocate resources in the manner most beneficial to the whole society, provided that government does not interfere with its operation.'

In other words, according to 'the flimsy intellectual structures of neo-classical theory...*any* interference by government, however well meant, was held to do harm'.[20]

Again, as Professor Robinson has repeated elsewhere: 'For fifty years

[20] Op. cit., pp. 46–7. Here is a similar statement by H. Sherman, 1972, p. 47: 'Neoclassical economics has nothing to say about the role of government except the common belief that the economy will work automatically and well without government.' If Jevons, Walras, Wieser, Wicksell, Marshall and Pigou are representative of 'neoclassical' economics, this generalisation is completely false. See Chapter 4 above.

before 1914 the established economists of various schools had *all* been preaching *one doctrine*, with great self-confidence and pomposity – the doctrine of *laissez-faire*.'[21]

It is very hard to see how this view can be sustained, at least for the leading neoclassicals: Jevons, Marshall, Wieser, Walras and Wicksell. Robinson and Eatwell do not provide sufficient evidence for their viewpoint (to put it mildly).

The basic theoretical changes of the 'neoclassicals' were (a) the development of the utility concept; (b) the development of the marginal concept; (c) *in Britain* the rejection of the Ricardo–Mill natural wage doctrine and hard-line Malthusianism.

These conceptual and theoretical changes were not primarily introduced for explicit or immediate policy purposes. But they led, in Britain, fairly rapidly to:

(1) The opening up of the poverty question;

(2) The building up of a case for progressive taxation in place of the classical proportionality rule;

(3) Concern with unemployment as a cause of poverty and hence to justifying relief works, contrary to Ricardian dogma;

(4) With regard to the marginal concept, to a far superior analysis of monopolistic processes, and of the policies of public utilities, than was possible with the classical apparatus (the rapidly growing problems of monopolistic developments being very early recognised by leading 'neoclassicals').

We have examined above in some detail the changing treatment of the principles of economic policy in Britain after 'the Jevonian revolution'. We saw, for example, how Professor Hobsbawm takes 'around 1860' as 'the peak of British *laissez-faire*', of which 'the foundations...crumbled in the 1860s and 1870s'.[22] We noted again, how, from an extremely different viewpoint, Professor Hayek regards the later views of Jevons on the role of government in the economy as a major turning-point: 'The end of the liberal era of principles might well be dated at the time when, more than eighty years ago, W. S. Jevons pronounced that in economic and social policy, "we can lay down no hard and fast rules, but must treat every case upon its merits"' (1973, p. 59).

We have mentioned also how the reintroduction of the utility concept into English political economy played a part in the move towards progressive taxation at the end of the century. J. S. Mill (in 1848) had described progressive taxation as 'a mild form of robbery',

[21] 1972, p. 2 (italics added). See also J. Robinson, 1974b, p. 61: 'Orthodox Teaching took a violent turn; the neo-classical school came into fashion. *Laissez-faire* was no longer a programme. It became a dogma.'

[22] 1969, pp. 226 and 237. See above Chapter 4, Section 1.

and proportionality had been the main classical doctrine, which obtained in practice in Britain with income tax at a flat rate of a few pence in the pound.

According to the most learned contemporary opponent of progressive taxation, it was Edgeworth who had the greatest influence among English economists in shifting opinion in its favour,[23] which is also the conclusion of Dr Shehab's leading monograph, who ranks Edgeworth's paper 'The Pure Theory of Taxation' as the most important contribution by an economist towards the introduction of progressive taxation in Britain.[24]

It was, in fact, the 'neoclassicals', and notably Edgeworth, who first raised, fundamentally and effectively, basic questions of equity in taxation and therefore in distribution.[25] But according to Professor Robinson: '*The whole point* of utility was to justify *laissez faire*' (1962, italics added).

This view is hard to sustain at least with respect to the great majority of economists in the latter part of the nineteenth century. Utility was not introduced into value analysis for any immediate policy purpose apart from public utility pricing (as with Dupuit). However, it soon came to be used – rightly or wrongly – for justifying redistribution and progresssive taxation, the actual rapid development of which in Britain, from the turn of the century onwards, was broadly approved by a majority of British economists.

The further great development in policy and theory, stemming

[23] F. A. Hayek, 1960, p. 517. See Chapter 4 above: 'The Jevonian revolution and economic policy in Britain'.

[24] 1953, p. 208. Dr Shehab's further conclusion should be noted regarding how neoclassical economists favoured 'the higher taxation of the rich in order to ameliorate the inequality of income distribution', as contrasted with the *laissez-faire* attitude to distribution of their predecessors (such as, notably, Ricardo). See the quotation above Chapter 4, Section v. On the other hand, according to Professor Robinson and Mr Eatwell, Edgeworth suggested 'a way out' of the egalitarian implications of the analysis of diminishing utility. They quote Edgeworth's objection to egalitarian conclusions but omit the preceding paragraph in which he emphasises 'equality, the right of equals to equal advantages and burdens, that large section of distributive justice, that deep principle which continually upheaves the crust of convention... All this mighty force is deducible from the practical principle of exact Utilitarianism combined with the simple laws of sentience' (*Mathematical Psychics*, 1881, p. 77).

[25] Edgeworth, it should be noted (in complete contrast with the way Marxists interpret their theories) was extremely modest and cautious in interpreting the marginal productivity theory, or its 'hints and metaphors and warnings'. He expressly rejected the view of F. A. Walker and J. B. Clark that competition 'affords the ideal condition for the distribution of wealth', when the labourer 'gets his product'. As Edgeworth maintains (1897): 'The coincidence of perfect competition with ideal justice is by no means evident to the impartial spectator: much less is it likely to be accepted by the majority of those concerned, whose views must be taken into account by those who would form a theory that has some relation to the facts. One who has closely observed popular movements in America testifies to "the growing belief that mechanical science and invention applied to industry are too closely held by private interests"' (vol. 1, p. 53).

originally from Jevons's and the neoclassicals' rejection of the Ricardian natural wage doctrine, was the opening up of the poverty question, which was of such major importance for Marshall. This led to the recognition of unemployment as a problem, since it was a major cause of poverty, and thus to proposals for relief works which were tentatively approved by Marshall in 1886 and strongly defended by Pigou in 1908, who exposed the fallacies in Ricardian dogma. We may perhaps remind readers that a recent very scholarly study has gone so far as to maintain: 'By 1914 fatalistic acceptance of the inevitability of the trade cycle and doctrinaire prejudice against the relief of unemployment seemed to have largely passed away' (J. Harris, 1972, p. 5).

Professor Robinson and Mr Eatwell also attempt to pin the *laissez-faire* label on Pigou, regarding whose views on the role of government in the economy, the beginner audience is simply told: 'In *The Economics of Welfare*, Pigou described a number of cases in which *laissez-faire* is not necessarily beneficial, but he treated them as exceptions to a rule which, in general, could not be questioned.'[26]

In fact, of the 800 pages of *The Economics of Welfare* the vast majority deal with cases and recommendations for intervention by government, either on the side of production or distribution. This quantitative indication of Pigou's views on the role of government is also supported by Pigou's earlier writings (1906, p. 379) where he said: 'In economics that doctrine affirms that complete industrial and commercial freedom conduces to the greatest possible sum of economic good...This argument is incorrect at once in its premises and its inferences.' In some directions Pigou elaborated more cases for various types of state action than did Keynes, though he did not share the latter's often optimistic views regarding the skill and integrity which politicians and bureaucrats would bring to the implementation of interventionist policies, for example with regard to tariffs and monetary management. Pigou, like Keynes, certainly supported the idea of a mixed economy and did not wish to eliminate private enterprise. He gave a very full outline of his proposals for government policy as follows:

> He would accept, for the time being, the general structure of capitalism; but he would modify it gradually. He would use the weapon of graduated death duties and graduated income tax, not merely as instruments of revenue, but with the deliberate purpose of diminishing the glaring inequalities of fortune and opportunity which deface our present civilization. He would take a leaf from the book of Soviet Russia and remember that the most important investment of all is investment in the health, intelligence and character of the people. To advocate 'economy' in this field would,

[26] Op. cit., p. 47.

under his government, be a criminal offence. All industries affected with a public interest, or capable of wielding monopoly power, he would subject at least to public supervision and control. Some of them, certainly the manufacture of armaments, probably the coal industry, possibly the railways, he would nationalise, not, of course, on the pattern of the Post Office, but through public boards or commissions. The Bank of England he would make in name – what it is already in effect – a public institution; with instructions to use its power to mitigate, so far as may be, violent fluctuations in industry and employment. If all went well, further steps towards nationalisation of important industries would be taken by degrees. In controlling and developing these nationalised industries, the central government would inevitably need to 'plan' an appropriate allocation for a large part of the country's annual investment in new capital [1937, pp, 137–8].[27]

This is how Pigou actually would have implemented 'the rule of *laissez-faire*'. In fact, Pigou is here sketching out, in 1937, the kind of transformation to the post-war mixed economy, which was broadly carried through in the following fifteen years in this country. Of course, if anyone who does *not* support the full range of Stalinist and Maoist methods of planning is to be described as 'upholding *laissez-faire*', as a rule 'which in general could not be questioned', then indeed Pigou can be said to have upheld *laissez-faire* as 'a rule which in general could not be questioned'.

Professor Robinson and Mr Eatwell then go on to explain to their beginner readers that to Keynes, 'Ricardo was just as bad as Pigou, because he did not allow for the possibility of a deficiency of effective demand' (1973, p. 49).

One may doubt whether Keynes would ever have made this suggestion. One trusts not, because as he himself admitted, writing (1937) of Pigou's book *Socialism versus Capitalism*, from which we have just quoted: '*When it comes to practice, there is really extremely little between us*' (1973, vol. XIV, p. 259, italics added).

This suggestion about Pigou and Ricardo is also very hard to reconcile with the fact that Ricardo was the great original propounder, before a Parliamentary Committee in 1819, of the so-called 'Treasury View' (which should *appropriately*, therefore, be called '*The Ricardo View*')[28] while Pigou was its first major twentieth-century opponent.

[27] We would remark that Mr P. M. Sweezy observes about this work of Pigou's that 'no future discussion of the economic merits of the rival systems of society can afford to neglect his cogently marshalled arguments'. Sweezy concludes that Pigou 'declares in effect for gradual socialisation – a Fabian among Fabians' (1953, pp. 263–5).

[28] Elsewhere Professor Robinson has written: 'We know what Marshall's pupils who had gone into the Treasury believed, from the famous White Paper of 1929 which was an example of neo-classical theory in action' (1962, p. 73). It is really necessary to identify the individuals involved here. It is clear that Sir Ralph Hawtrey never was a pupil of Marshall (Guillebaud, 1964, p. 75) and that Marshall's prime pupil Pigou was the leading attacker of the Ricardian theory in action in its twentieth century form, that is the so-called 'Treasury View' which restated Ricardo's preachings of 1819. In *Economic Heresies* (1972b, p. 50) Professor Robinson repeats that Marshall's 'pupils

Beginner students might also be misled by the following statement: 'In the great slump, when there was massive unemployment in all the industrial countries, economists were still maintaining that a free market tends to establish equilibrium and that interference with its delicate mechanism can only do harm.'[29]

Of course, if this statement is to be taken as merely suggesting that *some* economists, no more necessarily than a small extremist minority or fringe, held such views, it is undoubtedly true, but hardly very interesting or important. (There are few views about current issues so outlandish or bizarre that one cannot find one or two economists who support them.) On the other hand, if it is to be understood – as it well might be by beginners – as a broad generalisation about *the majority* of economists and their views, this statement conflicts with the plentiful evidence that a majority, and perhaps a large majority, of economists in Britain during the great slump, who expressed any views on the question, supported the kind of policy measures advocated by Keynes. This was certainly also the case in Sweden, and possibly, to a large extent in the USA and other countries.[30]

V

As we have noted, the two Cambridge accounts of the last hundred years or so of the history of economic thought, though on very

were propounding the truth of Say's Law and the Treasury View at the time they were struck by the great slump'. Again no names are provided.

[29] Op. cit., p. 47. A similar ambiguity is apparent in the generalisation: 'In the main, the teaching of orthodox economists and the beliefs that influenced policy were in line with each other' (p. 47). Of course, one can define 'orthodox' in a way which renders this proposition irrefutable and insignificant. What Keynes himself said at this time was that the 'experts' maintaining the Ricardo–Treasury view were completely mistaken in believing in their own orthodoxy, and 'were not familiar with modern economic thought... *Not one of the leading economists of the country who has published his views, or with whose opinion I am otherwise familiar, would endorse the general character of their argument*' (*Nation and Athenaeum*, 18 May 1929; see also Hutchison, 1953, p. 421; italics added).

In an earlier work, in similar vein, Professor Robinson wrote about Keynes's controversial methods in *The General Theory*: 'If he had used proper scholarly caution and reserve, his book would have slipped down unnoticed and millions of families rotting in unemployment would be so much the further from relief. He wanted the book to stick in the gizzards of orthodoxy, so that they would be forced either to spew it out or chew it properly. Pigou spewed it out.' But this invoking of 'families rotting in unemployment' is irrelevant tear-jerking. The arguments over *The General Theory* – and all the 'chewing' and 'spewing' so relished by Professor Robinson – had very little bearing or effect on policies for the 'relief' of unemployed families, regarding which there had long been widespread agreement and '*extremely little between*' Pigou and Keynes – as the latter agreed (see Robinson, 1962, p. 80, and Hutchison, 1968, p. 295).

[30] See above the essays on 'The Keynesian revolution and the history of economic thought', and on 'Demythologising the Keynesian revolution: Pigou, wage-cuts, and *The General Theory*' (Chapters 5 and 6).

different intellectual levels, bear a close Marxistic family likeness. But there is one important episode, that of the Keynesian revolution, regarding which Dobb, on the one hand, and Professor Robinson and Mr Eatwell, on the other, deviate from one another fundamentally and completely. In fact, the obvious contradictions between Dobb and Professor Robinson regarding 'the Keynesian revolution' are simply a reflection of the contradictions regarding the nature of the would-be 'revolution' in the subject which the 'radical' or Cambridge versions of the history of economics, and their variants, are seeking to promote. There is certainly nothing 'neo-' or 'post-Keynesian' in Dobb's variant.

Regarding Keynes's *General Theory*, in his later, more restrained, treatment, Dobb does no more than pose the question, without explicitly stating his own answer: 'Is *The General Theory* of J. Maynard Keynes to be regarded as a critique of (then existing) capitalism, or as an "apologetic theory of monopoly capitalism" as some Marxist writers of the time regarded it?' (1973, p. 29).

In an earlier paper, however, Dobb was much more explicit regarding Keynesian doctrine:

> As a practical doctrine it was always a 'save-capitalism', or 'make-capitalism-work', doctrine, and never pretended to be more. It was in no sense a socialist doctrine; and only by contrast with the spent and decayed ideology which it supplanted could it really pose as a fundamental critique of capitalism...To fail to appreciate this may make us the victims of 'the seven devils' of new illusions about the possibilities of 'full employment under capitalism', in place of old illusions from which we had complacently begun to think ourselves free. What this doctrine can be said to have reflected as an ideology is certain tendencies towards salvage-measures of State capitalism in a situation of general crisis for capitalism; and, for all its novel features, *it was an ideology which in essence stemmed from the tree of traditional bourgeois economic theory.*[31]

On the other hand, for Professor Robinson, an eager disciple of Keynes from the early 1930s, it must be difficult to relinquish the view that the Keynesian revolution was a comprehensively and fundamentally enlightening achievement. Now a recognition of the major and beneficent significance of the Keynesian revolution would seem natural enough for a supporter of a liberal–social–democratic, mixed economy – 'capitalist' or otherwise; and certainly Keynes himself was

[31] 1955, p. 218 (italics added). Mr P. M. Sweezy also takes the view that 'Keynes is both the most important and the most illustrious product of the neoclassical school...Keynes could never transcend the limitations of the neoclassical approach ...His shortcomings...are for the most part the shortcomings of bourgeois thought in general' (1953, pp. 255–61). In less genteel terms the Great Soviet Encyclopedia (1953) wrote of Keynes as follows: 'All the activity of Keynes, the zealous enemy of the working class and apologist of the fascist imperialist bourgeoisie, was directed to strengthening the power of the monopolies under the cover of demagogic "anti-crises" phrases' (quoted by J. M. Letiche, 1971, p. 44).

perfectly frank and explicit in intending his doctrines to serve the 'patching-up of Capitalism', or the imparting of a new lease of life to the existing system. But, in the 1930s, some socialist economists, who were enthusiastic disciples of Keynes, entertained the aspiration that some kind of comprehensive, socialist planning would be more or less inevitable for solving the problem of mass unemployment on Keynesian lines.[32] Apparently, this opinion is still clung to by Professor Robinson and Mr Eatwell. But for anyone claiming to pass muster today as a radical, anti-capitalist revolutionary – palaeo-Stalinist or neo-Ricardian – there can surely be no question that Dobb's attitude to Keynes shows more coherence, consistency and hard-headed logic than that of Professor Robinson and Mr Eatwell. After all, if the earlier 'neoclassicals' are condemned as trying vainly, in the face of the Paris Commune, to 'divert attention from the antagonism of social classes', what can be said regarding Keynes, who, it can be claimed, helped so significantly to rescue 'capitalism', and to give it – as Professor Robinson and Mr Eatwell have to admit – a further quarter of a century of 'boom' and 'success' (1973, p. 307).

In fact, as Mr Paul Sweezy has quite justifiably observed, Keynes can best be regarded as one of 'the most important and illustrious of the neo-classicals', who carried through (though hardly initiated) the second, macroeconomic leg of the anti-Ricardian revolution.

VI

In a contribution on rather similar lines to that of Dobb, Professor R. L. Meek has asserted: 'In the light of the "Sraffa revolution" of the

---

[32] Not that Professor Robinson, *at this earlier period*, encouraged any excessive or irresponsible views regarding the level of employment which it was feasible or desirable to aim at. In a paper of 1946 she maintained: 'Nor is completely full employment desirable. The attainment of full employment, in this absolute sense, would require strict controls, including direction of labour. To raise the average of employment from 86 per cent (the average of Great Britain 1921–38) to say 95 per cent, would be compatible with a much greater amount of individual liberty than to raise it from 95 per cent to 98 per cent. *To raise it from 95 per cent to 98 per cent (not momentarily – but on the average), would involve great sacrifices of liberty*, and to raise it from 98 per cent to 100 per cent would involve complete conscription of labour. *No one regards 100 per cent employment as a desirable objective.*' Again Professor Robinson insisted: '*In general it may be said that something appreciably short of full employment must be regarded as the optimum*' (see 1951, p. 106; and 1937 and 1947, p. 26). By 1966 of course Professor Robinson, following popular political trends, had abandoned such moderate views and was condemning those, like Mr J. C. R. Dow, who had held to them: 'There is one school of thought which contends that, since the trouble arises from near-full employment, let us give it up. Supporters of this view maintain that a "moderate" amount of unemployment, say between two and three per cent over all, would be sufficient to keep wages in check and secure stable prices. The evidence for this view is very sketchy. It might need much more. But, *in any case, deliberately to adopt such a cold-blooded policy is out of the question*' (1966, p. 20, italics added).

1960s, the Ricardian–Marxian analysis can no longer be plausibly considered by anyone as having been a mere "detour"' – as it was described by Schumpeter. Therefore, Professor Meek demands: 'A great deal of the history of value theory has to be rewritten' (1974, pp. 246–8).

Professor Meek, like Dobb, sees some vital line of development running from Ricardo to Marx and then to Sraffa (Keynes, quite logically, hardly comes into the Dobb–Meek account). The Ricardo–Marx sequence has been much proclaimed, and, in some respects, grossly exaggerated. It is the nearly century-long step from Marx to Sraffa which raises new and considerable questions.

First, regarding what might be called '*content*' – if there is any – Professor Meek is concerned to emphasise the closeness of the relationship between Marxian theory and the Sraffa models, as sharing what he describes as 'a production-oriented framework'. On the other hand, other Marxistic authorities emphasise the width of the gulf between the Sraffa analysis of 'the production of commodities by means of commodities', and Marx's analysis of the production of commodities by means of labour.[33]

Here we are primarily concerned, however, with the historical aspects of the long step from Marx to Sraffa, and with the course of this vital sequence and the intermediate stages. On this historical problem Professor Meek's *Studies in the Labour Theory of Value* (2nd ed., 1973) are illuminating. It emerges from Professor Meek's *Studies* that overwhelmingly the most creative and authoritative contribution between Marx and Sraffa, to a 'production-oriented framework', or to the labour theory, was that of Stalin and his *Economic Problems of Socialism in the U.S.S.R.* (1952). According to Professor Meek, the *Economic Problems*, 'the appearance of which in 1952 had a liberating effect... *may well remain the basis for serious scientific work on the operation of the law of value under socialism for some time to come*'.[34]

Certainly Stalin shared 'the production-oriented framework' of the Ricardo–Marx–Sraffa line of thought: 'Stalin would have had no truck with any economic laws, whether "universal" or otherwise, which in effect abstracted from men's relations of production. There is nothing whatever in Stalin's work which could possibly be construed as support

---

[33] E.g. R. Rowthorn in his article 'Neo-Ricardianism, Neo-Classicism or Marxism?', 1974.
[34] 1973, pp. xxx and 284 (italics added). In his second edition (1973a) Professor Meek substantially reaffirms, without modification, his treatment of Stalin's work in his first edition (1956). He writes (2nd ed., p. xxxi) that 'there do not seem to be many actual errors of substance in the section on Stalin' and he certainly does not specify any. Nor does Professor Meek mention as calling for any revision his earlier assessment of Stalin's *Economic Problems of Socialism* as 'one of Stalin's carefully rationed interventions', having behind it his 'unique authority', and his 'mastery of the *method* of Marxism', as a 'serious scientist' (see 1953, pp. 716 and 723; and Professor Meek's essay 'Stalin as an Economist', in the *Review of Economic Studies*, 1953–4, p. 234).

for an economics whose primary aim was to shake out the implications of the universal fact of choice' (1953, p. 721).

One can certainly appreciate that Stalin would have had 'no truck' with the 'implications of choice', or indeed with any sort of individual choice.[35] But in the rewriting of the history of value 'theory', as demanded by Professor Meek, how precisely should Stalin be accommodated? Professor Meek now tells us: 'The path from Ricardo to Sraffa, however, was not a wholly direct one. It also led through Marx and the Marxists' (1974, p. 257) – and presumably through Stalin and the Stalinists.

With the inclusion of this vital Stalin link it becomes possible to see something of the ideological significance (there is virtually no 'positive' or empirical significance) of this 'production-oriented framework' (or of the labour 'theory' of value) at the present juncture. For Stalinist, and similar, planning methods, basic and essential presuppositions are the dehumanising reduction of individual people to homogeneous units of 'socially necessary' labour, with the exclusion of individual choice, or any 'truck' with individual choice or freedom at all. In fact economists who are enthusiastic for Stalinist, or similar, planning methods, will be prepared to go to any lengths of over-simplification and arbitrary abstraction to exclude human, individual demand, or tastes, from their (pseudo-)'theory' of value. Therefore 'neoclassical' economics must be anathematised root and branch. Professor Meek has said (with dubious justification) of the critics of Ricardian economics, such as Longfield, in the 1830s: 'Their fundamental approach, in other words, was determined by a belief that what was socially dangerous could not possibly be true' (1967, p. 71).

In the 1970s, and indeed for a long time before, neoclassical theories, with such implications as they may suggest regarding individual freedom of choice and jobs, '*could not possibly be true*' for enthusiasts of totalitarian and bureaucratic planning systems, because these theories are 'socially dangerous to', or indeed 'contradictory of', such systems.

As is recognised by Professor Kornai, the Hungarian socialist: 'One of the basic ideas of the General Equilibrium school is that the economic system should be constructed in such a way that production,

[35] One can appreciate also the emphasis which Stalin would have placed on 'men's relations of production' in his Gulag Archipelago: 'The *zeks* of the Archipelago constitute a *class* of society. For, after all, this multitudinous group (of many millions) has a single (common to them all) relationship to *production* (namely: subordinate, attached, and without any right to direct that production). It also has a single common relationship to the *distribution of the products* of labor (namely: no relationship at all, receiving only that insignificant share of the products required for the meager support of their own existence). And, in addition, all their labor is no small thing, but one of the principal constituents of the whole state economy' (A. Solzhenitsyn, 1976, p. 484).

the utilization of resources, is adapted to the needs of the consumer. Production should serve man and not the opposite. This is a beautiful, humanistic idea, the importance of which cannot be stressed sufficiently.'[36]

In fact one could and should go appreciably further than Professor Kornai in recognising that 'one of the basic ideas' of the neoclassical theorists was not merely that production should serve the needs of the consumer, but that individuals, and not party bosses and bureaucrats, should be the judges of what their own needs as consumers and producers are.

As Professor Eagly has observed: 'The marginal utility approach permitted a calculus in which the vast majority of the general population would participate in voicing their preferences and voting their income in the market place...The marginal utility approach democratized economic theory and made every person influential, to some degree, in the outcome of economic activity' (1974, p. 137).

The marginal utility analysis did not, of course, assert that such a state of affairs existed, but suggested that it could be approached as an ideal. On the other hand Stalin would have 'had no truck' with theories which implied individual choice, and he certainly 'had no truck' with freedom of choice of goods and jobs in practice. Therefore, it is obvious enough that economists who have ardently championed Stalin's methods would be inclined to 'divert attention' from such ideas or implications as that production should serve the choices of individual consumers, if this might conflict with the plans of Stalin, or of similar planning authorities. It is, therefore, hardly a mere coincidence that leading exponents of the 'production-oriented framework' – and extreme opponents of 'neoclassical' economics – may be found expressing strong support for Stalinist economic policies.[37]

An aspect of Stalin's regime which is specially relevant here is the intellectual corruption of economic thought and ideas. This has been well described by Mr E. Mandel, who explains how Marxist economics is just as – or perhaps even more – liable to become imbued with 'the

---

[36] J. Kornai, 1971, p. 153. This Hungarian socialist planner, contradicting most emphatically the Cambridge version of the history of economics, concludes that neoclassical equilibrium theory '*is not "bourgeois" but rather politically neutral*' (p. 359, italics added).

[37] For enthusiastic eulogies, as late as 1952, of Stalin's methods of directing labour (and of Stalin's Moscow and the great 'joke' that foreigners were followed by the secret police), see *Conference Sketch-Book, Moscow 1952*. However, by 1969 Professor Robinson was remarking that 'nothing could be further than Mao's style from the vanity and paranoia of Stalin's last years' (see *The Cultural Revolution in China*,1969, p. 29, quoted by David Caute, 1973, p. 368). Mr Caute refers (p. 376) to the combination of 'gullibility with latent authoritarianism' possessed by enthusiasts for Stalin and/or Mao. We have already emphasised the obvious point that 'authoritarianism' (latent or not so latent) is likely to be combined with the most insistent rejection of the concept of subjective utility and of 'neo-classical' economics.

bad conscience and the evil intent of apologetic', as it in fact did with the economists who supported Stalin:

> From being an instrument of research into objective truth it was degraded to the role of justifying *a posteriori* the political or economic decisions taken by the government of the U.S.S.R. While a study of the various successive justifications of the 'twists and turns' of Soviet policy has now only a purely historical interest this does not apply to the *apologetic distortions* introduced into the corpus of Marxist economic theory itself [1971, p. 723].

Regarding Stalin's economic theories Mr Mandel continues:

> They were formulated in order to hide from the citizens of the U.S.S.R. the enormous gap which existed in that period between their standard of living and that of the citizens of the most advanced capitalist countries. By justifying the continued existence of commodity production under 'socialism' the authors of this thesis likewise justified the continued existence of social inequality and alienation of labour in this strange 'socialist society' [op. cit., p. 724].

So perhaps the celebrated passage in Marx's *Nachwort* has a wider application, or should be slightly reworded: 'It was thenceforth no longer a question, whether this theorem or that was true, but whether it was useful to Stalin – or some other totalitarian leader (or bureaucratic planner) – or harmful, expedient or inexpedient, politically dangerous or not.'

The labour-value theory, and the more extended 'production-oriented framework', as Professor Meek calls it, has never had much *empirical predictive content* and today has virtually none. Its significance always has been mainly, and today is almost entirely, ideological – that is why it may justifiably be described as a 'pseudo-theory' rather than a theory. Now ideological significance and function can and does change profoundly over time. As is well known, one of the earlier expositions of the labour-value pseudo-theory was developed by Locke as a defence of private property. Then in the era of the classical economists the labour pseudo-theory became a would-be empirical, but vastly over-simplified, explanation of relative values under such preposterously abstract assumptions as perfect competition (including, possibly or presumably, perfect knowledge), abstractions ridiculed by Marxists when employed by *bourgeois* economists. This Ricardian version of the labour-value theory has always, quite obviously, been useless so far as monopolistic and oligopolistic conditions obtain. Nor has the labour-value pseudo-theory been of the slightest assistance for any kind of practical or operational decisions by the managers of private firms or public utilities. In the Marxian adaptation of the labour-value theory, its function again, as with Locke, is purely ideological; that is, to serve in the denunciation of 'capitalism', and of the distribution of wealth under 'the capitalist system'. But for this purpose, a labour-value theory is totally unnecessary and superfluous since political or ethical judgments about distribution can, of course, rightly or wrongly, but perfectly reasonably, be advanced without any dependence on a labour theory of value of any kind (positive or 'pseudo-').[38]

Why then has the labour-value theory, or the 'production-oriented framework', with their empirically vacuous economics and rusty nineteenth-century sociological crudities, been so enthusiastically revived in the latter part of the twentieth century? The answer can hardly be merely in terms of antiquarianism and period charm.

A large part of the answer regarding the ideological functions and serviceability, in the latter part of the twentieth century, of 'production-oriented' and labour-value pseudo-theories, must rest in terms of the denunciation of neoclassical ideas about choice and demand which are subversive of Stalinist regimes and bureaucratic 'planning' generally: they can be used to justify the operation and imposition of such regimes.

Nevertheless, we would emphasise that all such questions of ideological significance and political motivation would be entirely irrelevant, or beside the point, in terms of any significant, non-trivial empirical or predictive content which the 'production-oriented framework', or the labour-value pseudo-theory, might possess – *if this 'framework' or 'theory' possessed any.*

VII

We have been focussing mainly on historical questions regarding the version of the history of economics designed to culminate in the 'Sraffa revolution', as Dobb and Professor Meek call it. Perhaps we cannot or should not avoid altogether the question of the *content* of 'the Sraffa revolution', and whether, in fact, it possesses any significant empirical or predictive content at all (as it might be held that it *should* possess if it is to have a 'revolutionary' place in the history of an empirical subject).

The Smithian revolution can be said to have contained – along with conceptual and analytical, as well as political, elements – a wide range

---

[38] In fact Friedrich Engels frankly, if abusively, admitted that the Marxian theory of value was not indispensable as a basis for socialist conclusions. He wrote of 'the rotten vulgarised economics of Jevons, which is so vulgarised that one can make anything out of it – even socialism'. He also admitted that the German 'vulgar economist', Wilhelm Lexis, had advanced an explanation of the profits of capital which 'amounts in practice to the same thing as the Marxian theory of surplus-value'). Lexis simply assumed that 'capitalists' were generally monopoly sellers in product markets and monopoly buyers in the labour market. (See a letter to F. A. Sorge quoted in *The Life of Friedrich Engels*, 1977, by W. O. Henderson, vol. II, p. 681, and Engels' preface to *Capital* by K. Marx, vol. III, 1961, p. 10.)

of highly significant, if not at all precise, predictions about how free markets worked, which, for better or for worse, were fairly rapidly and, on their own terms, *successfully*, applied to British economic policies in the decades after the appearance of *The Wealth of Nations*. The Keynesian revolution also contained some empirical predictions, of blinding obviousness, about government spending and fiscal policies, which were applied, not without initial success, within a few years of the appearance of the master text of the revolution – however serious the difficulties which their distortion and misapplication ran into nearly forty years later. The Jevonian revolution, in its negative aspect on the subject of distribution, that is, in denying finally the hard-line version of the Malthus–Ricardo–Mill population and natural-wage doctrine, had a massive empirical significance, widely and profoundly relevant to policy. Marginal analysis, in some of its earlier and most distinguished formulations was also developed with at least *some* new empirical or predictive policy-relevant content; for example, in Cournot's analysis of the policy of monopolists and of the effects of taxing them; in von Thünen's very practically and realistically based formulae regarding the allocation and location of resources on farms, in accordance with marginal productivity;[39] and in Dupuit's marginal utility analysis of public utility problems. The empirical and predictive content of the new and original theories of Cournot, von Thünen, and Dupuit was not *very* rich (nor was that of the Smithian or Keynesian theories) but it was not *non-existent*, and, such as it is, it helps *somewhat* still today with real-world problems (and was originally directed at real-world problems). In fact, a recent survey of the extent of agreement among economists shows that it is on the subject of public utilities and taxation policies, based on 'neoclassical' price theory, that the most significant positive consensus exists. In other branches of economic policy, apart from that based on neoclassical foundations, there is little positive, theoretical, economic consensus. (See S. Brittan, 1973.)

To what real-world problems does 'the Sraffa revolution' bring anything of empirical, explanatory, or predictive significance? In the decade and a half after the master text of this 'revolution' was published, it does not appear to have been applied fruitfully, or at all, to the explanation of *any* significant real-world problem, past or

---

[39] von Thünen deserves more than anyone else to be called the founder of marginal productivity analysis. As Marshall rightly said of von Thünen's down-to-earthness: 'You know von Thünen's *métier* was that of an agricultural reformer...He was up to his eyes in facts about rye and manure and so on' (in a letter to J. N. Keynes; I am indebted for this quotation to Professor R. H. Coase's paper, 'Marshall on Method', *Journal of Law and Economics*, April 1975). On the other hand, no real-world mud or manure can be discerned on the boots of 'the Sraffa revolutionaries', who, in Mr Dobb's own peculiar phraseology might rather be described as 'economists of gentry-breed', familiar only with 'the cloisters of ancient universities'.

present. It may well be asked whether there are *any* significant episodes in the economic history of any period or country, to which 'the Sraffa revolution' brings an element of valid explanation. Are there any significant real-world problems, for example, of the operation of a private firm or public utility, or of a socialist or development planner, in a rich or poor country, the solution of which would be assisted by any explanations or predictions yielded by 'the Sraffa revolution'? Professor R. Solow *may*, indeed, be totally unjustified in his defence of 'neoclassical' analysis – though this seems improbable. But he is surely undoubtedly justified in emphasising the almost total irrelevance, for any kind of practice or applicability, of this entire, hollow controversy or 'Great Charade' (as Professor Hahn has rightly described it, 1975, p. 364) out of which 'the Sraffa revolution' is supposed to have emerged: 'What is remarkable about this great tempest, however, is that it has no connexion with the practice of economics. If the debated points of mainstream "neo-classical" theory were officially declared to be overthrown to-morrow, hardly anyone, perhaps, no one, would do anything differently' (*Times Literary Supplement*, 14 March 1975).

If 'the Sraffa revolution' is to be assessed according to the criteria of pure mathematics, or of pure historical scholarship, so that practical policy applicability is irrelevant, well and good. But this should be admitted and clearly stated. Meanwhile, there seem to be no strong grounds, 'in the light' of its negligible real-world empirical content, for rewriting a significant part of the history of economics – if economics is to be regarded as an empirical study, concerned somehow to illuminate or assist with regard to policy-decisions.

It is fairly clear that criteria in terms of empirical content and policy-relevant predictions are not the appropriate ones to apply here. When one looks steadily at *the actual intellectual function, at the present day*, of labour-value pseudo-theories and 'the production-oriented framework', it is not difficult to discern what this is: they provide those who do not resort to mathematical elaboration with a complex impresssive jargon and an aura of bogus profundity (especially apparent, for example, in Stalin's pronouncements) which, moreover, exude a fashionable ideological aroma for those resentful of the economic performance of the Western world and who wish to justify systems of bureaucratic planning or the imposition of a neo- (or palaeo-) Stalinist type of economy. Certainly such an interpretation as this is in terms of political motivation rather than empirical content and policy-relevant predictions. But, in terms of the latter, the labour-value 'theory' and 'the production-oriented framework' possess nothing significant to appraise.

VIII

We would like to repeat that the two main 'revolutionary' versions with which we have been concerned, those of Dobb and of Professor Robinson and Mr Eatwell, are on *very* different intellectual levels. They also diverge crucially at certain points, especially with regard to the significance of Keynes's work. The implications of this particular difference are acute with respect to the nature and content of the would-be 'revolution' whose historical setting is being devised. For Dobb, Keynes's contribution should not be regarded as profoundly 'revolutionary', being directed to 'making capitalism work'. Dobb's would-be 'revolution' is certainly not 'neo-' or 'post-Keynesian'. On the other hand, for Professor Robinson, Keynes's work is profoundly 'revolutionary' and her would-be revolution derives essentially from Keynes (among others). This might seem to raise doubts as to whether it is really for the same would-be 'revolution' that Dobb and Professor Robinson are seeking to provide a scenario.

It is, in any case, extremely difficult to derive from Professor Robinson's outline scenario precisely what kind of 'revolution' it is intended to justify. At one point Professor Robinson was maintaining:

> I have been trying for the last twenty years to trace the confusions and sophistries of current neo-classical doctrines to their origin in the neglect of historical time in the static equilibrium theories of the neoclassics and at the same time to find a more hopeful alternative in the classical tradition, revived by Sraffa, which flows from Ricardo through Marx, diluted by Marshall and enriched by the analysis of effective demand of Keynes and Kalecki [1973(a), p. xii].

There are some extremely odd historical juxtapositions here. First, if one really wants to fix the origin of what Professor Robinson calls 'the neglect of historic time', the most obvious place to look for it is precisely in Ricardo's 'strong cases' of almost instant self-adjustment to equilibrium, with his quite explicit introduction of the perfect knowledge postulate. Certainly Marx was centrally concerned with historical, or rather, mainly historicist, processes. Marshall, also, wrestled heroically, though not entirely successfully, with the problems of meshing analysis and history as applied to industries and firms, only to have his efforts rejected by his Cambridge successors in the 1920s and 1930s, concerned with 'theories' of the firm and imperfect competition (notably Dr Sraffa and Professor Robinson) on the typically dubious grounds of his lack of 'rigour'.[40] Of course, as Ricardo's

---

[40] As Professor B. J. Loasby has accurately and trenchantly remarked: 'Economists attempted to improve on Marshall without appreciating what he was trying to do, and in the process created for themselves a logical dilemma which belonged to a dead world...Some of the sharpest minds of the twenties and thirties simply failed to appreciate what Marshall had done.' They ended up in 'one of the most notorious

follower, Dr Sraffa in his model-building 'neglects historical time', or historical processes, just as much as, or much more thoroughly and consequentially than, the most 'static' neoclassicals. Indeed Professor Robinson seems subsequently to have realised this point regarding Sraffa's 'models', when she later explained: 'The specification of a self-reproducing or self-expanding system such as that of Sraffa or von Neumann exists in logical time, not in history' (1974, p. 3).

In fact a history of concern for 'historical time' or historical processes in economics, which starts from Ricardo and leads up to Sraffa, is rather like a history of sexual asceticism in English literature which starts from Fanny Hill and leads up to Lady Chatterley. If one is really seeking to rediscover a tradition in economics seriously concerned with historical processes one should go back, in England, to Adam Smith, and then to the historical critic of Ricardo, Richard Jones – highly respected by both Marx and Marshall – and to such later historical rebels and critics as Cliffe Leslie and W. J. Ashley, not to mention the German historicals and the American institutionalists.

However, in addition to the contrasts, and indeed contradictions, among the various 'revolutionary' versions, there is also important common ground. First, they both start from the central stylised abstraction 'neoclassical economics'; for this is a term which, as Professor Galbraith has observed, 'is strongly suggestive of obsolescence' (1974, p. 9).

Then 'neoclassical economics' is assigned certain mythical characteristics which, in fact, few, or almost no, important economists in the last hundred years, and virtually none today, have ever asserted or believed in. On this point the game has been given away most revealingly by the 'radical' political scientist Professor C. B. Macpherson:

> The neo-classical theory *can* still be taken as providing a justification for a slightly modified system of capitalist enterprise. The modified market system can be held to be justified on the grounds that it distributes rewards according to marginal productivity. *It is true that few modern economists do explicitly use their theory to justify anything. Most of them decline to draw value judgments from technical theory. Indeed it is clearer to the economists than to the non-economists who have absorbed the elements of orthodox theory that the maximization of utility by the market can only be demonstrated by assuming a certain income*

blind alleys in twentieth century economics' (1976, pp. 174–5 and 200). In fact, one of the most decisive thrusts into the remoteness and irrelevance of the 'dead world', inhabited by much of what Professor Robinson now calls 'neo-neoclassical' analysis, was taken in the late 1920s and early 1930s by those who abandoned Marshall's attempt at a historical treatment of firms and industries, and equilibrating processes, thereby pushing the theory of the firm and equilibrium analysis towards more extreme and arbitrary abstractions. Prominent among the leaders (or 'young Turks') of this movement were, of course, Mr Sraffa, Mrs Robinson and Mr Kaldor – as they then were. (See Hutchison, 1977, pp. 74–81.)

distribution, and that the marginal productivity theory of distribution is not a demonstration of an ethically just distribution or wealth or income. It has, however, been easy for political theorists to overlook these limitations of economic theory [1972, p. 23].

It is always easy for propagandists and ideologues – whether political theorists or economists – to overlook limitations and qualifications, however important and however frequently they are repeated. The need to assume a certain income distribution in drawing conclusions about the competitive allocation of resources was recognised from the start by Walras; while the only documentary evidence ever produced, that the 'neoclassicals' maintained that the marginal productivity theory justified ethically the existing distribution of income and wealth dates usually from well before 1900, and is apt to consist of one or two constantly requoted sentences from J. B. Clark.[41]

Next, the upshot is much the same regarding the two Cambridge versions, whether more emphasis is placed on Marx's 1830 cut-off year (as by Dobb in his earlier account) or whether, alternatively, the emphasis is put on 1870 (as by Professor Robinson and Mr Eatwell) as the date when economic theory was fundamentally reconstructed, mainly for political reasons, in order to suppress any intimations of class conflict (out of 'fear and horror' of Marx and the Paris Commune). Subsequent economic theorising can be regarded as tainted and fundamentally distorted by political apologetics on the part of economists 'of gentry-breed'.[42]

[41] Actually J. B. Clark was extremely concerned with the dangers of monopolies and wrote extensively about them, as, for example, when he maintained: 'The industrial system which developed under a regime of freedom and competition has become perverted by the presence of monopoly... I know of no more startling and disquieting tendency of recent times than the growth of those great corporations which have gathered to themselves, each of its own field, nearly all the business that is there transacted' (1904, pp. v and 3).

[42] We have noted above how Marxist explanations of the 1870 transformation differ fundamentally about the facts. According to Professor Robinson and Mr Eatwell, it was 'fear and horror', and a desperate search for a cover-up to veil mounting class antagonism in the face of the new challenge by Marx, which motivated the abandonment of the Ricardo–Mill economics and the search for new theories of value and distribution. On the other hand, other Marxist explanations (by Mr Easlea and M. de Vroey) maintain that 'capitalism' was now much more firmly entrenched than earlier in the century, so that the change in the 1870s reflected a new complacency. This contradiction is an excellent example of how, for Marxists, what account one gives of historical events, or of what happens in history, *does not really matter. Whatever actually happened can always be explained by Marxism*, which is employed as a completely irrefutable pseudo-theory. So it *does not really matter* what account of the facts one gives, either in elementary textbooks or elsewhere. As Sir Karl Popper found at a crucial stage of his philosophical developments, whatever happens, or whatever historical events are reported in the newspapers, the Marxist theories are *always* confirmed. In fact, we are not dealing with empirical, refutable theories. Similarly in radical or Marxist versions of the history of economics, we are often (not *always*) dealing with irrefutable arguments. It is first stated that 'neoclassical economics' possessed certain characteristics or limitations (e.g. regarding their interpretation of

Finally, the nature of the approach to historical writing is crucial in radical or Marxist versions of history. A first-year student of sociology has aptly described teachers, 'whose criteria for the selection of material are purely political, and whose estimates of the great thinkers of history depend entirely on whether these persons can be fitted into some contrived evolutionary line preceding Marx, or if living later whether they agree with Marx' (K. Jacka et al., 1975, p. 44).

This approach is often accompanied by a denial of the possibility of objective truth. But as Barrington Moore has maintained:

> Different perspectives on the same set of events should lead to complementary and congruent interpretations, not to contradictory ones. Furthermore the denial that objective truth is possible in principle flings open the door to the worst forms of intellectual dishonesty. A crude version goes something like this: since neutrality is impossible I will take my stand with the underdog and write history to serve the underdog, helping in this way to reach a 'higher truth'. In plain language that is just cheating.[43]

Whether the 'cheating' is always on behalf of 'the underdog' (Stalin?) seems, in any case, to be doubtful. But the crucial point is whether *any* obligation is being accepted to control or reduce bias *or not*. It may well not be possible to eliminate every tinge or trace of bias, but it *can* be significantly reduced – especially by upholding, *as far as possible*, the principle of empirical testability. No one has been more concerned with value-loaded preconceptions in economics than Dr Gunnar Myrdal, whose views seem often to have been misunderstood and misrepresented. Recently Dr Myrdal has insisted:

> In the social sciences, we have to fight against the tendencies to bias...To keep concepts and terms clean, disinfected, logical and adequate to reality is a primary behest to the scientist. In this slippery field only the utmost purism can be accepted. *It is apparent that economists as well as other social scientists have in recent decades dangerously lowered their scientific sights and work standards*...We should never compromise with our duty to speak the language of strict science.[44]

marginal productivity and distribution). When it is pointed out that the majority of leading neoclassicals, such as Walras, Wieser, Böhm-Bawerk, Marshall and Edgeworth *actually said the opposite* of what 'neoclassical economics' is supposed to maintain, then it is explained that the doctrines of 'neoclassical economics' are to be found, not in the writings of leading 'neoclassicals' but in unspecified modern textbooks. Of course with perhaps hundreds of modern microeconomics texts to choose from it should be possible to extricate a relevant quotation. But in fact, nothing, or nothing in the least representative, is ever actually quoted.

[43] 1960, p. 522, quoted by M. Bronfenbrenner, 1974, p. 483.

[44] 1973, pp. 157 and 165–6 (italics added). It should be noted that Sir Karl Popper calls for just the same 'fight' as Dr Myrdal. Sir Karl agrees that: 'It is practically impossible to achieve the elimination of extra-scientific values from scientific activity. The situation is similar with respect to objectivity: we cannot rob the scientist of his partisanship without also robbing him of his humanity.' Nevertheless, Sir Karl insists that although 'the purity of science is an idea which is presumably unattainable', at the same time: '*It is an ideal for which we constantly fight – and should fight – by means of criticism*' (see 1976, p. 97).

There is obviously no point in Dr Myrdal urging us to 'fight' in this way unless he believes that there is a reasonable chance of *some* degree of success. In recent years obvious examples of the lowered standards referred to by Dr Myrdal have been displayed in radical or Marxist versions of history. It is pleasant to be able to note, however, that Dobb, in an 'explanatory note' of 1975, actually rejected the attribution to him of the Marxist view that 'effort devoted to minimising the ideological content of one's positive and normative statements...is a waste of time'.[45] This is an extremely important and necessary, if perhaps belated explanation. Moreover, the 'effort devoted to minimising ideological content' has an especially important role in the discussion of policy in a democracy. This point was emphasised by Keynes when, at the time of the setting up of the Economic Advisory Council (1930), he anticipated the growing role of the state in economic life and called for:

a recognition of the enormous part to be played in this by the scientific spirit as distinct from the sterility of the purely party attitude, which is never more out of place than in relation to complex matters of fact and interpretation involving technical difficulty. It would mean the beginning of ways of doing and thinking about political problems which are probably necessary for the efficient working of modern democracy.[46]

But, of course, Keynes is assuming a commitment to democracy in a genuine sense of the term (not 'peoples'' democracy). Meanwhile, on the other hand, Professor Robinson and Mr Eatwell have provided the most extreme example of a version of the history of economics and political economy – intended, incidentally, for beginners – which sets out the history of the subject simply in terms of a setting or scenario for their own would-be 'revolution'. In doing this they foster and encourage a quite opposite message to that of Dr Myrdal and Keynes. They advance the claim (for one part of their work, not, in fact, the historical part criticised here) that 'the authors intend their own prejudices to be sufficiently obvious for the reader to discount them as he feels right'.

But when, far from fighting against one's biases, one is 'using any stick' – as Mr G. F. Shove put it[47] – *on behalf of one's biases*, it is not to be expected that beginner students will be able to 'discount' them adequately.

It may be that economics is going through a period of fundamental,

---

[45] 1975, p. 358n. The attribution was by M. Bronfenbrenner, 1974, p. 483.
[46] In Prime Minister's Papers, 10 December 1929, quoted by S. Howson and D. Winch, 1977, p. 21.
[47] Mr Gerald Shove the Cambridge socialist, pacifist and theoretical economist, reviewing Professor Robinson's *Essay on Marxian Economics* wrote: 'She will seize on any stick with which to beat any doctrine that has been, or *might conceivably* be twisted into an apology for it [the present social system]'. See 1944, p. 60 (italics added).

critical debate. This is certainly long overdue. One may hope that the subject will emerge with such useful if fragmentary insights and concepts intact as have been inherited from 'neoclassical economics', in its microeconomic and macroeconomic branches, and that it will advance towards a richer historical and institutional content, rather than retreat into arid and vacuous neo-Ricardian abstractions.[48] As regards, however, the 'lowered standards' in economics, complained of recently by Dr Gunnar Myrdal, if he is right, a useful and necessary initial contribution to raising them again would be a wider cultivation of the disciplined study of the history of the subject. For it is probably the case that the standards generally maintained in writing the history of economics, including its contemporary history, may be taken as a reflection, or indicator, of how far economics is being pursued as a serious subject.

[48] An important element in clarification and the maintenance of standards would be regard, as far as possible, for the distinction between positive and normative. According to Professor Robinson: 'It is true that in Cambridge we had never been taught that...the positive and normative can be sharply divided' (1962, p. 74). This is quite incorrect. The sharp division of positive and normative was powerfully expounded in J. N. Keynes's *Scope and Method of Political Economy*, and Professor Friedman rightly invoked and quoted Keynes on positive and normative at the start of his essay on 'Positive Economics'. Not only is Keynes's book a thoroughly Cambridge one, on which the main influences are Sidgwick and Marshall, with its preface signed from 6 Harvey Road, it remains *the only* major Cambridge work on its general subject.

10

On the influence and effects on policies of economic ideas and theories

I

In this volume we have been concerned primarily with the influences and forces shaping economic theories and the major changes and choices in them, that is, with the origins, sources, or even 'causes', of changes and revolutions in economic theories, rather than with the influence and effects of such theories and ideas on policies. But these complex forces and influences are to some extent mutually interdependent; and what effects, in turn, economic theories are thought to be having, or going to have, on policies, has some part in the shaping and changing of these theories. So before summing up some conclusions in the next chapter we would like to look very briefly at the question as to how far economic ideas and theories may be said to have influenced and shaped policies. Various sweeping, but contrasting, generalisations have been put forward regarding this latter relationship.

Historians of ideas and of science, on the one hand, and economic historians on the other, will, as such, start with different interests and approaches regarding the history of economic thought and its relation with and effects on economic policies: for the historian of ideas, or of science, the history of 'economic thought', in any sense of that term, is not necessarily dependent for its value or interest on the existence, or on a belief in the existence, of any close or significant relationship between economic thought and policy, or on the determination, or partial determination, of policies by 'thought'. The historian of ideas can simply be satisfied with, for example, Clerk Maxwell's claim that: 'The history of the development, whether normal or abnormal, of ideas is of all subjects that in which we, as thinking men, take the deepest interest.'

Certainly the effect that many or most economists want, or try, to exercise on policy, or which they think, or claim, they are exercising or have exercised, may add an intriguing dimension to the interest in 'economic thought' of the historian of ideas. But it is not necessary for his interest for him to believe that economists actually have had any significant influence on policies.

On the other hand, as regards economic historians *as such*, if they are to be interested in the history of economic thought, this must surely be – as is not necessarily the case for historians of ideas – because economic thought, in one sense or another, is generally, or sometimes, among the significant determinants of, or helps to explain, the events of economic history, through its influence on action and policies.

As regards economists *as such*, those today who are interested in the history of economic thought may have a very wide variety of contrasting reasons for their interests, one of which may, or might, be a belief that in one way or another economic thought, in some sense, has had, and does have, a significant influence on policy.

II

Various confident generalisations about the influence on policies, and on history, of economic 'thought', 'theory', or 'ideas', have been made by economists. For example, just over a hundred years ago there was the exultant claim by Nassau Senior in explaining the prosperity and economic leadership of mid-Victorian Britain to a Frenchman: 'It is the triumph of theory. We are governed by philosophers and political economists' (1878, vol. I, p. 169).[1]

But much the most eloquent and forthright generalisation regarding the influence of economists on policies is that by Lord Keynes in the oft-quoted concluding paragraph of *The General Theory*:

> The ideas of economists and political philosophers, both when they are right and when they are wrong, are more powerful than is commonly understood. Indeed the world is ruled by little else. Practical men, who believe themselves to be quite exempt from any intellectual influences, are usually the slaves of some defunct economist. Madmen in authority, who hear voices in the air, are distilling their frenzy from some academic scribbler of a few years back. I am sure that the power of vested interests is vastly exaggerated, compared with the gradual encroachment of ideas [1936, p. 383].

We would underline two points here which are sometimes passed over by economists. *First*, that the claim for the influence of economists is not founded on any optimistic rationalism, for as often as not it is when they are wrong that their ideas take hold of the 'madmen in authority'. *Secondly*, in generalising about the power of economists' '*ideas*', and linking them with the ideas of political philosophers, Keynes seems to be suggesting that it is essentially or primarily a normative or even 'ideological' element that is essential for influence, rather than anything positive or 'scientific', whether this normative or ideological element is supplied by the economists themselves, or is infused by the

---

[1] This passage is quoted by A. Gerschenkron, 1969, p. 6.

'madmen in authority' when they take over, simplify, and perhaps distort, for their own purposes, the 'ideas' of economists.[2]

Lord Keynes's generalisation has been taken up and argued by Lord Robbins in his essay 'On the Relations between Politics and Economics' (1963). Lord Robbins seeks corroboration for Keynes's generalisation in the works of the English classical economists and in those of Karl Marx and Lord Keynes himself. Regarding the classical economists Lord Robbins maintains that their analysis:

> possessed sufficient intellectual coherence and persuasive power to exercise a most powerful influence on policy. Any account, for instance, of the coming of free trade in the United Kingdom which omitted the influence of economic thought and of economists would be defective and, indeed, absurd. And apart from spectacular episodes of this sort, in hundreds of subtler ways, Western policy and Western institutions have been influenced by this ideology [1963, p. 9].

We may notice that Lord Robbins refers here to the influence both of 'economic thought' and 'ideology', more or less interchangeably.

Regarding Karl Marx, though Lord Robbins would 'hesitate to describe the Messianic element in Marxian thought, *the element which gives it perhaps its main appeal and dynamic force*, as economic in character', he concludes:

> It is safe to say that if there had been no labour theory of value, no subsistence theory of wages, no exploitation theory of interest, the whole Marxian movement must have had an entirely different language; and the sense of *scientific* inevitability of the argument which, *ill-founded though it may be*, has influenced so many powerful intellects, would have been absent. And if anyone suggests that all that has had no influence on history, one can only say to him, look around! [op. cit., p. 10, italics added].

Thirdly, Lord Robbins cites 'the influence of the thought of Keynes himself' in the following terms:

> The whole episode of the reception of these views is a very apt illustration of the way in which thought may influence action...Public receptivity may indeed have been due to the depression. But what was received was economic thought of a specific character...It does not need much imagination to conceive alternative doctrines which might easily have suited the public mood: indeed, we know that there was strong competition on the Left. As it was, it was these ideas, argued with unsurpassable eloquence and expository skill, which gained the day [op. cit., p. 11].

In these three examples it may be noted that what Lord Robbins is ascribing influence to is the 'persuasive power' of the 'economic thought' or 'ideology' of the classical economists, 'the Messianic ele-

[2] The most recent exemplification of Keynes's generalisation, including both the elements in it noticed above, was the 'growth' policy of the British government of 1971–3, when the 'practical men' were simply 'distilling' their notions about 'going for growth', and 'putting growth first', from the academic fashions of the late 1950s and early 1960s.

ment', giving the 'main appeal and dynamic force' to Karl Marx's work, and 'the unsurpassable eloquence and expository skill' of Keynes, and how his ideas 'suited the public mood': that is, not (or not so much) to the weight of evidence marshalled on behalf of positive theories, or the strength of the empirical testing which they surmounted.[3]

Lord Robbins had begun by quoting Augustin Cournot to the effect that: 'Such questions as that of freedom of trade are not decided by the arguments of men of science...A higher power impels nations in one direction or another, and when a system of thought has had its day valid reasoning cannot restore its lost effectiveness any more than sophisms.'[4]

Lord Robbins agrees with Cournot: 'that scientific arguments alone are unlikely to settle the course of events', but concludes with Keynes that 'in the end, the world is governed by ideas and by little else' (1963, p. 23).

A pretty important distinction between 'scientific arguments' and 'ideas' seems to emerge. Anyhow, it would seem realistic to balance Keynes's confident claim for the 'ideas' of economists with a contrasting generalisation from J. S. Mill: 'Ideas, unless outward circumstances conspire with them, have in general no very rapid or immediate efficacy in human affairs' (1845, p. 503).

All the claims and generalisations regarding the importance of economic thought for policy which we have mentioned so far, have come from economists. Finally, we may cite the arguments of a historian as set out by Professor A. Gerschenkron. Professor Gerschenkron explains how he had 'believed that demonstrating the strong impact of economic doctrines upon economic history could serve as an additional argument for greater preoccupation with the history of doctrines' (1969, p. 1) – which he considers had come to be unduly neglected. But having surveyed the evidence for such an argument Professor Gerschenkron comes to strongly negative conclusions. He finds:

> a gap that separated economic analysis from economic history and was filled by ideology...For it is mainly as ideology, as varying mixtures of theories, or rather paratheories, conjoined with many other ingredients, that eco-

---

[3] It may be noted that Lord Robbins seems to be maintaining here that economists have only, or mainly, had influence when they have been exercising 'persuasive power', through an 'ideology', that is when they have been passing the kind of judgments which he had earlier maintained 'there is nothing in scientific Economics which warrants us in passing' (1935, p. 147).

[4] A. Cournot, 1927, p. 171. Cournot concludes with a comparison between economists and grammarians, which, though modest, may yet be over-optimistic: 'Up to a certain point it is possible to compare the influence of economic theories on society to that of grammarians on language. Languages are formed without the consent of grammarians and are corrupted in spite of them; but their works throw light on the laws of the formation and decadence of language; and their rules hasten the time when a language attains its perfection and delay a little the invasion of barbarism and bad taste which corrupt it.'

nomic doctrines may have had practical significance by hastening or obstructing as the case may be, the processes of economic change, the subject matter of economic history. Ideology then does two things: it reveals the impact of a doctrine, but also disguises its perversion, if not abandonment [op. cit., p. 2].

Taking as his thesis 'the limited role of economic analysis in influencing economic history', Professor Gerschenkron stresses 'certain dangers that arise when economic historians too readily regard contemporaneous economic theories as an integral part of the economic history of the times. One of the difficulties an economic historian experiences with the history of economic thought is precisely that at times, at least, it seems to obscure rather than clarify the course of events and its meaning' (op. cit., p. 2).

Professor Gerschenkron first cites 'mercantilism' as a case in point. Coming to the classical economists he claims that it was rather 'a popular mythology' or 'ideology' of *laissez-faire* that was influential, which was 'far removed from the actual scholarly contents of classical doctrines' (op. cit., p. 6).

Moreover: 'The *laissez-faire* ideology was quite selective in what it did and what it did not accept from classical economics...It was not the theories of the classical school, but convenient fragments thereof – at times words rather than concepts – that entered the *laissez-faire* ideology.'[5]

When he comes to Marx Professor Gerschenkron is even more emphatic. Though Marx

occupies a firm position in the history of economic doctrines...the total impact of Marx *as an economist* was very small if not negligible. What was accepted was the implied ethical message of the doctrine rather than the doctrine itself...What was received and worked as an intellectual yeast was not the theory in any reasonable sense of the word but the ethical norm in conjunction with a gospel-like promise of delivery. All the talk about scientific socialism could not change the fact that what was created was an ideology which contained, along with other things, paratheoretical elements and did so probably to a somewhat higher degree than most ideologies [1969, p. 14].

Professor Gerschenkron does not deny that 'Marxism affected the course of economic history. But here again I find it difficult to say

[5] The relationship between classical economic thought and policy has been much more positively described by Professor C. H. Wilson: 'These classical formulations of doctrine, whether by Thomas Mun or Adam Smith, had a special function in policy-making. They were neither short-sightedly commercial nor merely remotely academic. They seemed to reflect the current situation, to meet current needs so appropriately and so perfectly that they acquired a kind of controlling dynamism of their own, taking hold of men as a spirit is supposed to take hold of a human medium' (1968, p. 154). Professor Wilson is writing here of 'doctrine' which seems to lie somewhere between 'theory' and 'ideas' or 'ideology'.

that it was Marx as an economic theorist that produced the effect.' In fact Professor Gerschenkron concludes: 'Hardly anything in the momentous story of Soviet economic policies needs, or suffers, explanation in terms of its derivation from Karl Marx's economic theories.'[6]

It is important to realise that in taking as his theme '*Quantula theoria economica mundus regebatur*' Professor Gerschenkron is emphasising the inadequacies of economic 'theories' in positive scientific terms, as much as the irrationality or unwisdom of rulers in disregarding them: 'Had the theories been more operational, primarily in the narrow, pragmatic sense of the word, had there been, that is, a sufficiently large stock of empirical knowledge to support them, their impact upon events would have been much greater' (op. cit., p. 16).

Thus Professor Gerschenkron is led to take a much more hopeful, and probably quite excessively hopeful, view about the future, believing, with regard to the advance of economic knowledge, that 'we live in a new era'. The economics 'profession' today

> works with new and much more operational tools, and it has at its service the vastly increased body of primary quantitative information... If the past may look bleak, the future is bright. The economic historian of future times, in dealing with our own, in many other respects so unhappy, century will be forced to stress the strong impact of economic doctrines upon the course of economic events [op. cit., p. 17].

Summing up, we may agree with Professor Gerschenkron when he concedes that his 'mostly negative picture' is, in some respects, 'surely one-sided'. But we heartily agree also that: 'there may have been some merit in going over the bits of evidence that can be mustered in the service of a negative approach' (op. cit., p. 17).

Professor Gerschenkron has done especially well to emphasise *the identification problem*, as it might be called, of trying to sort out the directions in which the currents of influence run between 'thought', policies, and real-world events such as technological and other developments. Roughly simultaneously, a new dawn gradually begins to break, cocks crow, and people get out of bed. Claims by the birds that 'the world is ruled by little else' than their crowing should be treated with reserve, without denying them any influence whatsoever, on particular occasions, on the course of events.

Professor Gerschenkron also emphasises what he sees as the new relations between 'thought' and policies which have emerged, or may

---

[6] Op. cit., p. 16. As Oskar Lange said: 'It is obvious that Marshallian economics offers more for the current administration of the economic system of Soviet Russia than Marxian economics does' (*Marx and Modern Economics*, ed. D. Horowitz, 1968, p. 72n). When I delivered an earlier version of this paper in Leningrad, Professor Gerschenkron's judgments were not received with warm agreement by local and East European sections of the audience.

or will emerge, if economics becomes more positively disciplined and empirically based. However, there could be a great deal of over-optimism on this point. Anyhow, Professor Gerschenkron argues powerfully that it is through 'ideology', distorting and selective though it may have been, that, so far, economists have at times powerfully influenced policies and events. *If*, however, inadequate non-operational theories are being, or are going to be replaced by theories much more firmly and operationally grounded in 'primary quantitative information', economists *may possibly* come to exercise a very different kind of influence, in a different intellectual mode and manner, than they have in the past. But it is still far from clear just to what extent such changes have been, or are, taking place.

However, as regards past history perhaps the right balance was that of Leslie Stephen in his conclusions regarding the influence of the theory of political economy in the free trade victory of 1846, with the abolition of the Corn Laws:

> The triumph over the corn-laws seemed to establish the truth of the economic theory. Doctrines preached by professors and theorists had been accepted and applied by politicians on a grand scale. The result, as Cairnes, one of Mill's chief followers observes, was not altogether an advantage to the science. The popular mind identified political economy with free trade... The strict economic doctrine had been, as Cairnes held, adulterated in order to suit the tastes of the exoteric audience. This remark suggests the problem, not strictly soluble, as to the causes of the free trade victory. Did it mark a triumph of logic, or was it due to the simple fact that the class which wanted cheap bread was politically stronger than the class which wanted dear bread?...
>
> Later history, however, has shown that in such matters pure reason cannot by itself win the battle against interested prejudice [1900, vol. III, pp. 164–5].

III

The generalisations we have surveyed seem to present, on the surface at least, considerable contrasts. But the differences may be largely verbal. Anyhow, it is certainly essential to distinguish between the different modes or channels by which economists may influence policy and to fix on a terminology which clearly expresses these distinctions. In particular, it is highly desirable, in the interests of clarity, to use terms which distinguish between the political and the economic content in what economists write, as well as between very different types of economic propositions. For example, it seems desirable to achieve more precision and clarity regarding the term 'economic thought', along with, or in relation to, such other terms as 'economic doctrines', 'theory', 'analysis', and 'ideas'. Thus Professor Gerschenkron seems to be using 'economic thought', 'doctrines', 'theory', and 'analysis' more or less interchangeably while contrasting them all pretty sharply with what he calls 'ideology'. Lord Robbins, on the other hand, while contrasting the lack of influence of 'scientific arguments alone', with the power of 'ideas', stresses 'the influence of economic thought' and 'ideology', with regard to free trade, using 'thought' and 'ideology', in this particular context at any rate, in apparently more or less overlapping senses.

It seems that 'economic thought' might be taken as a broad, comprehensive, portmanteau term, covering the 'thought' about economic problems both of 'economists' and 'non-economists', and comprising both positive, 'scientific' 'theory' and 'analysis', as well as normative 'ideas' and 'ideology' – or, at any rate, 'ideas' and 'ideology' containing a significant normative element. Such a broad, inclusive coverage would seem to be in line with Schumpeter's definition of 'economic analysis' as 'the analytic or scientific aspects of economic thought' (1954, p. 3). However, Schumpeter also was not as precise and explicit as he might have been, and after emphasising 'the distinction between scientific economic analysis and economic thought', goes on to describe 'economic thought' as 'the ideas on economic policy that float in the public mind or may be attributed to legislators and administrators, whether or not embodied in elaborate systems' (op. cit., pp. 7 and 38). Certainly this phenomenon of 'ideas on economic policy in the minds of the public and of legislators and administrators' is of key importance. But it might, perhaps, be called '*economic opinion*', while 'economic thought' is used comprehensively to include economic opinion along with economic 'theory', 'analysis', and 'ideas'.[7] 'Economic opinion' will be, to an important extent, that of non-economists, among politicians, the public, and civil servants, who may be somewhat influenced by 'theories' and 'analysis', but who will mainly be swayed by the 'ideas' of economists, and will select from and distort these and infuse them with their own political purposes. But the main conclusion to emphasise is that economists' writings contain what are logically very different kinds of propositions and arguments, the influence of which, if any, must work in very different ways. It must be recognised that their influence on policy has been, and may be, according to very different modes, involving significantly more or significantly less, explicit or implicit, persuasion on their part. We would simply con-

---

[7] The term 'economic doctrines' is another vaguely comprehensive term which seems to cover both positive and normative elements emanating both from economists and non-economists. But it may be appropriate, and even vital to draw a sharp distinction between 'analysis' and 'theory' which is often not made by economists. The distinction is, for some purposes, essential, between empirically testable and refutable propositions on the one hand, and analytical or definitional propositions, not refutable empirically, on the other hand. Anyhow, Marshall considered it essential for clarity to distinguish between 'analysis' and 'theory' and criticised J. N. Keynes for not doing so. Incidentally, Marshall maintained that in economics there is 'no theory to speak of'. See 'Marshall on Method', by Professor R. H. Coase, 1975.

clude, regarding arguments in general terms as to the influence of economists and economic thought, that no short and simple general proposition on this subject is likely to score highly for *both* interest and validity. Each particular passage or episode in the history of thought and policy must be examined and unravelled, case by case, and the different possible channels or modes of influence, if any, sorted out. That is the point we would carry over from this brief discussion of the effects on policy of economic theories and ideas to our conclusions regarding the forces which shape, change and transform those theories and ideas.

11

On revolutions and progress in economic knowledge: definitions and conclusions

I

1. 1   In the foregoing chapters, including their titles, we have been making much use of the term 'revolution'. It may seem reasonable to hope (and believe) that the omission so far to define and analyse this term precisely or searchingly need not have, and has not, been a source of confusion. As we noted in the Foreword, the term 're-volution' has been very much used by economists, especially since Keynes, and for some time before the work of T. S. Kuhn appeared. It can therefore be used and understood without any of the implications regarding the history and philosophy of science attached to it in Kuhn's work.

1. 2   Presumably a 'revolution' is a process of comparatively funda-mental or comprehensive, and/or comparatively rapid, change, affect-ing either a part or the whole of the subject. We are concentrating here on 'revolutions' in, or appreciably affecting, the subject as a whole. For example, the Keynesian 'revolution' was only *directly* con-cerned with one major branch of the subject, but it might be con-sidered sufficiently important to have reshaped the subject as a whole. As we noted earlier, we are not concerned here with partial 'revolu-tions' in branches, or subdivisions too small to affect significantly the subject as a whole. We shall take up subsequently the concept of methodological 'revolutions'.

1. 3   It is impossible to be at all precise regarding the *rapidity* of the processes of fundamental change, if these are to be described as 'revolutionary'. The idea of 'a long revolution' does not seem to be contradictory (and has been, in fact, the title of a history of recent cultural changes in England). Also, complete conversions, or processes of change, may be, and usually have been spread out over a con-siderable period, although it may be possible to identify a decisive phase or episode with the publication of a particular book.

1. 4   Fundamental changes, or 'revolutions', have not, of course, begun and ended rapidly and immediately on the publication day of a particular historic book (9 March 1776 or 4 February 1936). Though *The Wealth of Nations* and *The General Theory* had comparatively powerful and rapid effects, Jevons's *Theory* did not. But, in any case, these books are useful landmarks, and processes of change were concentrated *around* their publication dates.

1. 5   'Revolutions' have destructive and constructive phases, one of which may be comparatively rapid, the other the reverse. For example, the comparatively rapid decline in the late 1860s in Britain of the classical regime was followed by a comparatively slow build-up of neoclassical theorising. With regard to the Keynesian 'revolution', it might be argued that the reverse was the case, with a comparatively long preceding phase of largely inexplicit disintegration or confusion, followed by a comparatively rapid constructive phase. 'Klassical' eco-nomics, in the Keynesian sense, had begun to disintegrate at least half a century before the appearance of *The General Theory*; and similarly with the 'Smithian revolution', the hold of 'mercantilist' doctrines had begun to weaken long before 1776.

1. 6   'Revolutions' in economics are not total and final in the way, or to the same extent, that they tend to be in some or most of the natural sciences. Acceptance of the new 'revolutionary' doctrines does not spread as rapidly, or to as high a degree of consensus, as in physics or chemistry. Moreover, theories once apparently eclipsed by a suc-cessful 'revolution' may sooner or later revive (e.g. the quantity theory of money). These are important qualifications, but they do not seem to invalidate the concept of 'revolutions' in economics.[1]

[1] See M. Bronfenbrenner, The 'Structure of Revolutions' in Economic Thought, 1971. Arthur Koestler has described 'revolutions' in literature and the arts as follows: 'Revolutions are both destructive and constructive. Old restraints and conventions are discarded, aspects of human experience previously neglected or repressed are suddenly high-lighted, there is a shift of emphasis, a reshuffling of data, a reordering of the hierarchy of values and of the criteria of relevance. This is what happened at each of the turning-points of narrative prose styles – classicism to romanticism, naturalism and so on.' Koestler outlines a cyclical process: 'As a rule, the life-cycle starts with a passionate dominant school, and a breakthrough towards new frontiers. The second phase in the cycle moves through a climate of optimism and euphoria in the footsteps of the conquering giants. Their followers move into the newly opened territories to explore and exploit its rich potentials. This is the phase *par excellence* of the cumulative progress described earlier on; a time for consolidating new insights, for elaborating and perfecting new styles and techniques. The third phase brings saturation, followed by frustration and decline.' Koestler describes the final phase as 'Crisis and New Departure', and defines a 'revolution' as 'a radical shift in selective emphasis and in the criteria of relevance'. (See *The Heel of Achilles*, 1974, pp. 122–3, 125–6 and 132.) See also J. G. A. Pocock (1972, pp. 13ff) for a discussion of Kuhn's ideas in relation to politics.

1. 7   It might be maintained that there have been *no* episodes, or phases, in the history of economics and political economy, which merit this description 'revolution'. This has been argued by Professor D. F. Gordon and Mr G. Routh (though it must be noted that they are using the term 'revolution' in the special Kuhnian sense, which we are not adopting here). Professor Gordon and Mr Routh hold, not unreasonably, that there has been *no* successful, major 'revolution' in 'orthodox' economics since the adoption of the central maximising and self-equilibrating models which began to emerge towards the end of the seventeenth century, and which came to full fruition and supremacy with *The Wealth of Nations* (or with what we have been calling the Smithian 'revolution'). There have been various historical and institutionalist attacks but, as Professor Gordon maintains, 'the potential revolutions have been suppressed'.[2]

There is a certain underlying validity in this view, which may be specially relevant in the 1970s. Nevertheless, change has not been continuously uniform in pace and profundity over the last 200 years and we are entitled to be interested in the limited number of relatively more fundamental changes or transformations that have taken place *within* this period, such as those associated with Jevons and Keynes, the outstanding significance of which have been emphasised by numerous economists. There could be a danger here, which we are anxious to avoid, of becoming involved in largely or purely terminological issues. But while recognising the sense in which it could be maintained that there has been no complete and successful 'revolution' since the maximising and self-equilibrating archetypal model first began gradually to emerge two to three centuries ago, we have been concentrating on the two or three major and more fundamental changes (or 'revolutions') – long and widely recognised and described as such in most histories of economic thought (though explained in widely contrasting ways) – as providing the main divisions or turning-points in the last two hundred years. Moreover, in not recognising *any* important turning-points within the last two hundred years, one

---

[2]   Professor D. F. Gordon has stated: 'Economics has never had a major revolution; its basic maximizing model has never been replaced...On the other hand, lacking basic revolutions, we have had major, if unsuccessful rebellions' (1965, p. 124). Similarly, Mr G. Routh has maintained that: 'The paradigm that provides the inner framework for economic thought has not changed since the seventeenth century...neither the advent of marginalism that distinguishes classical from neoclassical economics, nor the admission of the possibility of involuntary unemployment, that distinguishes Keynesian from neoclassical economics were revolutions in the Kuhnian sense. On the contrary, they were means by which the survival of the existing paradigm was ensured.' Alright: *first* we are not concerned here with 'revolutions *in the Kuhnin sense*' and *secondly*, in any case Mr Routh here recognises as outstanding two of the *major changes* we are prepared to describe as 'revolutions' (in a non-Kuhnian sense) (1976, p. 27 et passim).

would be missing at least one significant and profound *methodological* transformation, fully within the orthodox succession, which represented a vital change primarily in the formulation, but consequentially in the content, of the maximising, self-adjusting model: we are referring to the much underestimated methodological transformation as between *The Wealth of Nations* and Ricardo's *Principles*.

I. 8   Regarding the 'revolutions' which historically might be identified in political economy and economics over the last 200–300 years, though a variety of views have been put forward, there seems to be a considerable measure of support for the historical validity of (a) a Smithian; (b) a Jevonian; and (c) a Keynesian revolution. While agreeing, in substance, regarding these three main cases, one might reasonably hold that we have described them in too narrowly Anglocentric terms. The nomenclature of Professor Bronfenbrenner might well be preferred, i.e.: (a) the *laissez-faire* revolution, (b) the utility revolution, and (c) the macroeconomic revolution[3] (though it could be argued that there was never really a utility '*revolution*' apart from the Jevonian revolution *in Britain*).

II

II. 1   Are there any other worthy candidates? The following might be considered:

A Mercantilist revolution replacing Scholastic economics? The transition seems to have been *very* protracted and the two kinds of doctrines overlapped for centuries.

II. 2   A Physiocratic revolution? The Physiocrats have often been described as the first 'school' of political economy and they certainly possessed the requisite revolutionary, and even millennial, fervour. Their historian, or PRO, Mirabeau, put the invention of Quesnay's *Tableau* on a par with the inventions of writing and of money, as one of the three great discoveries in world history. Even McCulloch and Marx did not go as far as that. However, if the concept of the *laissez-faire* revolution is adopted, then the works of Quesnay and the Physiocrats could be ranged alongside *The Wealth of Nations*, and a number of earlier and lesser works, as making up a broader, international movement (which, however, contained some sharply distinguishable philosophical and political branches).

---

[3] M. Bronfenbrenner, op. cit., p. 150. Professor C. D. W. Goodwin upholds the same triad, calling them the Smithian, the Marginal and the Keynesian Revolutions (1973, p. 303).

II. 3   A Ricardian 'revolution'? We have not merely inserted inverted commas but (in the title of our essay on James Mill and Ricardo) have added a question-mark regarding this candidate. It has received, however, the support of both Sir John Hicks and Professor H. G. Johnson. We would certainly argue that the work of Ricardo brought about an extremely consequential *methodological* revolution. It could also be maintained that Ricardo crucially altered the *content* of Smithian political economy by hardening and sharpening basic propositions and assumptions, like the population and natural-wage proposition, the assumption of perfect knowledge and of much more smooth and rapid equilibrating processes. In so doing Ricardo could be held to have altered significantly the meaning or content of the Smithian doctrines of pricing and distribution.

However, on the other side, it could be maintained that there is not enough in the *substance* of Ricardo's doctrines that is basically new, or at variance, or in conflict, with those of Smith, to justify the concept of a 'Ricardian revolution'.[4] If – *apart from methodology* – there *was* a Ricardian 'revolution', it might seem, on the surface, to have had almost no destructive aspect as compared with the Smithian 'revolution', of which it could be regarded as a second phase. (We shall take up briefly below the idea of a methodological 'revolution'.)

II. 4   A Marxian 'revolution'? Marxists themselves would be the first to insist that Marx's economic doctrines and their historical develop-ment are to be fundamentally distinguished from those of Keynes or Jevons or Smith. Anyhow, we are not concerned here with 'might-have-beens' or 'ought-to-have-beens'. Within the time, space, and academic communities with which we are concerned, Marx's economic theories have not yet been sufficiently widely adopted. In the main areas in the world where Marx's theories, or some version of them, do dominate, it is because of propaganda ministries and police terror, not by the kind of relatively free consensus of anything which might be called a scientific community. (Furthermore, it would seem that, according to a stricter version of Marxist theory, an intellectual revolution – in economics or any other subject – cannot properly come about until the social revolution has taken place.)

II. 5   There have been various post-Keynesian candidates:
    (a) We have considered above one such would-be 'revolution' and

---

[4] We agree with Sir John Hicks that Ricardo's switch of emphasis on the subject of distribution – as contrasted with Smith's work – is not substantial: 'The general tendency of Ricardo's work is to treat distribution as secondary. He was interested in distribution because of the importance which he attached to the effects of dis-tribution on production, not because he had much interest in distribution *per se*' (1976, p. 212).

the historical scenario which has been constructed for it: that is, the Sraffa, or post-, or neo-Keynesian revolution.

(b) What has been called the mathematical or quantitative revolution does not qualify, as it hardly seems to have changed *very* significantly either the problems studied *or the empirical content* of economic theories (with the exception, presumably, of linear programming and operational research). We would hold that the mathematical or quantitative 'revolution' has not had nearly as significant consequences as what we have tentatively called the Ricardian methodological revolution.

(c) Professor H. G. Johnson has advanced considerable claims for a Monetarist Counter-Revolution which he subsequently withdraws, expecting it 'to peter out', and pointing out the less-than-fundamental character of its differences from its Keynesian opponent and predecessor. (We would not, however, agree that the problems of inflation, which has given impetus to the Monetarist Counter-Revolution is likely to prove insufficiently serious to sustain interest in it.) (1975, pp. 91–106.)

III

III. 1   Before we can explore the origins of these major turning-points, or their 'causation', we must distinguish the different elements of which they might be held to have consisted, and consider which of these elements should be regarded as essential or decisive, and which simply as accompanying changes.

The components and contents of the Smithian, Jevonian, and Keynesian 'revolutions' can certainly be regarded as very mixed in intellectual or epistemological terms and these components must be distinguished one from another. We set down the following outline list simply in the hope that it may·be of help in discerning and distinguishing *some* of the main, but very differing, components which have been intertwined with one another in the complex processes of 'revolutions', or rapid and comprehensive changes, in economics and political economy. We are certainly not suggesting that this list is necessarily complete.

III. 2   *New policy objectives are urged or given much greater priority than previously.* Part of the Keynesian revolution, for example, could be said to have involved persuading people and governments to put employment before the maintenance of the gold standard rules. Part of the Smithian revolution could be said to have consisted in normative political philosophising on behalf of individual initiative and against centralised regulation. There may have been no quite such immediate and clear-cut normative component in terms of particular policy objectives in the Jevonian revolution, but more attention to the poverty problem and to the problems of public utilities were forthcoming, together with a new questioning of the *laissez-faire* maxim. This kind of change does not, of course, necessarily, or by itself, entail that any theory has been refuted or amended, though it might be associated with such a refutation or amendment. Obviously, also, subjective valuations are involved in assessing such changes, which could be regarded as regressive, or involving *losses*, by those who did not share the valuations of the victorious consensus regarding policy-objectives.

III. 3   *Changes in interests, or research priorities, may well be a component* – or 'changes of attention' as Sir John Hicks has called them. We have, for example, noted, in the Jevonian revolution, the shift from problems of aggregate, average, or 'natural' wages to questions of relative wages and individual allocation, and there was an obvious change in intellectual priorities in the Keynesian revolution. Clearly such changes may be associated with changes of priorities in respect of policy-objectives, as discussed in III. 2 above. Here again no empirical refutation or amendment of any existing theory is *necessarily* involved. Which subject is the most 'interesting', 'important', or deserving of reseach priority or attention, obviously depends on subjective valuations, regarding which, losses, and regress, *may* be held to have taken place in respect of any particular change – whatever the extent of the consensus supporting it.[5] Again, changes of interest and attention cannot necessarily involve *any* refutations or amendments in respect of testable, empirical substance.

III. 4.1   *A new terminology, or a new 'conceptual framework', may well be part of a 'revolution'*, whether it is a matter of new terms for old concepts (e.g. 'the marginal efficiency of capital') or new (or relatively new) concepts (e.g. the 'final degree of utility'). This component may be taken to contain no empirically testable, or refutable, or predictive content. Valuations regarding convenience and elegance will obviously be involved.

III. 4.2   *A special form of this type of change has been the introduction, or the major extension, of the formulation of analysis and 'theory' in mathematical terms.* This occurred after 1870 in the development of marginal analysis in the closing decades of the nineteenth century, and also in the 1950s when there was a major extension of mathematical methods. Again, in these cases, no extensions of empirical or predictive content were *essentially* involved.

[5] See Hutchison, 1964, pp. 55–9.

III. 5.1   *Finally, there is the possible component of changes in testable, refutable, empirical content.*

In the first place, such changes in content may *appear* to be expressed in 'causal' propositions regarding what 'determines', or 'governs', the rate of interest, saving, investment, wages, value, etc. But such 'causal' propositions are liable to be extremely ambiguous. Jevons's apparently challenging statement of his '*catena*' on utility and the 'determination' of value is a case in point, and obvious 'Keynesian' or pseudo-Keynesian examples could be cited about what 'determines' or 'governs' saving, investment, the rate of interest, etc., etc., etc. The difficulty here is often in extricating what such allegedly 'causal' confrontations, or issues, regarding 'determination' precisely amount to, and in discerning just how far, if at all, what is at stake may be mainly, or entirely definitional, or may, on the other hand, be empirically resolvable and possess predictive content.

III. 5.2   A theory or proposition put forward as a universally, or virtually universally, valid empirical generalisation, or described as a 'Law', might be denied or abandoned, or so qualified and reduced, as to lose effective significance: an example might be the hard-line version of the Malthusian generalisation regarding population and the natural wage which, in Britain, finally lost credibility around the 1860s (it had been questioned much earlier).

III. 5.3   A proposition put forward as a relatively valid generalisation, or as stating a temporary trend, may be rejected because of historical or institutional changes. For example, Pigou maintained that a generalisation regarding a self-adjusting relationship between wage-flexibility and employment, which held good in Britain in the second half of the nineteenth century, had ceased to hold in the inter-war years of the twentieth century (because of the growth in trade union power and the introduction of unemployment benefit). Similarly it has been maintained that Keynes's assumption, in *The General Theory*, of workers' money illusion may have been valid in Britain in the 1930s, but not in other times and places. 'Absolute' and relative changes in empirical testable content may, of course, be combined.

III. 6   Which, if any, of the kinds of changes reviewed above in III. 2–III. 5 should be regarded as essential components of a 'revolution', and which merely as secondary accompaniments? Certainly, in terms of the development of what are frequently called the 'mature' sciences, such as physics or chemistry, such changes as III. 2, 3, and 4. 1 and 2 – that is, the advocacy of changes in policy objectives, or of the adoption of new policy objectives, and of the adoption of new terminologies, or 'conceptual frameworks', including new mathematical formulations – should and would be regarded as inessential, and partly 'external', accompaniments. *Insofar as we are concerned with 'revolutions' in the content of an empirical science it is changes under* III. 5 *above which primarily require explanation.*

Anyhow, it is necessary to clarify and distinguish the differing kinds of change of which 'revolutions' in economics may be regarded as consisting, before one can try to explain or account for these 'revolutions', and analyse the different kinds of factors or processes *via* which they come about.

IV

We earlier applied the term 'methodological revolution' to the transformation in method brought about by Ricardo's *Principles*, as contrasted with *The Wealth of Nations*. This transformation removed or destroyed the historical dimension in the subject which was so vital and pervasive for Adam Smith. The magnitude of this methodological change, or 'revolution', does not seem to have been recognised because of the superficial similarities in interests, concepts, and terminology as between the two works, or parts thereof. But the concepts and 'models' are so *much* more sharply drawn by Ricardo (for example, with regard to the 'natural' wage and the tendency to equilibrium) that his conclusions are different in mood and significance.

The Ricardian 'methodological revolution', in which James Mill and Senior also played very important parts, has unique features. For example, the development of more mathematical methods in the decades after 1870, and again in the 1950s, does not seem to have had the same hardening and sharpening effect, in particular in respect of economic policies, as had the Ricardian 'methodological revolution' but rather a generalising effect bringing a dilution of empirical content. Furthermore, the *Methodenstreit*, or the confrontation between the Austrian theoretical and the German historical economists, never resulted in a revolution, except perhaps locally in Germany when the historical school became prominent (though never exclusively so, and with perhaps something of a counter-revolution after 1945). But these methodological confrontations had *some* similarities with our three main revolutionary clashes associated with the names of Smith, Jevons, and Keynes. Only to a minor extent – as in Marshall's work – did a synthesis succeed the thesis and antithesis. It certainly did not in respect of the two contesting parties in the *Methodenstreit*. Why a synthesis was not more fully achieved was partly because the confrontations represented not so much differences in the methods adopted with regard to *the same* problems or questions, but differences in interest or 'attention', or differing value-judgments as to what was the 'appropriate' problem. The older historical school had been interested in economic development, while the Austrian theorists were mainly interested in allocation and 'catallactic' analysis. Historical and analytical methods could be combined or 'synthesised', as by Marshall, *with regard to the same particular subject* (for example, of pricing, firms and industries). But it was impossible to synthesise the treatment of quite different subjects which could simply be regarded as separate fields of attention. As we have suggested elsewhere:

> In fact the *Methodenstreit* was not basically a quarrel about methods so much as a clash of interests regarding what was the most important and interesting subject to study, pricing and allocation analysis, or the broad development and change of national economies and industries. As Menger himself agreed in his very generous obituary tribute to Roscher in 1894: 'The differences which have arisen between the Austrian school and some of the German historical economists were by no means ones of method in the proper sense of the word. If the German historical economists were often described – even in scientific works – as representatives of the inductive method, and the Austrian economists of the deductive method, this does not correspond with the facts. The true contrast between these two schools is not even remotely characterised as that between an empirical and a rationalist approach or an inductive and deductive one...The real foundation of the differences between the two schools, which are still not completely bridged, is something much more important: it relates to the different view regarding the *objectives* of research, and about the set of tasks which a science of economics has to solve.'[6]

It would seem, therefore, that major methodological controversies, clashes and 'revolutions', can often be regarded as turning on differences, or changes, in research priorities or in 'attention' (as described by Sir John Hicks) or regarding the appropriate subject for study (as discussed above in III. 3). However, this does not seem adequately to cover the methodological 'revolution' of James Mill and Ricardo, which may be regarded as, to a large extent, *sui generis*.

V

Philosophers of science have described and analysed processes of change in the natural sciences, or in the history thereof, in terms of 'internal' and 'external' factors, processes, or history. However, this pair of terms has been given significantly different senses by Kuhn, on the one hand, and Lakatos on the other, both of whose usages have been distilled from, and applied to, the more 'advanced' natural sciences. Though these terms, 'internal' and 'external', might seem to be largely self-explanatory, their application is not clear-cut in respect of economics and the social sciences, which possess a kind of

[6] See Carl Menger, vol. III, 1935, p. 279; and T. W. Hutchison, 1973, pp. 34–5.

historical dimension which is not nearly so important in the natural sciences. So we are not here going to redefine and apply these terms to the history of political economy and economics.

Instead of 'internal' and 'external' we propose to apply a threefold classification, or taxonomy, which would appear to be reasonably comprehensive, or which is capable of being interpreted comprehensively. We have not devised this classification so much by abstract *a priori* analysis, *but rather by setting out the main contrasting categories or types of historical explanation which we have found leading economists actually to have been applying, when seeking to analyse major processes of change, or revolution, in the history of economics.* Most of the views or interpretations of the economists whom we quote fit quite clearly under one or other of our three headings, though one or two require sub-headings in between our main three. We would emphasise from the start that these three types of history, or historical interpretation, are not necessarily or completely mutually exclusive, and should, in fact, be regarded as, in part, complementary.

v. 1   First, changes, 'revolutionary' or otherwise in economic theories, or shifting theory-choices, may be described and analysed in empirical–scientific terms, that is, to adopt the conceptual framework of Lakatos, in terms of expanding empirical content and the growth of 'objective knowledge'. This is to write, on Lakatos's definition, the 'internal' history of an empirical science, or to set out the 'rational reconstruction' of its development. Though he agrees that this 'internal' history needs to be 'supplemented' by empirical–sociological, 'external' history, Lakatos insists that: 'Internal history, so defined, is primary, and external history only secondary' (1971, p. 92).

This approach has been upheld for the history of economics by Professor Mark Blaug, who concludes:

> The object of the exercise is to show that most scientists join research programmes that have 'excess empirical content' and desert 'research programmes' that lack this characteristic. This is 'internal history' and every other reason for joining one camp rather than another is 'external'. It was Lakatos's claim that the 'rational reconstruction' of the history of science conceived in these terms would in fact need few footnotes referring to 'external history' [1976, p. 177].

Unfortunately, though we would certainly agree that it is extremely desirable, *so far as it is possible as an intellectual ideal,* to write the history of political economy and economics in these terms, as we shall see, very much of what leading economists have considered most important in this history, though not entirely or necessarily incompatible, would be, or would *have* to be, left out, or would be given a secondary place. In other words, much of the history of economic thought, as it has been written by economists, either would not be compatible with a 'rational reconstruction' according to the rules of empirical sciences, or, if compatible would have to be regarded as of subordinate importance to the primary, 'internal' history.

In fact, it seems rather optimistic of Professor Blaug to 'conclude that a Lakatosian "rational reconstruction" would suffice to explain virtually all past successes and failures of economic research programmes' (op. cit., p. 177).

For only just before reaching this conclusion Professor Blaug had complained: 'that the central weakness of modern economics is in fact the reluctance to produce theories which yield unambiguously refutable implications'.

In fact, Professor Blaug goes on to suggest that Lakatos's Methodology of Scientific Research Programmes

> may not fit the history of economics: economists may cling to 'degenerating' research programmes in the presence of rival 'progressive' research programmes while denying that the 'degenerating' programme is in need of resuscitation because they are suspicious of hard data, inclined to assign low priority to the discovery of novel facts, accustomed by long habit to deny the feedback of evidence on theory, or simply because they are deeply attached to the welfare implications of their theories [op. cit., pp. 172 and 176].

We shall shortly cite the views of several leading contemporary economists whose main explanations of major turning-points – or 'revolutions' – in the history of economics, in the last hundred years, would seem to be quite incompatible with the 'rational reconstructions' of strictly 'internal' scientific history, as conceived by Lakatos.

However, what deserves to be emphasised is that, even with the most scrupulous scientific intentions, owing to the nature of the material, and its historical changeability, it may be *practically impossible* to obtain clear-cut and agreed refutations with regard to economic theories, and so to obtain a historical record based on a broad scientific consensus.

Moreover, according to the Lakatos interpretation, or programme, this kind of 'internal' history, with which we are here concerned under heading 1 (v. 1), 'provides a rational explanation of the growth of objective knowledge' (1971, p. 91).

It would seem (and is presumably the case with regard to physics and the advanced natural sciences with which Lakatos was concerned) that no insuperable difficulties arise identifying 'the growth of objective knowledge', for which this kind of history accounts. But in economics and the social sciences it is, to start with, far from clear and unproblematic as to precisely when, at what points, and in what respects, there has been a 'growth of objective knowledge'. It may be difficult enough to assess the growth or progress of a branch of knowledge when, because of the constancy of the material, the components of the questions remain largely the same decade by decade and century by century. But when the material and the questions posed by it are changing, such assessments become far more problematic, like trying to assess changes in 'welfare' when there have been changes in tastes. Of course, most or all economists would say that there has been *some* growth or progress of knowledge, *but there would probably be much disagreement as to just when and where this growth took place and of what exactly it consisted.* Instead of 'internal' history providing a 'rational reconstruction' of growth, it would have – at least at some stages – to provide a rational (or irrational) reconstruction of loss.[7]

Nevertheless, we would strongly support any programme which was aimed at writing, in these 'internal' terms, a 'rational reconstruction' of the history of political economy and economics, *regarding whatever aspects or episodes for which it is possible, or insofar as the record makes this possible.* For only through such a history could it emerge how far economics qualifies as an empirical science, and, from any point of view, it is of interest and importance to realise just how far this is, and has been, the case.

v. 2   We come, secondly, to a kind of explanation or account of the history of political economy and economics which has, with regard to a number of major episodes, much support from leading economists. This kind of historical account would be excluded, or given a strictly secondary place by the upholders of the kind of internal, 'rationally reconstructed' history which we have just considered under heading 1, *though it would, in fact, appear to be largely complementary or compatible.*

It has been maintained by a number of leading economists that major changes (or 'revolutions') in the subject have come about as responses to major new problems posed by historical changes in economic conditions and institutions. This kind of historical interpretation has been put forward both in quite general terms, and specifically with regard to particular major changes, or 'revolutions', in the history of economics. For example, there have been the theses of Wesley Mitchell and Leo Rogin which assert the over-riding influence

[7] *For example*: (a) there would probably be much disagreement regarding 'progress' or 'regress' on the subject of effective demand and employment theory; was there 'growth' or 'loss' as between Sir James Steuart's contribution and that of Adam Smith nine years later, which subsequently became dominant? (b) Was there gain or loss in the abandonment of the wages-fund doctrine after 1871? (c) Was not the Keynesian revolution accompanied by significant losses in monetary theory? *Such ('Kuhnian') losses are surely much more important in economics than in the natural sciences, in that they may be lost sight of as irrelevant at the time of the revolution, while subsequent historical changes (e.g. from acute deflation to rampant inflation) may reveal their significance decades later. (See below p. 314.)*

on economic theorising of the problems thrown up by the events of economic history. As Mitchell put it:

> The important departures in economic theory have been intellectual responses to changing current problems...What has been true of the development of economics in the past is likely I think...to prove true of the development of economics in the future. That is, it seems to me the growth of our science will be shaped in very large measure by the appearance of new social problems [1949, vol. I, pp. 4–5].

Alternatively, as Leo Rogin argued regarding economic theories: 'To comprehend the problem, the criteria and the conditions which have endowed it with its distinctive character, it is necessary for historical research to devote particular attention to the practical social urgencies surrounding the inception of a theory' (1956, p. 4).

We may also cite, as upholding this kind of approach and explanation regarding particular episodes, or 'revolutions', the leading Chicago economists Professor F. H. Knight and Professor Milton Friedman. Regarding classical political economy Professor Knight maintained: 'The particular trend which the development of economics took in Great Britain after Smith was largely determined by the character of the economic problems which confronted the nation, partly by reason of rapid changes in its own industrial structure (the Industrial Revolution), and partly in consequence of the French Revolutionary and Napoleonic Wars' (1956, p. 10).

According to Professor Milton Friedman, two of the major developments of economic theorising in this century have been to a significant extent brought about by historical events. Regarding 'the Keynesian revolution', Professor Friedman writes: 'The basic source of the revolution and of the reaction against the quantity theory of money was a historical event, namely the great contraction or depression.'

Professor Friedman also cites a number of events or experiences after the Second World War which have contributed to 'the Monetary Counter-Revolution', including 'a number of dramatic episodes in our recent domestic experience' (1970, pp. 11, 15, and 18).

The kind of view of the history of economics represented in the foregoing quotations is not concerned with the epistemological criteria or methodological standards of economists, but with the forces which shape their choices of problems, and which set up new problems by producing anomalies or inadequacies in their previous answers. It seeks to relate historical changes in economic ideas and theories with the changes brought about by economic history. For example, the situation regarding protection for British agriculture after the Napoleonic wars, or regarding unemployment in Britain after the First World War, can be regarded as either, or both, setting up new problems or rendering inadequate the answers to earlier problems. Moreover, historical changes, in the social–economic environment, or in institutions, change *the content* of central concepts such as 'money', 'markets', and 'unemployment'. Such factors can be found at work in the decline and fall of English classical political economy and the Jevonian revolution, as well as in both the genesis and the decline, or degeneration, of the Keynesian revolution. More recently, the much higher inflation rates, beginning in the late 1960s, not only turned the attention of economists to the inflation question, but would, by many, have been held to require *some* new element in the answers (and some would say very largely *new answers*).

However, probably a considerable divergence of view would emerge, between historical and theoretical economists, as to how far the problems thrown up for economists by economic history can be treated adequately under a few '*general*' heads, corresponding to the three or four main branches of economic theory (such as the allocation or exchange of resources; the growth of resources; the aggregate level of employment; and the monetary framework). Alternatively, it could be held that the particular, specific, historically unique features of the 'problems', which the changes of economic history set for economists, are of overriding importance. For example, there used to be much disagreement as to how far the nineteenth – and early twentieth – century business cycle could usefully be generalised about and how far each cycle was historically unique. Again, as we saw in the discussion of the Keynesian interpretation of 'the mercantilists'' doctrines on unemployment (*Chapter 5, Section III*), it has been maintained that institutional changes had rendered the unemployment problem *completely* different as between the age of the 'mercantilists' and that of Keynes. Insofar as significant generality is denied to them, then the history of economic theories could not possess any continuity, but would have to be viewed simply as a series of particular, historically specific responses to particular, historically specific problems.

Finally we would mention a type of interpretation, or 'programme', which corresponds initially with what we have been considering under Heading 2 (v. 2), but which possesses also a vitally diverging element: this is the Marxist – or vulgar Marxist – interpretation of the history of political economy and economics. The Marxist account is concerned not only with the questions or problems posed, but with insisting how the answers given are biased and distorted by class interests. Mr Dobb (1955, p. 105), for example, writes of 'the traditional basis upon which economic theory in the nineteenth century was built as an elaborate apologetic of capitalism'. (Presumably, with roughly equal justice, one could describe late twentieth-century economic theory as being largely 'an elaborate apologetic' of bureaucratic vested interests and political jobbery.) The kind of historical interpretations, on the other hand, which we have included under Heading 2, are simply concerned with *how, or where, economists find their problems and how these change, not with how they reach their answers* – whether by the rules of empirical science, or under the influence of persistent and ineradicable prejudices and biases. We would conclude, therefore, that although the Marxist, or vulgar Marxist account, in terms of ineradicable prejudices and biases, is incompatible with the kind of 'internal' scientific history recommended by Lakatos and his followers above under Heading 1, the kind of explanations which we have mainly been concerned with in this section under Heading 2, can be regarded as quite compatible, complementary, or supplementary.

v. 3.1 Thirdly, changes (or 'revolutions') in the history of economics may be seen as coming about *via*, or consisting of, changes in the intellectual standards and criteria of economists, which changes might well come about, in turn, as the result of sociological changes in the economics 'profession' and its status or ambitions. Professor G. J. Stigler has accounted in these terms for the adoption of the marginal utility theory in the closing decades of the nineteenth century.

We may note, first, that Professor Stigler rejects completely and comprehensively the kind of historical interpretation set out above under our previous heading. He maintains:

> The dominant influence upon the working range of economic theorists is the set of *internal* values and pressures of the discipline. *The subjects for study are posed by the unfolding course of scientific developments...*
> Thus I assign a minor, even an accidental, role to the contemporary economic environment in the development of economic theory since it has become a professional discipline [1965, pp. 22–3].

Clearly Professor Stigler's generalisation is about highly general or abstract theories. The more general and abstract a theory the less will it tend to relate to, or be liable to have been influenced by, any particular, specific historical event. Professor Stigler states, for example: 'The nature of economic systems has changed little since Smith's time' (op. cit., p. 23).

Insofar as the subject-matter of economics is a kind of 'system' which has changed little in two hundred 'eventful' (even 'revolution-full'), years, then clearly it is the more likely that economists' 'theories' about such 'systems' will be uninfluenced by 'events'. Certainly, for example, general and abstract allocation formulae for conditions of scarcity can be developed with little or no regard to any particular economic environment or institutions, or to any historical 'events' consisting of changes in these. However, what can be said in terms of testable, falsifiable generalisations about economic phenomena, irrespective of the changing institutions or environments in which they take place (or of which they largely consist) is likely to be either highly qualified and questionable, or else somewhat jejune in terms of empirical, predictive content.

Professor Stigler's view of the kind of dominant influences shaping economics, as well as resting on a highly abstract or generalised conception of the subject, would seem to imply a definitely natural-scientific view of its subject-matter, likening it to that of physics. In physics, historical 'events', and the contemporary environment and its changes, do not pose the subjects for study in the way in which Professors Knight and Friedman claimed that they posed for study the important problems for economists in the early nineteenth century, during the 1920s and 1930s, and after the Second World War. But the *material* of economics differs significantly from that of physics, and it changes in the course of history in fundamental ways in which the materials of physics do not change, thus giving to economics a historical dimension which physics does not possess in the same way or to the same extent.

Subsequently Professor Stigler developed his own detailed account of the adoption of the marginal utility theory (which adoption, of course, comprised a, or the, major element in what we have called the Jevonian revolution). According to Professor Stigler, utility theory 'was at hand for at least three quarters of a century before it was accepted by the science' (1973, p. 310).

Before the last decades of the nineteenth century economics was 'a science conducted by non-academics whose main interest was in the policy-implications of the science; thereafter it was conducted by professors who accepted the ruling values and incentives of scholarly activity' (op. cit., p. 310).

This historical–sociological change in the economics 'profession' led to much greater importance being attached to generality, 'rigour', and mathematical formulation. The marginal utility analysis superseded – at any rate in Britain – the Ricardo–Mill economics, primarily because it appealed to the new intellectual values arising from these sociological changes. Actually, some leading pioneers of utility analysis (such as Bentham, Dupuit and Gossen) were not academics. However, Stigler maintains that: 'What utility theory contributed was precisely the values we attribute to the academic world' (1973, p. 312).[8] But for 'at least three quarters of a century' utility theory was not accepted by economists (*in Britain*) because these academic intellectual values were not sufficiently influential (*though this was hardly the case elsewhere, as, for example, in France*).

Professor Stigler, therefore, would appear to reject the presumption

[8] It is not clear whether the above statement covers the application of utility theory to progressive taxation.

that marginal utility analysis was adopted by Jevons, Marshall and others because it provided 'better' answers than their predecessors, in terms of excess empirical content, to general problems of value, pricing and distribution. The Jevons–Marshall answers were simply more 'appropriate' to the new academic, sociological status, and intellectual values, of economists after 1870. There was apparently no question of greater, well-tested empirical content and predictive capacity, with regard, say, to the activities of monopolies or public utilities, for example. The decisive factor in this main case of theory-choice was that, eventually, after at least three quarters of a century, *sociological* changes promoted *in Britain* a shift in intellectual values. It is not clear whether Professor Stigler would maintain that this sociologically based shift in intellectual values would have been sufficient to bring about a profound change in economic theory, *even if there had been no gain, or even a loss, in empirical content.* But it seems quite possible, according to Professor Stigler, that over a long period of the history of economic thought, a theory, or 'programme', which might reasonably have been held to score more highly in terms of well-tested empirical content and predictive capacity, would have failed to gain acceptance if it had scored *less* highly in terms of the prevailing 'professional' valuations, such as generality, elegance, and scope for mathematical formulations.[9] Professor Stigler's explanation of one of the major transformations, or revolutions, in the history of political economy and economics seems to contain some profoundly sceptical implications – *if* economics is to be regarded as an empirical science.[10]

Professor Stigler has written:

The explanation of the adoption of theories by sciences is an important and neglected subject of study. Once we accept the views that there are ruling theories in a science, and that these theories are replaced by new theories which are usually independently discovered by numerous persons, we are

[9] As an example of would-be 'professionalism' influencing the *methods* of economics and the social sciences, the 1950s and 1960s may offer richer evidence than the 1870s and 1880s. As was noted at the time: 'The search for pseudo-security seems to be on the increase among the younger generation of scholars, now in their graduate school apprenticeship. Harassed by financial and family worries, they are anxious to have a technique that is just mysterious enough so that a business-man or government administrator won't quite know what to make of it. In this way they can acquire a professional label and get on with the task of making a living' (Barrington Moore, 1958, p. 94).

[10] Anyhow, it would appear that Professor Stigler would not regard the marginal, or Jevonian revolution as possessing much content, holding that 'the essential elements of the classical theory were affected in no respect' (1969, p. 225). On the other hand, the most extreme view of the 'contrast' between the 'classical' system and the neoclassical, as representing a transition from what was 'completely wrong' to what was 'correct' was taken by Professor F. H. Knight (1956, pp. 37–8). Of course, if both classical and neoclassical systems are interpreted as possessing minimal empirical content, then, in such terms, there was minimal change. Then 'correctness' or 'incorrectness' relates to taxonomy, terminology or the choice of questions.

committed to the treatment of the change in scientific theories as a general scientific problem [1973, p. 318].

If and insofar as the relevant 'science' is a 'mature' natural, empirical science, there are some basic rules for the adoptions, changes, and choices, of theories, which have certainly not been 'a neglected subject of study', and as to which there is a significantly wide degree of general consensus – in spite of intense arguments over detailed formulations and historical examples. There is a *relatively* wide measure of agreement regarding the general nature of these rules, however fierce their disagreements, as between, say, Sir Karl Popper, Professor Kuhn and the late Professor Lakatos. But insofar as economics is *not* a 'mature', natural, empirical science, but a social–historical – and empirical – science, of questionable maturity, these rules would seem to require some crucial modifications or amplifications; and we would fully agree with Professor Stigler that they have been insufficiently studied. Meanwhile there will certainly be difficulties in trying to write the history of political economy and economics as an empirical science, if, or insofar as, the subject has not, historically, been cultivated as such, according to the rules thereof.

v. 3.2   Another leading economist who has examined the nature of revolutions in economics also puts great stress on intellectual–sociological factors in the case of a major change and choice of theories. Professor H. G. Johnson, in the course of an excursion into 'the economics and sociology of intellectual change', has analysed the determining 'characteristics' for the 'success' of the Keynesian revolution in the 1930s. (It is not quite clear how far these 'characteristics' have general significance for other, or all, major changes, or revolutions in the subject, or were specifically decisive, or important, *simply* in the historical conditions of the 1930s in England.)

According to Professor Johnson: 'A revolutionary theory had to depend for its success on five main characteristics' (1975, p. 95).

The *first* of these 'characteristics' was that it had 'to attack the central proposition of conservative orthodoxy – the assumed or inferred tendency of the economy to full employment – with a new but academically acceptable analysis that reversed the proposition'.

A vital question here is what makes a new theory or analysis 'academically acceptable'. This *first* 'characteristic' for the 'success' of 'a revolutionary theory' *might* be taken to require that the new theory contradicted, or somehow improved upon, its 'orthodox' predecessor to some extent in terms of well-tested, or at least testable, empirical content, and that this is the first and essential foundation for a successful 'scientific revolution' – or was in the 1930s. But 'academic acceptability', might, on the other hand, be interpreted simply in Professor Stigler's sociological terms of shifting professional conventions and values.

However, Professor Johnson then goes on to list four more 'characteristics' which, though describable as 'internal' to the study of economics (as in Professor Stigler's explanation of the adoption of the marginal utility analysis) are 'external' (in Lakatos's sense) in being related to the then prevailing sociology or organisation of the economics profession. Professor Johnson does not describe these four characteristics as being of any less importance than the first:

> Second, the theory had to appear to be new, yet absorb as much as possible of the valid or at least not readily disputable components of existing orthodox theory. In this process, it helps greatly to give old concepts new and confusing names, and to emphasise as crucial analytical steps that have previously been taken as platitudes...
>
> Third, the new theory had to have the appropriate degree of difficulty to understand...the new theory had to be so difficult to understand that senior academics would find it neither easy nor worthwhile to study...At the same time, the new theory had to appear both difficult enough to challenge the intellectual interest of younger colleagues and students, but actually easy enough for them to master adequately...
>
> Fourth, the new theory had to offer to the more gifted and less opportunistic scholars a new methodology more appealing than those currently available...
>
> Finally, the *General Theory* offered an important empirical relationship for the emerging tribe of econometricians to measure [op. cit., pp. 95–6].

Now these four of Professor Johnson's five 'characteristics', on which the success of the last major revolution in economics is held to have depended, might well be described as pertaining to intellectual–sociological cosmetics and the 'appeal' thereof.

Insofar as these 'characteristics' were decisive, the Keynesian revolution (some would say the only or certainly the most impressive case of a revolution in the history of political economy and economics) was successfully accomplished *not*, or *not mainly*, because a theory was discovered which provided more accurate predictions, of greater empirical content, than its predecessor, relevant to the reduction of instability and unemployment. On the contrary, what was largely decisive was how far the new theory could be dressed up to give an *appearance* (rather than the reality) of novelty; or possessed a suitably appealing degree of 'difficulty' and obscurity; or would play provocatively on inter-generational jealousies; and would help provide job opportunities for young research workers (or for economists in national bureaucracies).[11]

---

[11] We suggested above (Chapter 3) that a change of generations, or the arrival of a new 'cohort' of economists, may have been a significant factor in the anti-classical rebellion and Jevonian revolution of the late 1860s and early 1870s.

With regard to the provision of job opportunities, Mr Robert Skidelsky has suggested that opportunities in Washington for 'new' economists played a part in the

It certainly does not seem clear from Professor Johnson's account of the Keynesian revolution that the possibility can be ruled out that a theory which actually yielded significantly *more* empirical and predictive content would have lost, or failed to gain, acceptance, if it had scored weakly, instead of strongly, in terms of the various kinds of 'cosmetic' intellectual–sociological 'characteristics' analysed by Professor Johnson.

Anyhow, Professor Johnson's explanation is (like that of Professor Stigler) in strongly historical–relative terms. This is because: 'The question of success for a new theory, whether revolutionary or counter-revolutionary, depends upon its fitting appropriately into the intellectual climate of its time' (1975, p. 100). Moreover, success may significantly depend upon: 'techniques of scholarly chicanery used to promote a revolution or a counter-revolution in economic theory' (op. cit., p. 103).

It is certainly impossible to deny that the employment of 'techniques of scholarly chicanery' can be discovered throughout the history of political economy and economics and doubtless throughout all other sciences and subjects. Such techniques have been widespread in various versions of the history of economic thought. But one is inevitably forced to profoundly sceptical, and even cynical, conclusions regarding political economy or economics as a serious subject, unless such techniques of scholarly chicanery, and intellectual cosmetics, can be held to have had no more than fairly short-term local effects on theory-choice.

As with the relevance of equilibrium theory the issue turns on the length of the lags and adjustment processes, or on whether there can be said to be a 'tendency', in a genuine sense, for the 'irrational' factors to be overridden by the 'rational' factors making for consensus in some valid scientific sense. Unless the scientifically 'irrational' factors have been successfully overcome, after not too lengthy lags, the history of political economy and economics can hardly be written in terms of the history of science – as described, at any rate, by Lakatos.[12]

success of the Keynesian 'revolution' in America. (Mr Skidelsky's suggestion occurred in a lecture at the Third Keynes Seminar held at the University of Kent in November 1976.)

[12] Our conclusion is similar to that of Professor A. Leijonhufvud: 'From the standpoint of normative epistemology, the basic question is whether the actually observed behavior pattern of a disciplinary collective is "progressive" in the sense of producing Growth of *validated* Knowledge. Empirical confirmation of novel predictions, I have just suggested, plays less of a role in making economists change the direction of their work than it does in Lakatos's account of "progressiveness" in the natural sciences. Thus we have what appears to be a clear-cut isue: Either we weaken Lakatos's conception of progressiveness so as to accommodate the actual behavior of economists or else we recognise that one (at least) of the social sciences will not lend itself to "rational reconstruction" along Lakatosian lines' (1976, p. 79).

VI

We may cite, next, two kinds of historical explanation of change (and 'revolution') in political economy and economics which are not, as crucial points, sufficiently fully specified as to fall clearly and explicitly into one or other of the three headings just set out in Section v above.

VI. 1   Sir John Hicks's account of the main 'revolutions' in economics seems to be close to the kind of interpretation cited under Heading 2 above, which views the history of economics in terms of responses to changing policy problems.[13] Anyhow, Sir John describes the main 'revolutions' in economics as consisting of changes of 'interest' on the part of economists, or 'changes of attention', as he calls them. Such were, notably, what Sir John calls 'the Keynesian revolution'; and also the 'catallactic revolution', which was 'the chief "revolution" in non-Marxian economics between Ricardo and Keynes' (1975, p. 322).

Not that Sir John holds that 'revolutions' are all of one kind. There are also 'fields in which economics, like the natural sciences, advances. Techniques like econometrics and linear programming are invented; and their invention is a permanent gain' (1975, pp. 320–2). However, because of the historical character of economics, as contrasted with the natural sciences, Sir John maintains: 'Our facts are not permanent, or repeatable, like the facts of the natural sciences; they change incessantly and change without repetition' (op. cit., p. 320).

Consequently, with regard to economic theories:

> There are theories which at particular times are fairly appropriate, but which are subsequently rejected, or neglected, not because they have been superseded by a more powerful theory but because in the course of time, they have become inappropriate...
>
> We may then be right to reject our present theories, not because they are wrong but because they have become inappropriate [1976, p. 208].

According to this interpretation, Jevons and Keynes, and perhaps Smith too, were mistaken and unjustified in denouncing their predecessors as *wrong* in some empirical (and/or logical) sense. They should have held that the theories of 'the Ricardo–Mill economics', or of 'the classical school' – or perhaps of 'the mercantile system' – were simply 'inappropriate', and that economists should have turned their attention to different and more 'appropriate' problems. In fact it might seem that, on Sir John's interpretation, it is not often, or for long, that economists should be held to have been 'wrong' in any logical or empirical sense. Rather, they have lingered too long on 'inappropriate' subjects or cases.

Actually, Jevons and Keynes – and presumably Smith, too –

[13] See 1975, pp. 307–26; and 1976, pp. 207ff.

undoubtedly considered themselves to be putting forward '*general*' theories, and regarded their predecessors as having put forward 'general' theories that were 'wrong' empirically – and/or logically – and not *merely* 'inappropriate' in some particular historical context. But to regard the major turning-points, or 'revolutions', in economics as mainly 'changes of attention', would seem to imply the thoroughly historical–relative view that economists should not attempt, or claim, to put forward general or universal theories, 'appropriate' at all times and places, and should not interpret the theories of others, or of predecessors, as general, universal theories, whatever claims were made on their behalf. This historical–relative view also implies that the element of continuity in the history of economic theories is rather tenuous and insignificant, since the more substantial and important changes are changes of subject, or of 'attention'.

What is not clearly specified in Sir John Hicks's account is the factor, or factors, making for 'changes of attention', or rendering a previously 'appropriate' theory 'inappropriate'. According to Sir John these cannot be anomalies, or contradictions, which could conceivably *refute* the previously 'appropriate' theory or make it 'wrong'. It would seem that these factors must probably be found in the changing processes of economic history, along with institutional changes, which set new problems of theory and policy. But the factors making for 'changes in attention' *might* be more 'internal', relating to the changing intellectual values, and changing sociology, of economists and the economics profession (as insisted upon by Professors Stigler and Johnson under Heading 3 (v. 3) above). Sir John Hicks's account, therefore, seems classifiable as somewhere in between, our headings 2 and 3.

We would agree that the kind of 'change of attention' emphasised by Sir John has been an important *partial* component of the major turning-points, changes in research programmes, or 'revolutions' in economics. Moreover, we would go on to agree that it may well be sound advice to economists today that they should now, and in the future, abandon the elaboration of would-be general theories and concentrate mainly on discovering what is historically 'appropriate'. But we cannot agree that historically that is what Sir John's predecessors as analytical economists have been *trying to do, or thought that they were succeeding in doing*, in the past. Smith, Ricardo, Jevons and Keynes *thought they were, and aimed at*, putting forward 'general' theories, which contradicted, and were 'superior' to, those of their predecessors. *Moreover, to some extent, it seems, they may well have been justified in so thinking* (or, at any rate, Smith, Jevons and Keynes may have been). They were not *merely* concerned with 'changes of attention'. Indeed the change of attention between the classicals and neoclassicals was not a complete and clear-cut change from 'plutology' to 'catallactics' (to use Sir John's terms). Smith, Ricardo, Jevons and Marshall *were all, to an important extent, concerned with a general theory of exchange value or price* – though they approached this problem from different angles. In fact the latter pair were to some extent justified in holding that they had improved significantly on their predecessors' theory (although certainly Smith's chapter on Natural and Market Price was a major contribution). That Smith and Ricardo were concerned with a general theory of value and price as part of, or contributory to, the study of the growth of wealth, or 'plutology', rather than primarily with 'catallactics' itself, is quite another point. It is also, of course, another, and quite different kind of point, whether 'plutology' generally (in 1776 or 1871) should have been regarded as a more interesting, important, and research-worthy subject than 'catallactics'.

But the question today is what scope and fruitfulness now remain for 'research programmes' in terms of general, universal theories, and whether there is not more promise in programmes in terms of *appropriate cases* ('appropriate', that is, in terms of policy relevance) which therefore would imply recognising the historical dimension in economics. This seems to be the more important implication for the present and future which emerges from Sir John Hicks's treatment of 'revolutions' in economics; and we agree with it.

VI. 2   Another account which does not fall clearly and explicitly under one of our three headings is that of Professor Bronfenbrenner.

We have noted that Professor Bronfenbrenner identifies the same three main cases of 'revolutions' in the history of political economy and economics as we have – though he gives them the broader, and in some contexts more appropriate, titles of the *'laissez-faire'*, the 'utility', and the 'macroeconomic' revolutions (1971, p. 150).

In interpreting these processes of change Professor Bronfenbrenner rejects Kuhn's 'catastrophic' theory of (natural) scientific revolutions, as well as what he calls the theory of conventional 'incrementalism' in terms of the piecemeal advance of sciences 'from one volume of a journal to another'. He suggests that 'a crude Hegelian dialectic of thesis–antithesis–synthesis may fit the principal facts' of the history of economic thought better than any other kind of explanation (op. cit., p. 136).

One problem about the thesis–antithesis–synthesis pattern seems to be the difficulty in this context in distinguishing what is 'thesis' from what is 'synthesis'. On the same page (p. 142) Professor Bronfenbrenner writes of 'the classical or laissez-faire synthesis arising from the Hume–Smith economic revolution' and 'the classical *thesis* of Smith, Ricardo and the two Mills'. Of greater importance are fundamental ambiguities in Professor Bronfenbrenner's description of the decline and degeneration of 'theses', and of the emergence of 'antitheses': 'Because the thesis turns apologetic, repetitive, and lifeless, and also because problems arise for which the answers stemming from orthodox paradigms are either lacking or unacceptable, there develop antitheses to every thesis' (op. cit., p. 139).

This description indeed closely resembles the accounts of Walter Bagehot and others in the 1870s of classical political economy in decline,[14] and might also be considered relevant to the decline and degeneration of 'Keynesian' (or Pseudo-Keynesian) economics nearly a century later.

However (as in Sir John Hicks's essay), the 'dynamic' factors which impel Professor Bronfenbrenner's 'dialectical' processes are not clearly specified, that is, the factors which sooner or later render a once confidently – or probably over-confidently – held thesis 'apologetic, repetitive, and lifeless'. For it is not clear, but is highly significant for methodological comparisons between economics and the natural sciences, whether the 'problems' out of which 'antitheses' develop, are to be conceived of as arising out of emerging 'anomalies' discovered or confirmed by critical testing, in the orthodox 'answers' to mainly *unchanging* questions (as in the natural sciences); *or* as arising from *changes in the 'appropriate' questions*, which have come about from the kind of historical–institutional changes which the natural sciences, unlike economics, do not have to take so seriously into account. To the extent that 'thesis' and 'antithesis', or contrasting models and theories, represent 'changes of attention', and are addressed to *differing* questions, 'syntheses' cannot come about in the way they might as between contrasting answers to *unchanged* questions (as in astronomy, physics, and chemistry). The sequence of 'thesis', 'antithesis', and 'synthesis', would seem to relate to *unchanging* general questions. Insofar as the 'appropriate' questions change, or there are 'changes of attention', it is hardly surprising that in the history of political economy and economics relatively little '*synthesising*' has, for the most part, come about. It might seem that the idea of a 'synthesis' should point the way, normatively, for the resolving of the great perennial *general* confrontations in the history of economic theorising, such as those between (satisfactorily) self-adjusting and non-self-adjusting models; or between cost and demand theories of value and price; or between quantity-of-money, and income (or effective demand) theories in macro-economics. Perhaps also with regard to recurring methodological confrontations the notion of synthesis may have much to offer. But the limited scope of the synthesising tendency may partly be due to the fact that 'synthetic' models will usually

---

[14] 'It lies rather dead in the public mind. Not only does it not excite, the same interest as formerly but there is not exactly the same confidence in it' (1895, p. 3).

be more general and more obviously empty, simply recognising that anything may happen. Another 'irrational' obstruction to the achievement of syntheses are the political overtones of the contrasting models. It is, of course, quite justifiable to hold political principles in an unqualified, or even extreme form. But unqualified political principles *may* unjustifiably promote, or be associated with, the dog- matic adhesion to allegedly empirical models in unqualified or extreme terms, or to the dogmatic rejection of contrasting models. However, though contrasting models may be regarded, in part, in terms of general confrontations and contradictions, which may be reconcilable in terms of a synthesis, they may also be treated as alternatives, appropriate in different historical or institutional conditions. As Professor Bronfenbrenner suggests, changes, or advances, in economic thought should be seen 'to be major accretions without any corresponding rejections of existing paradigms' (op. cit., p. 150).

This would rather imply that alternative models or theories should be regarded as 'appropriate' under different historical conditions. This brings us near to the strongly historical–relative viewpoint of Sir John Hicks, discussed above.

However, another much more serious and irrational source of 'anomalies' and degeneration is suggested by Professor Bronfen- brenner when he describes the processes by which a 'thesis', or 'pro- gramme', may be rendered 'apologetic, repetitive and lifeless': 'With the passing of the generations, a thesis hardens from doctrine to dogma. Its choirs of angels become choirs of parrots, chanting "supply and demand", "full employment", or "planned society" as the case may be. At the same time...there is leached out of the original thesis whatever implications seem threatening to the ruling class' (1971, p. 139).

Two kinds of degeneration are to be noted here: (a) 'hardening from doctrine to dogma', and *secondly*, (b) the tendency towards apologetic.

As regards the hardening into dogma, the over-confidence and pretentiousness – or the appearance or proclamation thereof – generated by the initial revolution may be reinforced by short-run, and/or apparent, policy success. That nothing fails like success is liable to be true also in the history of economic thought. For when, and insofar as, the original doctrines are hardened over-confidently into dogmas, and protected against testing and retesting, the flexibility and sensitiveness to changing real-world conditions which made for the success of the work of the original 'revolutionary' leader may be lost by the epigoni. Furthermore, the attitude of regarding economic theories – including especially a new 'revolutionary' theory – as on a par, epistemologically, with the theories of the natural sciences – and Keynes was compared with Einstein – may encourage a more

exaggerated belief than is justified in the relative durability and resistance to obsolescence of the new economic theory or discovery. A
more serious development may be that the hardening into dogma and
mystique of the original theory may bring a significant *alteration* in
the theory or doctrine, as original qualifications and exceptions are forgotten or modified. The transitions from Smith to the Ricardians and
from Keynes to his Pseudo-Keynesian successors might be examples
of such processes, which are much furthered by popularisation.

It may be most serious of all when the epigoni also seek to bend
the original doctrine in favour of their own policy predilections, or
in favour of newly emerging political forces on whose bandwagon they
may wish to secure a place. Professor Bronfenbrenner noted how
implications threatening to a new ruling class are liable to get strained
out of a current orthodoxy, and it is likely that this kind of political
distortion will in due course weaken empirical validity or relevance
(Hutchison, 1977b).

Whether in the classical or Ricardian case this kind of slippage into
degeneration and political bias was important, depends largely on how
the role of J. S. Mill and his *Principles* is regarded. According to the
Marxists, J. S. Mill was guilty of just the kind of political bowdlerising
regarding implications 'threatening to the ruling class' described by
Professor Bronfenbrenner. But it is quite reasonable, on the other
hand, to regard J. S. Mill's restatement, or revision, as having immensely *improved* the original Ricardian doctrines. On this issue, we are
not concerned to pronounce here. However, Keynes's *General Theory*,
in any case, was not followed by any work corresponding to J. S. Mill's
Principles, unless what is called the 'neoclassical synthesis', propounded
by Samuelson, Hicks and others, can be regarded as a kind of corresponding development (which has also been denounced for betraying
and emasculating the original, as J. S. Mill's *Principles* was denounced
by Marxists). But there is plenty of evidence for the view that in terms
of *policy* doctrines, Keynes's original teachings, at any rate in their
country of origin, came to be crucially altered as 'the Keynesian
revolution' proceeded after the master's death (Hutchison, 1977b).

VII

We shall now state here somewhat briefly and summarily our own
standpoint and conclusions regarding the various interpretations (just
reviewed in Sections v and vi) of the history of political economy and
economics, and of the various 'programmes' for the writing of it. We
stated at the start of our review that these various interpretations, or
'programmes', were not necessarily mutually exclusive, but in fact
should be regarded as, to an important extent, complementary. Cer-

tainly, insofar as the history of political economy and economics is not necessarily epistemologically homogeneous, it may well be that some types of interpretation, or explanation, are valid, adequate, and relevant, regarding some phases (or 'revolutions'), while other types are more applicable in other cases. For example, the kind of intellectual–sociological factors invoked by Professor Stigler for explaining the adoption of marginal utility theory may have much more importance and relevance for that episode, or revolution, than for others. But we would definitely go further than this. In particular, interpretations, or 'programmes', of our types 1 and 2 should be regarded as, up to a point, complementary, those of type 2 being concerned with how the *questions* posed to economists change (to an extent and in a manner different from the natural sciences); while those of type 1 are concerned with showing how economists follow (insofar as they do) particular rules, criteria, and epistemological objectives (those of empirical science) in trying to provide *answers*.

However, insofar as the more extreme historical–relative interpretations of type 2 were adopted, it would follow that economic theories had closer affinities with historical explanations than with those of science. Moreover, some kinds of sociological–intellectual interpretation (belonging under our Heading 3) *might* imply that the intellectual criteria and objectives of (political) economists could not be described, or 'rationally reconstructed', in accordance with rules of empirical science, as required by the interpretations, and 'programmes', of our type 1.

But we would repeat that the Lakatosian 'programme' of type 1 should certainly be carried *as far as it can* in the history of political economy and economics. It simply seems that it will not be possible, because of the nature of the material, to demonstrate such interpretations, in any clear-cut or relatively definitive or uncontroversial manner, for significant phases of the history of the subject. We would not, however, attempt to insist, with Lakatos, that, as regards the history of economics, this kind of interpretation or programme *must* be regarded as primary, and others as merely secondary or tertiary. There would not be much point in such a claim if such a programme, to an important extent, cannot be completed *reasonably* definitely and uncontroversially, and without leaving out very important factors in theory change. We would come to the same conclusion for the history of economics regarding our type 1 – as well as for the most part type 2, and to some extent even type 3.1 and also 3.2 – as Kuhn does regarding what he calls 'internal' and 'external' approaches to the history of science: 'They are, in fact, complementary concerns. Until they are practised as such, each drawing from the other, important aspects of scientific development are unlikely to be understood' (1968, vol. xiv, p. 81).

VIII

We would include here some points regarding the relation between the concept of 'revolutions' in political economy and economics, as used in this chapter and volume, and Professor Kuhn's concept of 'scientific revolutions' as developed in his much discussed work.

VIII. 1   As emphasised in the Foreword to this volume, we have not been using the term 'revolution' in the relatively elaborate sense which it had in the work of Professor T. S. Kuhn. We would stress again that the account of Kuhn – and that of Popper and Lakatos – of the development of the sciences was distilled mainly from physics and chemistry. It may be very seriously misleading and presumptuous to assume that concepts and patterns applicable to astronomy, physics, and chemistry (assuming that they are applicable and illuminating as regards these sciences) will also yield accurate and significant lessons in the case of economics and the social sciences. However, some useful parallels and analogies may be forthcoming.

VIII. 2   Two Kuhnian notions which *do* seem to apply significantly in the history of economic thought are (a) that, as already noted, development is discontinuous, insofar as changes have taken place with a highly unequal pace and profundity; and (b) that major turning-points or revolutions have involved 'losses': 'There are losses as well as gains in scientific revolutions, and scientists tend to be peculiarly blind to the former' (1970a, p. 167).

Whether this is true for astronomy, physics, and chemistry (or whether it is not) it is *a fortiori, and much more*, true and important regarding economics. In fact, as Kuhn himself says regarding what he calls 'proto-sciences', or 'many of the social sciences today': 'No more than in philosophy and the arts...do they result in clear-cut progress.'[15] This brings us to 'the historical dimension'.

VIII. 3   Anyhow, there is one essential basic elaboration of the Kuhnian framework which arises out of the inevitable historical dimension which is so much more important for economics and the social sciences than it is for the natural sciences, with which Kuhn was concerned. This point has been cogently developed by Professors Kunin and Weaver:

[15] 1970a, p. 244. Professor P. A. Samuelson in his celebrated textbook seems to describe 'revolutions' in economics in rather blithely confident Kuhnian terms as representing unqualified '*progress*'. Of the Keynesian 'revolution', Professor Samuelson writes: 'Once again it was a case where, funeral by funeral, science progressed.' In the first place this may be a rather over-simplified summary of Kuhn's account; and secondly, it begs the question of the complete applicability of Kuhn's theory, derived from physics, or 'mature' natural sciences, to the history of political economy and economics (1976, pp. 843 and 845).

It is important to note that the 'nature' which the physical scientist learns to see in a new way is a historically unchanging one. By this we mean that the structure and behaviour of the physical universe toward which these sciences are directed do not exhibit change on a time scale which would alter significantly any important characteristics of the population of that universe. Economics, however, like other social sciences, is manifestly different from physical science in that it is a profoundly historical science; its roots lie in the attempt to understand a particular configuration of human (social) institutions...

Normal economic research is vulnerable to anomalies not only from the internal dynamics of the scientific enterprise itself but also from sources external to the science as such – stemming from changes in the economic universe being studied. This latter source of anomaly, distinguishing economics (and the social sciences in general) from the natural sciences, means that a model of paradigm change tailored for the natural sciences must be opened up to include the more complex set of forces involved in the progress of paradigm selection in the social sciences [1971, pp. 394-5].

This 'more complex set of forces' includes both changes in interest brought about by political changes (e.g. more interest in questions of poverty and distribution following the extension of the franchise in Britain in the last third of the nineteenth century); as well as the invalidation of previous answers by historical–institutional changes amounting to the posing of new or different questions (as with the final breakdown of the Ricardian natural wage theory).

VIII. 4   As Professor Bronfenbrenner has emphasised, Kuhn's cataclysmic account of 'revolutions' does not apply so drastically in economics (whether or not it applies to the natural sciences). Theories and 'programmes' in economics have not, for the most part, been displaced and destroyed *very* rapidly, completely, and lastingly, 'with a total victory for one of the two opposing camps' (Kuhn, 1970a, p. 166), because the possibilities of *relatively* decisive testing do not exist to the same extent in economics as, for the most part, in the natural sciences, and because political–ideological factors make for greater tenacity.

VIII. 5   Because no 'theory', 'programme', or 'paradigm', can *validly* achieve the degree of 'revolutionary' supremacy obtained, in leading cases, in the history of physics, 'normal' science can never be based on the same kind of *relatively* firm presumptions. 'Normal Science' must always, in economics, involve a more questionable and blinkered approach. Even regarding sciences like physics and chemistry, Sir Karl Popper denounced the presumptions of 'normal science', while recognising its existence:

'Normal' science, in Kuhn's sense, exists. It is the activity of the non-revolutionary, or more precisely, the not-too-critical professional: of the science student who accepts the ruling dogma of the day; who does not wish to challenge it; and who accepts a new revolutionary theory only if almost everybody else is ready to accept it – if it becomes fashionable by a kind of bandwagon effect. To resist a new fashion needs perhaps as much courage as was needed to bring it about...

The 'normal' scientist, as described by Kuhn, has been badly taught. He has been taught in a dogmatic spirit: he is a victim of indoctrination [1970, pp. 52–3].

Whether or not this kind of 'normal' science is prevalent, and whether or not Sir Karl's severe judgment is justified in the case of the natural sciences, this account has much justification regarding 'normal science' in economics (whatever its kind or degree of 'normality'). In fact, it seems that various schools in economics have been inclined to promote pseudo-normality along the lines outlined by Professor Feyerabend:

More than one social scientist has pointed out to me that now at last he had learned how to turn his field into a 'science' – by which of course he meant that he had learned how to *improve* it. The recipe, according to these people, is to restrict criticism, to reduce the number of comprehensive theories to one, and to create a normal science that has this one theory as its paradigm. Students must be prevented from speculating along different lines and the more restless colleagues must be made to conform and 'to do serious work' [1970, p. 198].

Most 'schools' in economics since the Physiocrats have, to a lesser or greater extent, followed this line.

VIII. 6   Finally, with regard to comparisons and contrasts with Kuhnian concepts, we would agree with Professor Bronfenbrenner that it does *not* hold in economics that, as Kuhn has it for the natural sciences: 'Once it has achieved the status of a paradigm, a scientific theory is declared invalid *only if an alternate candidate is available to take its place*...The decision to reject one paradigm is always simultaneously the decision to accept another' (1971, p. 140, and Kuhn, 1970, p. 77).

However, we would *dis*agree with Professor Bronfenbrenner insofar as he regards the *failure* of economists to uphold the principle of 'the king is dead, long live the king', as a kind of unfortunate 'illogical negativism' on the part of economists and social scientists as contrasted with natural scientists. According to Professor Bronfenbrenner, economists, unfortunately, 'have such great patience' with the man, 'who says of received doctrine, "It simply isn't so. It's just theory. I don't know what's wrong with it, but it isn't helpful, it isn't relevant, and I won't accept it." (This kind of thought substitute is unfortunately more prevalent among social scientists, including economists, than among natural scientists)' (1971, p. 140).

Now it is one thing to demand that someone who rejects a doctrine – 'received' or otherwise – should formulate his objections in a clear and arguable form. But it is quite another thing to demand that if he rejects one theory he *must* straightway commit himself to an alternative (assuming that this demand is not tautological and that agnosticism is not an 'alternative theory'). On the contrary, it would be very healthy if explicit agnosticism was much more widespread than it is among economists. The man of action, it can be argued, *has* to act (for even doing nothing is a kind of action) on *some kind* of 'theory'. But this does not have to be a formalised theory of the kind academics develop: and, in any case, an academic does not *have* to have an immediate replacement, or *any* replacement, for a theory which he regards as invalidated. There is always the perfectly valid and justifiable position of the agnostic. In fact historically, after 1870, after the loss of confidence in the 'classical', or Ricardo–Mill, distribution theory, though there was hardly a state of general agnosticism, there was, for a decade or two, no replacement around which an orthodox consensus gathered. (But absence of consensus does not imply that *individuals* were taking up agnostic positions – quite probably the reverse.)

IX

There are one or two further conclusions we would summarise:

IX. 1   Any account of the changes, or shifting theory-choices, major or minor (or 'normal' or 'revolutionary') in the history of economic thought, must take full account of the complexity of the material and of its various kinds of components. That this renders the account untidy and indecisive may be inevitable in view of the nature of the material. A neatly exclusivist or monistic account will not do justice to the complexity of the actual processes.

The main distinction is between (1) changes with regard to the empirical content of theories concerned with processes assumed to be unchanged; and (2) changes of 'attention' with regard to the processes considered most appropriate for study, or in the nature of the problems which deserve attention. There are further types of changes which we have already listed. In the complex major changes described as 'revolutions' in economics and political economy these different kinds of changes are mixed together pretty intricately.

IX. 2   Moreover, these different kinds of changes are involved with different kinds of causal relationships. Changes in empirical content will primarily come about through the 'internal' processes of economists accepting theories, or joining 'research programmes', which show an extension of empirical content; while 'changes in attention', or in the processes studied, may probably mainly come about either through the changes of political and economic history and institutions, or through sociological–intellectual changes in the professional status and interests of economists.

IX. 3   In the major changes, or 'revolutions', with which we have been concerned – the Smithian, or *laissez-faire*; the Jevonian, or utility, or 'marginalist', and the Keynesian or macro-economic, – these different kinds of elements have been blended together in differing mixes. The changes in these various elements have also been shaped by different kinds of 'causes', or causal relationships. It is the task of the historian of economic thought to distinguish and appraise these variegated processes without over-simplifying them.

IX. 4   The complexity and variety of the changes involved in the history of political economy and economics, and the growth or 'progress' of knowledge in the subject, may be superficially, but perhaps usefully, compared with economic changes, and with economic growth and 'progress', in the course of economic history. On highly simplified assumptions, index-numbers of 'economic growth' can, of course, be constructed, though the significance of these will at once become highly problematic if changes in tastes are to be taken into account. With regard to growth and 'progress' in economic knowledge, changes in tastes or interests may clearly be of major importance, while changes in economic institutions or behaviour may invalidate what had been justifiably regarded as valid economic knowledge. Hence change *may* bring what can reasonably be regarded as losses and may represent 'regress' rather than progress.

IX. 5   Of course there are certain kinds or components of economic knowledge in which more or less unqualified, clear-cut growth or progress might be said to take place. This is notably the case with basic empirical and statistical material and also with regard to mathematical and statistical techniques. The steady growth of historical and statistical material might well be regarded as the most solid basis for a belief in the progress of economic knowledge. But even here there might be historical changes in economic behaviour, or in the more important economic problems, which might render both material and techniques irrelevant, or less useful – especially if they were accompanied by changes in intellectual tastes or interests. Anyhow, changes or extensions in the empirical content of theories and programmes, whether regarded as gains or losses, or a balance of the two, are much more difficult to assess, especially when there may well be important changes in intellectual tastes and interests, or in the problems considered important.

IX. 6   It might seem remarkable that leading theoretical economists (e.g. Sir John Hicks, and Professors H. G. Johnson and G. J. Stigler) emphasise changes originating mainly 'externally', in the problems considered appropriate or needing attention, or in intellectual criteria and tastes, as major and *possibly decisive* components in the more important turning-points, or 'revolutions', in the history of economic thought.

IX. 7   Perhaps economics has grown too massive, in terms both of its subject-matter and the numbers concerned with it, for any new 'revolution' in terms of general theories, or in economics as a whole, to be feasible. In fact the subject as a whole may have grown into something too extensive, sprawling, and decentralised to be transformable, or much affected, as an entirety or in large part, by a single 'revolutionary' process. The busy new suburbs sprawling out in all directions – public utility economics, transport, health, education, defence, urban, regional economics, etc., etc. – go their own ways largely in intellectual independence of the run-down city centre of 'general theory', now increasingly abandoned for residential purposes, and given over to political gang warfare and attempted 'putsches', coups, and counter-coups at City Hall.

Perhaps there is a pointer here as to the direction of a further 'revolution', if it emerges as that. This would be a methodological 'revolution', away from the ever more refined cultivation of 'general' models or 'theories', usually extremely abstract and possessing a very tenuous empirical content, if any. The programme of constructing 'general theory' (or theories) was launched with the emergence of political economy in the late seventeenth century. It supplemented the limited, historical–relative, empirical efforts of those who Schumpeter called 'consultant administrators', as political economy became an autonomous discipline. In *The Wealth of Nations* the general self-adjusting model was based on, as well as qualified and fortified by, extensive historical, psychological and institutional studies. But since the methodological 'revolution' of James Mill and Ricardo, the 'programme' or 'paradigm' has often consisted of the cultivation of ever more precise, and frequently extremely abstract, maximising, self-equilibrating 'models'. Useful results of limited validity have certainly been achieved, which will continue to be useful and valid, and which should be taught – with due warnings – in textbooks. But the costs, in terms of the kind of extreme and arbitrary abstractions introduced by Ricardo, have always been high, and have perhaps, for a long time, hardly been covered by the diminishing returns (diminishing, that is, in terms of the kind of empirical, predictive, policy-relevant content, which economists have usually and traditionally aimed at and claimed).

For this evergreen type of 'model' became highly dependent on the perfect knowledge postulate, and the extremely restrictive abstractions involved in this assumption have seldom been adequately recognised or admitted since its emergence with the James Mill–Ricardo methodological 'revolution' more than a century and a half ago. Perhaps the programme, or 'paradigm', based on these kinds of abstract 'models' should now be phased out, or relegated to a minor role in a new kind of 'consultant–administrative' economics, which in a primitive form had been dominant in the seventeenth and eighteenth centuries. This is certainly *not* to say that self-adjusting processes are not worth further exploration. Quite the reverse. They deserve even more study in rapidly changing institutional conditions. But they should be studied much more specifically, in terms of historical and institutional methods, rather than in terms of extreme general abstractions.

J. S. Mill, over a century ago, and Alfred Marshall, about three quarters of a century ago, both had the idea that the general 'theory' of the subject, or the 'organon', as Marshall strangely called it, was reasonably complete, and that what usefully remained for economists were particular applications of the 'organon' to the developing problems which social and economic history threw up. J. S. Mill was soon shown to be rather seriously wrong, while Marshall's 'organon' emerged as gravely inadequate for the monetary and macroeconomic problems of the twentieth century. But the instincts of these two great minds may probably not have been *completely* at fault in holding that general theories would, in the longer, or not so much longer, run, yield sharply diminishing returns in terms of the intellectual objectives traditionally aimed at and claimed by economists. It might seem that the insights of Mill and Marshall were by no means fundamentally misconceived, but simply, as the finest predictive insights sometimes are, premature in respect of the time scale.

General theories or theorising in political economy set out in the eighteenth century with the grandiose intellectual ambition of 'doing a Newton' for the political and economic world. To a very limited and questionable extent this aim was carried out in the general, Smithian self-adjusting model. Certainly, considerable advances were, in some directions, forthcoming. But the parallel with Newtonian physics was always profoundly misconceived and misleading. To-day it seems very doubtful whether the way forward should be sought in programmes for a new 'general' theory, or in terms of what has been called 'the waiting for Newton syndrome' (more often among economists expressed as a 'waiting for a new Keynes syndrome'). Instead of waiting for Newton, or a new Keynes, it may be more promising to seek to restore the historical, institutional and psychological components of the subject, so masterfully incorporated in *The Wealth of Nations*.

Bibliography

Foreword

Blaug, M., 1973: 'Was There a Marginal Revolution?', in *The Marginal Revolution in Economics*, ed. R. D. C. Black, A. W. Coats and C. D. W. Goodwin, pp. 3ff.

Bronfenbrenner, M., 1971: 'The "Structure of Revolutions" in Economic Thought', *History of Political Economy*, vol. 3, pp. 136ff.

Coats, A. W., 1969: 'Is there a Structure of Scientific Revolutions in Economics?', *Kyklos*, vol. 22, pp. 289ff.

Dobb, M. H., 1973: *Theories of Value and Distribution since Adam Smith.*

Goodwin, C. D. W., 1973: 'Marginalism Moves to the New World', in *The Marginal Revolution in Economics*, ed. R. D. C. Black, A. W. Coats and C. D. W. Goodwin, pp. 285ff.

Gordon, D. F., 1965: 'The Role of the History of Economic Thought in the Understanding of Modern Economic Theory', *Papers and Proceedings of the AEA*, vol. 55, pp. 119ff.

Hicks, Sir John, 1975: 'The Scope and Status of Welfare Economics', *Oxford Economic Papers*, vol. 27, pp. 307ff.

1976: '"Revolutions" in Economics', in *Method and Appraisal in Economics*, ed. S. Latsis, pp. 207ff.

Hutchison, T. W., 1977: *Knowledge and Ignorance in Economics.*

Johnson, H. G., 1975: 'The Keynesian Revolution and the Monetarist Counter-revolution', in *Economics and Society*, pp. 91ff.

Kuhn, T. S., 1970: *The Structure of Scientific Revolutions*, 2nd ed.

Kunin, L. and Weaver, F. S., 1971: 'On the Structure of Scientific Revolutions in Economics', in *History of Political Economy*, vol. 3, pp. 391ff.

Leijonhufvud, A., 1976: 'Schools, "revolutions" and research programmes in economic theory', in *Method and Appraisal in Economics*, ed. S. Latsis, pp. 65ff.

Routh, G., 1975: *The Origins of Economic Ideas*, 1975.

Chapter 1: The Wealth of Nations *and the Smithian Revolution*

Ashley, W. J., 1900: 'The Historical School of Economists', *Dictionary of Political Economy*, ed. R. H. I. Palgrave, vol. 1, p. 310.

Bagehot, W., 1881: 'Adam Smith as a Person', in *Biographical Studies*, ed. R. H. Hutton, pp. 125ff.

1895: 'Adam Smith and our Modern Economy', in *Economic Studies*, ed. R. H. Hutton, pp. 125ff.

Bitterman, H. J., 1940: 'Smith's Empiricism and the Law of Nature', *Journal of Political Economy*, vol. XLVII, pp. 487ff and 703ff.

Bonar, J., 1922: *Philosophy and Political Economy*, 3rd ed.
Bowley, M., 1973: *Studies in the History of Economic Theory before 1870.*
Brittan, S., 1973: *Capitalism and the Permissive Society.*
Buchanan, J. M., 1976: 'Public Goods and Natural Liberty', in *The Market and the State*, ed. T. Wilson and A. Skinner, pp. 271ff.
Campbell, T. D., 1971: *Adam Smith's Science of Morals.*
Checkland, S. G., 1976: 'Adam Smith and the Bankers', *Essays on Adam Smith*, ed. A. Skinner and T. Wilson, pp. 504ff.
Clark, G. N., 1932: 'The Study of Economic History', in *The Study of Economic History*, ed. N. B. Harte, 1971.
Cropsey, J., 1957: *Polity and Economy.*
Douglas, P. H., 1928: 'Smith's Theory of Value and Distribution', in J. H. Hollander et al., *Adam Smith, 1776–1926*, pp. 77ff.
Fay, C. R., 1956: *Adam Smith and the Scotland of his Day.*
Finlay, James, and Co., 1951: *James Finlay & Co, 1750–1950.*
Forbes, D., 1954: '"Scientific" Whiggism: Adam Smith and John Millar', *Cambridge Journal*, vol. VII, 11, pp. 643ff.
Hollander, S., 1973: *The Economics of Adam Smith.*
Hutcheson, F., 1755: *A System of Moral Philosophy*, 2 vols.
Hutchison, T. W., 1953a: *A Review of Economic Doctrines 1870–1929.*
    1953b: 'Berkeley's *Querist* and its Place in the Economic Thought of the 18th Century', *British Journal for the Philosophy of Science*, vol. IV, 13, pp. 52ff.
    1958: 'Keynes und die Geschichte der Klassischen Nationalökonomie', *Zeitschrift für Nationalökonomie*, Bd VIII, Heft 5, pp. 393ff.
Keynes, J. M., 1938: Review of W. R. Scott, *Adam Smith as Student and Professor*, *Economic History*, vol. 3, pp. 33ff.
Keynes, J. N., 1917: *Scope and Method of Political Economy*, 4th ed.
Leslie, Cliffe, n.d.: *Essays in Political and Moral Philosophy*, 2nd ed.
Lindgren, J. R., 1973: *The Social Philosophy of Adam Smith.*
Macfie, A. L., 1967: *The Individual in Society.*
Marshall, A., 1975: *The Early Writings of Alfred Marshall*, ed. J. K. Whitaker.
Meek, R. L., 1971: 'Smith, Turgot and the "Four Stages" Theory', *History of Political Economy*, vol. 3, pp. 9ff.
    1973: *Studies in the Labour Theory of Value*, 2nd ed.
Morrow, Glen, 1928: 'Adam Smith: Moralist and Philosopher', in J. H. Hollander et al., *Adam Smith, 1776–1926*, pp. 156ff.
O'Brien, D., 1975: *The Classical Economists.*
Pascal, R., 1938: 'Property and Society, The Scottish Historical School of the 18th Century', *Modern Quarterly*, pp. 167ff.
Pigou, A. C., 1929: *Economics of Welfare*, 3rd ed.
Political Economy Club, 1876: *Revised Report of the Proceedings at the Dinner of 31st May 1876.*
Rae, J., 1895: *Life of Adam Smith.*
Reisman, D. A., 1976: *Adam Smith's Sociological Economics.*
Richardson, G. B., 1976: 'Adam Smith on Competition and Increasing Returns', in *Essays on Adam Smith*, ed. A. Skinner and T. Wilson, pp. 350ff.
Robertson, H. M., 1976: 'Euge! Belle! Dear Mr. Smith', *South African Journal of Economics*, vol. 44 (4), pp. 378ff.
Schumpeter, J. A., 1954: *History of Economic Analysis.*
Scott, W. R., 1937: *Adam Smith as Student and Professor.*
    1938: *Adam Smith, an Oration.*
Senior, N., 1836: *Outline of Political Economy.*

Small, A., 1907: *Adam Smith and Modern Sociology.*
Smith, A., 1795: *Essays on Philosophical Subjects.*
1797: *Theory of Moral Sentiments*, 8th ed.
1895: Letter to the Duc de la Rochefoucauld, reproduced in *Economic Journal*, vol. 5, p. 165.
1937: *An Inquiry into the Nature and Causes of the Wealth of Nations*, Modern Library edition.
1963: *Lectures on Rhetoric and Belles Lettres*, ed. J. M. Lothian.
Stigler, G. J., 1950: *Five Lectures on Economic Problems.*
Tawney, R. H., 1932: 'The Study of Economic History', in *The Study of Economic History*, ed. N. B. Harte, 1971.
Thomson, J., 1859: *An Account of the Life, Lectures and Writings of W. Cullen, M.D.*, 2 vols.
Unwin, G., 1908: 'The Aims of Economic History', in *The Study of Economic History*, ed. N. B. Harte, 1971.
Viner, J., 1928: 'Adam Smith and Laissez-faire', in J. H. Hollander et al., *Adam Smith 1776–1926*, pp. 116ff.
1965: *Guide to John Rae's Life of Adam Smith.*
1968: 'Adam Smith', in *Encyclopaedia of the Social Sciences*, vol. 14.
Young, A. A., 1928: 'Increasing Returns and Economic Progress', *Economic Journal*, vol. 38, pp. 527ff.

Chapter 2: *James Mill and Ricardian economics: a methodological revolution?*

Bagehot, W., 1895: 'Ricardo', in *Economic Studies*, ed. R. H. Hutton, pp. 197ff.
Bain, A., 1882: *James Mill, a Biography.*
Cannan, E., 1917: *History of the Theories of Production and Distribution, 1776–1848*, 3rd ed.
Duncan, G., 1973: *Marx and Mill*, 1973.
Fetter, F. W., 1969: 'The Rise and Decline of Ricardian Economics', *History of Political Economy*, vol. 1, pp. 67ff.
Forbes, D., 1951 (October): 'James Mill and India', *Cambridge Journal*, pp. 19ff.
Halévy, E., 1928: *The Growth of Philosophic Radicalism*, translated by M. Morris.
Harte, N. B. (ed.), 1971: *The Study of Economic History.*
Hayek, F. A., 1949: 'Individualism: True and False', in *Individualism and Economic Order*, pp. 1ff.
Hicks, Sir John, 1975: 'The Scope and Status of Welfare Economics', *Oxford Economic Papers*, vol. 27, pp. 307ff.
1976: '"Revolutions" in Economics', in *Method and Appraisal in Economics*, ed. S. Latsis, pp. 207ff.
Hollander, S., 1974: 'Ricardo and the Corn Laws: A Revision', A paper for the 6th International Congress on Economic History.
Hutchison, T. W., 1952: 'Some Questions about Ricardo', *Economica*, vol. 19 (N.S.), pp. 415ff.
1953: 'Ricardo's Correspondence', *Economica*, vol. 20 (N.S.), pp. 263ff.
1956: 'Bentham as an Economist', *Economic Journal*, vol. 66, pp. 288ff.
Inglis, B., 1972: *Poverty and the Industrial Revolution*, Paperback ed.
Johnson, H. G., 1975: 'The Keynesian Revolution and the Monetarist Counter-revolution', in *On Economics and Society*, pp. 91ff.
Keynes, J. M., 1933: *Essays in Biography.*
1937: 'The General Theory of Employment', *Quarterly Journal of Economics*, vol. 51, pp. 209ff.

Koot, G., 1975: 'Cliffe Leslie and the Historical School', *History of Political Economy*, vol. 7.

Malthus, T. R., 1836: *Principles of Political Economy*, 2nd ed.

Marx, K., 1961: *Capital*, English translation, Moscow.

Mill, J., translated, 1805: C. Villers: *An Essay on the Spirit and Influence of the Reformation of Luther*.

1858: *History of India*, ed. H. H. Wilson.

1966: *Selected Economic Writings*, ed. D. Winch.

Mill, J. S., 1909: *Principles of Political Economy*, ed. W. J. Ashley.

1924: *Autobiography*, Worlds Classics.

Myrdal, G., 1953: *The Political Element in the Development of Economic Theory*.

Pigou, A. C. (ed.), 1925: *Memorials of Alfred Marshall*.

Ricardo, D., 1951 and 1952: *Works of D. Ricardo*, ed. P. Sraffa, vols. I–IV, and vols. V–IX.

Rima, I., 1975: 'James Mill and Classical Economics: a Reappraisal', *Eastern Economic Journal*, vol. 2, pp. 113ff.

Robbins, L. C., 1952: *The Theory of Economic Policy in English Classical Political Economy*.

Sayers, R. S., 1971: 'Ricardo's Views on Monetary Questions', in A. W. Coats, ed., *The Classical Economists and Economic Policy*, pp. 33ff.

Schumpeter, J. A., 1954: *History of Economic Analysis*.

Smith, A., 1937: *The Wealth of Nations*, Modern Library edition.

Sowell, T., 1974: *Classical Economics Reconsidered*.

Sraffa, P. (ed.), 1951 and 1952: *Works of D. Ricardo*, vols. I–IV (1951), vols. V–IX (1952).

Stigler, G. J., 1950: *Five Lectures on Economic Problems*.

1965: *Essays in the History of Economics*.

Thweatt, W. O., 1976: 'James Mill and the Early Development of Comparative Advantage', *History of Political Economy*, vol. 8, pp. 207ff.

Tucker, G. S. L., 1960: *Progress and Profits in British Economic Thought*.

Wilson, H. H. (ed.), 1858: James Mill: *History of India*.

Winch, D. (ed.), 1966: James Mill: *Selected Economic Writings*.

Chapter 3: *The decline and fall of English classical political economy and the Jevonian revolution*

Arrow, K. J., 1968: 'Economic Equilibrium', *International Encyclopedia of the Social Sciences*, vol. 4.

Arrow, K. J. and Starrett, D. A., 1973: 'Cost – and Demand – Theoretical Approaches to the Theory of Price Determination', in *Carl Menger and the Austrian School of Economics*, ed. J. R. Hicks and W. Weber, pp. 129ff.

Ashley, W. J., 1893: 'On the Study of Economic History', *Quarterly Journal of Economics*, vol. VII, pp. 115ff.

Bagehot, W., 1895: *Economic Studies*, ed. R. H. Hutton.

Barucci, P., 1973: 'The Spread of Marginalism in Italy', in *The Marginal Revolution in Economics*, ed. R. D. C. Black, A. W. Coats and C. D. W. Goodwin, pp. 246ff.

Bastable, C. F., 1962: 'Comparison Between the Position of Economic Science in 1860 and 1894', in *Essays in Economic Method*, ed. R. L. Smyth, pp. 126ff.

Black, R. D. C. (ed.), 1970: Jevons's *Theory of Political Economy*, Pelican Books.

Blaug, M., 1956: 'The Empirical Content of Ricardian Economics', *Journal of Political Economy*, vol. 64, pp. 41ff.

1962: *Economic Theory in Retrospect*.

Cairnes, J. E., 1873: 'Political Economy and *Laissez Faire*', (1870) in *Essays in Political Economy*.
   1874: *Some Leading Principles of Political Economy*.
Cannan, E., 1929: *A Review of Economic Theory*.
Checkland, S. G., 1951: 'Economic Opinion in England as Jevons Found It', *Manchester School*, vol. 19, pp. 143ff.
Clark, J. B., 1904: *The Problem of Monopoly*.
Court, W. H. B., 1964: *A Concise Economic History of Britain*.
Dobb, M. H., 1973: *Theories of Value and Distribution since Adam Smith*.
Edgeworth, F. Y., 1881: *Mathematical Psychics*.
Galton, F., 1877: *Journal of the Statistical Society*, pp. 468ff.
Gerschenkron, A., 1969: 'History of Economic Doctrines and Economic History', *Papers and Proceedings of the American Economic Association*, vol. 59, p. 1.
Hicks, J. R., 1934: 'Leon Walras', *Econometrica*, vol. 2, pp. 338ff.
Hicks, Sir John, 1975: 'The Scope and Status of Welfare Economics', *Oxford Economic Papers*, vol. 27, pp. 307ff.
Hicks, Sir John, 1976: Review of *The Early Writings of Afred Marshall*, *Economic Journal*, vol. 86, pp. 376–9.
Hicks, J. R. and Weber, W. (ed.), 1973: *Carl Menger and the Austrian School of Economics*.
Hollander, S., 1968: 'The Role of the State in Vocational Training: the Classical Economists' View', *Southern Economic Journal*, vol. 34, pp. 513ff.
Hutchison, T. W., 1953: *A Review of Economic Doctrines 1870–1929*.
   1955: 'Insularity and Cosmopolitanism in Economic Ideas', *Papers and Proceedings of the American Economic Association*, vol. 45, May, pp. 1ff.
   1966: *Markets and Elections*, IEA Occasional Paper.
   1973: 'Some Themes from "Investigations into Method"', in J. R. Hicks and W. Weber ed., *Carl Menger and the Austrian School of Economics*, pp. 15ff.
Jenkin, F., 1931: *The Graphic Representation of the Laws of Supply and Demand* (reprinted).
Jevons, W. S., 1886: *Letters and Journal*, edited by his wife.
   1905: *The Principles of Economics*, ed. H. Higgs.
   1931: *Theory of Political Economy*, 4th ed.
Koot, G. M., 1975: 'Cliffe Leslie and the Historical School', *History of Political Economy*, vol. 7.
Leslie, Cliffe, 1870: *Land System and Industrial Economy of Ireland, England and Continental Countries*.
   n.d.: *Lectures in Political and Moral Philosophy*.
de Marchi, 1973: 'Mill and Cairnes and the Emergence of Marginalism in England', in *The Marginal Revolution in Economics*, ed. R. D. C. Black, A. W. Coats and C. D. W. Goodwin, pp. 78ff.
Marshall, A., 1925: *Memorials of Alfred Marshall*, ed. A. C. Pigou.
   1926: *Official Papers*.
   1961: *Principles of Economics*, ed. C. W. Guillebaud, 2 vols.
Marshall, A. and M. P., 1879: *The Economics of Industry*.
Marx, K., 1935: *Value, Price and Profit* (reprinted).
   1961: *Capital*, English translation (Moscow).
Menger, C., 1934–5: *Collected Works*, 4 vols.
   1950: *Principles of Economics*, translated by J. Dingwall and B. F. Hoselitz.
   1963: *Problems of Economics and Society*, translated by F. J. Nock.
Mill, James, 1966: *Selected Economic Writings*, ed. D. Winch.
Mill, J. S., 1909: *Principles of Political Economy*, ed. W. J. Ashley.

1967 and 1972: *Collected Works*, vols. IV and V, *Essays and Economics and Society*, ed. J. M. Robson, and vol. XVI, *Letters 1849–1873*, ed. F. E. Mineka and D. N. Lindley.

Milner, Lord, 1905: Introduction to A. Toynbee, *Lectures on the Industrial Revolution*.

Ricardo, D., 1951: *Works*, ed. P. Sraffa, vol. I, *The Principles of Political Economy and Taxation*.

Sayers, R. S., 1967: *Economic Change in England 1880–1939*.

Schumpeter, J. A., 1954: *History of Economic Analysis*.

Schwartz, P., 1972: *The New Political Economy of J. S. Mill*.

Senior, N. W., 1878: *Conversations with M. Thiers, M. Guizot, and other Distinguished Persons During the Second Empire*.

Sidgwick, H., 1883: *Principles of Political Economy*.

Sowell, T., 1972: *Say's Law*.

Stigler, G. J., 1965: *Essays in the History of Economics*.

1973: 'The Adoption of the Marginal Utility Theory', in *The Marginal Revolution in Economics*, ed. R. D. C. Black, A. W. Coats, and C. D. W. Goodwin, pp. 305ff.

Taussig, F. W., 1896: *Wages and Capital*.

Toynbee, A., 1908: *Lectures on the Industrial Revolution*.

Walras, L., 1954: *Elements of Pure Economics*, translated and edited by W. Jaffé.

Whitaker, J. K., 1975: *The Early Writings of Alfred Marshall*.

Wieser, F., 1893: *Natural Value*, translated by C. A. Malloch.

Winch, D. (ed.), 1966: *James Mill: Selected Economic Writings*.

Winch, D., 1971: *The Emergence of Economics as a Science 1750–1870*.

Chapter 4: *The Jevonian revolution and economic policy in Britain*

Annan, N., 1951: *Leslie Stephen*.

Bowley, M., 1949: *Nassau Senior and Classical Political Economy*.

Cairnes, J. E., 1873: *Essays in Political Economy*.

1874: *Some Leading Principles of Political Economy*.

Cannan, E., 1917: *Theories of Production and Distribution*, 1893, 3rd ed.

Clapham, J. H., 1932–8: *An Economic History of Modern Britain*, vol. II and vol. III.

Edgeworth, F. Y., 1925: *Papers Relating to Political Economy*, 3 vols.

Fetter, F. W., 1965: *The Development of British Monetary Orthodoxy 1797–1875*.

Foxwell, H. S., 1886: *Irregularity of Employment and Fluctuations of Prices*.

Garvin, J. L., 1933: *Life of Joseph Chamberlain*.

Harris, J., 1972: *Unemployment and Politics 1886–1914*.

Hayek, F. A., 1960: *The Constitution of Liberty*.

1973: *Law, Legislation and Liberty*, vol. I.

Hobsbawm, E. J., 1969: *Industry and Empire*, Pelican ed.

Hutchison, T. W., 1953: *Review of Economic Doctrines 1870–1929*.

1968: 'Jevons', in *International Encyclopedia of the Social Sciences*, vol. 8.

Jevons, W. S., 1857: 'Comparison of the Land and Railway Policy of New South Wales', in *Empire*, Sydney.

1870 and 1962: 'Economic Policy', (1870) in *Essays in Economic Method*, ed. R. L. Smyth.

1878: *Primer of Political Economy*.

1879 and 1911: *Theory of Political Economy*, 2nd ed. and 4th ed.

1882: *The State in Relation to Labour*.

1883: *Methods of Social Reform.*

1905: *The Principles of Economics and other Papers,* ed. H. Higgs.

Keynes, J. M., 1973: *The Collected Writings,* ed. D. E. Moggridge, vol. xiv.

Marshall, A., 1885: Paper to the Industrial Remuneration Conference in *Report of the Proceedings and Papers.*

1919: *Industry and Trade.*

1920 and 1961: *Principles of Economics,* 8th ed., ed. C. W. Guillebaud, 2 vols.

1925: *Memorials,* ed. A. C. Pigou.

1926: *Official Papers.*

Matthews, R. C. D., 1968: 'Why has Britain had Full Employment since the War?', *Economic Journal,* Sept. 1968, pp. 555ff.

Pigou, A. C., 1929: *Economics of Welfare,* 3rd ed.

1939: Presidential Address, *Economic Journal,* 49, pp. 215ff.

Robinson, J., 1972: 'The Second Crisis of Economic Theory', *Papers and Proceedings of the A.E.A.,* vol. 62, pp. 1ff.

Robinson, J. and Eatwell, J., 1973: *An Introduction to Modern Economics.*

Senior, N. W., 1847 and 1852: *Lectures on Political Economy.*

Shehab, F., 1953: *Progressive Taxation.*

Sidgwick, H., 1883 and 1887: *Principles of Political Economy,* 1st and 2nd eds.

Stigler, G. J., 1973: 'The Adoption of the Marginal Utility Theory', in *The Marginal Revolution,* ed. R. D. C. Black, A. W. Coats, and C. D. W. Goodwin, pp. 305ff.

Toynbee, A., 1894 and 1905: *Lectures on the Industrial Revolution.*

Tullberg, R. McW., 1975: 'Marshall's Tendency to Socialism', *History of Political Economy,* vol. 7, pp. 75ff.

Chapter 5: *The Keynesian revolution and the history of economic thought*

Ashton, T. S., 1955: *The Eighteenth Century.*

1959: *Economic Fluctuations in England, 1700–1800.*

Barber, W. J., 1967: *A History of Economic Thought.*

Barkai, H., 1969: 'A Smithian Growth Model', *Quarterly Journal of Economics,* vol. 83, pp. 396ff.

Barucci, P., 1975: 'Sismondi Revisited', *Rivista Internazionale di Scienze Economiche e Commerciali,* vol. 22 (10), pp. 977ff.

Becher, J. J., 1673: *Politische Discours von den eigentichen Ursachen des Auf und Abnehmens der Städte, Länder und Republiken,* 2nd ed.

Black, R. D. C., 1967: 'Parson Malthus, the General and the Captain', *Economic Journal,* vol. 77, pp. 59ff.

Blaug, M., 1962: *Economic Theory in Retrospect.*

1964: 'Economic Theory and Economic History in Britain 1650–1776', *Past and Present* No. 28, pp. 111ff.

Böhm-Bawerk, E., 1921: *Kapital und Kapitalzins,* 4th ed.

Boisguilbert, P. de, 1695: *Le Détail de la France.*

1707: *Dissertation sur la nature des richesses, de l'argent et des tributs.*

Cannan, E., 1901: 'Saving', in *Dictionary of Political Economy,* ed. R. H. I. Palgrave, vol. 3.

Cantillon, R., 1931: *Essai sur la nature du commerce en général,* ed. H. Higgs.

Cassel, G., 1903: *The Nature and Necessity of Interest.*

Chamley, P., 1962: 'Sir James Steuart inspirateur de la théorie générale de Lord Keynes', *Revue d'économie politique,* vol. 72, pp. 303ff.

Checkland, S. G., 1976: 'Adam Smith and the Bankers', in *Essays on Adam Smith,* ed. A. Skinner and T. Wilson, pp. 504ff.

Clark, G. N., 1947: *The Seventeenth Century.*
Clark, J. B., 1898: Introduction to *Overproduction & Crises,* by K. Rodbertus.
Corry, B. A., 1962: *Money, Saving and Investment in English Economics 1800–1850.*
Ferguson, A., 1767: *Essay on Civil Society.*
Fetter, F. W., 1965: *The Development of British Monetary Orthodoxy 1797–1875.*
Foxwell, H. S., 1886: *Irregularity of Employment and Fluctuations of Prices.*
Furniss, E. S., 1920: *The Position of the Laborer in a System of Nationalism.*
Galbraith, J. K., 1976: *Money,* Pelican ed.
Galiani, F., 1959: *Dialogues sur le Commerce des Bleds,* ed. F. Nicolini.
Garegnani, P., 1972: 'Heterogeneous Capital, the Production Function and the Theory of Distribution', in *A Critique of Economic Theory,* eds. E. K. Hunt and J. G. Schwartz, pp. 245ff.
Gordon, B. J., 1965: 'Say's Law, Effective Demand and the Contemporary British Periodicals', *Economica,* vol. 32 (N.S.), pp. 438ff.
    1967: *The Anti-Ricardian Tradition: Some Neglected Critics of Economic Orthodoxy.*
Grampp, W. D., 1952: 'The Liberal Elements in English Mercantilism', *Quarterly Journal of Economics,* vol. 66, pp. 465ff.
    1965: *Economic Liberalism,* 2 vols.
Harris, J., 1972: *Unemployment and Politics 1886–1914.*
Harrod, R. F., 1951: *Life of J. M. Keynes.*
Hawtrey, R. G., 1913: *Good and Bad Trade.*
Hayek, F. A., 1939: *Profits, Interest and Investment and other essays.*
    1941: *The Pure Theory of Capital.*
Heckscher, E., 1955: *Mercantilism,* 2 vols., 2nd ed.
Hegeland, H., 1954: *The Multiplier Theory.*
Henderson, H. D., 1934: 'The Slump and the Growth of Productive Power', *The Listener,* 17 October 1934, pp. 646–7.
    1955: *The Inter-War Years.*
Hicks, Sir John, 1965: *Capital and Growth.*
    1969: 'Monetary Theory and History: An Attempt At Perspective', in *Readings in Monetary Theory,* ed. R. Clower, pp. 254ff.
Hinton, R. W. K., 1955: 'The Mercantile System in the Time of Thomas Mun', *Economic History Review,* vol. 7, No. 3, pp. 277ff.
Hobson, J. A., 1910: *The Industrial System.*
Hollander, S., 1969: 'Malthus and the Post-Napoleonic Depression', *History of Political Economy,* vol. 1, pp. 306ff.
Howell, G., 1878: *The Conflicts of Labour and Capital.*
Howson, S. and Winch, D., 1977: *The Economic Advisory Council 1930–1939.*
Hume, D., 1955: *Writings on Economics,* ed. E. Rotwein.
Hutcheson, F., 1727 and 1750: *Remarks upon the Fable of the Bees.*
Hutchison, T. W., 1952: 'Some Questions about Ricardo', *Economica,* vol. 19 (N.S.), pp. 415ff.
    1953a: *A Review of Economic Doctrines 1870–1929.*
    1953b: 'Berkeley's *Querist* and its Place in the Economic Thought of the Eighteenth Century', *British Journal for the Philosophy of Science,* vol. 4, No. 13.
    1956: 'Bentham as an Economist', *Economic Journal,* vol. 66, pp. 288ff.
    1960: 'George Berkeley as an Economist: a Comment', *Journal of Political Economy,* vol. 68, pp. 302ff.
Johannsen, N., 1908: *A Neglected Point in Connection with Crises.*

Kauder, E., 1962: 'Aus Mengers Nachgelassenen Papieren', *Weltwirtschaftliches Archiv*, Bd. 89, pp. 1ff.

Keynes, J. M., 1924: 'A Comment on Professor Cannan's Article', *Economic Journal*, vol. 34, p. 68.

1929: 'A New Sort of White Paper', *The Nation and Athenaeum*, 18 May.

1931a: *Essays in Persuasion.*

1931b: 'An Economic Analysis of Unemployment', in *Unemployment as a World Problem*, ed. Q. Wright.

1933: *Essays in Biography.*

1936: *The General Theory of Employment, Interest and Money.*

1937: 'The General Theory of Employment', *Quarterly Journal of Economics*, vol. 51, pp. 209ff.

1946: 'The Balance of Payments of the United States', *Economic Journal*, vol. 56, pp. 172ff.

1973: *The Collected Writings*, vols. XIII and XIV, ed. D. Moggridge.

Klaveren, J. von, 1969: 'Fiscalism, Mercantilism and Corruption', in *Revisions in Mercantilism*, ed. D. C. Coleman.

Lambert, P., 1956: 'The Law of Markets Prior to J. B. Say and the Say–Malthus Debate', *International Economic Papers*, No. 6.

Leigh, A. H., 1974: 'Locke and the Quantity Theory of Money', *History of Political Economy*, vol. 6, pp. 200ff.

Lekachman, R. (ed.), 1964: *Keynes' General Theory, Reports of Three Decades.*

Link, R. G., 1959: *English Theories of Economic Fluctuations, 1815–1848.*

MacGregor, D. H., 1949: *Economic Thought and Policy.*

McDonald, S., 1954: 'Boisguilbert: A Neglected Precursor of Aggregate Demand Theories', *Quarterly Journal of Economics*, vol. 68, pp. 401ff.

Malthus, T. R., 1798–1926: *Essay on Population.*

1836: *Principles of Political Economy*, 2nd ed.

Mandeville, B. de, 1970: *Fable of the Bees*, Pelican Classics.

Marshall, A., 1879a: *The Pure Theory of Domestic Values.*

1925: *Memorials*, ed. A. C. Pigou.

1926: *Official Papers.*

Marshall, A. and M. P., 1879b: *The Economics of Industry.*

Marx, K., 1973: *Grundrisse, Introduction to the Critique of Political Economy*, Pelican ed.

Meek, R. L., 1962: *The Economics of Physiocracy*, 1962.

1967: *Economics and Ideology.*

Meoli, U., n.d.: *The Problem of Luxury in the Economic Thought of Condillac* (unpublished paper).

Mill, J., 1966: *Selected Economic Writings*, ed. D. Winch.

Mill, J.S., 1844 and 1948: *Essays on Some Unsettled Questions of Political Economy*, 1844, reprinted 1948.

1909: *Principles of Political Economy*, ed. W. J. Ahley.

Miller, M. H. and Upton, C. W., 1974: *Macroeconomics, a Neoclassical Introduction.*

Moggridge, D. (ed.), 1973: *The Collected Writings of J. M. Keynes*, vols. XIII and XIV.

Morize, A., 1909: *L'Apologie du Luxe au XVIIIe Siècle.*

Muchmore, L., 1969: 'G. de Malynes and Mercantile Economics', *History of Political Economy*, vol. 1, pp. 336ff.

Paglin, M., 1961: *Malthus and Lauderdale.*

Patinkin, D., 1975: 'J. M. Keynes from the *Tract* to *The General Theory*', *Economic Journal*, vol. 85, pp. 249ff.
Petty, Sir W., 1899: *The Economic Writings*, ed. C. H. Hull, 2 vols.
Pigou, A. C. (ed.), 1925: *Memorials of A. Marshall*, 1925.
    1949: *Employment & Equilibrium*, 2nd ed.
Pullen, J., 1974: *The First and Second Editions of Malthus's Political Economy*.
Ricardo, D., 1951–2: *Works and Correspondence*, ed. P. Sraffa.
Robbins, Lord, 1968: *The Theory of Economic Development in the History of Economic Thought*.
    1976: *Political Economy: Past and Present*.

Robertson, D. H., 1952: *Utility and All That*.
Robinson, J., 1966: *An Essay on Marxian Economics*, 2nd ed.
Roscher, W., 1849: *Ansichten der Volkswirtschaft*.
Say, J. B., 1817–1936: *Letters to T. R. Malthus*, reprinted.
    1841: *Traité d'économie politique*, 6th ed.
Schnack, H., 1951: *Der Wirtschaftskreislauf bei N. Johannsen und J. M. Keynes*.
Schumpeter, J. A., 1954: *History of Economic Analysis*.
Schwartz, P., 1972: *The New Political Economy of J. S. Mill*.
Sen, S. R., 1947: 'Sir James Steuart's General Theory of Employment, Interest and Money', *Economica*, vol. 14 (N.S.), pp. 19ff.
Skinner, A. S. (ed.), 1966: Sir James Steuart's *An Inquiry into the Principles of Political Economy*.
    1969: 'Of Malthus, Lauderdale and Say's Law', *Scottish Journal of Political Economy*, vol. 16, pp. 177ff.
Smith, A., 1797: *Theory of Moral Sentiments*, 8th ed.
    1896: *Lectures*, ed. E. Cannan.
    1937: *The Wealth of Nations*, Modern Library edition.
Sowell, T., 1972: *Say's Law*.
Steiger, O., 1971: *Studien zur Entstehung der neuen Wirtschaftslehre in Schweden*.
Stigler, G. J., 1965: *Essays in the History of Economics*.
Supple, B. E., 1959: *Commercial Crisis and Change in England 1600–1642*.
Suviranta, B., 1923: *The Theory of the Balance of Trade in England*.
Torrens, R., 1815: *Essays on the External Corn Trade*.
Tsuru, S., 1968: 'Keynes v Marx: the Methodology of Aggregates', in *Marx and Modern Economics*, ed. D. Horowitz, pp. 176ff.
Tucker, G. S. L., 1960: *Progress and Profits in British Economic Thought 1650–1850*.
Tucker, J., 1751: *Reflections on the Expediency of a Law for the Naturalisation of Foreign Protestants, Part II*.
Turgot, A. R. J., 1898: *Reflections on the Formation and Distribution of Riches*, ed. W. J. Ashley.
Upton, C. W. and Miller, M. H., 1974: *Macroeconomics, a Neoclassical Introduction*.
Vickers, D. W., 1959: *Studies in the Theory of Money 1690–1776*.
Viner, J., 1937: *Studies in the Theory of International Trade*.
    1964: Comment, in *Keynes' General Theory*, ed. R. Lekachman, pp. 253ff.
Ward, I. D. S., 1959: 'George Berkeley: Precursor of Keynes or Moral Economist of Underdevelopment', *Journal of Political Economy*, vol. 67, pp. 31ff.
Wicksell, K., 1936: *Interest and Prices*.
Wilson, C. H., 1958: *Mercantilism*.
    1967: *Economic History and the Historian*.
Winch, D. (ed.), 1966: *Selected Economic Writings of James Mill*.
Winch, D. and Howson, S., 1977: *The Economic Advisory Council 1930–1939*.
Wood, J., 1972: *Money and Output: Keynes and Friedman in Historical Perspective*.

Chapter 6: *Demythologising the Keynesian revolution: Pigou, wage-cuts, and* The General Theory

Alford, B. W. E; (ed.), 1972: *Depresssion and Recovery, British Economic Growth 1918–1939* (prepared for the Economic History Society).

Churchill, R., 1967: *Life of Winston Churchill*, vol. II.

Clay, H., 1929: 'The Public Regulation of Wages in Great Britain', *Economic Journal*, vol. 39, pp. 323ff.

Currie, L., 1972: 'The Keynesian Revolution and its Pioneers: Comment', *Papers and Proceedings of the A.E.A.*, vol. 62, pp. 139ff.

Davis, J. R., 1971: *The New Economics and the Old Economics*, 1971.

    1972: 'A Study in Caricatures: Keynes and the Classics' (Cyclostyled).

Dillard, D., 1948: *The Economics of J. M. Keynes.*

Galbraith, J. K., 1971: *A Contemporary Guide to Economics, Peace and Laughter.*

Harrod, R. F., 1951: *Life of J. M. Keynes.*

Hobsbawm, E. J., 1969: *Industry and Empire*, Pelican ed.

Howson, S. and Winch, D., 1977: *The Economic Advisory Council 1930–1939.*

Hutchison, T. W., 1953: *Review of Economic Doctrines 1870–1929.*

    1956: 'Bentham as an Economist', *Economic Journal*, vol. 66, pp. 288ff.

    1977: *Keynes versus the 'Keynesians'. . .?*, IEA.

Johnson, H. G., 1975: *On Economics and Society*, 1975.

Keynes, J. M., 1930: 'The Question of High Wages', *Political Quarterly*, vol. I.

    1931a: 'An Economic Analysis of Unemployment', in *Unemployment as a World Problem*, ed. Q. Wright.

    1931b: *Essays in Persuasion.*

    1936: *The General Theory of Employment, Interest and Money.*

    1973: *Collected Writings*, vol. XIV, ed. D. Moggridge.

Klein, L. R., 1947 and 1966: *The Keynesian Revolution*, 1st and 2nd eds.

Lekachman, R. (ed.), 1964: *Keynes' General Theory.*

Lekachman, R., 1967: *The Age of Keynes.*

Macmillan, Lord, 1931: Committee on Finance and Industry, *Report and Minutes of Evidence*, 2 vols.

Mill, J. S., 1844 and 1948: *Essays on Some Unsettled Questions of Political Economy*, reprinted.

Moggridge, D., 1976: *Keynes.*

Myrdal, G., 1973: *Against the Stream.*

Patinkin, D., 1972: 'Keynesian Monetary Theory and the Cambridge School', *Banca Nazionale del Lavoro, Quarterly Review*, vol. 25, pp. 138ff.

    1975: 'J. M. Keynes: from the *Tract* to *The General Theory*', *Economic Journal*, vol. 85, pp. 249ff.

    1976: 'Keynes' Monetary Thought', *History of Political Economy*, vol. 8, pp. 1ff.

Pigou, A. C., 1908: *Economic Science in Relation to Practice.*

    1913: *Unemployment.*

    1927: 'Wage Policy and Unemployment', *Economic Journal*, vol. 37, pp. 355ff.

    1933: *The Theory of Unemployment.*

    1935: *Economics in Practice.*

    1936: Review of *The General Theory of Employment, Interest and Money* of J. M. Keynes, *Economica*, vol. 3 (N.S.), pp. 115ff.

    1944: 'Employment Policy and Sir William Beveridge', *Agenda*, vol. 3, pp. 18ff.

    1945: *Lapses from Full Employment.*

1947: *Aspects of British Economic History, 1918–1925.*
1949: *Employment and Equilibrium,* 2nd ed.
Robinson, Sir Austin, 1967: Review of R. Lekachman, *The Age of Keynes, Economic Journal,* vol. 77, pp. 647ff.
Robson, W. A., 1963: *Introduction to English Poor Law History* by S. and B. Webb, new ed.
Sayers, R. S., 1976: *The Bank of England,* 3 vols.
Shackle, G. L. S., 1967: *The Years of High Theory.*
Skidelsky, R., 1967: *Politicians and the Slump.*
1975: 'The Reception of the Keynesian Revolution', in *Essays on J. M. Keynes,* ed. M. Keynes.
Steiger, O., 1971: *Studien zur Entstehung der neuen Wirtschaftslehre in Schweden.*
Stein, H., 1969: *The Fiscal Revolution in America.*
Stewart, M., 1967 and 1972: *Keynes and After,* 1st and 2nd eds.
Winch, D. and Howson, S., 1977: *The Economic Advisory Council 1930–1939.*
Wright, Q. (ed.), 1931: *Unemployment as a World Problem.*

Chapter 7: *The Keynesian revolution, uncertainty, and deductive general theory*

Bentham, J., 1859: *Works,* vol. I, edited J. Bowring.
Edgeworth, F. Y., 1925: 'The Pure Theory of Monopoly' (1897), in *Papers relating to Political Economy,* vol. I, pp. 111ff.
Gordon, D. F., 1965: 'The Role of the History of Economic Thought in the Understanding of Modern Economic Theory', *Papers and Proceedings of the A.E.A.,* vol. 55, pp. 119ff.
Hicks, Sir John, 1946: *Value and Capital,* 2nd ed.
Hutchison, T. W., 1937: 'Expectation and Rational Conduct', *Zeitschrift für Nationalökonomie,* Band VIII, Heft 5, pp. 636ff.
1938 and 1960: *The Significance and Basic Postulates of Economic Theory.*
1977: *Knowledge and Ignorance in Economics.*
Keynes, J. M., 1936: *The General Theory of Employment, Interest and Money.*
1937: 'The General Theory of Employment', *Quarterly Journal of Economics,* vol. 51, pp. 209ff.
1946: 'On the Balance of Payments of the United States', *Economic Journal,* vol. 56, pp. 172ff.
1971: *Collected Writings of J. M. Keynes,* vol. xv, ed. E. Johnson.
Klein, L. R., 1947: *The Keynesian Revolution.*
Knight, F. H., 1921: *Risk, Uncertainty and Profit.*
Kregel, J. A., 1976: 'Economic Methodology in the Face of Uncertainty', *Economic Journal,* vol. 86, pp. 209ff.
Latsis, S. J., 1972: 'Situational Determinism in Economics', *British Journal for the Philosophy of Science,* vol. 23, pp. 207ff.
Leijonhufvud, A., 1968: *On Keynesian Economics and the Economics of Keynes.*
Leslie, Cliffe, n.d.: *Essays in Political and Moral Philosophy.*
Marshall, A., 1961: *Principles of Economics,* ed. C. W. Guillebaud, 2 vols.
Menger, C., 1963: *Problems of Economics and Sociology,* translated F. J. Nock.
Mill, J. S., 1844 and 1948: *Essays on some Unsettled Questions in Political Economy,* reprinted.
1909: *Principles of Political Economy,* ed. W. J. Ashley.
Patinkin, D., 1976: 'Keynes' Monetary Thought: a study of its development', *History of Political Economy,* vol. 8, pp. 1ff.
Phelps Brown, Sir Henry, 1972: 'The Under-development of Economics', *Economic Journal,* vol. 82, pp. 1ff.

Ricardo, D., 1951: *Works*, vol. I, *The Principles of Political Economy and Taxation*, ed. P. Sraffa, 1951.
Robinson, J., 1933: *Economics of Imperfect Competition*.
  1936 and 1947: *Essays in the Theory of Employment*, 1st and 2nd eds.
  1937: *Introduction to the Theory of Employment*.
Shackle, G. L. S., 1967: *The Years of High Theory*.
Simon, H., 1976: 'From Substantive to Procedural Rationality', *Method and Appraisal in Economics*, edited S. Latsis, pp. 129ff.
Smith, A., 1937: *The Wealth of Nations*, Modern Library edition.
Weintraub, E. Roy, 1975: '"Uncertainty" and the Keynesian Revolution', *History of Political Economy*, vol. 7, pp. 530ff.

Chapter 8: *Economists and the history of economics: revolutionary and traditional versions*

Ashley, W. J., 1891: 'The Rehabilitation of Ricardo', *Economic Journal*, vol. I, pp. 474ff.
Blanqui, J. A., 1837: *Histoire de l'économie politique*.
Bronfenbrenner, M., 1974: Review of M. H. Dobb, *Theories of Value and Distribution since Adam Smith*, *History of Political Economy*, vol. 6, p. 483.
Burns, E., 1951: Introduction to Marx (1951).
Cairnes, J. E., 1875: *Character and Logical Method of Political Economy*, 2nd ed.
Cannan, E., 1903: *Theories of Production and Distribution, 1776–1848*.
Dobb, M. H., 1937: *Political Economy and Capitalism*.
  1973: *Theories of Value and Distribution since Adam Smith*.
Engels, F., 1959: Preface to *Capital*, K. Marx, vol. III, English translation (Moscow).
Fawcett, H., 1863: *Manual of Political Economy*.
Fetter, F. W., 1969: 'The Rise and Decline of Ricardian Economics', *History of Political Economy*, vol. I, pp. 67ff.
Gide, C. and Rist, C., 1948: *A History of Economic Doctrines*, 2nd English edition.
Guillebaud, C. W., 1971: 'Some Personal Reminiscences of Alfred Marshall', *History of Political Economy*, vol. 3, pp. 1ff.
Harrod, Sir Roy, 1951: *Life of J. M. Keynes*.
Henderson, W. O., 1977: *The Life of Friedrich Engels*, 2 vols.
Hicks, Sir John, 1975: 'The Scope and Status of Welfare Economics', *Oxford Economic Papers*, vol. 27, pp. 307ff.
Hines, A. G., 1973: in *Times Higher Educational Supplement*, 30 March.
Hobsbawm, E. J., 1969: *Industry and Empire*, Pelican ed.
Howard, M. C. and King, J. E., 1975: *The Political Economy of Marx*.
Hunt, E. K. and Schwartz, J. G. (ed.), 1972: *A Critique of Economic Theory*.
Hutchison, T. W., 1977: *Knowledge and Ignorance in Economics*.
James, E. J. (ed.), 1907: *History of Political Economy* by J. K. Ingram.
Jevons, W. S., 1931: *The Theory of Political Economy*, 4th ed.
King, J. E., 1975–6: *Marx as an Historian of Economic Thought*, Discussion Papers, La Trobe University and University of Lancaster.
Kuhn, T. S., 1970: *The Structure of Scientific Revolutions*, 2nd ed.
McClellan, D., 1973: *Karl Marx: his Life and Thought*.
McCulloch, J. R., 1824: *A Discourse on the Rise, Progress, Peculiar Objects, and Importance of Political Economy*.
  1845: *The Literature of Political Economy*.
  1856: *A Select Collection of Early English Tracts on Commerce*.
  (ed.), 1863: *The Wealth of Nations*, by Adam Smith.

Malthus, T. R., 1827: *Definitions in Political Economy*.
    1836: *Principles of Political Economy*.
Marshall, A., 1925: *Memorials of Alfred Marshall*, ed. A. C. Pigou.
    1961: *Principles of Economics*, edited C. W. Guillebaud.
Marx, K., 1951: *Theories of Surplus Value*, translated by G. A. Bonner and
    E. Burns.
    1953: 'The German Ideology', in *Die Frühschriften*, ed. S. Landshut.
    1961: *Capital*, vol. 1, Moscow.
    1962: 'Randglossen zu A. Wagner's "Lehrbuch der Politischen Ökonomie"'
    (1879–80), in Marx and Engels: *Werke*, Bd. 19, p. 383.
    1973: *Grundrisse*, Pelican ed.
Mill, J., 1821: *Elements of Political Economy*.
    1966a: 'Whether Political Economy is Useful' (1836), *Selected Writings*, ed.
    D. Winch.
    1966b: 'Commerce Defended' (1808), *Selected Economic Writings*, ed.
    D. Winch.
Mill, J. S., 1844 and 1948: *Essays on some Unsettled Questions* (reprinted).
    1909: *Principles of Political Economy*, ed. W. J. Ashley.
    1967: *Essays on Economics and Society*, vol. II, ed. L. Robbins and J. M. Robson.
Moore, Barrington, 1960: *Social Origins of Dictatorship and Democracy*.
O'Brien, D. P., 1974: *Whither Economics?*
Patinkin, D., 1969: 'The Chicago Tradition, the Quantity Theory, and
    Friedman', *Journal of Money, Credit and Banking*, February, pp. 46ff.
Read, S., 1829: *An Inquiry into the Natural Grounds of Right to Vendible Property
    or Wealth*.
Robertson, H. M., 1976: 'Euge! Belle! Dear Mr. Smith', *South African Journal
    of Economics*, vol. 44 (4), pp. 378ff.
Say, J. B., 1828–9: *Cours Complet d'Economie Politique Pratique*, vol. II.
    1841: *Traité d'économie politique*, 6th ed.
Schumpeter, J. A., 1954: *History of Economic Analysis*.
Schwartz, P., 1972: *The New Political Economy of J. S. Mill*.
Senior, N. W., 1928: *Industrial Efficiency and Social Economy*.
Steedman, I., 1972: 'Jevons' Theory of Capital and Interest', *Manchester School*,
    vol. 40, pp. 31ff.
Thompson, W., 1827: *Labour Rewarded*.
Torrens, R., 1821: *An Essay on the Production of Wealth*.
Vroey, M. de, 1975: 'The Transition from Classical to Neoclassical Economics:
    a Scientific Revolution', *Journal of Economic Issues*, vol. 9, pp. 415ff.
Wicksell, K., 1958: 'Ends and Means in Economics', *Selected Papers on Economic
    Theory*, ed. E. Lindahl.
Winch, D., 1962: 'What Price the History of Economic Thought?', *Scottish
    Journal of Political Economy*, vol. 19, pp. 193ff.

Chapter 9: *On recent revolutionary versions of the history of economics*

Böhm-Bawerk, E., 1962: *Shorter Classics of E. von Böhm-Bawerk*, translated by
    J. R. Mez.
Brittan, S., 1973: *Is there an Economic Consensus? An Attitude Survey*.
Bronfenbrenner, M., 1974: Review of M. H. Dobb, *Theories of Value and
    Distribution since Adam Smith*, *History of Political Economy*, vol. 6, p. 483.
Caute, D., 1973: *The Fellow-Travellers*.
Clark, J. B., 1904: *The Problem of Monopoly*.

Coase, R. H., 1975: 'Marshall on Method', *Journal of Law and Economics*, vol. XVIII (1).
Dobb, M. H., 1937: *Political Economy and Capitalism*.
1955: *On Economic Theory and Socialism*.
1972: 'The Sraffa System and Critique of the Neo-Classical Theory of Distribution', in *A Critique of Economic Theory*, E. K. Hunt and J. G. Schwartz, pp. 205ff.
1973: *Theories of Value and Distribution since Adam Smith*.
1975: 'Revival of Political Economy: an Explanatory Note', *Economic Record*, vol. 51, pp. 357ff.
Eagly, R. V., 1974: *The Structure of Classical Economic Theory*.
Easlea, B., 1973: *Liberation and the Aims of Science*.
Edgeworth, F. Y., 1881: *Mathematical Psychics*.
1897 and 1925: 'The Pure Theory of Taxation', *Economic Journal*, vol. 7, reprinted in *Papers Relating to Political Economy*, 1925, vol. 2, pp. 63ff.
Galbraith, J. K., 1974: *Economics and the Public Purpose*.
Gordon, B., 1967: *The Anti-Ricardian Tradition: Some Neglected Critics of Economic Orthodoxy, 1800–1830*.
Guillebaud, C. W., 1964: Review of E. Eshag: From Marshall to Keynes, *Economic Journal*, vol. 74, pp. 474ff.
Hahn, F. H., 1975: 'Revival of Political Economy: The Wrong Issues and the Wrong Argument', *Economic Record*, vol. 51, pp. 360ff.
Halévy, E., 1956: *Thomas Hodgskin*, translated by A. J. Taylor.
Harris, J., 1972: *Unemployment and Politics, 1886–1914*.
Hayek, F. A, 1960: *The Constitution of Liberty*.
Hobsbawm, E. J., 1969: *Industry and Empire*, Pelican ed.
Hollander, S., 1973: 'Ricardo's Analysis of the Profit Rate', *Economica*, vol. 40 (N.S.), pp. 260ff.
1976: 'Ricardianism, J. S. Mill and the Neoclassical Challenge', in *Essays on James and J. S. Mill*, ed. Laine and Robson.
Howson, S. and Winch, D., 1977: *The Economic Advisory Council 1930–1939*.
Hunt, E. K. and Schwartz, J. G., 1972: *A Critique of Economic Theory*.
Hutchison, T. W., 1938 and 1960: *The Significance and Basic Postulates of Economic Theory*.
1953: *A Review of Economic Doctrines, 1870–1929*.
1957: Review of *Thomas Hodgskin*, by E. Halévy, *Economica*, 1957, p. 89.
1968: *Economists and Economic Policy 1946–1966*.
1977: *Knowledge and Ignorance in Economics*.
Jacka, K., Cox, C. and Marks, J., 1975: *The Rape of Reason*.
Jones, R., 1831: *Essay on the Distribution of Wealth*.
Keynes, J. M., 1929: 'A New Sort of White Paper', *The Nation and Athenaeum*, 18 May.
1946: 'The Balance of Payments of the United States', *Economic Journal*, vol. 56, pp. 172ff.
1973: *Collected Writings of J. M. Keynes*, vols. XIII and XIV, ed. D. Moggridge.
Keynes, J. N., 1891: *The Scope and Method of Political Economy*.
Kornai, J., 1971: *Anti-Equilibrium*.
Leslie, T. E. C., n.d.: *Essays in Political and Moral Philosophy*.
Letiche, J. M., 1971: 'Soviet Views on Keynes', *Journal of Economic Literature*, vol. 9, pp. 442ff.
Lloyd, W. F., 1835: *Four Lectures on Poor-Laws*.
1836: *Two Lectures on the Justice of Poor Laws and One Lecture on Rent*.

Loasby, B. J., 1976: *Choice, Complexity and Ignorance.*
Lowenthal, E., 1911: *The Ricardian Socialists.*
Macpherson, C. B., 1972: 'Politics: Post Liberal Democracy', in *Ideology in Social Science*, ed. R. Blackburn, pp. 17ff.
McLellan, D., 1973: *Karl Marx His Life and Thought.*
Mandel, E., 1971: *Marxist Economic Theory.*
Marshall, A., 1961: *Principles of Economics*, ed. C. W. Guillebaud.
Marx, K., 1961: *Capital*, English translation, Moscow.
   n.d.: *Theories of Surplus Value*, Moscow ed.
Meek, R. L., 1953: Review of J. Stalin, *Economic Problems of Socialism in the U.S.S.R.*, *Economic Journal*, vol. 63, pp. 716ff.
   1953-4: 'Stalin as an Economist', *Review of Economic Studies*, vol. 21, pp. 232ff.
   1967: *Economics and Ideology.*
   1973a: *Studies in the Labour Theory of Value*, 2nd ed.
   1973b: 'Marginalism and Marxism' in *The Marginal Revolution in Economics*, ed. R. D. C. Black, A. W. Coats and C. D. W. Goodwin, pp. 233ff.
   1974: 'Value in the History of Econoimic Thought', *History of Political Economy*, vol. 6, pp. 246ff.
Menger, C., 1950: *Principles of Economics*, translated J. Dingwall and B. F. Hoselitz.
Mill, J. S., 1909: *Principles of Political Economy*, ed. W. J. Ashley.
Moore, Barrington, 1960: *Social Origins of Dictatorship and Democracy.*
Myrdal, G., 1973: *Against the Stream.*
Pareto, V., 1935: *The Mind and Society.*
Pigou, A. C., 1906: 'The Unity of Political and Economic Science', *Economic Journal*, vol. 16, pp. 372ff.
   1937: *Socialism versus Capitalism.*
Popper, Sir Karl, 1963: *Conjectures and Refutations.*
   1976: in *The Positivist Dispute in German Sociology*, ed. G. Adey and D. Frisby.
Robinson, J., 1937 and 1947: *Essays in the Theory of Employment.*
   1951: *Collected Economic Papers*, vol. 1.
   1952: *Conference Sketch-Book, Moscow 1952.*
   1962: *Economic Philosophy.*
   1966: *Economics: An Awkward Corner.*
   1969: *The Cultural Revolution in China.*
   1972a: 'The Second Crisis of Economic Theory', *Papers and Proceedings of the A.E.A.*, vol. 62, pp. 1ff.
   1972b: *Economic Heresies.*
   1973a: Foreword to *The Reconstruction of Political Economy: an Introduction to Post-Keynesian Economics*, by J. A. Kregel.
   1974a: *History versus Equilibrium.*
   1974b: *Collected Papers*, vol. 4.
Robinson, J. and Eatwell, J., 1973b: *An Introduction to Modern Economics.*
Romano, R. M., 1971: 'W. F. Lloyd – A Comment', *Oxford Economic Papers*, vol. 23, pp 285ff.
Routh, G., 1975: *The Origins of Economic Ideas.*
Rowthorn, R., 1974: Neo-Ricardianism, Neo-Classicism, or Marxism?, *New Left Review*, No. 86, pp. 63ff.
Schumpeter, J. A., 1917: 'Das Grundprinzip der Verteilungstheorie', *Archiv für Sozialwissenschaft und Sozialpolitik*, Bd. 42.
Shehab, F., 1953: *Progressive Taxation.*
Sherman, H., 1972: *Radical Political Economy.*

Shove, G. F., 1944: Review of J. Robinson, *An Essay on Marxian Economics*, *Economic Journal*, April, p. 60.

Solow, R., 1975: *Times Literary Supplement*, 14 March.

Solzhenitsyn, A., 1976: *The Gulag Archipelago*, vol. 2, Fontana ed.

Sweezy, P. M., 1953: *The Present as History*.

    1942: *Theory of Capitalist Development*.

Tugan-Baranovsky, M., 1913: *Die Soziale Theorie der Verteilung*.

Vroey. M. de, 1975: 'The Transition from Classical to Neoclassical Economics: a Scientific Revolution', *Journal of Economic Issues*, vol. 9, pp. 415ff.

Walras, L., 1896: *Etudes d'économie sociale*.

    1954: *Elements of Pure Economics*, edited and translated by W. Jaffé.

Wicksteed, P., 1933: *The Common Sense of Political Economy and Selected Papers*, ed. L. Robbins.

Wieser, F., 1926: *Das Gesetz der Macht*.

    1927: *Social Economics*, translated by A. F. Hinrichs.

    1956: *Natural Value*, translated by C. A. Malloch (reprinted).

Chapter 10: *On the influence and effects on policies of economic ideas and theories*

Coase, R. H., 1975: 'Marshall on Method', in *Journal of Law and Economics*, vol. XVIII (1).

Cournot, A., 1927: *Researches into the Mathematical Principles of the Theory of Wealth*, translated by N. T. Bacon.

Gerschenkron, A., 1969: 'History of Economic Doctrines and Economic History', *Papers and Proceedings of the A.E.A.*, vol. 59, pp. 1ff.

Keynes, J. M., 1936: *The General Theory of Employment, Interest and Money*.

Lange, O., 1968: 'Marxian Economics and Modern Economic Theory', in *Marx and Modern Economics*, ed. D. Horowitz, pp. 68ff.

Mill, J. S., 1845: 'The Claims of Labour', *Edinburgh Review*.

Robbins, Lord, 1935: *An Essay on the Nature and Significance of Economic Science*, 2nd ed.

    1963: 'On the Relations between Politics and Economics', in *Economics and Politics*.

Schumpeter, J. A., 1954: *History of Economic Analysis*.

Senior, N. W., 1878: *Conversations with M. Thiers, M. Guizot, and other Distinguished Persons during the Second Empire*.

Stephen, L., 1900: *The English Utilitarians*, reprinted 1950.

Wilson, C. H., 1968: *Economic History and the Historian*.

Chapter 11: *On revolutions and progress in economic knowledge: definitions and conclusions*

Bagehot, W., 1895: *Economic Studies*, ed. R. H. Hutton.

Blaug, M., 1976: 'Paradigms versus Research Programmes in the History of Economics', *Method and Appraisal in Economics*, ed. S. Latsis, 1976, pp. 149ff.

Bronfenbrenner, M., 1971: 'The "Structure of Revolutions" in Economic Thought', *History of Political Economy*, vol. 3, pp. 136ff.

    1974: Review of M. H. Dobb, *Theories of Value and Distribution since Adam Smith*, *History of Political Economy*, vol. 6.

Dobb, M. H., 1955: *On Economic Theory and Socialism*.

Feyerabend, P. K., 1970: 'Consolations for the specialist', in *Criticism and the Growth of Knowledge*, ed. I. Lakatos and A. Musgrave, pp. 197ff.
Friedman, M., 1970: *The Counter-revolution in Monetary Theory*, IEA.
1974: *Inflation; Causes, Consequences, Cures*, IEA.
Goodwin, C. D. W., 1973: *The Marginal Revolution in Economics*, ed. R. D. Black, A. W. Coats and C. D. W. Goodwin, pp. 285ff.
Gordon, D. F., 1965: 'The Role of the History of Economic Thought in the Understanding of Modern Economic Theory', *Papers and Proceedings of the A.E.A.*, vol. 55, pp. 119ff.
Hicks, Sir John, 1975: 'The Scope and Status of Welfare Economics', *Oxford Economic Papers*, vol. 27, pp. 307ff.
1976: '"Revolutions" in Economics', *Method and Appraisal in Economics*, ed. S. Latsis, pp. 207ff.
Hutchison, T. W., 1964: *'Positive' Economics and Policy Objectives.*
1973: 'Some Themes from "Investigations into Method"', *Carl Menger and the Austrian School of Economics*, ed. J. R. Hicks and W. Weber, pp. 15ff.
1977a: *Knowledge and Ignorance in Economics.*
1977b: *Keynes versus the 'Keynesians'?*, IEA.
Johnson, H. G., 1975: 'The Keynesian Revolution and the Monetarist Counter-revolution', *On Economics and Society*, pp. 91ff.
Keynes, J. N., 1917: *The Scope and Method of Political Economy*, 4th ed.
Knight, F. H., 1956: *On the History and Method of Economics.*
Koestler, A., 1974: *The Heel of Achilles.*
Kuhn, T. S., 1968: 'Science, History of', in *International Encyclopaedia of the Social Sciences*, vol. 14.
1970a: *The Structure of Scientific Revolutions*, 2nd ed.
1970b: 'Reflections on my Critics', *Criticism and the Growth of Knowledge*, ed. I. Lakatos and A. Musgrave, pp. 231ff.
Kunin, L. and Weaver, F. S., 1971: 'On the Structure of Scientific Revolutions in Economics', *History of Political Economy*, vol. 3, pp. 391ff.
Lakatos, I., 1971: 'History of Science and its Rational Reconstruction', *Boston Studies in the Philosophy of Science*, vol. 8, ed. R. C. Buck and R. S. Cohen.
Leijonhufvud, A., 1976: 'Schools, "Revolutions" and Research programmes in economic theory', *Method and Appraisal in Economics*, ed. S. Latsis, pp. 65ff.
Menger, C., 1935: *Collected Works of Carl Menger*, 4 vols., reprinted.
Mitchell, Wesley, 1949: *Lecture Notes on Types of Economic Theory.*
Moore, Barrington, 1958: *Political Power and Social Theory.*
Pocock, J. G. A., 1972: *Politics, Language and Time.*
Popper, K., 1970: 'Normal Science and its Dangers', *Criticism and the Growth of Knowledge*, ed. I. Lakatos and A. Musgrave, pp. 51ff.
Rogin, L., 1956: *The Meaning and Validity of Economic Theory.*
Routh, G., 1976: *The Origins of Economic Ideas.*
Samuelson, P. A., 1976: *Economics*, 10th ed.
Stigler, G. J., 1965: 'The Influence of Events and Policies on Economic Theory', *Essays in the History of Economics*, pp. 16ff.
1973: 'The Adoption of the Marginal Utility Theory', *The Marginal Revolution in Economics*, ed. R. D. C. Black, A. W. Coats, and C. D. W. Goodwin, pp. 305ff.

Index of subjects

Index of names (pp. 1–320)